# WEAPONS OF WORLD WAR II

# WEAPONS OF WORLD WAR II

ALEXANDER LÜDEKE

Parragon

Bath • New York • Singapore • Hong Kong • Cologne • Delhi
Melbourne • Amsterdam • Johannesburg • Auckland • Shenzhen

This edition published by Parragon in 2011

Parragon
Queen Street House
4 Queen Street
Bath BA1 1HE, UK

Production: akapit Verlagsservice, Berlin-Saarbrücken
Project coordination and provision of illustrations: akapit Verlagsservice
Author: Alexander Lüdeke
Layout and composition: Geert Möbius, KONTUR Media Team, Bergisch
Gladbach
UK edition produced by: Cambridge Publishing Management Ltd
Translation: Richard Elliott, John Kelly, James Taylor
Editing: Gillian Delaforce
Proofreading: Kate Knight/Ian Faulkner

ISBN: 978-1-4454-2435-4

Printed in China

# CONTENTS

# INTRODUCTION

The Greek philosopher Heraclitus wrote: 'War is the father of all things.' As terrible as the Second World War was, there is no doubt that this saying applies to its technological dimensions. The war that raged from 1939 to 1945 was an out-and-out conflict of technology. The courage, determination and personal aptitude of the individual had only a limited ability to determine victory or defeat. What was far more important for victory was the equipment and, in particular, the technological advantage over the opponent.

While fighting spirit, leadership qualities and clever tactics were repeatedly able to decide the result of individual engagements or even campaigns, it was no longer possible to win the whole war in this manner. The countries engaged in this war placed their total scientific and industrial capacity at the service of the military so as not to be left behind by their opponents. Therefore the development of weapons technology accelerated in the years between 1939 and 1945 to an extent never before seen, and all the major countries engaged in the war produced weapons and vehicles in quantities and varieties never witnessed either before or after this time. Within less than six years weapons technology progressed remarkably to an extent that would otherwise have required decades. One can find striking examples of this phenomenon in every field of military technology. While in 1939 most tanks were still fitted with cannon of 40 mm calibre or less, and most weighed not more than 15 tonnes, in 1945 heavy monsters of up to 70 tonnes fitted with weapons of calibres of up to 128 mm ranged over the battlefields. In the infantry one can also observe a similar trend. While at the outbreak of war many soldiers went into combat with weapons that would have been familiar to their fathers in 1914–18, by 1945 modern models were in use, some of which are still produced today. The best example of this is the German MG 42 machine gun. In 1939 almost all countries still possessed biplanes, whose performance hardly differed from that of machines at the start of the 1920s. By 1945, however, aircraft driven by jet or rocket propulsion hunted in the skies at up to 1,000 km/h, and multi-engine bombers carried ten times the load of their predecessors at the start of the war. To understand the pattern of events and the outcome of this war it is also necessary to become acquainted with the dimensions of weapons technology.

*Red Army T-34s on the advance.*

Without an appreciation of progress and developments in this field anyone who is interested in its history cannot review and classify all aspects of this dreadful war. This book therefore provides a comprehensive overview of the rapid progress of weapons technology and the variety of design and development from 1939 to 1945. It presents all the important and forward-looking weapons and vehicles that were in use at this time in the countries engaged in the conflict. Wherever possible details are also provided concerning the production quantities for the models in question so that their relevance can be better assessed. The countries are classified according to whether they were members of the Axis or one of the Allied nations, and are listed in the order in which they entered the war. May the study of this subject lead to a clear understanding that a conflict of this kind must never be repeated. For each one of the more than 50 million sacrifices on all sides was one too many.

*The Boeing B-17 Flying Fortress is, with the P-51 Mustang, one of the best-known American Second World War combat aircraft.*

*Russia, 1943: an MG 42 machine gunner from the Grossdeutschland Division.*

# INFANTRY WEAPONS

## MODEL 08 SEMI-AUTOMATIC PISTOL 9 MM

The development of this pistol is closely linked with the names of two world-famous designers: Hugo Borchardt and Georg Luger. The predecessors of this weapon originated as early as the last decade of the 19th century, and various stages of development led to the 08 pistol, which in 1908 was introduced as the standard handgun of the German Imperial Army. By the end of the First World War more than 1.5 million of these weapons had been produced. After 1918 civil and military versions of this model were exported, not least on account of its excellent reputation, to many countries such as Finland, Sweden, the Netherlands, Switzerland, Portugal, Spain, Brazil, Latvia, Turkey, Iran and the USA.

From 1930 onwards the pistol was mainly manufactured by the Mauser factories in Oberndorf. By the time production of the weapon ceased in

June 1942 more than 900,000 had been made for the Wehrmacht (German armed forces) and for export. The 08 was used by the Luftwaffe and the Navy, and proved its worth. It was rated as accurate and reliable, but was expensive and complicated to manufacture.

| Calibre: | 9 mm |
|---|---|
| Cartridge: | 9 x 19 mm Parabellum |
| Muzzle velocity: | 320 m/s |
| Weight with full magazine: | 0.968 kg |
| Magazine capacity: | 8 rounds |
| Operational range: | 50 m |

## WALTHER SEMI-AUTOMATIC PISTOL MODEL P 38 9 MM

The Wehrmacht high command had recognized since the mid-1930s that the 08 could only be produced by expending vast resources in terms of materials, time and costs. The search was therefore under way for a new pistol that would supplement the 08 as a military weapon and even replace it. However, the first model put forward by the Walther weapons factory in Thuringia did not meet requirements; the third version was only introduced

| Calibre: | 9 mm |
|---|---|
| Cartridge: | 9 x 19 mm Parabellum |
| Muzzle velocity: | 355 m/s |
| Weight with full magazine: | 0.89 kg |
| Magazine capacity: | 8 rounds |
| Operational range: | 50 m |

in 1938 as a military side arm called the P 38 pistol. It soon became clear that the P 38 was not much cheaper

than the P 08, but it was faster and no more complicated to manufacture. Since Walther could not meet the demands of the Wehrmacht alone the P 38 was also produced by other companies, such as the Mauser factories in Oberndorf. By the end of the war in 1945 more than 1.2 million P 38s had been produced. While the first models were of excellent quality and made from high-quality materials, workmanship steadily declined from 1943 onwards. Nevertheless, the P 38 was rated as a thoroughly good weapon with excellent characteristics. Many experimental models were produced during the war, including a short version, the P 38 k, which was originally destined for special units.

In 1957 Walther (now based in Ulm) resumed production. Under the name P 1, the weapon has been introduced into the Bundeswehr, police units of several of the Federal states, and armies of other countries.

## MP 38 AND MP 40 MACHINE PISTOLS 9 MM

| Calibre: | 9 mm |
|---|---|
| Cartridge: | 9 x 19 mm Parabellum |
| Muzzle velocity: | 380 m/s |
| Firing rate: | 400 rounds/min |
| Weight with full magazine: | 3.61 kg |
| Magazine capacity: | 32 rounds |
| Operational range: | 200 m |

This weapon, often incorrectly called the 'Schmeisser MP', originated in 1938 at the request of the German Tank Corps, which, as a result of its experiences in the Spanish Civil War, was looking for a close combat weapon. Even in later models the origin of the MP 38 as a weapon for tank crews is still clear in the form of the 'nose' under the barrel, which was designed to hook into firing slits, and the downward-pointing box magazine. For infantrymen who had to shoot lying down this type of magazine was a real hindrance. The designer of the weapon was not, as is often assumed, Hugo Schmeisser, but Heinrich Vollmer, who was working at the ERMA (ERfurter MAschinenfabrik) weapons factory.

In the MP 38 the wooden stock that was usual up to that time was dispensed with, and the pistol was made completely out of metal and plastic. Also the shoulder stock was foldable for the first time, to allow better handling in a small space – another indication of its origin as a weapon for the Tank Corps. The MP 38 was rated as an excellent, forward-looking design that was easy to operate, with good accuracy and stability. However, if not well maintained it tended to jam during loading, and the safety record of the pistol gave rise to criticism because of its ability to cause accidents time and again. Since the metal parts of the MP 38 were machined, the manufacturing costs were extremely high. From 1940 onwards a version therefore appeared that was manufactured using sheet metal pressing technology: the MP 40. This model was also meant to remove the weak points of the MP 38, but in this it was not altogether successful. Nevertheless the MP 38 and 40 were popular with troops, since they had significantly higher firepower than the Mauser 98 k standard carbine.

To provide a further increase in firepower the model MP 40/1 was developed with a magazine that was twice the size – i.e. with 64 rounds – but this design proved not to be effective. The MP 38/40 was never available in sufficient numbers. Even the paratrooper units were mainly equipped with the Mauser 98 k carbine. By the end of the war around 1 million MP 38/40s had been produced.

*The MP 40 in Stalingrad.*

## 44 STG 44 / MP 43 / MP 44 ASSAULT RIFLE 7.92 MM

| Calibre: | 7.92 mm |
|---|---|
| Cartridge: | 7.92 x 33 mm |
| Muzzle velocity: | 685 m/s |
| Firing rate: | 500 rounds/min |
| Weight with full magazine: | 5.5 kg |
| Magazine capacity: | 30 rounds |
| Operational range: | 400 m |

*The StG 44 was the first rifle of its kind worldwide, and the predecessor of a whole series of assault rifles.*

This weapon, designed by Hugo Schmeisser, utilized the advantages of the newly developed 7.92 x 33 mm short cartridge. This cartridge had in fact a lower muzzle velocity and range than conventional ammunition, but it had been found that the maximum range of conventional weapons was almost never fully utilized. More important was the firepower. Machine pistols were not a perfect solution since their pistol ammunition possessed too low a penetration capability. With the new cartridge, which weighed significantly less and was smaller than the 7.92 x 57 mm, more ammunition could be carried; 150 cartridges weighed only 2.5 kg instead of 3.9 kg. First tests were carried out from 1940 onwards, and in 1943 Albert Speer authorized mass production under the designation 'MP 43'. This name was chosen as a kind of camouflage, since in spite of all the positive reports Hitler had decided against the introduction of the machine carbine.

In September 1943 the first large-scale trial took place on the Eastern Front. Finally Hitler was persuaded to change his mind as a result of pleas from troops at the front – supported by Speer and the Army Ordnance Office – and authorized production. In 1944 the designation was first altered to MP 44 and then, apparently at Hitler's instigation, to Sturmgewehr (assault rifle) 44, without any further modifications being made to the weapon. The MP 44 was reliable, easy to dismantle and accurate. The recoil force was less than half the strength of that of the 98 k. In total some 424,000 rifles were produced. After the war the weapon was used by the People's Police of the German Democratic Republic and the Yugoslav Army. MP 44s have even surfaced in Africa, probably originating from Soviet stocks of appropriated weapons.

## MAUSER CARBINE 98 K 7.92 MM

The 98 k carbine was the standard weapon of the soldiers of the Wehrmacht from 1935 onwards and during the whole of the Second World War. Altogether 12.8 million carbines were manufactured – of which more than 2.26 million were produced in 1944 – and they were also manufactured under licence in other countries. The origins of the carbine go back to the rifle that was introduced into the Imperial German Army in 1898, and which was also the standard infantry weapon from 1914 to 1918. The main difference was a shorter barrel (thus 98 'k' for 'kurz', i.e. 'short'). After 1918 rifles of this type were exported across the world from the Mauser factories. In the war many different versions were built, e.g. with a target telescope, or as a launcher for rifle grenades. Because of its large stocks the 98 k continued to be used after the war, for example in Norway, Spain, and Portugal. Also the armed forces and police of both the German Federal Republic and the GDR used the weapon in their early years.

| Calibre: | 7.92 mm |
|---|---|
| Cartridge: | 7.92 x 57 mm |
| Muzzle velocity: | 755 m/s |
| Weight with empty magazine: | 3.7–4.1 kg |
| Magazine capacity: | 5 rounds |
| Operational range: | 400 m, max 2,000 m |

# MG 34 UNIVERSAL MACHINE GUN MODEL 34 7.92 MM

| Calibre: | 7.92 mm |
|---|---|
| Cartridge: | 7.92 x 57 mm |
| Muzzle velocity: | 755 m/s |
| Firing rate: | 800–900 rounds/min |
| Weight with bipod: | 11.5 kg |
| Magazine capacity: | 50 or 75 rounds drum or 300 rounds belt |
| Operational range (bipod): | 1,200 m |

In the First World War machine guns demonstrated their devastating effect and thus their value in battle. However, the majority of the machine guns of this time were too heavy, so an attempt was made to find a new weapon that could be universally used and was also light enough to be carried by a soldier in an attack. First tests began in 1929 and continued until 1933. Officially the new machine gun was introduced as early as 1934 as the MG 34, but series production actually began only in 1936. The MG was designed to be used as a light machine gun on a bipod, as a heavy machine gun on a tripod, as a weapon in armoured vehicles and bunkers, and also as an anti-aircraft weapon. The MG 34 was extremely accurate and versatile, but because of the complicated method of manufacture was expensive and time-consuming to produce. Moreover, the gun mechanisms were very sensitive, requiring a well-trained crew, and it malfunctioned if there was any lack of maintenance. For this reason the MG 34 was later supplemented and in part replaced by the MG 42. In vehicles these disadvantages were not so important, and for this reason the MG 34 remained the standard German armoured vehicle machine gun until the end of the war. The armies of Axis-aligned countries such as Hungary, Italy, Slovakia and Finland also used the MG 34.

After 1945 the MG 34 continued to be produced for some years in Czechoslovakia, both for its own army and for export (factories there had to work for the Wehrmacht during the German occupation). After the war the MG 34 could also be found in France, Israel, Vietnam and Portugal as well as in a number of African countries. It featured in many conflicts including the war in Indochina, the Middle Eastern wars between Israel and its neighbours, and the wars in Angola and Mozambique in the mid-1970s.

*An MG 34 on a tripod mounting.*

*In the first years of the war the MG 34 was the standard machine gun for the Wehrmacht.*

# MG 42 UNIVERSAL MACHINE GUN MODEL 42 7.92 MM

The war clearly demonstrated the weaknesses of the inherently outstanding MG 34: it was not only too expensive, but also too sensitive to dirt, snow and ice. An attempt was therefore made to simplify the production methods. However, this design – called the MG 34/41 – was not introduced; instead a decision was made in favour of a new design, the MG 42. As events turned out, this would become one of the best, if not indeed the best, machine gun designs of all time. The MG 42 was developed under the leadership of Dr Werner Gruner in the Grossfuss factories at Döbeln in Saxony. Dr Gruner was in fact not a weapons specialist, but rather a specialist in sheet metal pressing technology. He simply combined the principles of other machine guns into the design of the MG 42. Instead of resource-intensive manufacture involving tight tolerances he decided in favour of the production of pressings utilizing forming and moulding technologies, and developed the gun from sheet metal pressed parts, investment castings and plastics. This robust method of manufacture proved to be outstandingly successful. Both the number of machine tools and the number of working operations could be reduced, and thus the price of each gun was also reduced. With its extremely high rate of fire of 1,500 rounds per minute, not previously achieved by universal machine guns, the MG 42 entered into mythology on both sides of the front. The Allied soldiers feared it and used the MG 42 whenever they could get hold of it. Among the German soldiers it enjoyed a very high reputation, achieving up to 75–80% of the firepower of a section armed only with carbines.

| | |
|---|---|
| Calibre: | 7.92 mm |
| Cartridge: | 7.92 x 57 mm |
| Muzzle velocity: | 750 m/s |
| Firing rate: | 1,500 rounds/min |
| Weight with bipod: | 11.6 kg |
| Magazine capacity: | belt with 50 or 250 rounds |
| Operational range (bipod): | 1,200 m |

*After the war the MG 42 continued to be produced and – adapted to the NATO 7.62 x 51 mm calibre – was introduced into the Bundeswehr as the MG 1 and MG 3. The model was also used in Italy, Norway, Pakistan, Turkey and Austria. In the former Yugoslavia the MG 42* *continued to be produced with its original 7.92 x 57 mm calibre and was used in the Balkan wars of the 1990s. Even today, more than 60 years after its debut, this weapon continues to be manufactured, which speaks eloquently for its quality.*

*The MG 42 proved itself, even in the mud and snow of the Eastern Front.*

*Russia, 1943: an MG 42 machine gunner of the Grossdeutschland Division.*

# PANZERFAUST MODEL 30, 60, 100, 150

The Panzerfaust (meaning 'armoured fist') was in principle a small recoilless gun of the simplest form of construction that fired a high-calibre shaped charge projectile with an armour-piercing capability. Germany's desperate state required the availability of a more effective anti-tank weapon that was simpler to produce in large numbers than the Panzerschreck anti-tank rocket launcher. The design concept of the Panzerfaust was developed in 1941, but the first prototypes were tested only from 1943 onwards. From mid-1944 onwards the Panzerfaust was introduced into the Wehrmacht in various models (30 small, 30, 60, 100, 150). These types differed from each other only slightly; it was just the range that differed. The Panzerfaust was designed for one-time use only. After firing, the barrel could be thrown away, although empty barrels were often gathered up and reloaded in the factory. Operation was very simple: the soldier firing the weapon raised the sight, released the safety catch, located the target and pressed the trigger. Thus the Panzerfaust became the ideal weapon for the poorly trained soldiers of the last phase of the war, and also for the children and old men of the Volkssturm (literally 'People's Storm'). Nevertheless use of the weapon was not without its problems. As in the case of the Panzerschreck it was inadvisable for anyone to be in the area behind the Panzerfaust when it was fired. Moreover, the shaped charge very often did not explode on impact. It is no longer possible to establish exact production numbers, but the Panzerfaust was manufactured in very large quantities. In November 1944 alone the Wehrmacht had more than half a million at its disposal,

of which more than half were fired in the same month.

Despite all its disadvantages, most of which were caused by quality defects resulting from the adverse military situation and lack of training, the Panzerfaust was a feared weapon. Many armoured units attempted to provide their vehicles with additional protection in the form of improvised 'armouring'. The mode of operation of the Panzerfaust meant that rolls of wire mesh or similar were often sufficient for this purpose; these 'softly' captured the slow-moving, shaped charge

| Calibre of the barrel | |
|---|---|
| (Panzerfaust 30): | 45 mm |
| Muzzle velocity: | 45 m/s |
| Length: | 1,030 mm |
| Weight: | 5.1 kg |
| Weight of explosive charge: | 1.5 kg |
| Max. operational range: | 30–40 m |
| Penetration capability: | 140 mm |
| | armoured steel |

and triggered a premature detonation. Similar devices can be seen today on vehicles of the US and British Armies in Iraq.

*The Panzerfaust gave infantrymen the ability to fight against even heavy tanks with a good prospect of success.*

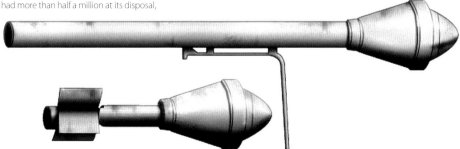

GERMANY

## PANZERSCHRECK ANTI-TANK ROCKET LAUNCHER 54 88 MM AND 100 MM

The Panzerschreck (which literally means 'armour fear') was introduced into the Grenadier units at the start of 1944. The motive for the development of this recoilless rocket launcher to fight against tanks was the desperate position of the infantry in the face of armoured attacks. The Panzerbüchsen 39 anti-tank rifles with a 7.92 mm calibre that were available at the start of the war had demonstrated a lack of capability as early as 1939. The Grenadiers were forced to use demolition charges, magnetic hollow charges or Molotov cocktails; they even resorted to jamming anti-tank mines between the turret and deck of a tank. All these devices required the soldier to enter into the immediate vicinity of the tank, to allow it to roll over him, or even to clamber on to the vehicle. At the end of 1942 and the start of 1943 US Army rocket weapons of the Bazooka type were captured in Tunisia; these were studied with great haste and it was recognized that this weapon could provide anti-tank defence forces with an unimagined strike power. An improved weapon, based on the Bazooka but with a greater calibre (88 mm instead of 60 mm), was developed; because of its shape this was first called the 'Ofenrohr' ('Stovepipe') and then later the 'Panzerschreck'. It fired a rocket projectile with a shaped charge. In its original form the weapon still had no shield for the soldier firing the weapon; he had to wear a fireproof mask so that the exhaust from the rocket charge did not burn him. Nevertheless, this could still happen to another soldier if he was directly behind a Panzerschreck when it was being fired. A special 100 mm version

with an improved penetration capability was manufactured only in small numbers. From 1943 to mid-March 1945, 314,895 anti-tank rocket launchers 54 and more than 2.2 million charges were produced. The Panzerschreck together with the Panzerfaust was part of the so-called 'wonder weapon programme', which with the aid of a massive propaganda campaign was designed to ensure that belief in the final victory remained intact.

| | |
|---|---|
| Calibre: | 88 mm |
| Muzzle velocity: | 130 m/s |
| Length: | 1,640 mm |
| Weight: | 9.5 kg |
| Weight of grenade: | 2.4–3.3 kg |
| Operational range: | 100–200 m |
| Penetration capability (armoured steel): | 150–220 mm at 90° |

*The loading procedure for the Panzerschreck: the soldier on the right places a rocket charge in the barrel from the rear. Wisely he is kneeling alongside, and not behind, the weapon.*

## FLAMETHROWER 35

Flamethrowers were used for the first time on the German side in the First World War and proved to be very successful – for the most part because of their psychological effect, since the equipment itself was heavy, difficult to handle, with a limited range, and quite dangerous for the soldier using it. If the flammable liquid tank on his back was hit this could set him alight. The Wehrmacht also used flamethrowers in the Second World War (as did the other countries engaged in it) against bunkers, secure positions and armoured vehicles. The flamethrowers used by the Germans worked on the following principle: each flamethrower had two tanks – one for a flammable liquid, and the other for a propellant, usually nitrogen. When the valve was opened, the propellant pushed the flammable liquid through the flame tube, at the front end of which it was ignited. The range was dependent on the flow rate of the nozzle, the initial velocity of the flammable liquid and the wind direction. In turn the initial velocity was determined by the pressure in the tank and the length of hose. The first German one-man flamethrower was the Flamethrower 35. It weighed 35.8 kg and was really too heavy to use. The tank contained 11.8 litres of flammable liquid. The jet of flame extended for 25–30 m. Depending on the length of the individual bursts, up to 15 strikes could be delivered. The Flamethrower 35 was produced until 1941. Thereafter various other models (Flamethrower 40, 41, 43, 44, 46) went into production, all of which were lighter and easier to handle than the 35 version.

| Weight: | 35.8 kg |
|---|---|
| Propellant: | nitrogen |
| Quantity of flammable liquid: | 11.8 litres |
| Number of possible strikes: | 2–15 |
| Operational range: | 25–30 m |

*German soldier with a Flamethrower 35.*

## 8 CM MODEL 34 MORTAR

From 1932 onwards the Rheinmetall company developed the 8 cm 34 mortar. The weapon was a smooth-barrelled muzzle-loader with a weight of 57 kg. The mortar consisted of the barrel with cover, bipod with aiming and elevating mechanisms, baseplate and sight mounting. The barrel was 1,143 mm long; the calibre was 81.4 mm. With a muzzle velocity of 172 m/sec the heavy 3.5 kg mortar 34 shell could be fired up to 2,400 m. Scatter at the maximum range was of the order of 65 m. The first weapons were made available to the troops in 1937, and at the outbreak of war they had access to more than 3,625 pieces. When the mortar was mounted on a self-propelled carriage (e.g. Sd.Kfz. 250/7), it was called the

67 mortar. More than 73,000 mortars of this model had been produced by March 1945. In addition the Wehrmacht used many captured mortars of French, Polish, Czech or Russian origin.

| Calibre: | 81.4 mm |
|---|---|
| Muzzle velocity: | 172 m/s |
| Length: | 1,143 mm |
| Weight: | 57 kg |
| Weight of mortar shell: | 3.5 kg |
| Max. operational range: | 2,400 m |

*A 34 mortar team takes cover while firing.*

## BERETTA MODEL 1938/42 MACHINE PISTOL AND VARIANTS 9 MM

| Calibre: | 9 mm |
|---|---|
| Cartridge: | 9 x 19 mm Parabellum |
| Muzzle velocity: | 370 m/s |
| Firing rate: | 400 rounds/min |
| Weight without magazine: | 3.27–4.3 kg |
| Magazine capacity: | 20 or 40 rounds |
| Operational range: | 200 m |

the Beretta models from the First World War. The Model 38 used the 9 mm Parabellum ammunition, was rated as extremely robust and was very popular. Two different triggers allowed an uncomplicated choice between single or continuous fire. From the end of 1942 onwards the 38/42 variant was

manufactured, which was designed to remove the main disadvantage of the machine pistol, namely the excessive resources required for its production. The Model 38/44 was a further simplification. Both variants were also produced for the Wehrmacht, where they saw operation as the MP.738 and MP.739.

This weapon was the Italian Army's standard machine pistol during the Second World War. The Model 1938A was introduced in 1938, and variants were in production until 1975. The weapon was an ongoing development of

## MANNLICHER-CARCANO REPEATING RIFLES 6.5 MM AND 7.35 MM

| Calibre (Model 1938): | 7.35 mm |
|---|---|
| Cartridge: | 7.35 x 52 mm |
| Muzzle velocity: | 755 m/s |
| Weight with empty magazine: | 3.09 kg |
| Magazine capacity: | 6 rounds |
| Operational range: | 600 m |

The rifles and carbines of the Mannlicher-Carcano family, used during the Second World War by the Italian armed forces in more than 15 variants, can be traced back to a rifle

*Mannlicher-Carcano rifles were rated as unreliable and not particularly accurate.*

introduced for the first time in 1891 – the Model 1891. Fundamentally nothing had altered up to the start of the Second World War in the design of this conventionally built and manually operated weapon. The design, and in particular the 6.5 mm calibre cartridge that was developed for it, were rated as hopelessly out of date even at the beginning of the 20th century. An attempt was therefore made in 1938 to remove its worst weak spots by introducing a new 7.35 mm calibre cartridge and shortening the weapon, but this was unsuccessful. In the absence of any alternative the Italian troops had to remain equipped with 7.35 mm and 6.5 mm calibre weapons of this type until the end of the war.

## NAMBU TAISHO SEMI-AUTOMATIC PISTOL MODEL 14 8 MM

This weapon was designed by Major (later General) Nambu in the 14th year of the reign of the Emperor Taisho, hence its designation. It was the standard pistol of the Japanese armed forces from 1941 to 1945 and was issued primarily to officers. In total more than 320,000 were produced. In appearance it is somewhat similar to the German P 08, but is significantly simpler in its construction, and never achieved the reliability or quality of manufacture of the latter at any time. Moreover, the Japanese 8 mm cartridge was greatly inferior to the German Parabellum ammunition in all respects, and the weapon could react unpleasantly if it was not handled with care. A version with a 7 mm calibre was also manufactured. This variant, originally intended for the civilian market, was issued primarily to Japanese pilots. After the defeat and the subsequent demilitarization of Japan in 1945 many Nambu pistols found their way to the USA, since returning GIs often took weapons of this type home as souvenirs or trophies, even though it was against the regulations.

| Calibre: | 8 mm |
|---|---|
| Cartridge: | 8 x 21.5 mm |
| Muzzle velocity: | 290 m/s |
| Weight with empty magazine: | 0.96 kg |
| Magazine capacity: | 8 rounds |
| Operational range: | 50 m |

## ARISAKA MODEL 99 REPEATING RIFLE AND VARIANTS 7.7 MM

Like many other nations, the Japanese during the Second World War employed rifles and carbines that were already in use between 1914 and 1918, e.g. the Arisaka Model 38 with a 6.5 mm calibre. It had, however, been recognized during the Sino-Japanese War at the end of the 1930s that these rifles and their ammunition no longer satisfied requirements. In 1939 therefore a slightly modified and easier-to-handle 7.7 mm calibre rifle was introduced. These weapons were conventional manual repeaters, similar to the European Mauser 98k or Mannlicher-Carcano. Although this very average design should have been the standard weapon for the Japanese troops, sufficient numbers were never produced to allow all troop units to be equipped with them. The Model 38 therefore remained in service up to 1945. Altogether more than 10 million rifles of the Arisaka type are believed to have been manufactured between 1897 and 1945.

| Calibre: | 7.7 mm |
|---|---|
| Cartridge: | 7.7 x 58 mm |
| Muzzle velocity: | 755 m/s |
| Weight with empty magazine: | 3.79 kg |
| Magazine capacity: | 5 rounds |
| Operational range: | 600 m |

## LIGHT MACHINE GUN MODEL 99 7.7 MM

| Calibre: | 7.7 mm |
|---|---|
| Cartridge: | 7.7 x 58 mm |
| Muzzle velocity: | 715 m/s |
| Firing rate: | 800 rounds/min |
| Weight with empty magazine and bipod: | 10.01 kg |
| Magazine capacity: | 30 rounds |
| Operational range: | 800 m |

As was the case for the Arisaka rifles, it likewise became clear during the Sino-Japanese War that the 6.5 mm calibre ammunition used for the machine guns up to that time no longer satisfied requirements. The Model 96 light machine gun that had been introduced shortly before this war was thus already out of date. In addition this weapon had the disadvantage that the cartridges had to be greased before loading in order to guarantee trouble-free operation. In 1939 therefore a new machine gun was introduced, the Model 99 with a 7.7 mm calibre. Although it was declared to be a standard weapon it was never manufactured in sufficient numbers and older models also remained in service up to the end of the war.

The Model 99 appears to have been based on the Czech ZB 1926 and was likewise reliable and accurate as well as being a weapon that was highly prized by soldiers. It is believed that 100,000 were produced up to 1945.

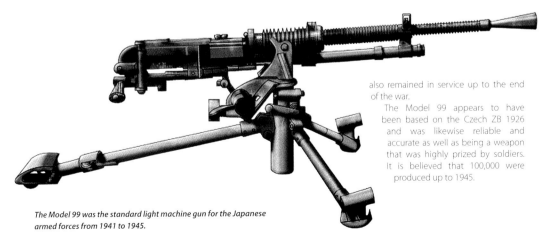

*The Model 99 was the standard light machine gun for the Japanese armed forces from 1941 to 1945.*

# HEAVY MACHINE GUN MODEL 92 7.7 MM

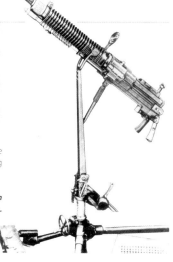

Machine guns of this type were identical to the Taisho 3 Model of 1914 apart from the calibre (which was 7.7 mm instead of 6.5 mm). Externally these weapons were easily recognized by the massive cooling ribs on the barrel, although extended continuous fire was still not possible. Another disadvantage was the great weight, which made any change of firing position difficult. Also the cartridges had to be oiled before they were inserted. Malfunctions occurred if this procedure was not carried out carefully enough. Nevertheless the Model 92 was the machine gun most often used by Japanese troops between 1941 and 1945.

| | |
|---|---|
| Calibre: | 7.7 mm |
| Cartridge: | 7.7 x 58 mm |
| Muzzle velocity: | 730 m/s |
| Firing rate: | 450 rounds/min |
| Weight with tripod: | 55.3 kg |
| Magazine capacity (loading clips): | 30 rounds |
| Operational range: | 1,000 m |

The Allied forces named it the 'Woodpecker' because of its stuttering tone when firing.

*A Model 92 heavy machine gun on an anti-aircraft mounting.*

# 50 MM MODEL 89 MORTAR

This weapon emerged from the need to bridge the gap between the range of thrown hand grenades and the minimum range of the larger mortars. The mortar was introduced in 1929 and at first was only issued to special units. By the start of the Second World War, however, it was part of standard infantry ordnance. The mortar had a 50 mm calibre, weighed only 4.54 kg and had a barrel length of just 254 mm. It fired a shell weighing 0.793 kg over a maximum range of 640 m, and could also fire the standard Japanese Model 91 hand grenade instead of a dedicated shell.

| | |
|---|---|
| Calibre: | 50 mm |
| Muzzle velocity: | not known |
| Length: | 254 mm |
| Weight: | 4.54 kg |
| Weight of mortar shell: | 0.793 kg |
| Max. operational range: | 640 m |

*Since the mortar did not feature a bipod, the soldier firing the weapon had to hold the barrel steady during firing. Therefore the firing procedure usually meant that the soldier firing the mortar knelt behind it. Thus the mortar acquired the nickname 'Knee Mortar'. Apparently some US Marines are believed to have taken this all too literally and tried to fire captured weapons with the baseplate located on their knees – which inevitably resulted in broken bones. Despite its small size the mortar had a massive recoil.*

## MAS 1938 MACHINE PISTOL 7.65 MM

As a consequence of the First World War, the French government weapons factories began to work on the design of machine pistols from the mid-1920s onwards. However, it took until 1938 before any useful results were achieved. Series production started up only slowly, so that by the time France was invaded in 1940 only a few weapons were available. However, production continued in the unoccupied part of France after its defeat. Overall the weapon was rated as accurate, but also complicated and expensive to manufacture. Its greatest disadvantage was the poor performance of the 7.65 mm calibre ammunition, which was unable to match the 9 mm Parabellum cartridge. Nevertheless, the MAS 1938 continued to be used after the war.

| | |
|---|---|
| Calibre: | 7.65 mm |
| Cartridge: | 7.65 x 20 mm |
| Muzzle velocity: | 350 m/s |
| Firing rate: | 600 rounds/min |
| Weight with full magazine: | 3.4 kg |
| Magazine capacity: | 32 rounds |
| Operational range: | 150 m |

## MAS 1936 REPEATING RIFLE 7.5 MM

| | |
|---|---|
| Calibre: | 7.5 mm |
| Cartridge: | 7.5 x 54 mm |
| Muzzle velocity: | 825 m/s |
| Weight with empty magazine: | 3.78 kg |
| Magazine capacity: | 5 rounds |
| Operational range: | 600 m |

In 1886 the French Army led the world when it introduced smokeless rifle ammunition in the form of the 8 mm Lebel cartridge. In the 1920s, however, this ammunition began to be dated. After a number of unsuccessful attempts a new standard cartridge with a calibre of 7.5 x 54 mm was introduced in 1929. Attempts to retrofit the old Lebelund Berthier rifles, which originated in the First World War and were still available in large numbers, were not successful, so development started on a new weapon, which was introduced in 1936 as the MAS 1936. However, series production of this model also started only slowly. It is believed that only 250,000 were produced by 10 May 1940. The MAS 1936 was one of the last manually actuated conventional repeaters. Captured weapons were also used by German occupation troops. After 1945 the MAS 1936 continued to remain part of the equipment of the French Army for some years. Subsequently the weapon was to be found in the armies of several of the former French colonies.

*The MAS 1936 was the last manually loaded rifle in the world to be adopted by an army.*

## CHÂTELLERAULT LIGHT MACHINE GUN MODEL 1924/29 7.5 MM

| Calibre: | 7.5 mm |
|---|---|
| Cartridge: | 7.5 x 54 mm |
| Muzzle velocity: | 790 m/s |
| Firing rate: | 550 rounds/min |
| Weight with empty magazine and bipod: | 8.93 kg |
| Magazine capacity: | 25 rounds |
| Operational range: | 800 m |

In the First World War France was one of the first countries to introduce light machine guns, the majority of which were of the Chauchat Model 1915 type. Although this 8 mm calibre machine gun provided the soldiers with valuable

firepower, it was anything but a mature, reliable weapon. In 1920 a contract was therefore awarded to the government weapons factory in Châtellerault to design a successor model that was to use the 7.5 mm calibre ammunition being developed at that time. The gun was modelled on the US Browning BAR M 1918. In 1924

the new machine gun entered service in the French Army. However, it had the habit of sometimes exploding when in continuous fire mode. It was discovered that lower-quality steel had been used in its production, which conducted the heat away so poorly that cartridges ignited even as they were being fed in. An improved model appeared in 1929. In addition there were variants for installation in aircraft and fortifications. After the victory over France the Wehrmacht captured large stocks of the machine gun and called it the MG Model 24/29 (f). After the war the French Army continued to use it for some years.

## BRANDT 81 MM MORTAR MODEL 1927/31

In the trench warfare of the First World War a new weapon emerged: the grenade or mine launcher, otherwise known as a mortar. This mortar originated in 1927 as an improvement of the British Stokes model from the First World War. It was Edgar Brandt's masterpiece, exported to many countries and at the same time an archetype for many similar models across the world. The mortar was a simple smooth-barrelled weapon that was muzzle loaded and weighed 59.7 kg together with a baseplate and bipod, on which were fitted both an elevating and traversing mechanism and also a sighting device. A shell with a maximum weight of 6.5 kg was fired out of the 1,270 mm long barrel with a muzzle velocity of 174 m per second. The maximum range was 2,850 m.

| Calibre: | 81 mm |
|---|---|
| Muzzle velocity: | 174 m/s |
| Length: | 1,270 mm |
| Weight: | 59.7 kg |
| Weight of shell: | 3.25 kg |
| Max. operational range: | 2,850 m |

*The design of this mortar was so accomplished that even today almost all mortars of whatever kind are descendants of the Brandt mortar.*

## ENFIELD REVOLVER MODEL NO. 2 MK. 1 CALIBRE .380

This revolver was developed in the Enfield government weapons factory (Royal Small Arms Factory Enfield, RSA) at the start of the 1920s to replace the many different Webley and Enfield revolvers in the British Army that originated during the First World War and in some cases were even significantly older. The British stayed with the revolver, although most other countries developed semi-automatic pistols. The reason for this was a deeply rooted tradition as well as the indestructible properties and the great efficiency of the Webley and Enfield revolvers. Disadvantages, however, included the heavy weight and the massive recoil

of these older .455 calibre models (approximately 11.5 mm) that required a practised marksman. The decision was therefore made to stay with the revolver, but with a smaller calibre and less weight. The result was a compromise, since, although the Enfield No. 2 was robust and required little maintenance, its stopping power was not always adequate. Nevertheless by the end of the war 380,000 revolvers of the military variant had been produced.

| Calibre: | .380 (ca. 9 mm) |
| --- | --- |
| Cartridge: | .380 (9 x 20 mm) |
| Muzzle velocity: | 200 m/s |
| Weight unloaded: | 0.78 kg |
| Magazine capacity: | 6 rounds |
| Operational range: | 45 m |

## STEN MACHINE PISTOL 9 MM

| Calibre: | 9 mm |
| --- | --- |
| Cartridge: | 9 x 19 mm |
| Muzzle velocity: | 380 m/s |
| Firing rate: | 500 rounds/min |
| Weight without magazine: | 3 kg |
| Magazine capacity: | 32 rounds |
| Operational range: | 200 m |

The designation 'Sten gun' was used for a series of very simply and cost-effectively constructed, but nevertheless reliable and effective, British Army machine pistols that originated in the Second World War. The name was derived from those of the two designers,

R. V. Shepperd and H. J. Turpin, who were working in the Enfield government weapons factory. The design of the pistol began in 1940 in response to the German victories on the continent when it appeared likely that the Wehrmacht would carry out an invasion of the United Kingdom in 'Operation Sea Lion'. What the British Army required in this situation – particularly after the heavy losses of equipment at Dunkirk – was an effective and inexpensive automatic weapon. In 1941 production began of the Sten Mk. 1, of which more than 100,000 were produced. The success of these crude and cheap-looking weapons led to a number

of improved models in the shape of Mk. 2 to Mk. 6, of which in total more than 3.5 million were manufactured. Not only was the Sten standard equipment for the British armed forces during the war, but also those dropped by parachute were used by many partisan and resistance groups in occupied Europe. The greatest compliment to the potency and effectiveness of the Sten was without doubt that paid by the Germans, when shortly before the end of the war they planned a replica under the names 'Gerät Potsdam' ('Potsdam equipment') and 'Gerät Neumünster' ('Neumünster equipment') so that they could arm the Volkssturm effectively and cheaply. However, only a few thousand were delivered by the end of the war. The original Sten machine pistol remained in use up to the 1960s in various armed forces, and was always highly prized because of its reliability and simplicity.

*Sten MP Mk. 2.*

## LEE-ENFIELD REPEATING RIFLE .303 (7.7 MM)

| Calibre (all versions Lee-Enfield No. 4 Mk. 1): | .303 (7.7 mm) |
|---|---|
| Cartridge: | .303 (7.7 x 56 mm) |
| Muzzle velocity: | 745 m/s |
| Weight with empty magazine: | 4.12 kg |
| Magazine capacity: | 10 rounds |
| Operational range: | 800 m |

In the Second World War the British Army used rifles of the same type as were used in the First World War. Some of the weapons were still available from war stocks, but some were also improved versions. The original Lee-Enfield rifle was developed in 1895 and in 1902 was designated a standard weapon. At that time it was rated as one of the best rifles of its kind, particularly because of the 10 round magazine and what was a high firing rate for a manually loaded rifle. Various trial weapons were developed between the wars, but were unable to achieve acceptance for economic reasons. The large stocks of .303 calibre ammunition and the corresponding Lee-Enfield rifles from the First World War ensured that this type continued to be used in the form of various models. Thus it remained in service with only minimal modifications, but the designations of the different variants are confusing. Most heavily used was definitely the Type No. 4 Mk. 1, series production of which began in the 1930s and continued until 1945. Alongside special sniper models there was also a shortened version for the jungle, but this failed to prove itself.

## BREN LIGHT MACHINE GUN MODEL .303 (7.7 MM)

The name of this machine gun is based on the first letters of the locations 'Brno' and 'Enfield'. Brno indicates the Czech origin of this weapon, which was designed in that country in 1933 and was based on the MG ZB v.b.26. The Bren fired the same ammunition as the Lee-Enfield rifle. In general the Bren was rated as a very reliable weapon. Particular emphasis was given to the easy changeover of the barrel when this became overheated with continuous fire. The drawbacks were the rather heavy weight and the low rate of fire of 500 rounds/min compared with the MG 42's 1,500 rounds/min. The British .303 cartridge was also not ideal for automatic weapons, so loading jams could occur. It was therefore recommended that the curved magazine inserted on top of the weapon should be loaded with only 28 rounds instead of 30. This was, of course, inadequate for a machine gun: a belt feed would have been preferable, but this was never

| Calibre: | .303 (7.7 mm) |
|---|---|
| Cartridge: | .303 (7.7 x 56 mm) |
| Muzzle velocity: | 745 m/s |
| Firing rate: | 500 rounds/min |
| Weight with empty magazine and bipod: | 10.2 kg |
| Magazine capacity: | 30 rounds |
| Operational range: | 650 m |

introduced. During the war the gun was manufactured not only in Enfield but also in Canada and Australia. After 1945 the Bren was retrofitted to take the NATO 7.62 x 51 mm calibre and was used by the British up to the 1990s.

*The Bren was the standard light machine gun for Commonwealth troops until well after 1945.*

## VICKERS HEAVY MACHINE GUN MODEL .303 (7.7 MM)

This machine gun was manufactured by Vickers from 1912 onwards. It was a development of the Maxim machine gun developed in 1885 by Hiram Maxim, whose patent Vickers bought in 1896. The Vickers gun was the British Army's standard machine gun in the First World War, and from 1916 onwards formed the standard armament of British and French fighter aircraft. The British standard ammunition with a .303 calibre was used for the Vickers machine gun. The cartridges usually had to be loaded by hand into the ammunition belts, which were made of fabric. Operation of the machine gun required six men: one fired

the weapon, a second man had to feed in the ammunition belt, while the others carried ancillary equipment and looked after the ammunition logistics. The Vickers was popular with soldiers because of its reliability and solid workmanship. As a result of its water cooling it was exceptionally well suited for continuous fire. The ammunition boxes, each holding 250 rounds, weighed 10 kg. As aircraft armament the gun operated in an air-cooled mode and was fitted with an interrupter gear to provide synchronization with the propeller. There

| | |
|---|---|
| Calibre: | .303 (7.7 mm) |
| Cartridge: | .303 (7.7 x 56 mm) |
| Muzzle velocity: | 745 m/s |
| Firing rate: | 450 rounds/min |
| Weight with tripod: | 41.27 kg |
| Magazine capacity: | 250 rounds/belt |
| Max. operational range: | 4,000 m |

were many versions for installation in aircraft, armoured vehicles, and even ships, including a .50 calibre (12.7 mm) version.

*The Vickers remained in service with the British Army until well into the 1960s.*

## BOYS ANTI-TANK RIFLE .55 MK. 1

| | |
|---|---|
| Calibre: | .55 (13.97 mm) |
| Cartridge: | .55 (13.97 x 99 mm) |
| Muzzle velocity: | 760 m/s |
| Penetration capability: | 20 mm/90 m/90° |
| Weight with empty magazine and bipod: | 16.32 kg |
| Magazine capacity: | 5 rounds |
| Operational range: | 90 m |
| (further against armoured targets) | |

This rifle was developed from 1934 onwards by the British weapons expert Captain Boys in response to the start of rearmament in Germany, and was introduced officially into the British armed forces in November 1937. Its penetration capability of 20 mm of armoured steel at a distance of 90 m was already inadequate at this time. The German 39 anti-tank rifle with a 7.92 mm

calibre could penetrate 30 mm at a distance of 100 m! Therefore an improved version (Mk. 2) was designed during the war, but this in turn was quickly overtaken by developments in vehicle armour. At the outbreak of war in 1939 the Boys was only effective to a limited extent against modern tanks, but could still be used against lightly armoured

scout cars or personnel carriers, and also later against light Japanese tanks. In 1940 the Germans captured quite a number of these weapons at Dunkirk and used them temporarily. In North Africa the Boys was often installed in armoured vehicles by Commonwealth troops. Besides its low penetration capability further disadvantages included its great weight and heavy recoil. Nevertheless approximately 63,000 were produced up to 1942.

# PIAT

| Calibre of the tube: | 76 mm |
| --- | --- |
| Muzzle velocity: | 106 m/s |
| Length of tube: | 991 mm |
| Weight unloaded: | 14.52 kg |
| Weight of explosive charge: | 1.13 kg |
| Max. operational range: | 25–90 m |
| Penetration capability: (armoured steel) | 75 mm/90° |

The PIAT (Projector Infantry Anti Tank) arose out of the need to equip the British troops with a more effective anti-tank weapon than the Boys anti-tank rifle – this, however, had to be light enough such that it could also be used by parachute troops. In the same manner as the Panzerfaust and the Bazooka the PIAT used the shaped charge principle to achieve the greatest possible effect on the target. At the same time this weapon had its own particular features. Thus it functioned in principle like a crossbow, using spring tension: the projectile had a hollow tailpiece, fitted with vanes for stabilization, which held the propellant charge. In the barrel were a strong spiral spring and a metal rod. When the soldier

firing the weapon pressed the trigger, the rod sprang forward, ejected the round and at the same time ignited the propellant charge. In theory this process should have put the spring under tension again, but this did not always happen. Tensioning by hand was laborious, since it required a pulling force of 90 kg!

*The PIAT, introduced into service from the end of 1942, was a simple design which at the same time was heavy and difficult to handle. Nevertheless it proved itself as an anti-tank weapon and in street fighting, and continued to be used even after 1945.*

# 76.2 MM MORTAR

This mortar originated as an improved version of the British Stokes model from the First World War, when the British Army was planning at the end of the 1920s to improve the immediate fire support for their infantry. At first, light guns were envisaged, but for reasons of cost and weight the decision was made in favour of a mortar, 50.8 kg in weight, with a 76.2 mm calibre, which fired a 4.53 kg shell with a muzzle velocity of 198 m/sec from a 1,370 mm barrel. The maximum range of the first models was approximately 1,460 m. During the war, however, it emerged that the German 8 cm mortar 34 had a significantly greater range (2,400 m). Therefore a variant was designed with a longer barrel and a projectile

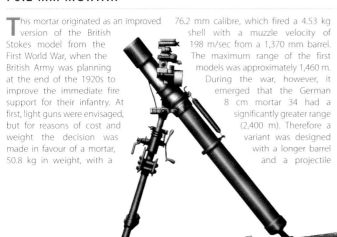

| Calibre: | 76.2 mm |
| --- | --- |
| Muzzle velocity: | 198 m/s |
| Length: | 1,370 mm |
| Weight: | 50.8 kg |
| Weight of projectile: | 4.53 kg |
| Max. operational range: | Mk. 1: 1,460 m |
| | Mk. 2: 2,560 m |

with a more powerful propellant charge, which brought the range up to 2,560 m (Mk. 2).

## TULA-TOKAREV SEMI-AUTOMATIC PISTOL MODEL TT 1933 7.62 MM

| | |
|---|---|
| Calibre: | 7.62 mm |
| Cartridge: | 7.62 x 25 mm |
| Muzzle velocity: | 420 m/s |
| Weight with empty magazine: | 0.854 kg |
| Magazine capacity: | 8 rounds |
| Operational range: | 50 m |

The Tokarev TT-33 was the standard pistol of the Red Army from the 1930s and in that respect was the successor to a number of older revolvers. The mechanism was based on that of the Browning models. It was designed to fire the 7.62 mm calibre Tokarev cartridge, which was almost identical to the very powerful German 7.63 mm Mauser cartridge, which could also be used. The weapon was rated as very robust, reliable, safe and accurate. The TT-33 was produced up until 1952 in enormous numbers and introduced into the whole of the Eastern Bloc. Some models remained in service into the 1970s. Copies of the TT-33 are also known to originate from China and Egypt, among other countries.

## SHPAGIN MACHINE PISTOL MODEL PPSH 1941 7.62 MM

The PPSh machine pistol was designed and developed by the Russian designer Georgii Shpagin. The first model appeared in 1940 and was tested together with other designs in the same year. In these tests the weapons were fired with artificially contaminated magazines and were unlubricated (to do this individual parts were cleaned with kerosene and rubbed dry). Moreover, 5,000 rounds were fired without cleaning the machine pistol. Since it performed the best in these rigorous tests, the PPSh was introduced into the Red Army in December 1940. It was designed to be in service for a minimum of 30,000 rounds with the requirement that afterwards the weapon should demonstrate satisfactory accuracy and reliability. When the PPSh-41 was introduced, sheet metal pressing procedures were not yet widely used. Nevertheless many of the machine pistol's parts were manufactured using metal pressing technology. Since most of the individual parts were no longer cast but manufactured from 2–5 mm thick sheet metal, metal could be saved and production costs lowered. The most expensive parts to produce were the barrel and the drum magazine, which was taken from the earlier PPD-40 weapon. The machine pistol only had two threaded connections. In total almost 6 million of these were manufactured. The Wehrmacht thought highly of the indestructible weapon. Captured examples not only were used unofficially by soldiers, but also became part of the official armament. The designation was MP 717(r); there were also models that were retrofitted to take the 9 mm Parabellum cartridge. The PPSh was one of the best weapons of its class. Its primary advantages were its superior firepower, the uncomplicated production methods and also its indestructibility, but its heavy weight was a disadvantage.

| | |
|---|---|
| Calibre: | 7.62 mm |
| Cartridge: | 7.62 x 25 mm |
| Muzzle velocity: | 500 m/s |
| Firing rate: | 900 rounds/min |
| Weight with full magazine: | 4.1–5.3 kg |
| Magazine capacity: | 35 or 71 rounds |
| Max. operational range: | 200 m |

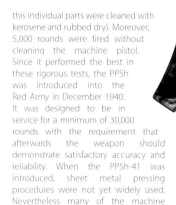

*A PPSh with a 35-round box magazine.*

## MOSIN-NAGANT REPEATING RIFLE 91/30 7.62 MM

| | |
|---|---|
| Calibre: | 7.62 mm |
| Cartridge: | 7.62 x 54 mm |
| Muzzle velocity: | 865 m/s |
| Weight with empty magazine: | 4.5 kg |
| Magazine capacity: | 5 rounds |
| Operational range: | 600 m |

Weapons of this type were in service over seven decades in Russia and subsequently the Soviet Union. The original model was a repeating rifle designed in 1891 by Sergei Mosin and introduced into the Tsarist Army. This rifle was called the Mosin-Nagant, since the magazine had been designed by the Belgian Nagant brothers. A new 7.62 x 54 mm cartridge was introduced with the Mosin-Nagant. During the First World War this rifle was the standard weapon of the Russian infantry and remained so until after the Second World War; it was prized on account of its robust design and accuracy. Various versions were also introduced into many other armies in the Eastern Bloc. In China the M1938 carbine version and its M1944 variant were produced under licence as the Type 53. Licensed versions and further developments were also produced in Czechoslovakia (the Model 54 sniper rifle) and Yugoslavia. The 7.62 x 54 mm R rimmed cartridge developed for this rifle has meanwhile become the oldest rifle cartridge in use in the world and is still produced worldwide and used in modern weapons such as the Dragunov sniper rifle and heavy machine guns, primarily those made in Russia and China.

## DEGTYAREV LIGHT MACHINE GUN MODEL DP 1928 AND DPM 1944 7.62 MM

The Degtyarev DP 1928 was the standard light machine gun of the Red Army during the Second World War and thereafter. Its origin goes back to 1924 when the designer Degtyarev began to develop a new machine gun for the Soviet armed forces that was required to be as simple as possible, robust, cost-effective and usable under widely varying conditions. In tests in the summer of 1927 its new design proved to be superior to all others – including foreign machine guns – and it was therefore introduced into the Red Army in 1928. Although Degtyarev's objectives had been more than achieved and the weapon was rated as reliable, light and robust, there were still a few weak points. Thus from their experience on the Eastern Front the troops complained

| | |
|---|---|
| Calibre: | 7.62 mm |
| Cartridge: | 7.62 x 54 mm |
| Muzzle velocity: | 840 m/s |
| Firing rate: | 600 rounds/min |
| Weight with bipod: | 8.4 kg |
| Magazine capacity (pan magazine): | 49 (47) rounds |
| Operational range: | 800 m |

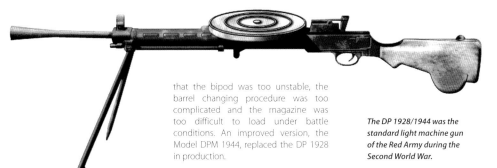

that the bipod was too unstable, the barrel changing procedure was too complicated and the magazine was too difficult to load under battle conditions. An improved version, the Model DPM 1944, replaced the DP 1928 in production.

*The DP 1928/1944 was the standard light machine gun of the Red Army during the Second World War.*

## MAXIM HEAVY MACHINE GUN MODEL PM 1910 7.62 MM

As the name suggests, this veteran went into production in 1910 for the Tsarist Army. The Model PM 1910 is an improved version of the Model 1905 that in turn was based on the first successful automatic weapon ever, the Maxim machine gun. The American Hiram Maxim developed this machine gun in 1885; it was the first weapon to use the recoil gases generated during firing in an automatic loading and ejection procedure. The previously developed weapons, e.g. the Gatling or Gardener guns, were still reliant on manual operation. The British armaments company Vickers acquired the licence rights from Maxim and exported these machine guns all over the world. By the start of the 20th century weapons based on the Maxim system were very widespread and found many imitators, among them the German MG 08, the French Hotchkiss and the Vickers machine gun. The Russian PM 1910 variant was manufactured in enormous numbers up to 1942; in that year alone 55,258 were produced. Because of its robust design and reliability it continued to be used even after 1945. The Soviet Union gave large numbers of this machine gun to China and North Korea, where the PM 1910 (and its successors) were in use until the 1970s.

| | |
|---|---|
| Calibre: | 7.62 mm |
| Cartridge: | 7.62 x 54 mm |
| Muzzle velocity: | 860 m/s |
| Firing rate: | 520 rounds/min |
| Weight with mounting: | 45.27 kg |
| Magazine capacity (textile belt): | 250 rounds |
| Operational range: | 1,000 m |

*The PM 1910 proved itself in 1941–45.*

## DEGTYAREV-SHPAGIN MACHINE GUN DSHK 1938 12.7 MM

This weapon is a real classic and has now been in use for more than seven decades. Its origin goes back to 1930 when the Red Army awarded a contract for a heavy machine gun utilizing the 12.7 x 108 mm cartridge to counter lightly armoured and aerial targets. The designer Degtyarev therefore brought across features of his 7.62 mm DP 27 machine gun using the principle of gas pressure loading. The machine gun, designated the DK, was built from 1934 onwards in small numbers, but was not satisfactory because of its low firing rate of only 360 rounds/min. To increase the firing rate, Shpagin developed a modified cartridge feed, which brought the rate of fire up to approximately 600 rounds/min. This machine gun, now named the DShK, was tested in 1938 and became part of the weaponry of the Red Army in 1939. The machine gun was not only introduced into infantry units as an infantry support and anti-aircraft machine gun, but also used as turret armament for light tanks, and as an anti-aircraft machine gun on ships and armoured trains. The first Soviet tank to receive a machine gun of this type was the IS-2 from 1943 onwards.

| | |
|---|---|
| Calibre: | 12.7 mm |
| Cartridge: | 12.7 x 108 mm |
| Muzzle velocity: | 850 m/s |
| Firing rate: | 600 rounds/min |
| Weight without mounting: | 33.3 kg |
| Magazine capacity (metal belt): | 50 rounds |
| Operational range: | 2,000 m |

During the war the feed mechanism was modified (cartridge feed via belt boxes), the mounting was improved, the changeover of the barrel was simplified, and the length of service of essential parts was increased. Overall the DShK was rated as a reliable, indestructible weapon with a high efficiency on target. After the war a modernized version was designated the DShKM 38/46. When modified as anti-aircraft armament for medium tanks, the machine gun was called the DShKMT. The former Soviet Union exported weapons of this type in large numbers and even today the DShK is in service in more than 40 countries worldwide.

## DEGTYAREV ANTI-TANK RIFLE MODEL PTRD 1941 14.5 MM

In the Second World War the Red Army used two types of anti-tank rifle: the Degtyarev PTRD with single cartridges and the five-round, semi-automatic Simonov PTRS. Both were developed to meet the requirement to supply an anti-tank rifle using the 14.5 x 114 mm cartridge in the shortest possible time. In the space of just one month both weapons were tested, but neither one seemed to be better than the other. Therefore the Soviet armed forces introduced both weapons into active service in 1941. Despite a view that was

widely held at that time, anti-tank rifles were not completely useless. On the battlefield there were a large number of only lightly armoured vehicles, whose armour could easily be penetrated by an anti-tank rifle. The side armour of the early German battle tanks was also vulnerable against the anti-tank rifles of the Red Army. At first glance the PTRD appears to be a primitive weapon but in reality it is

| | |
|---|---|
| Calibre: | 14.5 mm |
| Cartridge: | 14.5 x 114 mm |
| Muzzle velocity: | 1,010 m/s |
| Penetration capability: | 40 mm/100 m/90° |
| Weight with empty magazine and bipod: | 17.3 kg |
| Magazine capacity: | 1 round |
| Operational range: (further against unarmoured targets) | 400 m |

complex. The barrel moves a certain amount back into the shaft as a result of the recoil during firing, which results in the bolt rotating and unlocking. At the end of this

movement the bolt engages, while the barrel is pushed back into its initial position. This opens the breech and the empty cartridge shell is ejected. Now the soldier firing the weapon can load a new cartridge and close the breech manually.

## 82 MM MORTAR MODEL PM-37

| | |
|---|---|
| Calibre: | 82 mm |
| Muzzle velocity: | 211 m/s |
| Barrel length: | 1,220 mm |
| Weight: | 45 kg |
| Missile weight: | 3.05 kg |
| Max. operational range: | 3,040 m |

The Red Army always placed great value on artillery support for the infantry, and, when in the mid-1930s it was looking for a support weapon that would be immediately available to the infantry units, the decision was made in favour of mortars. In 1936 the Soviet Union therefore acquired a number of French 81 mm Brandt mortars. The evaluation of these weapons was essentially positive and with a few modifications an unlicensed copy of the Brandt mortar was produced from 1937 onwards. The calibre was increased to 82 mm and the Russians inserted a spring mechanism between the barrel and the bipod; in addition the aiming mechanism was improved and instead of a rectangular baseplate the copies were given a round one.

*Budapest, 1945: soldiers of the Red Army using an 82 mm mortar in street fighting. This design was extremely successful and more than 165,000 of them were produced – with only a few modifications – by 1945. Production also continued after the Second World War. Many mortars were exported all over the world or produced under licence. Even today this mortar is used in many armies with hardly any modifications.*

USA

## COLT SEMI-AUTOMATIC PISTOL M 1911 A1 .45 (11.43 MM)

From its introduction in 1911 through to its replacement in 1992 by the Beretta 92 FS, the Colt M 1911 was a standard weapon in the US Army. Even today its popularity is undiminished and this model is still manufactured and in use.

At the start of the 20th century the US Army, in its search for a new pistol, needed nearly five years for rigorous fundamental tests in which the new Colt, designed by Browning, distinguished itself as the best and most reliable weapon. As a result it was adopted by the army in 1911, and, although Colt had reckoned on this outcome of the test series, the company needed some time in order to be able to deliver large numbers of the pistols. When the First World War broke out, across the world various other companies also produced the pistol under licence. After the war a number of improvements were introduced and standardized into the Model 1911 A1. The American armed forces also went into the Second World War using this pistol.

| Calibre: | .45 (11.43 mm) |
|---|---|
| Cartridge: | .45 ACP (11.43 x 23 mm) |
| Muzzle velocity: | 260 m/s |
| Weight with empty magazine: | 1.13 kg |
| Magazine capacity: | 7 rounds |
| Operational range: | 50 m |

Countless weapons have been generated since 1911, including unlicensed copies made in China. Among the advantages of the Colt M 1911 are its extreme robustness, its reliability, and the efficiency of the .45 (11.43 mm) bullet. At the same time, however, this results in a heavy weapon that is somewhat difficult to handle and has a really hard recoil. Many of its users are nevertheless happy to accept these features and consider this to be one of the best pistols in the world.

## THOMPSON M1928 MACHINE PISTOL .45 (11.43 MM)

| Calibre: | .45 (11.43 mm) |
|---|---|
| Cartridge: | .45 ACP (11.43 x 23 mm) |
| Muzzle velocity: | 280 m/s |
| Firing rate: | 675 rounds/min |
| Weight without magazine: | 4.88 kg |
| Magazine capacity: | according to the type of magazine 20, 30, 50 or 100 rounds |
| Max. operational range: | 200 m |

The Thompson M1928 machine pistol – also known as the 'Thompson A1' or 'Tommy Gun' – was developed during the First World War with contributions from the US General Thompson and was designed to be a 'trench cleaner'. However, in the 1920s it became famous when it was used by many American gangsters, such as Al Capone. They called the Thompson the 'Chicago Typewriter' and it was prized because of its superior firepower, which the police at this time had nothing to counter. Because of this feature, however, the US Army was also interested in the pistol and introduced it as the M1928 A1, although in significant numbers only from 1938 onwards. The Thompson ran through many modifications during its military service, almost all of which were related to the reduction of production costs and times. It was finally replaced in 1944 by the M3 'grease gun'. By that time more than 1.5 million of all models had been produced. The Thompson was generally valued on account of its stable platform when firing, its high quality and its firepower, but it was also thought to be heavy and expensive.

## MODEL M3 MACHINE PISTOL CALIBRE .45 (11.43 MM) AND .35 (9 MM)

*An M3 .45 (11.43 mm) calibre.*

| Calibre: | .45 (11.43 mm) |
|---|---|
| Cartridge: | .45 ACP (11.43 x 23 mm) |
| Muzzle velocity: | approx. 400 m/s |
| Firing rate: | 270 rounds/min |
| Weight without magazine: | 3.7 kg |
| Magazine capacity: | box magazine |
| | 30 rounds |
| Max. operational range: | 100 m |

The recoil-loading M3 machine pistol was also called the 'grease gun' or 'cake decorator'. It fired the .45 calibre ACP and was developed in December 1942 by the designer George J. Hyde, who originated from Germany, to replace the Thompson machine pistol, which was expensive and complicated to manufacture. The British Sten gun and the German MP 38/40 served as the basis for the design. The M3 can fire only in fully automatic mode, and its magazine contains 30 rounds. One interesting feature of the M3 was that it could quickly be converted from .45 calibre to .35 (9 mm) Parabellum, which enabled captured German ammunition to be used. As a result this weapon was also very popular with partisans and resistance fighters. Although it was almost primitive in its construction, the M3 was extremely accurate and resistant to dirt and contamination, although it sometimes had problems with the ammunition feed. This was rectified with the M3 A 1 version. After 1945 the USA exported many M3s. Overall more than 655,000 of them were believed to have been manufactured in the USA and some models were also produced under licence in Argentina, Taiwan and Portugal. Even in the 1990s weapons of this type could still be found in used by armed forces.

## SPRINGFIELD SEMI-AUTOMATIC RIFLE M 1903 AND VARIANTS .30 CALIBRE (7.62 MM)

The Springfield rifle was another veteran from the First World War that remained in use until 1945 and later. The reason for that was not so much the properties of the rifle – a design of high quality – but rather the lack of a modern replacement. As early as the mid-1930s the US Army planned the replacement of the M 1903 by the new M1 Garand design. But the production of this new weapon did not proceed at the required pace, so that when the USA entered the war in December 1941 large sections of the US Army continued to carry the Springfield rifle. The new units that were subsequently formed had to be equipped in the first instance with the M 1903 from storage stocks, so that the Springfield was not completely replaced, even by 1945.

| Calibre: | .30 (7.62 mm) |
|---|---|
| Cartridge: | .30-06 (7.62 x 63 mm) |
| Muzzle velocity: | 815 m/s |
| Weight with empty magazine: | 3.94 kg |
| Magazine capacity: | 5 rounds |
| Operational range: | 600 m |

*The Springfield semi-automatic rifle.*

American soldiers with a Bazooka, 1944.

At the end of 1942 the Bazooka was first used by the US Army in the battles against the German Afrikakorps in Tunisia. There some of them were captured by the Germans and after careful examination were developed into the Panzerschreck. In 1943 the Model M1A1 appeared with an improved aiming device and from 1944 onwards the significantly improved M9 version appeared with a two-part light metal barrel, which greatly simplified handling. In addition to a warhead for tank fighting with a shaped charge, high explosive and phosphorus warheads were also available. Bazookas were produced in large numbers and enjoyed great popularity with the troops. The M1 can be said to be the prototype of many similar weapons that continue to be used today.

## BROWNING EXTRA-HEAVY MACHINE GUN M 2 AND M 2 HB .50 (12.7 MM)

After the First World War the Type M 1917 machine gun was converted to a new 12.7 mm calibre cartridge based on captured German Mauser ammunition. This machine gun was intended for the defence of armoured vehicles and aircraft and was designated the M 1921. In the mid-1930s the heavy Browning M 1921 was fitted with an air-cooled barrel and renamed the M 2 Browning, but this version tended to overheat. A heavier barrel was therefore introduced, and the M 2 HB (Heavy Barrel) that thus emerged became the standard 12.7 mm machine gun of the US armed forces and also of some of the other Allied forces. The M 2 proved to be extremely durable and became a real classic. Even today the 'Fifty Cal' is to be found in the USA and another 20 countries. It found and continues to find service in planes and helicopters, in tanks and other armoured vehicles, as a heavy infantry

machine gun, and also on ships. The great weight and the relatively low firing rate are the result of the use of the heavy 12.7 x 99 mm M 2 cartridge, which because of its enormous power of penetration and hard recoil demands a robust design. Against unprotected targets the ammunition is effective at a distance of up to 2,000 m. At 500 m armour of up to 34 mm thickness can still be penetrated. In the newer versions of the M 2 modifications allow the barrels to be changed more quickly than in earlier variants, in which a laborious adjustment of the barrel to the shell was required. Some sources give the number of M 2s manufactured as more than 3 million. During the whole of the Second World War the air-cooled version of the M 2 was also used as aircraft armament – using either a fixed or movable mounting. The main difference from the HB version was the barrel, which was shortened and also

| Calibre: | .50 (12.7 mm) |
| --- | --- |
| Cartridge: | .50 (12.7 x 99 mm) |
| Muzzle velocity: | approx. 895 m/s |
| Firing rate: | 500 rounds/min |
| Weight without tripod: | 38.11 kg |
| Magazine capacity: (metal belt in box): | 110 rounds |
| Max. operational range: | 2,000 m |

wrapped in a perforated jacket in order to improve the cooling, since no change of barrel was possible. The water-cooled versions of the M 2 were primarily used as light anti-aircraft machine guns. A tank surrounded the barrel with cooling fluid, which circulated inside the weapon.

*An M 2 on a mounting used in armoured vehicles.*

## BAZOOKA MODELS M1, M1A1 AND M9 2.36 (60 MM)

| Calibre: | 60 mm |
| --- | --- |
| Muzzle velocity: | 105 m/s |
| Length: | 1,390 mm |
| Weight: | 5.8 kg |
| Weight of shell: | 1.54–2.8 kg |
| Operational range: | 200 m |
| Penetration capability (armoured steel): | approx. 100 mm/ 90° |

After the entry of the USA into the war the US Army was looking for a new high-performance anti-tank weapon for the infantry. When in 1942 a test demonstration of new anti-tank rifles took place, the weapons expert Leslie Skinner was able to demonstrate in a quasi non-competitive manner his rocket

weapon based on the shaped charge principle, and this outclassed all other designs. As a result a contract for production of the weapon, called the M1, was immediately awarded. Skinner's design was in principle little more than a metal barrel open at both ends that was used to fire an electrically ignited rocket projectile with a shaped charge warhead of 2.36 (60 mm) calibre. Nevertheless this was a revolution, since for the first time an individual soldier was provided with the

possibility of fighting successfully and at some distance against heavily armoured targets. Since the propulsive jet of the rocket projectile exited rearwards out of the open barrel. there was no recoil, which enabled the use of a thin wall barrel and control of the weapon by an individual soldier. The soldiers christened the weapon the 'Bazooka' – the name owed something to a similar-looking musical instrument used by the American radio comic Bob Burns.

*A Bazooka M1A1.*

## GARAND SEMI-AUTOMATIC RIFLE M1 .30 CALIBRE (7.62 MM)

John C. Garand developed as early as the 1920s the first semi-automatic rifles, from which came the M1 in the mid-1930s. While the plan was to replace the manually loaded model M 1903 by the new model relatively quickly, this only happened completely after 1945. The M1, a reliable robust gas pressure loader, was the first semi-automatic rifle in military service and helped the US Army to achieve increased firepower. Its considerable weight was a disadvantage, but this ensured a stable platform for the weapon and a relatively low recoil that

placed less load on the soldier firing the weapon. The magazine of the M1 had to be filled with special loading strips that could only be reloaded when they fell out of the weapon after the last round. This generated a characteristic noise that betrayed to the enemy that the rifleman was out of ammunition, and also where he was located. However, the M1 riflemen utilized this disadvantage, in that they simulated this noise and so lured the enemy out of cover. Up to the discontinuation of production in 1957 more than 5.5 million M1 Garand rifles

| Calibre: | .30 (7.62 mm) |
| Cartridge: | .30-06 (7.62 x 63 mm) |
| Muzzle velocity: | 855 m/s |
| Firing rate: | 30 rounds/min |
| Weight unloaded: | 4.37 kg |
| Magazine capacity: | 8 rounds |
| Operational range: | 600 m |

had been produced. After 1945 it was also used by other countries and was, for example, manufactured in Italy by Beretta under licence.

## M1 CARBINE SEMI-AUTOMATIC RIFLE .30 CALIBRE (7.62 MM)

| Calibre: | .30 (7.62 mm) |
| Cartridge: | .30 M1 Carbine (7.62 x 33 mm) |
| Muzzle velocity: | 610 m/s |
| Firing rate: | 45 rounds/min |
| Weight unloaded: | 2.48 kg |
| Magazine capacity: | 15 rounds box magazine |
| Operational range: | 250 m |

During the late 1920s the US Army decided to develop an automatic weapon for troop units that were not in service in the immediate front line. This weapon was required to be more compact than a normal rifle and more

effective than a pistol or a machine pistol. Since the new M1 Garand was also being introduced at this time, this project progressed only slowly for financial reasons. In 1940, however, the situation in Europe forced the USA into action and a competition was announced for an automatic infantry weapon that had to be a maximum of 2.5 kg in weight. It quickly became clear, however, that this requirement could not be fulfilled with existing ammunition. Thus emerged the new 30 M1 Carbine cartridge with a 7.62 mm calibre. From October 1941 production of the new weapon began under the designation of M1 Carbine. Despite the original service objective the

M1 Carbine was also used in the front line and, for example, played a role in the landing of US troops in North Africa and in Normandy. Although the range and penetration capability were less than for the Garand, the Carbine had a higher firing rate and a lower weight. The M1 Carbine is not dissimilar to the design of the M1 Garand. In addition to the M1 standard version there was also the model M1 A1 with a folding shoulder stock, the M2 version for continuous fire, and the M3 sniper rifle. By 1945 a total of 6,117,827 of these weapons had been manufactured.

## BROWNING AUTOMATIC RIFLE LIGHT MACHINE GUN (BAR)
## MODEL M 1922 AND M 1918 A1 AND A2 .30 (7.62 MM)

When the USA went into the First World War in 1917 the Army was equipped with a total of 1,150 heavy machine guns and a few light machine guns. Trials with the French Chauchat machine gun were not very successful, so the development of new weapons was put out to contract. The weapons designer John Moses Browning thereupon developed two different models: the heavy machine gun M 1917 and a type of light machine gun with the designation Browning Automatic Rifle (BAR), which was used by the Army from September 1918.

The BAR, although a gas pressure loader, is not a machine gun in the true sense, but rather an automatic rapid-firing rifle. This is also confirmed by the magazine capacity, too small for a machine gun, of only 20 rounds, which is more suited for targeted individual rounds and short volleys than for continuous fire. A further disadvantage of the BAR was its great weight of more than 10 kg (loaded). The 1918 version was further developed to become the M 1922. The firing rate could be adapted from 350 rounds/min to 550 rounds/min, but in practice it was only 60–80 rounds. The further improved M 1918 A1 and M 1918

| | |
|---|---|
| Calibre: | .30 (7.62 mm) |
| Cartridge: | .30-06 (7.62 x 63 mm) |
| Muzzle velocity: | approx. 855 m/s |
| Firing rate: | 350–550 rounds/min |
| Weight without magazine: | 9.5 kg |
| Magazine capacity: | 20 rounds |
| | trapezoidal magazine |
| Operational range: | 800 m |

A2 models (introduced in 1937 and 1940 respectively) were given barrels with greater wall thicknesses that were better suited for continuous fire, but the magazine capacity remained the same. Although the BAR did not match the requirements of a light machine gun, it was astonishingly rated as one of the most important automatic weapons in the Second World War. Various BAR models were also used in the Korean War and at the start of the Vietnam War. The number of all versions of the BAR produced amounted to more than 350,000.

## BROWNING HEAVY MACHINE GUN M 1919 A4 AND VARIANTS

| | |
|---|---|
| Calibre: | .30 (7.62 mm) |
| Cartridge: | .30-06 (7.62 x 63 mm) |
| Muzzle velocity: | approx. 855 m/s |
| Firing rate: | 500 rounds/min |
| Weight without tripod: | 14.1 kg |
| Magazine capacity | 250 rounds |
| (fabric belt in box): | |
| Operational range: | 1,400 m |

In 1917 the weapons designer J. M. Browning built the heavy, water-cooled M 1917 machine gun that was the standard machine gun of the US Army up until the start of the Second World War. As early as 1919 a lighter weapon with air cooling for installation in aircraft and armoured vehicles was developed: the M 1919. Since the BAR was not a true machine gun and the M 1917 was too heavy on account of its water cooling, these versions were further developed into the M 1919 A4 and used by the Allies in large numbers. Nevertheless

the weight of the M 1919 A4 was still too great compared with other air-cooled weapons of that time: 14.1 kg compared with the 10.2 kg of the Bren machine gun. Moreover, it was fitted with a tripod mounting that weighed an additional 6.35 kg. In total therefore the M 1919 A4 was almost twice as heavy as the Bren.

Also it did not always function correctly because of insufficient recoil energy. Nevertheless this machine gun was a solid design that was used by the US Army until the 1960s, and in other countries up until the end of the 1980s.

*An M 1919 A4 on a mounting used in armoured vehicles.*

*Italy, November 1944: a mortar section of the 92nd US Infantry Division fires on Wehrmacht positions. Mortars of this type were also mounted in half-track vehicles of the M3 model, which were then designated as 'M21 mortar carriers'. US troops were still using this mortar during the Korean War.*

## FLAMETHROWER M1, M1 A1 AND M 2-2

The first American flamethrower, the M1 model, was introduced in 1942. In principle it functioned in exactly the same way as the flamethrowers of the Wehrmacht. However, the US Army used manual flamethrowers in Europe only very infrequently. More often they were used in the Pacific theatre where these dreadful weapons were often the only option for breaking the fanatical resistance of Japanese troops. The greatest disadvantage of the M1 and its successor the M1 A1 – which used napalm for an increased range – was the electrical ignition of the flame jet, which often failed, so that the soldier had to use his lighter to fire the weapon! The M 2-2 model, introduced from 1944 onwards, used special ignition cartridges that were in a revolver-type drum at the tip of the flame tube instead of the problematical electrical ignition. Because of the risk that the soldier firing the weapon would be

engulfed in flames if the flammable liquid tank was hit, the US Army and US Marines gradually replaced these weapons with flamethrowers that were installed in Sherman tanks; these, moreover, had a higher range and a greater flammable liquid capacity.

| | |
|---|---|
| Weight (M1): | 31.75 kg |
| Propellant: | nitrogen |
| Flammable liquid quantity: | 18 litres |
| Number of possible flamethrows: | 5, each of 2 seconds |
| Range: | 40–45 m |

*Training in the USA: a GI learns how to handle a flamethrower.*

## MODEL M1 81 MM MORTAR

| | |
|---|---|
| Calibre: | 81 mm |
| Muzzle velocity: | 213 m/s |
| Barrel length: | 1,158 mm |
| Weight: | 61.74 kg |
| Shell weight (high explosive): | 3.12–6.81 kg |
| Max. operational range: | 3,010 m |

As was the case with many other mortars of that time the M1 was based on the French Brandt model

1927–31. As a simple smooth-bore weapon which fired only in a high angle trajectory, the M1 was loaded from the muzzle. The projectile slipped down to the end of the barrel, where it was ignited by a firing pin. Since the barrel did not have any rifling to set the shell in rotation to stabilize the flight path, the shell was stabilized by fins at the rear. In addition to a light high-explosive shrapnel shell with which ranges of more than 3,000 m were

achieved, the M1 mortar also made use of special ammunition with a greater explosive force that was correspondingly heavier and therefore achieved a range of only around 1,190 m. Smoke and flare shells were also available for the M1.

# UNARMOURED VEHICLES

## HEAVY 750 CC MOTORCYCLES WITH SIDECARS
## BMW R 75, ZÜNDAPP KS 750

The Wehrmacht used many different motorcycles, which were divided into three categories: light (up to 350 cc), medium (up to 500 cc) and heavy (more than 500 cc). Their prime suppliers were BMW, Zündapp and NSU. Two of the best-known machines were without doubt the BMW R 75 and Zündapp KS 750 motorcycle combinations. Both models emerged in the autumn of 1940 and were intended in the first instance only for the Mediterranean region and in particular

for the Afrikakorps. They had permanently mounted, powered sidecars. In addition, they were fitted with a reverse gear. In the first instance it was also planned to use the large heavy machines to tow light ordnance for parachute troops. When towing, however, the front wheel lifted off the ground, so this idea was abandoned. Both machines were designed for three

men and were often armed with a Model 34 machine gun. They were mostly used by motorcycle units and reconnaissance units. The motorcycle combinations proved to be robust and reliable, but a machine cost around twice as much as a VW Kübelwagen. BMW manufactured in total 16,510 motorcycle combinations, while Zündapp manufactured 18,635.

*A BMW R 75.*

|  | BMW R 75 | Zündapp KS 750 |
|---|---|---|
| Empty weight: | 420 kg | 400 kg |
| Payload: | 250 kg | 270 kg |
| Dimensions in mm (length/width/height): | 2,400/1,730/1,000 | 2,385/1,650/1,010 |
| Engine: | BMW 2-cylinder horizontally opposed, air-cooled, 746 cc, 26 hp | Zündapp 2-cylinder horizontally opposed, air-cooled, 751 cc, 26 hp |
| Speed: | max. 92 km/h | max. 95 km/h |
| Range: | approx. 340 km road, 270 km cross-country | approx. 330 km road, 260 km cross-country |
| Armament: | 7.92 mm Model 34 machine gun on occasion | 7.92 mm Model 34 machine gun on occasion |
| Fording depth: | 0.35 m | 0.4 m |

## VW TYPE 82 'KÜBELWAGEN'

The Volkswagen Type 82 was manufactured in larger numbers than any other Wehrmacht personnel transport. Its modest design and reliability made it famous and popular. In particular the air-cooling proved its worth in icy temperatures. The soldiers called it the 'Kübelwagen' (literally 'bucket car') or 'Kübel' ('bucket') for short because of its bucket-type seats. From 1939 onwards the Type 82 was developed by Professor Porsche on the basis of the VW Beetle. To improve its cross-country capability the ground clearance was increased to 29 cm, the chassis was strengthened, and the bodywork was simplified, lightened and adapted for military service. The gearbox was fitted with a limited slip differential and a lesser overall transmission ratio, and the air filter was increased in size. In this way the 'Kübel' was able to get through in circumstances where few other vehicles could follow.

According to various sources either 50,000 or 55,000 vehicles had been built by 1945. The bodywork was not in fact made by VW, but by Ambi-Budd in Berlin, and then brought by train to VW for assembly. In addition to the standard version there were also trial models and special models that never went into production. In 1943 the lack of working materials led to a new variant with a wood gas generator – this could be recognized by the 'bump' in the front bonnet. There were also versions that operated with brown coal, anthracite or wood.

| Empty weight: | 750 kg |
|---|---|
| Payload: | 400 kg |
| Dimensions in mm (length/width/height): | 3,773/1,600/1,650 (with cover) |
| Engine: | up to March 1943: 4-cylinder horizontally opposed, air-cooled, 985 cc, 24 hp; later: 1,131 cc, 25 hp |
| Speed: | max. 80 km/h |
| Range: | 400–450 km |
| Armament: | 7.92 mm Model 34 or Model 42 machine gun on occasion |
| Fording depth: | 0.45 m |

*Type 82, Afrikakorps, Libya, 1942.*

## VW TYPE 166 'SCHWIMMWAGEN'

Although the Type 82 proved itself in service it did not have unlimited cross-country and amphibious capability. In particular, reconnaissance units and pioneer units wanted a vehicle in which they did not need to make a detour around rivers or lakes. Professor Porsche therefore developed the Type 128, which had watertight tub-shaped bodywork and all-wheel drive. After only 30 had been built, however, the production of the model was terminated, since it proved to be too complex and heavy. Thus there emerged the Type 166, the bodywork of which was once again built by Ambi-Budd in Berlin. The tub of the Type 166 was without doors, was welded out of steel plate and had a shape similar to that of a boat. The engine and gearbox were taken from the Type 128. The new Schwimmwagen offered space for four fully equipped soldiers and was fitted with all-wheel drive. For travel on water a

three-bladed ship's propeller was folded down into the water at the rear of the vehicle, steered by swivelling the propeller. On the Eastern Front and in the desert the Schwimmwagen proved its worth and was often used in reconnaissance units. The real advantage was, however, its cross-country capability, which was almost equal to that of tracked vehicles. For this reason the Schwimmwagen was a valued command and reconnaissance vehicle. Between 1942 and 1944 around 14,300 of them were produced.

| Empty weight: | 910 kg |
|---|---|
| Payload: | 435 kg |
| Dimensions in mm (length/width/height): | 3,825/1,480/1,615 (with cover) |
| Engine: | 4-cylinder horizontally opposed, air-cooled, 1,131 cc, 25 hp |
| Speed: | max. 80 km/h, in water 10 km/h |
| Range: | approx. 520 km |
| Armament: | 7.92 mm Model 34 or Model 42 machine gun on occasion |
| Fording depth: | amphibious |

*VW TYPE 166, the 'Schwimmwagen' ('Swimming Car').*

## LIGHT ALL-TERRAIN STANDARD PERSONNEL VEHICLE

Initially the Reichswehr (1919–35) and Wehrmacht were equipped with a large number of commercial vehicles. Between 1934 and 1936 the Army Ordnance Office therefore began a simplification of its fleet of personnel vehicles. The objective was to have a standard personnel vehicle in three weight classes: light, medium

and heavy. These personnel vehicles were to display the following features: permanent all-wheel drive, limited slip differential, integral chassis and replaceability of parts subject to wear. The light standard personnel vehicle was manufactured by BMW with a BMW 325 engine (45 hp/32.85 kW), by Hanomag

| Empty weight: | 1,775 kg |
|---|---|
| Payload: | 425 kg |
| Dimensions in mm (length/width/height): | 3,580/1,570/1,780 (with cover) |
| Engine: | 4-cylinder petrol, water-cooled, 45–50 hp |
| Speed: | max. 100 km/h |
| Range: | approx. 400 km |
| Armament: as Kfz. 4: | two 92 mm Model 34 machine guns |
| Fording depth: | 0.6 m |

*Kfz. 1, light all-terrain personnel vehicle.*

with the 20 b engine (50 hp/36.8 kW) and by Stöwer with the R-180-W engine or AW-2 engine (both 50 hp/36.8 kW). According to application and bodywork the vehicles received different Kfz. ('vehicle') numbers: Kfz. 1 was the light personnel all-terrain vehicle; Kfz. 4 was a personnel vehicle fitted with a twin anti-aircraft machine gun, the Model 34. In total around 14,500 of these were built.

## MEDIUM ALL-TERRAIN STANDARD PERSONNEL VEHICLE

| | |
|---|---|
| Empty weight: | 2,700 kg |
| Payload: | 600 kg |
| Dimensions in mm | 4,440/1,680/1,730 |
| (length/width/height): | (with cover) |
| Engine: | Opel: 6-cylinder inline, petrol, water-cooled, 3,600 cc, 68 hp; Horch: V8, 3,800 cc, 75 hp, otherwise data identical |
| Speed: | max. 90 km/h |
| Range: | approx. 400 km |
| Armament: | none |
| Fording depth: | 0.6 m |

The medium standard personnel vehicle was built by the Auto-Union and Opel companies. Because of the long wheelbase all such personnel vehicles in the first instance had spare wheels fitted at the side on a special support axle in order to prevent grounding. From 1940 onwards, however, the vehicles were also manufactured without this feature by Auto-Union with a Horch V8 3,800 cc engine. In total some 12,000 vehicles

were manufactured, and according to their duties were fitted with varying bodywork with which the Kfz. numbers were then aligned. The Kfz. 11 was the medium all-terrain personnel vehicle without a trailer coupling, the Kfz. 15 included a trailer coupling, while Kfz. 16

and 17 were signals vehicles. The Opel engine was much more robust and simple, and was therefore preferred by the soldiers to the Horch engine. However, in the war, particularly on the Eastern Front, these vehicles proved to be too heavy and complicated.

*Medium all-terrain personnel vehicle Kfz. 15 Horch, 16th Infantry Division (Motorized).*

## HEAVY ALL-TERRAIN STANDARD PERSONNEL VEHICLE

The chassis of the heavy standard personnel vehicle, i.e. Wanderer, was produced exclusively by Auto-Union and was driven by a Horch engine. There were two versions: A with a total weight of 3,000 kg and B with a total weight of almost 5,000 kg. The vehicles were

given different identification numbers according to their function; for example, the eight-seater personnel vehicle had the designation Kfz. 18. Others included an ambulance (Kfz. 31), a tug vehicle (Kfz. 69) for the towing of light ordnance, a signals vehicle (Kfz. 81) and a personnel

| | |
|---|---|
| Empty weight: | A: 3,000 kg, B: 5,000 kg |
| Payload: | 900 kg |
| Dimensions in mm | 4,440/1,680/1,730 |
| (length/width/height): | (with cover) |
| Engine: | A: Horch V8, petrol, water-cooled, 3,500 cc, 75 hp, B: 3,800 cc, 90 hp, otherwise data identical |
| Speed: | max. 90 km/h |
| Range: | approx. 400 km |
| Armament: | as Kfz. 70: 2 cm in anti-aircraft cannon 30/38 |
| Fording depth: | 0.6 m |

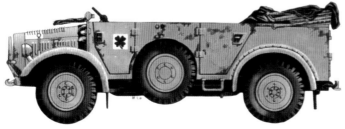

*Heavy all-terrain personnel vehicle Kfz. 18 Horch, 606 Artillery Regiment, Africa, 1942.*

carrier (Kfz. 70). The latter were sometimes fitted out as an improvised self-propelled platform for the Model 30 or Model 38 2 cm anti-aircraft cannon. In the course of the war these vehicles also generally proved to be too expensive, complicated and heavy.

## KRUPP 1.5 TONNE 'KRUPP-TUG'

*Krupp 1.5 tonne truck.*

| Empty weight: | 2,450 kg |
|---|---|
| Payload: | 1,500 kg |
| Dimensions in mm | 4,950/1,950/2,300 |
| (length/width/height): | (with cover) |
| Engine: | Krupp 4-cylinder horizontally opposed, M304, air-cooled, 3,308 cc, 60 hp |
| Speed: | max. 70 km/h |
| Range: | approx. 400 km road, 275 km cross-country |
| Armament: | provisionally 2 cm anti-aircraft cannon 30/38 or 3.7 cm anti-tank cannon 36 |
| Fording depth: | 0.6 m |

There were two versions of this vehicle: the L 2 H 43 and the L 2 H 143. The difference between the two models lay in the wheel spacing on the rear axle. The vehicles were fitted with the following types of bodywork: tug vehicle for the towing of ordnance (Kfz. 69 'Krupp Tug'), personnel vehicle (Kfz. 70) and light searchlight vehicle (Kfz. 83). A 2 cm anti-aircraft cannon or 3.7 cm anti-tank cannon was sometimes fitted to the Kfz. 69, thus creating improvised self-propelled platforms. The Krupp engine proved to be problematical, since it required a high-octane petrol that was not always available. Around 7,000 Krupp vehicles of this kind were built between 1934 and the beginning of 1942.

## OPEL BLITZ 1.5 AND 3 TONNE TRUCKS

The truck that was best known and that saw the most service with the Wehrmacht was the Opel Blitz, of which some 130,000 were supplied up to 1945, but only about 25,000 of them were the four-wheel drive 6700A military version. At that time the Opel Blitz was one of the most reliable trucks. The engine was built in a modular manner, and many parts were exchangeable with the four-cylinder engine from the personnel vehicle series, which was also used in the NSU Kettenkrad. As a result of continuous development from 1931, onwards the Blitz surpassed its competitors from Daimler-Benz, Borgward or Magirus. It proved to be reliable, easy to maintain and docile under all conditions. The high regard in which it was held was shown when Daimler-Benz was forced to manufacture it unmodified under licence and to cease production of its own 3 tonne range of trucks. The Opel was manufactured from July 1944 onwards as the DB 701 with the standard Wehrmacht driver's cab (but without Opel identification). The Blitz was produced in many versions: as a 1.5 or 3 tonne truck, with pallet, van or bus bodywork, and with different wheelbases and types of transmission. Even a half-tracked version – the Opel Maultier ('Mule')

| | 1.5 tonne Type 2.3–32 | 3 tonne Type 3.6–6700A |
|---|---|---|
| Empty weight: | 1,525 kg | 3,350 kg |
| Payload: | 1,675 kg | 3,100 kg |
| Dimensions in mm (length/width/height): | 5,400/1,940/1,845 | 5,950/2,340/3,180 (with cover) |
| Engine: | Opel 6-cylinder inline, water-cooled, 2,473 cc, 55 hp | Opel 6-cylinder inline, water-cooled, 3,600 cc, 75 hp |
| Speed: | max. 80 km/h | max. 80 km/h |
| Range: | approx. 340 km road | 300 km road, 230 km cross-country |
| Armament: | | provisionally 2 cm anti-aircraft cannon 30/38 or 3.7 cm anti-aircraft cannon 36 |
| Fording depth: | 0.5 m | 0.5 m |

– was built. The Maultier and truck versions were occasionally armed by units with 2 cm or 3.7 cm anti-aircraft cannon and used as self-propelled gun platforms. Production of the Blitz was continued by Opel after 1945.

*Opel Blitz.*

## HALF-TRACKED MOTORIZED TRACTION VEHICLES SD.KFZ. 6, 7, 8, 9, 10 AND 11

In the course of motorization of the Wehrmacht the Army Ordnance Office developed the concept of a range of six different motorized traction vehicle models, each of which was to possess standard design features. The individual types were divided into different groups according to their towed load capacity. The main purpose of the vehicles was to pull artillery pieces. Contracts for development and production of the models were awarded to various German manufacturers (see table).

Common to all models was the relatively long crawler track drive with large running wheels in a typical nested configuration with a drive wheel at the front. The front wheels, which were fitted with pneumatic tyres, were not driven

and had no brakes; they served only to provide steering, although above a certain steering angle track steering also contributed. All the motorized traction vehicles proved their worth in the war, and indeed some of them did so outstandingly well. Technically, however, they were peacetime designs that were too complex, and the variety of models was too great to withstand the tough demands of mass production under most difficult conditions. This fact was also clearly demonstrated by the designs that succeeded them in wartime – the Wehrmacht tractor and the Ost crawler tractor – which were far more primitive, but also more cost-effective.

Nevertheless an astonishing number of the motorized traction vehicles were

produced. The 1 tonne model served primarily as a means of pulling light anti-aircraft and anti-tank cannon, which in the course of the war were also mounted on the loading bed. Versions included the Sd.Kfz. 10/4 with a 2 cm anti-aircraft cannon and the Sd.Kfz. 10/5 with a 5 cm anti-tank cannon. The 1 tonne motorized traction vehicle also formed the basis for the Sd.Kfz. 250 armoured personnel carrier. The Sd.Kfz. 11 (the 3 tonne model) was mainly used for pulling howitzers and rocket launchers. The chassis of this model provided the basis for the Sd.Kfz. 251 armoured personnel carrier.

The 5 tonne motorized traction vehicles saw little service, and were used in a similar manner to the 3 tonne models.

*Sd.Kfz. 7 8 tonne medium motorized traction vehicle.*

| | Sd.Kfz. 10; 1 tonne Demag | Sd.Kfz. 11; 3 tonne Hanomag | Sd.Kfz. 6; 5 tonne Büssing-NAG | Sd.Kfz. 7; 8 tonne Krauss-Maffei | Sd.Kfz. 8; 12 tonne Daimler-Benz | Sd.Kfz. 9; 18 tonne Famo |
|---|---|---|---|---|---|---|
| Empty weight: | 3,400 kg | 5,550 kg | 7,500 kg | 9,750 kg | 12,700 kg | 15,200 kg |
| Payload: | 1,500 kg | 1,550 kg | 1,500 kg | 1,800 kg | 2,000 kg | 2,800 kg |
| Towed load: | 1,000 kg | 3,000 kg | 5,000 kg | 8,000 kg | 14,000 kg | 18,000 kg |
| Dimensions in mm (length/width/height): | 4,750/1,930/1,620 | 5,550/2,000/2,150 | 6,325/2,260/2,500 | 6,850/2,350/2,620 | 7,350/2,500/2,770 | 8,250/2,600/2,850 |
| Engine: | Maybach HL-42, 6-cylinder inline, water-cooled, 4,170 cc, 100 hp | Maybach HL-42, 6-cylinder inline, water-cooled, 4,170 cc, 100 hp | Maybach HL-54, 6-cylinder inline, water-cooled, 5,420 cc, 115 hp | Maybach HL-62, 6-cylinder inline, water-cooled, 6,191 cc, 140 hp | Maybach HL-85, V-12, water-cooled, 8,520 cc, 185 hp | Maybach HL-108, V-12, water-cooled, 10,830 cc, 250 hp |
| Speed: | max. 65 km/h | max. 52.5 km/h | max. 50 km/h | max. 50 km/h | max. 51 km/h | max. 50 km/h |
| Range: | 300 km road, 170 km cross-country | 240 km road, 140 km cross-country | 310 km road, 150 km cross-country | 250 km road, 120 km cross-country | 250 km road, 110 km cross-country | 240 km road, 100 km cross-country |
| Fording depth: | 0.7 m | 0.5 m | 0.6 m | 0.65 m | 0.63 m | 0.8 m |
| Number manufactured: | approx. 25,000 | approx. 25,000 | approx. 3,000 | approx. 12,000 | approx. 4,000 | approx. 2,500 |

Sd.Kfz. 9 18 tonne heavy motorized traction vehicle.

The 8 tonne tractor (Sd.Kfz. 7) achieved a certain fame as the means of traction for the legendary 'Acht-Acht'. It also formed the basis for self-propelled gun carriages for anti-aircraft cannon. The Sd.Kfz. 8 (the 12 tonne model) was intended to pull the heavier artillery pieces, such as the 15 cm howitzers and 21 cm mortars. In 1940 some were even fitted with 8.8 cm anti-aircraft cannon, but these did not prove to be successful. The largest and heaviest model, the Sd.Kfz. 9 (18 tonnes) was mainly used as a recovery vehicle for tanks that had become stuck. When it was a matter of recovering heavy tanks, however, three 18 tonners were required to move these vehicles, and so the Sd.Kfz 9 finally had to be replaced by recovery tanks.

Sd.Kfz. 10/4 1 tonne vehicle with a Model 30 2 cm anti-aircraft cannon.

Sd.Kfz. 10 with a Model 38 5 cm anti-tank cannon.

## SD.KFZ. 2 LIGHT TRACKED MOTORCYCLE NSU HK-101

| Empty weight: | 1,280 kg |
|---|---|
| Payload: | 325 kg |
| Dimensions in mm (length/width/height): | 3,000/1,000/1,200 |
| Engine: | Opel-Olympia, 4-cylinder inline, water-cooled, 1,500 cc, 36 hp |
| Speed: | max. 70 km/h |
| Range: | approx. 250 km road, 175 km cross-country |
| Fording depth: | 0.44 m |

*NSU tracked motorcycle.*

In 1939 the Army Ordnance Office was looking for a means of pulling smaller loads, such as the light weapons of parachute troops, mortars or field cables. The engineer Heinrich Ernst developed a vehicle with a front wheel and controls similar to those of a motorcycle and a rear crawler track drive. Production was undertaken by NSU in Neckarsulm, and later under licence by the Stöwer factory in Stettin. The first 500 were delivered from July 1940. On 5 June 1941 the vehicle was officially introduced into service as the Sd.Kfz. 2. Although particularly valuable in winter and in the mud, the tracked motorcycle was both too expensive and too complicated (with 124 lubrication points!). Further versions were the Sd.Kfz. 2/1 for field cables and the Sd.Kfz. 2/2 for heavy field cables. In total 8,733 were built by 1944.

## 2 TONNE CRAWLER TRACKED TRUCK 'MAULTIER'

As a result of the very poor weather and road conditions in the Soviet Union an attempt was made to give the trucks of the German logistical support troops a better cross-country capability. A research vehicle of the Waffen-SS was requisitioned for this purpose. This vehicle featured a British Carden-Loyd transmission that had been installed under a normal 3 tonne truck. The installation of this simple crawler track drive in place of the rear axle proved to be a success and the vehicles were introduced into the Wehrmacht under the name 'Maultier' ('Mule') (Sd.Kfz. 3). Later versions were produced by Opel (Type 3.6–36 S), by Klöckner-Humboldt-Deutz (Type 3000 S with a diesel engine) and by Ford (Type G 398 TS/V 3000 S). In 1942, 635 vehicles were manufactured, in 1943 around 13,000 and in 1944 another 7,310.

Some Maultiers were fitted with a 2 cm or 3.7 cm anti-aircraft cannon. Three hundred vehicles were provided with an armoured body and acquired the Model 41 15 cm rocket launcher, whose ten tubes could be swivelled through 360° (Model 42 rocket launcher), and 90 unarmed vehicles were used as ammunition carriers for the launchers. A 4.5 tonne design was developed by Daimler-Benz, using the undercarriage of a Model II tank, and 1,480 of this heavy model were produced. The Magirus model proved to be the best and most reliable Maultier because of its indestructible diesel engine.

| Empty weight: | 3,930 kg |
|---|---|
| Payload: | 2,000 kg |
| Dimensions in mm (length/width/height): | 6,000/2,880/2,710 |
| Engine: | Opel, 6-cylinder inline, water-cooled, 3,600 cc, 75 hp |
| Speed: | max. 38 km/h |
| Range: | 160 km road, 80 km cross-country |
| Fording depth: | 0.44 m |

*Maultier based on the Opel Blitz.*

# OST CRAWLER TRACTOR RSO/01

| | |
|---|---|
| Empty weight: | 3,500 kg |
| Payload: | 1,700 kg |
| Towed load: | 3,000 kg |
| Dimensions in mm (length/width/height): | 4,425/1,990/2,530 |
| Engine: | Steyr V-8, air-cooled, 3,517 cc, 70 hp |
| Speed: | max. 17 km/h |
| Range: | 300 km road, 150 km cross-country |
| Armament: | variants with a 7.5 cm anti-tank cannon or a 7.5 cm howitzer |
| Fording depth: | 0.85 m |

*An Ost crawler tractor with a 75 mm anti-tank cannon.*

Since the trucks operated by the Wehrmacht were often stuck fast in the Russian mud and ice, and production of the half-tracked motorized traction vehicles was too complex, a fully tracked vehicle simple to manufacture but capable of movement under the most adverse conditions was designed: the Ost (East) crawler tractor, abbreviated to RSO.

The pattern for this design was provided by the extremely robust and reliable tracked tractors that were captured during the advance on the Eastern Front. The RSO/01 was manufactured from 1942 onwards by Steyr. In 1944, because of the great need for such a vehicle, Klöckner-Humboldt-Deutz, Gräf & Stift and Auto-Union also participated in its manufacture.

In total almost 26,000 Osts were built by the end of the war. A self-propelled gun carriage with a 7.5 cm anti-tank cannon was also built on the basis of the RSO, but this variant was not a success.

For mountain infantry units the Gebirge (Mountain) crawler tractor (RSG) was produced, which carried a Model 34 7.5 cm mountain howitzer.

# HEAVY WEHRMACHT TRACTOR S.WS

| | |
|---|---|
| Empty weight: | 13,500 kg |
| Payload: | 4,000 kg |
| Towed load: | 8,000 kg |
| Dimensions in mm (length/width/height): | 6,675/2,500/2,830 |
| Engine: | Maybach HL-42, 6-cylinder inline, water-cooled, 4,170 cc, 100 hp |
| Speed: | max. 27 km/h |
| Range: | 300 km road, 150 km cross-country |
| Armament: | variant with a 3.7 cm anti-aircraft cannon |
| Fording depth: | 1 m |

Only two different vehicles were to be built as the successors to the motorized traction vehicle (as opposed to the previous six), and these had to be simple and cost-effective to produce, but very robust: these were the light and heavy Wehrmacht tractors. Only prototypes were ever produced of the former, but the heavy version went into production at Büssing-NAG in

the autumn of 1943. Although the requirements were met, the vehicle's cruising speed had to be severely reduced, with the result that it could no longer be used in tank units, but only in infantry divisions. As variants there emerged a model with a 3.7 cm anti-aircraft cannon and a partially armoured model for the supply of front-line units.

*Only 825 heavy Wehrmacht tractors had been produced by March 1945.*

## CAMIONETTA 42 SAHARIANA SPA AS 42

These unamoured vehicles were created by SPA (at that time part of the Fiat group) especially for use in North Africa – hence the designation AS ('Africa Settentrionale', which can be approximately translated as 'North Africa'). They were based on the chassis of the AB-41 armoured scout car.

The vehicles were fitted with oversize tyres for use on sand, together with a large fuel tank and fixtures for a great number of additional fuel cans to achieve a long range. The scout cars were mainly used by reconnaissance units and special troops, for example, for excursions behind enemy lines. The armament for the

| Empty weight: | 3,950 kg |
|---|---|
| Payload: | 800 kg |
| Dimensions in mm (length/width/height): | 5,750/2,250/2,150 |
| Engine: | SPA, 6-cylinder inline, petrol, 4,995 cc, water-cooled, 88 hp |
| Speed: | max. 80 km/h |
| Range: | 800 km |
| Armament: | from an 8 mm machine gun up to a 4.7 cm anti-tank cannon |
| Fording depth: | 0.6 m |

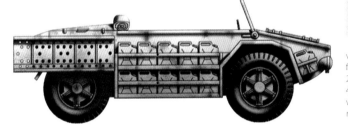

vehicles was very varied, and ranged from an 8 mm Breda machine gun, via a 2 cm Breda anti-aircraft cannon, up to a 4.7 cm anti-tank gun. Among other weapons, 2 cm anti-tank rifles or 12.7 mm machine guns were also used.

## BEDFORD MWD 4 × 2 15 CWT 0.75-TONNER

Bedford MWD vehicles were the light trucks most frequently used by British troops. The first pre-production models appeared in 1937. Series production was carried out for the duration of the war by Vauxhall Motors, where a total of 66,000 trucks was produced. In addition to a pallet bed version there was also a version with an enclosed body fitted with signals equipment, and a tanker variant with a capacity of 200 gallons (approximately 900 litres). More than 230,000 vehicles in the 15 cwt class as a whole were produced in the United Kingdom during the war. The armies of the British Empire defined the payload of their trucks in terms of hundredweight (cwt). This unit of weight corresponds to 112 British pounds (lb) or 50.8 kg. A payload of 15 cwt was therefore 1,680 lb (762 kg). Highly prized as a versatile and robust transport vehicle, Bedford MWDs continued in service with the British armed forces into the late 1950s. Light trucks of the Bedford MWD type (and countless other vehicles) were captured by the Wehrmacht in substantial numbers in France – particularly during the British retreat from Dunkirk – and also in Norway. Since the Wehrmacht was chronically

short of vehicles of all kinds, captured vehicles were absorbed into its own fleet and used for as long as replacement parts were available. Sometimes conversions and adaptations of the original vehicles were even undertaken to meet German needs. The Bedford MWD also proved its worth in the service of the Wehrmacht.

*A Bedford MWD.*

| Empty weight: | 2,140 kg |
|---|---|
| Payload: | 762 kg |
| Dimensions in mm (length/width/height): | 4,380/1,990/2,290 (with cover) |
| Engine: | Bedford OHV, 6-cylinder inline, 3,518 cc, water-cooled, 72 hp |
| Speed: | max. 80 km/h |
| Range: | 385 km |
| Fording depth: | 0.7 m |

# BEDFORD QLD 4 × 4 3-TONNER

The Bedford QLD was the most frequently manufactured British 3-tonner. The design of the all-wheel drive vehicle began shortly after the outbreak of war and in 1941 the first trucks were delivered to units. Vauxhall in Luton built 52,245 QLDs, which were not only deployed in the British Army.

In 1942 the Soviet Union also received a number of these vehicles as part of Allied military aid. The versatile and reliable truck was used in a wide variety of roles, from acting as a tractor unit for artillery, via transport duties, through to a tanker vehicle. The weakest feature of the Bedford was its low-powered engine.

| | |
|---|---|
| Empty weight: | 9,700 kg |
| Payload: | 3,000 kg |
| Dimensions in mm (length/width/height): | 5,990/2,260/3,000 |
| Engine: | Bedford OHV, 6-cylinder inline, 3,518 cc, water-cooled, 72 hp |
| Speed: | max. 60 km/h |
| Range: | 370 km |
| Fording depth: | 0.4 m |

*Bedford QLD.*

# MORRIS COMMERCIAL C 8 'QUAD' ARTILLERY TRACTOR UNIT

| | |
|---|---|
| Empty weight: | 3,400 kg |
| Payload: | No details |
| Dimensions in mm (length/width/height): | 4,490/2,200/2,280 |
| Engine: | Morris inline 4-cylinder, 3,600 cc, water-cooled, 70 hp |
| Speed: | max. 80 km/h |
| Range: | 250 km |
| Fording depth: | 0.4 m |

In 1937 the Guy Motors company originally developed an artillery tractor unit for 25-pounder guns on the basis of the all-wheel drive transmission of the Morris Commercial C 8. With the outbreak of war the need for such vehicles rose sharply and Morris itself began to produce this vehicle. Later on Chevrolet Canada also manufactured a large number of the vehicles. Generally known as the 'Quad', these tractor units offered sufficient space for a crew and

ammunition. Because of its four-wheel drive it had an extremely high towing capacity and was outstandingly good at cross-country duties. In addition the 'Quads' were fitted with a winch with a 4,000 kg pulling force. Alongside models

with enclosed metal bodywork there were later some that also acquired a canvas cover. In total more than 10,000 were produced by all the manufacturers and used by the Commonwealth armed forces.

*Morris Commercial C 8 'Quad'.*

# FORD F15A 4 × 4 15 CWT 0.75-TONNER

| | |
|---|---|
| Empty weight: | 2,490 kg |
| Payload: | 762 kg |
| Dimensions in mm (length/width/height): | 4,216/2,100/2,188 |
| Engine: | Ford V-8, water-cooled, 95 hp |
| Speed: | max. 90 km/h |
| Range: | 350 km |
| Armament: | variant with a 2 cm anti-aircraft cannon |
| Fording depth: | 0.6 m |

*A Ford 15A with all-wheel drive*

During the war Canada produced more than 710,000 trucks of all kinds, which were used by the Commonwealth armed forces. Many were similar to each other, since they were manufactured in accordance with the Canadian Military Pattern (CMP). As early as 1937 planning started at Ford of Canada on a light military truck with four-wheel drive on the basis of a British requirements specification. A year later Chevrolet joined in the planning activities and vehicles of different classes were designed that were to have a maximum number of components in common. The result was the series of CMP trucks, which mainly differed from each other only in terms of power units. The first prototypes were subjected to rigorous testing in 1939, and series production began in 1940. The 0.75-tonners (15 cwt) built by Ford and Chevrolet were the most numerous light trucks in this programme. They were versatile and robust, and were utilized in every sector of the armed forces. Ford's 0.75-tonner appeared in the widest number of variants: the Ford 15A featured all-wheel drive, while the Ford 15 variant only had rear-wheel drive. In addition there were models that had a canvas cover over the driver's cab. Others had a metal roof. The same was true for the 0.75-tonner built by Chevrolet to the same pattern. There was also a version of the Ford 15A that had a 2 cm Polsten anti-aircraft cannon, a variant of the well-known 2 cm Oerlikon.

# CHEVROLET C60L 4 × 4 3-TONNER

Chevrolet of Canada, part of the enormous General Motors group, built large numbers of standardized military vehicles during the Second World War, as did Ford of Canada. One of these CMP vehicles was the C60L. The Chevrolet differed primarily from the Ford truck of the same pattern in terms of having a different engine. For those who are not experts, the two variants can be distinguished from each other only by the company badge, and the same is true for almost all the CMP vehicles. In total around 209,000 CMP 3-tonners were built. While they were in fact rated as under-powered and slow, they were also judged to be indestructible and reliable. Thanks to their four-wheel drive they were also suitable as

| | |
|---|---|
| Empty weight: | 3,023 kg |
| Payload: | 3,048 kg |
| Dimensions in mm (length/width/height): | 5,664/2,100/2,276 |
| Engine: | Chevrolet, 6-cylinder inline, water-cooled, 3,600 cc, 85 hp |
| Speed: | max. 70 km/h |
| Range: | 270 km |
| Fording depth: | 0.5 m |

tractor units. The payload of 3 tonnes could be exceeded to a considerable extent without causing any problems. Many variants were built that differed primarily in terms of their bodywork, long or short wheelbases, and drivers' cabs. As in the case of the 0.75-tonner the 3-tonners were also adapted to almost every conceivable purpose, from a pallet bed vehicle to an enclosed body forming an observation post. Some of these trucks were also delivered to the Soviet Union.

# GAZ-AA AND GAZ-AAA

| | |
|---|---|
| Empty weight: | 1,810 kg |
| Payload: | 1,500 kg |
| Dimensions in mm (length/width/height): | 5,300/2,000/1,950 |
| Engine: | GAZ, 6-cylinder inline, water-cooled, 3,285 cc, 40 hp |
| Speed: | max. 70 km/h |
| Range: | 200 km |
| Fording depth: | 0.4 m |

This antiquated truck was the Soviet standard 1.5-tonner, and was based on the Ford AA of the late 1920s. The leadership of the Soviet Communist Party did not shrink from collaboration with capitalists in its efforts to convert the young Soviet Union quickly into an industrial nation. Thus Ford first won the contest for the supply of vehicles in kits of parts, and later for the licensed production of trucks. In 1930 the first kits arrived from the USA, and from 1932 licensed production began in Gorky. The GAZ-AA, as the Ford model was now called, was a simple vehicle, but one that was outstandingly well matched to the Russian conditions. In 1941 and 1942 the Germans captured large numbers of GAZ 1.5-tonners, and these were in turn used by the Wehrmacht.

*The GAZ was very robust, and despite the lack of all-wheel drive had an excellent cross-country capability. Since only one 1.5-tonner was produced in the Soviet Union, huge numbers of vehicles and parts were available. From 1932 to 1946 more than 1 million GAZ-AAs and GAZ-AAAs (the three-axle version) were manufactured.*

# ZIS-5 3-TONNER

As was the case with the 1.5 tonne class, only one 3-tonner model was built in the Soviet Union before and during the war. The ZIS-5 was also based on a US model, in this case a truck of the Autocar brand. From 1933 onwards trucks of this type were manufactured in the ZIS factory (ZIS: Zavod Imeni Stalina – that is Stalin Factory) in Moscow. When in the autumn of 1941 the Wehrmacht advance threatened to reach Moscow the factory was moved to the east, but production was quickly restored. Although similar to the GAZ 1.5-tonner the ZIS-5 was even more primitive, but extremely robust and resilient. The Wehrmacht were happy to use captured trucks, since under Russian conditions they performed better than most German models. In June 1941 the Red Army had around 105,000 ZIS-5s in service, and up to 1945 another 84,000 were built. However, during the war the

| | |
|---|---|
| Empty weight: | not known |
| Payload: | 3,000 kg |
| Dimensions in mm (length/width/height): | 6,060/2,235/2,160 |
| Engine: | GAZ, 6-cylinder inline, water-cooled, 5,557 cc, 73 hp |
| Speed: | max. 70 km/h |
| Range: | 200 km |
| Fording depth: | 0.5 m |

Red Army for the most part depended on deliveries of trucks from the USA. Some 500,000 3-tonners and 50,000 Jeeps were supplied under the terms of the Lend-Lease agreement.

*Many Red Army trucks were fitted with drivers' cabs made of wood because of the shortage of materials, as in the case of this ZIS-5.*

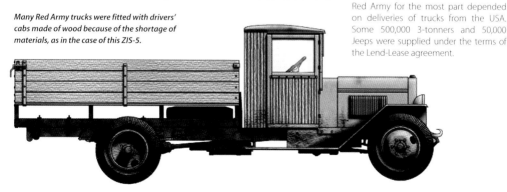

## STALINETS 65SG FULLY TRACKED TRACTOR

In the 1930s 'Stalinets' (Russian for 'Stalinist') was the proud name given to a whole series of agricultural vehicles in the Soviet Union. In addition to their peacetime uses, however, various models were also used as artillery tractors, as was the Stalinets 65SG. Because of the road conditions, at times extremely poor with both mud and deep snow, fully tracked tractors were the only vehicles that could always guarantee mobility. This bitter truth also had to be learnt by the German units when their vehicles were stuck fast

in the Russian mud and snow. Captured fully tracked tractors were therefore highly prized by the Wehrmacht. Although of almost primitive appearance they were extremely well matched to the hard climatic conditions. Broad tracks and tough engines ensured a slow but steady progress in the deepest mud and snow. Thanks to a pre-heating system these tractors sprang into life at even the coldest temperatures. For pulling artillery pieces, or recovering vehicles that had been abandoned, the tractors were

| Empty weight: | 11,200 kg |
| Towed load: | 4,000 kg |
| Dimensions in mm (length/width/height): | 4,086/2,416/2,803 |
| Engine: | Stalinets 17, 4-cylinder diesel, water-cooled, 18,500 cc, 75 hp |
| Speed: | 7 km/h |
| Range: | 300 km road |
| Fording depth: | 0.8 m |

indispensable on both sides. The Ost crawler tractor of the German Wehrmacht was designed on the pattern of these vehicles. Between 1937 and 1941, 37,626 Stalinets 65s and 65SGs were built in total. The number of variants was very great. Details such as the bodywork varied from one version to the next, depending on the factory from which the tractor unit came.

*A Stalin tractor operating as a tractor unit for a 15.2 cm ML-20 howitzer.*

*What was previously a Soviet tractor here serves as a tractor unit for a German 8.8 cm anti-aircraft cannon.*

# WILLYS MB 'JEEP'

| Empty weight: | 1,106 kg |
|---|---|
| Payload: | 500 kg road, |
| | 360 kg cross-country |
| Dimensions in mm | 3,370/1,570/1,303 |
| (length/width/height): | (windscreen folded down) |
| Engine: | Willys 442, 4-cylinder |
| | inline, petrol, |
| | water-cooled, |
| | 2,199 cc, 60 hp |
| Speed: | 100 km/h road, |
| | 80 km/h cross-country |
| Range: | 450 km |
| Armament: | 12.7 mm machine gun |
| | on occasion |
| Fording depth: | 0.5 m |

The Jeep was definitely the best-known military vehicle of the Second World War, and the 'Jeep' designation has today become synonymous with cross-country vehicles. The history of the Jeep began in 1940 when the US Army was looking for a small, convenient, off-road vehicle that was suitable for mass production. Pre-production vehicles from three factories (Bantam, Ford and Willys) were subjected to rigorous tests, as a result of which the MA design from the Willys-Overland company emerged as the victor. In the course of 1941 18,600 were manufactured, but neither Willys nor the US Army was as yet fully happy with its performance. Willys therefore reworked the design and put forward a definitive version under the MB designation. Alongside Willys Ford also

entered into series production. The vehicles produced by Ford carried the designation GPW, but differed only in small details from the MB. By the end of the war the two companies together produced around 640,000 Jeeps (by comparison, only approximately 52,000 VW Kübels were manufactured!). Wherever the Allied units were in action, the Jeep was there, right on the front line. As a result of its four-wheel drive and low weight the MB had extremely good cross-country capability, and it was also robust and reliable. For the troops the Jeeps were 'maids of all work', and many variants were therefore built or refitted on-site. Among the most important of these were models armed with machine guns, a signals version fitted with antenna equipment and ambulance versions.

Together with Marmon-Herrington and Sparkman & Stevens, Ford developed an amphibious version, but this failed to be a success with the troops, and production was halted in 1943. Most of the 'Seeps' (Sea Jeeps) were delivered to the Red Army, where they created such a good impression that the Soviet Union developed its own model. Among the most famous were the Jeeps of the British Special Air Service (SAS), an elite unit that carried out attacks behind enemy lines. These Jeeps were heavily armed, and partially armoured, and carried so much equipment with them that all 'unnecessary' items, such as bumpers and radiator grille, were removed to save weight.

*This amphibious design of Jeep was in service with the Red Army – as one of 50,000 supplied under the terms of the Lend-Lease agreement.*

# DODGE 0.75-TONNER OF THE T-214 SERIES

Dodge, part of the Chrysler group, built a bewildering number of different types of 0.75-tonners during the Second World War. The series was named T-214, to which were added codes to identify the type of body. The main version was the command and reconnaissance vehicle (WC-56). There were also various weapons carriers, which sometimes were armed with a 3.7 cm anti-tank cannon (WC-55), signals and workshop vehicles, as well as versions with a van body. Common to all were the engine, chassis and four-wheel drive. The WC-36 version was manufactured in larger numbers than any other 0.75-tonner, and was mainly used as a communications vehicle, as a vehicle for senior officers, or in reconnaissance units. According to its duties the vehicle was fitted with signals equipment, a map table and a removable canvas cover. The Dodge T-214 series stood out in terms of its great reliability and robust engine, which also withstood the worst kind of treatment. Dodge built around 253,000 vehicles of this type, which continued to be used for decades after 1945 by armed forces across the world.

| | |
|---|---|
| Empty weight: | 2,443 kg |
| Payload: | 750 kg |
| Dimensions in mm (length/width/height): | 4,240/1,980/2,060 |
| Engine: | Dodge T-214, 6-cylinder inline, OHV, petrol, water-cooled, 3,772 cc, 92 hp |
| Speed: | 110 km/h road, 80 km/h cross-country |
| Range: | 380 km |
| Armament: | 3.7 cm anti-tank cannon (WC-55) |
| Fording depth: | 0.86 m |

A Dodge WC-51.

A Dodge ambulance.

This Dodge WC-52 was in service with the Red Army – as one of 25,000 supplied under the terms of the Lend-Lease agreement.

# GMC CCKW 2.5-TONNER

From 1939 onwards the standardization programme for the US Armed Forces envisaged only two different vehicles in each class. One of these vehicle classes was the 2.5 tonne truck, of which more than 800,000 units were built up to 1945. The largest manufacturer was General Motors (GMC) with – according to the source – 562,750 or 625,000 units, but companies such as Studebaker, Reo and International also manufactured 2.5-tonners during the war. GMC built a large number of different versions. There were chassis with short (CCKW-352) and long (CCKW-353) wheelbases, 6 x 6 or 6 x 4 transmissions, and even types with only two axles instead of the usual three. Early models featured an enclosed driver's cab, while later versions had a canvas roof. A very wide variety of bodies were placed on these different chassis, from a van body, via tanks for petrol or water, crane systems, through to bodies for workshop or fire vehicles. The most common version was, however, the one pictured here with load restraints and tarpaulins.

| | |
|---|---|
| Empty weight: | 5,420 kg |
| Payload: | 2,500 kg |
| Dimensions in mm (length/width/height): | 6,928/2,235/2,200 |
| Engine: | GMC, 6-cylinder inline, OHV, petrol, water-cooled, 4,420 cc, 90 hp |
| Speed: | 80 km/h |
| Range: | 280 km |
| Armament: | 12.7 mm anti-aircraft machine gun |
| Fording depth: | 0.75 m |

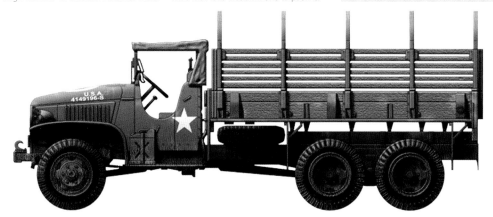

# DUKW AMPHIBIOUS TRUCK

| | |
|---|---|
| Empty weight: | 7,400 kg |
| Payload: | 2,500 kg |
| Dimensions in mm (length/width/height): | 9,449/2,515/2,841 |
| Engine: | GMC, 6-cylinder inline, OHV, petrol, water-cooled, 4,420 cc, 90 hp |
| Speed: | 80 km/h (in water 10 km/h) |
| Range: | 280 km |
| Fording depth: | 0.75 m |

Army required a transport vehicle that could convey soldiers and equipment from the ships on to the beach, and also further into the interior of the country. GMC therefore developed, together with the Sparkman & Stevens boatyard, an amphibious version of the proven GMC 2.5-tonner. The DUKW was fitted with powerful bilge pumps that enabled it to remain afloat after having been damaged by gunfire. Although of tubby appearance the DUKW was very seaworthy and proved its worth in the Pacific, and in 1944 also in Normandy. By 1945 more than 21,000 DUKWs had been built.

This vehicle, named the 'Duck' on account of its military designation DUKW, was basically nothing more than a GMC 2.5-tonner with a boat-shaped hull. For its amphibious landings the US

# M4 FULLY TRACKED TRACTOR UNIT

| | |
|---|---|
| Empty weight: | 14,288 kg |
| Payload: | 17,000 kg |
| Dimensions in mm (length/width/height): | 5,230/2,460/2,520 |
| Engine: | 6-cylinder inline, petrol, water-cooled, 210 hp |
| Speed: | 53 km/h road |
| Range: | 280 km road |
| Armament: | 12.7 mm M2HB anti-aircraft machine gun on occasion |
| Fording depth: | 1 m |

The M4 'High-Speed Tractor' was created in response to a US Army requirement for a new mobile tractor unit for heavy artillery and anti-aircraft guns, such as the M1 9 cm anti-aircraft cannon, the M2 15.5 cm 'Long Tom' cannon, or the M1 20.3 cm howitzer. The development of the M4 began in 1941, and was based on the chassis of the M2A1 light tank. In 1942 the new tractor unit, produced by Allis-Chalmers, received the designation M4 and was delivered to units. In addition to ten seats for the whole of the gun crew in the forward zone, the M4 also featured stowage for sufficient ammunition so that limbers were unnecessary. The engine was located in the central zone. For loading heavy shells a small crane was also fitted. A cable winch with a 13 tonne pulling force was installed in the rear above the trailer coupling. Often a rotary mount was fitted on the roof of the crew cabin with a 12.7 mm anti-aircraft machine gun of the Browning M2HB type. Between 1943 and 1945 Allis-Chalmers built around 5,500 vehicles of this type, which proved themselves exceptionally well in all duties – not only on the roads but also when travelling cross-country. After the war fully tracked tractor units of this kind were delivered by the USA in the course of military aid programmes to many countries, for example Brazil, Japan, Pakistan and Yugoslavia. The newly formed Bundeswehr also profited from these supplies, and until the start of the 1960s used a number of M4s to pull its heavy guns.

*The M4 fully tracked tractor unit.*

# M29 WEASEL

Originally this crawler vehicle was developed for special units that were to attack factories in Norway in which the Nazis were producing 'heavy water' (deuterium), which was required for the construction of atomic bombs. Since it was thought that the troops would have to overcome snow and ice, the decision was made to equip them with a new vehicle. Studebaker was granted the contract on 17 May 1942, and only 34 days later the first prototype was produced, but this did not immediately fulfil all requirements. Therefore modifications were undertaken on two prototypes, but shortly thereafter the planned attack was abandoned. Nevertheless the US Army recognized the potential of the vehicle, named the 'Weasel', and equipped mountain troops and pioneer units with it. The M29 was used primarily to transport supplies and wounded. In remote regions such as Alaska, Greenland or Iceland M29s were also employed for rescue duties. While early production models were designated the M28, the main production model was the M29. Although even the basic version could float, it was very difficult to steer in the water. Therefore an amphibious version was generated, the M29C, with a boat-shaped front end, buoyancy aids and a cable winch. In total Studebaker built around 15,124 vehicles between 1942 and 1945. After the war the M29 continued to be used by the US armed forces and in the civilian sector it was used for polar exploration. The last M29s were in service up until the 1980s in Norway, in other words, in the terrain for which they had been developed.

| | |
|---|---|
| Empty weight: | 1,851 kg |
| Payload: | 545 kg |
| Dimensions in mm (length/width/height): | 3,194/1,708/1,524 |
| Engine: | Studebaker, 6-cylinder inline, petrol, watercooled, 75 hp |
| Speed: | 58 km/h |
| Range: | 250 km |
| Fording depth: | 0.8 m |

*The M29 'Weasel' of the US Army.*

ARMOURED VEHICLES

## LIGHT ARMOURED CARS SD.KFZ. 221, 222, 223

*Sd.Kfz. 223 of the 15th
Panzer Division, Libya, 1942.*

| | Sd.Kfz. 223 Ausführung B |
|---|---|
| Combat weight: | 4,400 kg |
| Crew: | 3 |
| Dimensions in mm (length, width, height): | 4,800/1,950/1,800; height with antenna: 2,060 |
| Engine: | Horch V8 petrol, water-cooled, 3,823 cc, 81 hp |
| Power/weight ratio: | 16.9 hp/tonne |
| Max. speed: | 80 km/h road |
| Range: | 280 km road 200 km cross-country |
| Armament: | 1 x 7.92 mm MG 34 machine gun |
| Armour: | 8–14.5 mm, later up to 30 mm |
| Fording depth: | 0.6 m |

The Wehrmacht used a whole series of armoured cars based on the same chassis. The Sd.Kfz. 221 – armed at first with no more than an MG 34 – was brought into service in 1936. From 1942 onwards, it was equipped with the 2.8 cm Panzerbüchse anti-tank rifle. These light reconnaissance vehicles consisted in essence of an armoured superstructure with a rotating turret mounted on a traditional chassis. In addition to an MG 34, the Sd.Kfz. 222 also carried a 2 cm KwK cannon and had a larger turret. The Sd.Kfz. 223 was an Sd.Kfz. 221 with a large, conspicuous frame antenna and high-performance radio system. Vehicles of this series were deployed in the armoured car units of the reconnaissance battalions, mostly in teams made up of gun and radio vehicles. Sd.Kfz. 220 and 261, known officially as 'small armoured communications vehicles', were turretless, unarmed versions of the Sd.Kfz. 223. They carried a full set of radio equipment and were used mainly at headquarters and in armoured communications companies. All models remained in service up to the end of the war and were based on good if somewhat over-complicated designs. In Russia their role was eventually taken over by special half-track vehicles. Altogether 2,118 vehicles were built.

## HEAVY ARMOURED CARS SD.KFZ. 231 AND 232 (6-WHEEL)

| | Sd.Kfz. 231 Type G31 (Büssing-NAG) |
|---|---|
| Combat weight: | 5,700 kg |
| Crew: | 4 |
| Dimensions in mm (length, width, height): | 5,570/1,820/2,250; height with antenna: 2,900 |
| Engine: | Büssing-NAG Type G inline 4-cylinder petrol, water-cooled, 3,920 cc, 60 hp |
| Power/weight ratio: | 10.5 hp/tonne |
| Max. speed: | 40 km/h road |
| Range: | 260 km road, 140 km cross-country |
| Armament: | 1 x 2 cm KwK 30 cannon 1 x 7.92 mm MG 34 machine gun |
| Armour: | 8–14.5 mm |
| Fording depth: | 0.5 m |

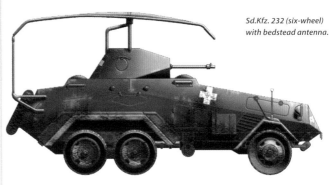

*Sd.Kfz. 232 (six-wheel)
with bedstead antenna.*

These heavy armoured cars comprised an armour-plated superstructure and rotating turret mounted on a normal commercial truck chassis. Starting in the early 1930s, three different companies (Daimler-Benz, Büssing and Magirus) manufactured versions of this vehicle which varied slightly from one another. None of them had all-wheel drive and their cross-country capability was therefore limited. They were no longer used on the front after 1940. The Sd.Kfz. 231 (six-wheel) was the so-called Kanonenwagen (gun vehicle) while the Sd.Kfz. 232 (6-wheel) was equipped with a radio and large bedstead antenna. Small numbers were also produced of another model, the Sd.Kfz. 263, which served as a command vehicle and had a high superstructure in place of a turret. An unusual feature of all the different versions was that they had duplicate front and rear controls. In total 928 six-wheel reconnaissance vehicles were built.

# HEAVY ARMOURED CARS SD.KFZ. 231 AND 232 (8-WHEEL)

*Sd.Kfz. 232 (eight-wheel).*

| | Sd.Kfz. 232 |
|---|---|
| Combat weight: | 8,800 kg |
| Crew: | 4 |
| Dimensions in mm (length, width, height): | 5,850/2,200/2,340; height with antenna: 2,900 |
| Engine: | Büssing-NAG Type L 8V-GS V8 petrol, water-cooled, 8,360 cc, 180 hp |
| Power/weight ratio: | 20.5 hp/tonne |
| Max. speed: | 85 km/h road |
| Range: | 300 km road, 160 km cross-country |
| Armament: | 1 x 2 cm KwK 30 cannon, 1 x 7.92 mm MG 34 machine gun |
| Armour: | 8–14.5 mm; later 30 mm |
| Fording depth: | 1 m |

Army command soon became aware of the limitations of the six-wheel reconnaissance vehicles and awarded contracts for a successor as early as 1934. Büssing-NAG delivered the first of the new vehicles to the Wehrmacht in 1937. Because they were designed to perform the same role as the six-wheel versions, the new models were again named 'Sd.Kfz. 231' and 'Sd.Kfz. 232'. They were the best models of their day with the greatest cross-country capability. This was only

achieved, however, at the expense of an extremely complex chassis with all-wheel drive and steering. They were also relatively large and high – something of a disadvantage for a reconnaissance vehicle. Like their six-wheel predecessors, the eight-wheel versions also had front and rear controls. Because of their size, they proved to be relatively vulnerable during the war and were therefore fitted with an anti-tank-gun shield mounted some distance in front of the vehicle's

nose. The thickness of the front armour was later increased to 30 mm. In addition to the two main versions there was also a command vehicle (Sd.Kfz. 263) with a high superstructure as well as a support variant (Sd.Kfz. 233) with an open turret and short 7.5 cm StuK L/24 assault gun. By the time production finally ceased in 1942, 1,235 had been built.

# HEAVY ARMOURED CAR SD.KFZ. 234 PUMA

Although the first generation of eight-wheel reconnaissance vehicles had been relatively successful, they also had a number of major drawbacks, not least the

| | Sd.Kfz. 234/2 |
|---|---|
| Combat weight: | 11,700 kg |
| Crew: | 4 |
| Dimensions in mm (length, width, height): | 6,000/2,330/2,380 |
| Engine: | Tatra 103 V12 diesel, air-cooled, 14,825cc, 210 hp |
| Power/weight ratio: | 18.2 hp/tonne |
| Max. speed: | 90 km/h road |
| Range: | 900 km road, 600 km cross-country |
| Armament: | 1 x 5 cm KwK 39 cannon 1 x 7.92 mm MG 34 (or MG 42) machine gun |
| Armour: | 8–30 mm |
| Fording depth: | 1 m |

risers that supported the large frame antenna and the vehicles' limited off-road range. Büssing-NAG therefore designed a vehicle with a monocoque hull that dispensed with the frame antenna, thereby reducing the height. It also featured a new Tatra air-cooled diesel engine and large fuel tanks which extended the range to 900 km, a decision taken with North Africa and the Russian steppes in mind. The new vehicle, named the Sd.Kfz. 234, went into production in

1943 in four different versions: the Sd.Kfz. 234/1 had a turret similar to the Sd.Kfz. 222 with a 2 cm KwK cannon; the Sd.Kfz. 234/2 had the same turret as the Leopard light tank and the 5 cm KwK cannon; the Sd.Kfz. 234/3 had a short 7.5 cm StuK 24 assault gun mounted in its open, fixed turret; while the Sd.Kfz. 234/4 mounted the long 7.5 cm Pak 40 L/46. Technically, these vehicles were way ahead of their time and were to influence the development of reconnaissance vehicles for years to come. Around 1,000 units were manufactured.

*Sd.Kfz. 234/2.*

# LIGHT ARMOURED PERSONNEL CARRIER SD.KFZ. 250

| | Sd.Kfz. 250/1 |
|---|---|
| Combat weight: | 5,700 kg |
| Crew: | 2 + 4 |
| Dimensions in mm (length, width, height): | 4,560/1,950/1,660 (without machine gun shield) |
| Engine: | Maybach HL 42 TRKM inline 6-cylinder, water-cooled, 4,170 cc, 100 hp |
| Power/weight ratio: | 17.5 hp/tonne |
| Max. speed: | 65 km/h road |
| Range: | 350 km road, 200 km cross-country |
| Armament: | 2 x 7.92 mm MG 34 or 42 machine guns |
| Armour: | 8–12 mm |
| Fording depth: | 0.7 m |

*Sd.Kfz. 250/1 of the Grossdeutschland Division, Eastern Front.*

The Blitzkrieg concept was based largely on swift, deep tank advances with infantry support. The Wehrmacht was the first army in the world to develop special armoured personnel carriers that enabled the infantry to keep pace with the tanks. This strategy required all kinds of additional support vehicles, which were based on the same chassis. The army's light armoured personnel carriers were based on the chassis of the 1 tonne tractor and were manufactured in a wide range of variants. The basic model was the Sd.Kfz. 250/1, a simple troop carrier often used by platoon or company sergeants and equipped with a machine gun. There were also radio/command vehicles with or without a frame antenna

(e.g. Rommel's Sd.Kfz. 250/3, known as the 'Greif' – 'Griffin') and armoured artillery observation vehicles with binocular periscope and other special equipment (Sd.Kfz. 250/5). So-called 'Kanonenwagen' (gun vehicles) were intended to provide the mechanized infantry with supporting fire and were equipped with either the 3.7 cm Pak (Sd.Kfz. 250/10) or 7.5 cm StuK 24 (Sd.Kfz. 250/8). The Sd.Kfz. 250/9 was a special reconnaissance variant and was fitted with the Sd.Kfz. 222 turret and a 2 cm KwK cannon. There were also mortar carriers

and ammunition transporters based on the Sd.Kfz. 250. In 1943 the vehicle's complex angular hull was greatly simplified in order to make production easier. The Sd.Kfz. 252, an ammunition transporter also based on the light armoured personnel carrier, had a closed, foreshortened superstructure and – like the observation variant Sd.Kfz. 253 – was assigned to assault gun units. All the vehicles in this series proved outstandingly successful and were highly valued by the army. By 1945 around 7,500 units had been built.

*Sd.Kfz. 250/3.*

# MEDIUM ARMOURED PERSONNEL CARRIER SD.KFZ. 251

This medium armoured personnel carrier was based on the chassis of the 3 tonne tractor and had in common with it a front axle that was neither powered nor equipped with brakes and served solely to steer the vehicle. A chain brake came into play during extreme steering manoeuvres, however. The first vehicles were supplied to the Army in 1939 and received a baptism of fire in the Polish campaign. Like the light armoured personnel carrier, the medium personnel carrier was manufactured in a wide range of variants. There were 22 officially designated models. The basic model (Sd.Kfz. 251/1) was a ten-man troop carrier and was armed with two machine guns. The numerous special versions included radio, command, ambulance, engineers', ammmunition and artillery observation vehicles. There was great variety in the vehicles' armaments too. The Sd.Kfz. 251/10 was often fitted out as a platoon leader's vehicle with the 3.7 cm Pak anti-tank gun and the Sd.Kfz. 251/9, in its role as provider of supporting fire, with the short 7.5 cm StuK assault gun. From the end of 1944 the 7.5 cm StuK 40 was also fitted in one model (Sd.Kfz. 251/22). Other variants of the medium armoured personnel carrier included mortar carriers, rocket launchers, flamethrowers and self-propelled anti-aircraft guns (such as the Sd.Kfz. 251/21 equipped with the 1.5 cm Drilling 151 MG). The hull underwent minor modifications a number of times during the war and was greatly simplified in 1944. The medium armoured personnel carrier proved extremely successful on all fronts and pretty well represented a new generation of armoured vehicle. Wherever German troops were to be found, the

| | Sd.Kfz. 251/1 |
|---|---|
| Combat weight: | 8,500 kg |
| Crew: | 2 + 10 |
| Dimensions in mm (length, width, height): | 5,800/2,000/1,750 (without machine gun shield) |
| Engine: | Maybach HL 42 TRKM inline 6-cylinder, water-cooled, 4,170 cc, 100 hp |
| Power/weight ratio: | 11.8 hp/tonne |
| Max. speed: | 52.5 km/h road |
| Range: | 320 km road, 180 km cross-country |
| Armament: | 2 x 7.92 mm MG 34 or 42 machine guns |
| Armour: | 8–12 mm |
| Fording depth: | 0.5 m |

Sd.Kfz. 251 could be found alongside them and in this respect the vehicle could be said to have been a defining feature of the Wehrmacht. By 1945 around 16,000 medium armoured personnel carriers had been built.

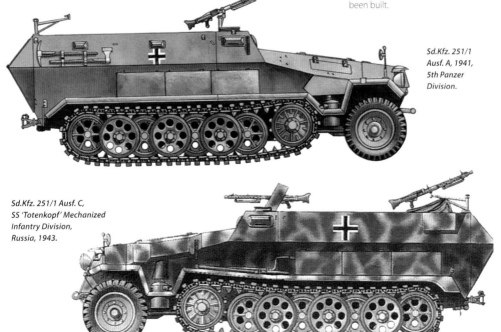

*Sd.Kfz. 251/1 Ausf. A, 1941, 5th Panzer Division.*

*Sd.Kfz. 251/1 Ausf. C, SS 'Totenkopf' Mechanized Infantry Division, Russia, 1943.*

## PANZER I SD.KFZ. 101

*Panzer Command
Vehicle I, 11th Panzer
Division, Tula, 1941.*

|  | Pz.Kpfw. I Ausführung A |
|---|---|
| Combat weight: | 5,400 kg |
| Crew: | 2 |
| Dimensions in mm (length, width, height): | 4,020/2,060/1,720 |
| Engine: | Krupp 4-cylinder boxer petrol, air-cooled, 3,460 cc, 60 hp |
| Power/weight ratio: | 19.5 hp/tonne |
| Max. speed: | 37 km/h |
| Range: | 200 km road, 140 km cross-country |
| Armament: | 2 x 7.92 mm machine guns |
| Armour: | 6–13 mm |
| Fording depth: | 0.6 m |

*Panzer I Ausf. A, 5th Panzer
Regiment, Libya 1941.*

Germany was prohibited under the Treaty of Versailles from building armoured vehicles but this did not stop the National Socialists from embarking upon a secret programme of tank design and construction after they seized power in 1933. A number of prototypes of a new tank – referred to initially, for reasons of secrecy, as a 'Landwirtschaftlicher Schlepper' (agricultural towing vehicle) before being renamed 'Panzerkampf-wagen I'– were tested as early as 1934. The new tank's armament consisted solely of two 7.92 mm machine guns mounted in a rotating turret. Ausf. A was powered by a 60 hp engine which was upgraded to 100 hp in Ausf. B. The later version was also extended by some 40 cm. Although its firepower was relatively modest, the Panzer I was used in the Polish and French campaigns. After the Battle of France it was withdrawn from the front line but remained in service for the whole of the war either as a special variant of one kind or another, or as a training tank. One of the Wehrmacht's first self-propelled guns was based on the Panzer I. The 15 cm SIG-33 heavy infantry gun – complete with wheels and carriage – was mounted on a Panzer I hull and the whole structure covered with armour plating. Another Panzer I variant that pointed the way forward was the tank command vehicle that facilitated the mobile command of tank battles for the first time. Attempts were also made to build a Panzer I direct infantry support vehicle by equipping the basic design with armour 80 mm thick but this idea never progressed beyond the prototype stage. Around 2,800 Panzer Is of all types were built between 1934 and 1939.

*SIG-33 heavy infantry gun mounted on a Panzer I.*

# PANZER II SD.KFZ. 121

Like the Panzer I, the Panzer II was initially regarded as a stopgap that would have to do until Panzers III and IV were ready. Krupp, Henschel and MAN developed proposals for a 10 tonne tank designated for reasons of secrecy the 'Landwirtschaftlicher Schlepper 100'. Army high command decided in favour of the MAN version and the first vehicles were delivered to the Wehrmacht in 1935. The earliest versions, which were only produced in small numbers, had a chassis with six small road wheels fitted to a single arm. Only with Ausf. A did the Panzer II adopt its final form with five medium-sized wheels. This design continued to be used for versions B, C and F, which differed only in terms of their armour. Versions D and E were equipped with a Christie-type suspension with four large wheels and a more powerful engine. They were capable of up to 55 km/h and were intended as fast fighting vehicles. Although the Panzer II was well made, its armour and armament were considered rather inadequate. It nevertheless remained in service as a battle tank until 1941; after this it was used mainly in a reconnaissance role. Ausf. L was developed specifically as a reconnaissance tank although only a few were actually built. Flamethrowers (the 'Flamingo') and submergible versions for the planned invasion of the United

*Panzer II Ausf. B, 6th Panzer Regiment, September 1938.*

Kingdom were also based on the Panzer II design. Far better known and more successful than these, however, were the self-propelled Marder and Wespe anti-tank and artillery guns.

*Panzer II Ausf. C, 8th Panzer Regiment, Libya, 1941.*

*Panzer II Ausf. C, 7th Panzer Division.*

| | Pz.Kpfw. II Ausführung C |
|---|---|
| Combat weight: | 9,500 kg |
| Crew: | 3 |
| Dimensions in mm (length, width, height): | 4,810/2,280/2,020 |
| Engine: | Maybach HL 62 TRM inline 6-cylinder petrol, air-cooled, 6,190cc, 140 hp |
| Power/weight ratio: | 14.7 hp/tonne |
| Max. speed: | 40 km/h road, 19 km/h cross-country |
| Range: | 150 km road, 100 km cross-country |
| Armament: | 2 cm KwK 30 cannon, 1 x 7.92 mm MG 34 machine gun |
| Armour: | 5–30 mm |
| Fording depth: | 0.92 m |

# PANZER 35(T) ŠKODA LT 35

This tank was built by Škoda in Czechoslovakia in the 1930s and was introduced into the Czech armed forces in 1936. Following the annexation of Czechoslovakia in 1939, numerous Czech tanks fell into the Wehrmacht's hands including this model. The Škoda Model LT 35 carried a 3.7 cm gun and proved extremely reliable. Named 'Panzerkampfwagen 35(t)' by the Wehrmacht, it was at least as good as the Panzer II and played an important part in the equipping of the German tank divisions. The (t) in its new name stood for 'tschechisch' (Czech). The tag (f) was used for captured French weapons, (r) for Russian weapons and so on. Although its

armour plating was riveted, which to some extent impaired its fighting strength, the general quality of the 35(t)'s construction was outstanding. The drive sprocket was located at the rear in order to create more space in the crew compartment. The gears and steering were driven by compressed air in an attempt to make the driver's job easier. On the Eastern Front in winter, however, this system proved extremely temperamental and the compressed air was replaced by mechanical components. The tank's suspension was extremely well designed and the lifespan of the tracks was almost 7,000 km. The Panzer 35(t) was integrated

|  | Pz.Kpfw. 35(t) |
|---|---|
| Combat weight: | 11,000 kg |
| Crew: | 4 |
| Dimensions in mm (length, width, height): | 4,650/2,250/2,350 |
| Engine: | Škoda inline 4-cylinder petrol, water-cooled, 8,620 cc, 115 hp |
| Power/weight ratio: | 10.5 hp/tonne |
| Max. speed: | 34 km/h road |
| Range: | 190 km road, 120 km cross-country |
| Armament: | 3.7 cm Škoda cannon, 2 x 7.92 mm MG 34 machine guns |
| Armour: | 16–25 mm |
| Fording depth: | 0.77 m |

into German tank divisions and was used in Poland and France as well as on the Eastern Front as late as 1942, by which time it was considered obsolete. The remaining vehicles were converted into recovery tanks or towing vehicles. The Wehrmacht had brought around 300 LT 35s into service. Before the Second World War, Škoda had supplied a number of tanks of this type to Romania, which deployed them alongside the Wehrmacht in Russia. Having thoroughly overhauled the Škoda design, Hungary started to build its own version of it, the Turan, in a range of different models in 1940.

*Panzer 35(t).*

*A Škoda R-2 of the 1st Romanian Panzer Division, Eastern Front, November 1942.*

# PANZER 38(T) PRAGA TNHP-S LT 38

|  | Pz.Kpfw. 38(t) |
|---|---|
| Combat weight: | 10,500 kg |
| Crew: | 4 |
| Dimensions in mm (length, width, height): | 4,650/2,250/2,350 |
| Engine: | Praga inline 6-cylinder petrol, water-cooled, 7,754 cc, 125 hp |
| Power/weight ratio: | 11.9 hp/tonne |
| Max. speed: | 42 km/h road |
| Range: | 240 km road, 160 km cross-country |
| Armament: | 3.7 cm cannon, 2 x 7.92 mm MG 34 machine guns |
| Armour: | 15–25 mm; later up to 50 mm |
| Fording depth: | 0.9 m |

*A Panzer 38(t) on the advance in the West in 1940.*

The second Czech tank to be adopted by the Wehrmacht was the LT 38, made by CKD. These vehicles were trialled from May 1939 onwards and proved significantly superior to Germany's Panzers I and II. The Army Ordnance Office therefore ordered that production continued and the manufacturer's name was changed to 'Böhmisch-Mährische-Maschinenfabrik' (BMM). By the start of the war the Army had taken receipt of 98 vehicles, which were given the official designation Panzer 38(t) Ausführung A. The tanks carried 90 rounds for their

3.7 cm KwK 38(t) L/48 cannon. With a muzzle velocity of 740 m per second, this weapon was capable of penetrating armour plating up to 35 mm thick from a distance of around 500 m. The 38(t)'s armour was very weak, however, and, like that of the 35(t), riveted, which meant that if the vehicle were hit, the rivets would turn into dangerous projectiles and explode into the interior of the tank. Four large road wheels benefited from simple but effective leaf spring suspension that ensured good handling. The vehicle was well designed and

proved extremely reliable and versatile. Later versions B, C and D differed only in minor details. Versions E and F were given additional 25-mm-thick riveted armour at the front. The final version, Ausf. G, remained in production until 1942. Ausf. S was an export version supplied to Hungary (102 units), Slovakia (69 units), Romania (50 units) and Bulgaria (10 units). Sweden had ordered 92 vehicles from CKD which were not supplied (the Wehrmacht took delivery of them instead). In December 1942, however, Sweden was granted the right to manufacture the tank under licence. In 1943, 70 units of a 38 reconnaissance tank based on the 38(t) were built. This involved fitting the turret of the Sd.Kfz. 222 on to the unmodified 38(t) hull and equipping it with a 2 cm KwK 38 cannon and MG 42 machine gun. A far more familiar sight was the numerous self-propelled guns based on the 38(t), which played an important role for the Wehrmacht. The German forces employed around 1,500 38(t)s although they no longer used them as battle tanks after 1942.

*A Panzer 38(t) Ausf. E, 8th Panzer Division, 1941.*

# PANZER III SD.KFZ. 141

| | Pz.Kpfw. III Ausführung J |
|---|---|
| Combat weight: | 22,300 kg |
| Crew: | 5 |
| Dimensions in mm (length, width, height): | 5,560/2,950/2,510 (length without gun barrel) |
| Engine: | Maybach HL 120 TRM V12 petrol, water-cooled, 11,870 cc, 300 hp |
| Power/weight ratio: | 12.2 hp/tonne |
| Max. speed: | 40 km/h road, 19 km/h cross-country |
| Range: | 140 km road, 90 km cross-country |
| Armament: | 5 cm KwK 39 L/60 cannon, 2 x 7.92 mm MG 34 machine guns |
| Armour: | 18–50 mm |
| Fording depth: | 1 m |

*A Panzer III Ausf. F in Russia in winter 1941.*

The Panzer III was intended as a standard battle tank and for logistical reasons (the infantry was already using the 3.7 cm Pak anti-tank gun) was initially to have been equipped with a 3.7 cm KwK cannon. Leading generals such as Heinz Guderian, however, wanted a 5 cm gun. In 1935, development contracts were awarded to MAN, Daimler-Benz,

Rheinmetall and Krupp and in 1936 the Daimler-Benz design emerged victorious. The first models (Ausf. A to D) were used mainly to test different kinds of running gear. Only with Ausf. E in 1939 did the Panzer III assume its typical appearance with six medium-sized wheels. Although the tank was reasonably well made, it suffered from the outset from inadequate

weaponry. This became particularly apparent in 1940 and so later models were equipped with more powerful guns (the 5 cm L/42 and later the L/60). The thickness of armour was also steadily increased (30 mm maximum for Ausf. E; 70 mm maximum for Ausf. L). Ultimately the tank was fitted with a spaced turret girdle and side skirts. The final production model was Ausf. N, which mounted a short 7.5 cm KwK L/24. Compared to the Panzer IV, which had similar dimensions, the Panzer III was always underarmed. The size of its turret ring prohibited it from being fitted with the long 7.5 cm KwK, which would have been necessary against the Soviet T-34 from 1943. Nevertheless, with its advanced design (five-man crew, radio equipment, torsion bar suspension), the Panzer III was forward-looking and effective in combat. From 1942, however, it could no longer be relied upon to be the match of any opponent and was clearly inferior to the T-34 or KV-1. In addition to the command and flamethrower versions, an amphibious model was made for Operation Sea Lion. By 1943 around 5,700 Panzer IIIs of all variants had been built although many of these were assault guns based on the Panzer III chassis. The Russians also found that (captured) Panzer IIIs made a useful base for an assault gun (e.g. the SU-76i).

*A Panzer III Ausf. N, Kursk, July 1943.*

*A Panzer III Ausf. J with 5 cm KwK L/60 cannon, 'Wiking' Panzer Division, 1942.*

# PANZER IV SD.KFZ. 161

*A Panzer IV Ausf. D1, Hungarian Panzer Division 'Don 09', September 1942.*

wore a coating of Zimmerit paste to impede magnetic charges. With Ausf. J (April 1944 to the end of the war) it was decided to sacrifice the electric turret traversing gear in order to make room for an additional fuel tank, which extended the vehicle's range to around 260 km. From September 1944, skirts of wire mesh were commonly used in order to save weight. The Panzer IV remained a serious battlefield opponent through to the end of the war – not a bad outcome for a design that dated back to 1934. There were also ammunition transporter, bridgelaying and recovery variants as well as a series of self-propelled guns. Around 9,200 Panzer IV units were produced. In addition to the Wehrmacht, the tank was used by Germany's allies as well as by a number of neutral states. The last Panzer IVs in service were probably those deployed in 1973 by Syria, which had bought them cheaply from the Soviet Union's stock of captured tanks.

The Panzer IV was initially conceived as a heavy support vehicle. During the course of the war, however, it became the backbone of the German tank fleet. Development was begun by Krupp in 1934. The first 35 units of the 17.3 tonne Ausf. A, equipped with a 7.5 cm KwK L/24, two machine guns and 14.5 mm armour all over, were delivered by 1938. The Panzer IV had pretty well found its final form with this first version because no significant modifications were undertaken during the war other than the upgrading of its gun and armour. From the middle of 1942, Ausf. F2 was equipped with the 7.5 cm KwK-40 L/43 and its armour was reinforced through the addition of 30 mm-thick plates on the nose and at the front of the turret, finally producing a match for the T-34. Ausf. G carried the even better KwK-40 L/48. Ausf. H (May 1943 onwards), was given reinforced turret roof armour, 80 mm-thick front armour, side skirts to protect it from anti-tank rifles and hollow charge projectiles and wider tracks for use in the snow and mud of the East. From September 1943 onwards, Panzer IVs

| | Pz.Kpfw. IV Ausführung H |
|---|---|
| Combat weight: | 25,000 kg |
| Crew: | 5 |
| Dimensions in mm (length, width, height): | 5,930/2,880/2,680 without barrel or skirts; 7,020/3,350/2,680 with barrel and skirts |
| Engine: | Maybach HL 120 TRM V12 petrol, water-cooled, 11,870 cc, 300 hp |
| Power/weight ratio: | 12 hp/tonne |
| Max. speed: | 38 km/h road, 16 km/h cross-country |
| Range: | 180 km road, 120 km cross-country |
| Armament: | 7.5 cm KwK 40 L/48 cannon & 2 x 7.92 mm MG 34 machine guns |
| Armour: | 10–80 mm; skirts 5 mm |
| Fording depth: | 1.2 m |

*A Panzer IV H of an assault gun unit on the Eastern Front.*

## PANZER V SD.KFZ. 171 (PANTHER)

*A Panzer V Ausf. D1, 'Das Reich' Panzer Division.*

*A Panzer V Ausf. D2, 9th Panzer Division ('Hohenstaufen'), Normandy, 1944.*

| | Pz.Kpfw. V Ausführung D |
|---|---|
| Combat weight: | 45,500 kg |
| Crew: | 5 |
| Dimensions in mm (length, width, height): | 6,870/3,270/3,100 without barrel or skirts; 8,650/3,420/3,100 with barrel and skirts |
| Engine: | Maybach HL 230 P30 V12 petrol, water-cooled, 23,880 cc, 700 hp |
| Power/weight ratio: | 15.3 hp/tonne |
| Max. speed: | 46 km/h road, 24 km/h cross-country |
| Range: | 160 km road, 100 km cross-country |
| Armament: | 7.5 cm KwK 42 L/70 cannon, 2–3 x 7.92 mm MG 34 machine guns |
| Armour: | 26–100 mm |
| Fording depth: | 1.7 m |

The development of the Panther was largely influenced by the emergence of the Soviet T-34, which set new standards in tank construction. The Army Ordnance Office contracted MAN and Daimler-Benz to develop a 35 tonne tank with the same outstanding properties as the T-34: a ballistically effective shape (providing effective shot deflection), powerful weaponry and good manoeuvrability. The MAN design was chosen and the tank went into production at the end of 1942. The Panther had its debut at the Battle of Kursk (Operation Citadel) in July 1943 – albeit without success as the first Panthers were still suffering from teething problems as a result of having been sent into battle prematurely. Their gearboxes and running gear failed and many broke down before they had even reached the front. Once these defects had been rectified, the Panther went on to become one of the best, if not *the* best, tank of the Second World War. It combined firepower, effective armour and manoeuvrability and was justifiably feared by opposing tank crews. Its 7.5 cm KwK L/70 could pierce the armour of almost any tank at around 1 km. Even the Panther had its defects, however: its turret traversing gear was so weak that the turret would not rotate if the tank was on a slope; its engine had a lifetime of little more than 1,000 km; the side and rear armour was relatively thin – only frontally did the tank offer first-class protection, which was why Panzer IVs were often deployed to protect the flanks. Another problem was the shape of the gun mantlet: hits were known to have ricocheted off it and penetrated the roof of the hull. In addition to battle tank versions D, A and G, a number of special recovery Panthers were also built because the usual 18 tonne towing machines were not powerful enough to tow either Panthers or Tigers. By the end of the war around 6,000 Panthers had been built. The French Army continued to use captured Panthers for some time afterwards.

*A Panther on difficult terrain. Despite weighing 45 tonnes, the tank was extremely manoeuvrable.*

# JAGDPANTHER 8.8 CM TANK DESTROYER SD.KFZ. 173

After a number of attempts to use the excellent but unwieldy 8.8 cm Pak 43 in a variety of self-propelled guns, resulting in vehicles such as the Nashorn and Elefant, the decision was finally taken to mount the anti-tank gun on the chassis of the highly successful Panther tank. The first prototype was unveiled in October 1943. At the beginning of 1944, the new fighting vehicle was given the name 'Jagdpanther' at Hitler's suggestion, and went into production at MIAG in February. By the end of the war just 382 Jagdpanthers had been built. The Jagdpanther was extremely mobile and well armoured with sloped armour that was highly

*The Jagdpanther's sloping sides are particularly conspicuous from the front.*

| Combat weight: | 46,000 kg |
| --- | --- |
| Crew: | 5 |
| Dimensions in mm (length, width, height): | 6,870/3,270/2,715 without barrel or skirts; 9,860/3,420/2,715 with barrel and skirts |
| Engine: | Maybach HL 230 P30 V12 petrol, water-cooled, 23,880 cc, 700 hp |
| Power/weight ratio: | 15.2 hp/tonne |
| Max. speed: | 46 km/h road, 24 km/h cross-country |
| Range: | 150 km road, 100 km cross-country |
| Armament: | 88 cm Pak 43/3 L/71 anti-tank gun, 7.92 mm MG 34 machine gun |
| Armour: | 17–80 mm |
| Fording depth: | 1.55 m |

*A Jagdpanther with the Panzer Lehr Division, Uelzen area, March 1945.*

effective from a ballistics point of view. Like other German assault guns and tank destroyers, however, the vehicle had to be pointing in the approximate direction of the target because the gun had a very limited traverse. The superstructure was roomy and Krupp was therefore commissioned to design an upgraded version with a 12.8 cm Pak. The combination of 8.8 cm Pak and Panther chassis proved extremely successful. The gun was capable of destroying any Allied tank in existence and the chassis was mobile and robust. As a result the vehicle was loved by its crews and feared by the Allies. The Jagdpanther is widely regarded as a masterpiece of middle-period tank design.

*A Jagdpanther in the Tank Museum, Münster, Germany.*

## PANZER VI TIGER SD.KFZ. 181

| | Pz.Kpfw. VI Ausführung E |
|---|---|
| Combat weight: | 55,000 kg |
| Crew: | 5 |
| Dimensions in mm (length, width, height): | 6,200/3,550/2,880 without barrel or skirts; 8,240/3,730/2,880 with barrel and skirts |
| Engine: | Maybach HL 230 P45 V12 petrol, water-cooled, 21,353 cc, 700 hp |
| Power/weight ratio: | 12.3 hp/tonne |
| Max. speed: | 38 km/h road, 20 km/h cross-country |
| Range: | 90 km road, 60 km cross-country |
| Armament: | 8.8 cm KwK-36 L/56, 2 x 7.92 mm MG 34 machine guns |
| Armour: | 26–110 mm |
| Fording depth: | 1.2 m; first units capable of submerging to a depth of 4 m |

*A Sturmtiger assault gun of the Sturmmörser (mortar) Company 1002 in the Ardennes, winter 1944–45.*

*A Tiger Ausf. E, 101st Heavy SS Panzer Battalion, Normandy, 1944.*

*A Tiger Ausf. H1, 503rd Heavy Panzer Battalion, Rostov, 1943.*

Experience in the Battle of France in 1940 and the appearance of the Soviet T-34 and KV-1 confirmed the Wehrmacht's pressing need for a heavy tank. In 1941, therefore, the Army Ordnance Office commissioned Porsche and Henschel to develop an appropriate vehicle. Both firms turned to designs and prototypes they had been working on since 1937. The Porsche design proved too technically complex; Henschel's was more conventional and was chosen for production. Confident that his design would be selected, however, Professor Porsche had already manufactured 90 chassis, which were later turned into the Elefant tank destroyer. Henschel's design was heavily armoured but did not share the T-34's innovative sloping design. The turret was made by Krupp and was equipped with an 8.8 cm gun based on the legendary 8.8 cm anti-aircraft gun. This gave the new tank, which by now had been named the Tiger, the ability to penetrate the armour of any opponent. Production began in 1942 and the first Tigers were sent to North Africa and the Eastern Front in late summer. As a consequence of the hasty development process, the tank was mechanically unreliable and furthermore the right

battlefield tactics had yet to be devised for the 55 tonne colossus. Once these weaknesses were rectified, the Tiger began to be greatly feared by the enemy. Although it was not sloped, the thickness of its armour (100 mm at the front and 80 mm at the sides) meant it could withstand most shells. The Tiger was therefore capable of taking extremely heavy punishment and still penetrating the armour of a T-34/76 over 1.5 km away with its 8.8 cm KwK 36.

When properly deployed, the Tiger dominated battlefields on both the Eastern and Western fronts. In 1944, for example, a single Tiger destroyed 25 Allied tanks, holding up an entire division before being hit itself. But the mighty Tiger also had its weak points. Its great weight was the cause of numerous

difficulties – there were many bridges it could not cross, for example. Its width was also a problem because narrow transport tracks had to be fitted (a slow and laborious process) before it could be loaded on to railway trucks. In heavy mud or freezing snow its interleaved running gear had a tendency to become blocked. One Tiger variant was a tractor designed specifically to tow other Tigers. Another was the so-called 'Sturmtiger', whose turret was replaced with an armour-plated superstructure accommodating a 38 cm rocket mortar, although only 18 of these were manufactured. Production of the Tiger came to a halt in August 1944 after only 1,350 or so had been built – not many when one stops to consider the legendary reputation the tank had acquired.

# TIGER (P) TANK DESTROYER SD.KFZ.184 (FERDINAND/ELEFANT)

| | Jagdpanzer Tiger (P) Ferdinand |
|---|---|
| Combat weight: | 68,000 kg |
| Crew: | 6 |
| Dimensions in mm (length, width, height): | 6,800/3,430/2,970 |
| Engine: | 2 x Maybach HL 120 TRM/ 112 V12 petrol, water- cooled, 11,870 cc, 300 hp |
| Power/weight ratio: | 8.8 hp/tonne |
| Max. speed: | 20 km/h road |
| Range: | 130 km road, 90 km cross-country |
| Armament: | 8.8 cm Pak 43/2 L/71 anti-tank gun |
| Armour: | sides and rear 80 mm front 200 mm |
| Fording depth: | 1 m |

*A Ferdinand tank destroyer with its long 8.8 cm Pak 43.*

After losing out to the Henschel Tiger design, an alternative use was sought for the chassis units that had already been manufactured by Porsche. Back in 1942, Hitler had called for an armoured fighting vehicle capable of mounting the 8.8 cm KwK L/71 and in September 1942 a vehicle of this type was commissioned based on the Porsche Tiger. In February 1943, Hitler ordered that the weapon be delivered as soon as possible. The Jagdpanzer Tiger (P) Sd.Kfz. 184 adopted the Porsche Tiger's running gear unchanged. The fighting compartment with its fixed superstructure up to 200 mm thick was located at the rear with

the engine in the middle. The vehicle had an interesting drive system which offered a number of distinct advantages from a mechanical and constructional point of view: two Maybach HL 120 TRM tank engines powered generators that delivered current to electric motors that drove the sprockets positioned at the front of the vehicle. The tank had a powerful gun and thick armour, making it extremely heavy and slow. Another disadvantage was that it had no means of defending itself against infantry attack, not even a machine gun. Ninety vehicles were produced in total. This tank destroyer, initially named the 'Ferdinand',

first saw combat at the Battle of Kursk in 1943. The 90 Ferdinands deployed there are thought to have knocked out over 500 enemy tanks but they in turn broke down by the dozen. Only 48 vehicles remained after the battle and nearly all were damaged. Following this debacle, they were recalled for modifications and finally fitted with a machine gun and turret hatch. Their name was changed to 'Elefant' and from this point on they saw battle mainly in Italy, where they impressed when used defensively as a kind of mobile bunker. Essentially, however, the vehicle was too heavy, slow and unreliable.

*A Tiger on the Eastern Front in winter 1943.*

*An Elefant tank destroyer with modified front machine gun.*

## TIGER II SD.KFZ. 182

*A 'King Tiger' with Henschel turret. 502nd Heavy Panzer Division, Ardennes, winter 1944–45.*

| Pz.Kpfw. VI B (Henschel turret) | |
|---|---|
| Combat weight: | 69,700 kg |
| Crew: | 5 |
| Dimensions in mm (length, width, height): | 7,260/3,625/3,090 without barrel or skirts: 10,286/3,755/3,090 with barrel and skirts |
| Engine: | Maybach HL 230 P30 V12 petrol, water-cooled, 23,889 cc, 700 hp |
| Power/weight ratio: | 10 hp/tonne |
| Max. speed: | 38 km/h road, 17 km/h cross-country |
| Range: | 120 km road, 80 km cross-country |
| Armament: | 8.8 cm KwK 43 L/71, 2 x 7.92 mm MG 34 machine guns |
| Armour: | 40–185 mm |
| Fording depth: | 1.6 m |

Although production of the Tiger had only just started, the Army Ordnance Office immediately commissioned designs for a successor with a ballistically more efficient shape that would be equipped with the 8.8 cm KwK 43. Once again Porsche and Henschel were in competition, and once again Professor Porsche was so sure of victory that he started production of the tank turret before waiting for the decision. The Army Ordnance Office, meanwhile, preferred yet again the Henschel design. The Porsche turrets were incorporated into the first 50 Henschel vehicles, which went into production in December 1943. Nicknamed the 'King Tiger' or 'Royal Tiger' by the Allies, the Tiger II featured near-indestructible sloped armour and one of the most powerful tank guns of the Second World War. It was also, however, extremely heavy. Its engine was under constant strain, rendering the vehicle ponderous and mechanically unreliable. The Maybach power plant consumed over 1,000 litres of valuable petrol for every 100 km of terrain it covered. By 1944–45 the necessary fuel was often simply not available. Most Tiger IIs were put out of action not by enemy hits but by engine failure or a shortage of petrol. In spite of this – or perhaps because of it – the tank acquired a legendary reputation for its firepower and the strength of its armour. By the end of the war only 485 Tiger IIs had been built.

## JAGDTIGER TANK DESTROYER SD.KFZ. 186

| | Jagdtiger Ausführung B |
|---|---|
| Combat weight: | 72,000 kg |
| Crew: | 5 |
| Dimensions in mm (length, width, height): | 7,800/3,625/2,945; length with barrel: 10,654 |
| Engine: | Maybach HL 230 P30 V12 petrol, water-cooled, 23,889 cc, 700 hp |
| Power/weight ratio: | 9.8 hp/tonne |
| Max. speed: | 35 km/h road, 16 km/h cross-country |
| Range: | 120 km road, 80 km cross-country |
| Armament: | 12.8 cm Pak 44 L/55 anti-tank gun, 2 x 7.92 mm MG 34 machine guns |
| Armour: | 30–250 mm |
| Fording depth: | 1.75 m |

*A Jagdtiger with the 653rd Heavy Tank Destroyer Battalion, Westphalia, April 1945*

The Tiger II also provided the basis for a tank destroyer with a fixed superstructure and limited field of fire. Contracts for this vehicle were awarded in February 1943 and the initial prototype was completed by the Nibelungen Works in April 1944. The first Jagdtigers were delivered to the Army in November 1944. Professor Porsche was again involved and the first two vehicles were provided with running gear of his design. This system did not prove successful, however, and was replaced by the Henschel-designed Tiger II running gear. The Jagdtiger was designed to be able to deal effectively with even the heaviest Allied tank, from a long distance. Its 12.8 cm Pak 44 was indeed up to the task. With a muzzle velocity of 920 m per second, its 28.3 kg tank shell was capable of penetrating 170 mm of armour from 3,000 m away. Unsurprisingly, the ammunition was very heavy and charge and shell had to be loaded separately each time, resulting in a low rate of fire. The Jagdtiger's solid 250 mm frontal armour made it almost invulnerable to attack from this angle although its sides and rear, where the armour was just 80 mm thick, were highly susceptible. The weight of this armour made the tank extremely heavy. Its engine and gears were constantly under strain and consequently the Jagdtiger was often out of action. Because of its great weight it was seldom used as a tank destroyer but rather in an infantry support role. The tank was unpopular with its crews and only 74 of them were built.

# PANZERJÄGER I (SELF-PROPELLED GUN BASED ON PANZER I AUSF. B)

*Panzerjäger I, 'Leibstandarte Adolf Hitler' Division, France, 1942.*

| | Panzerjäger I |
|---|---|
| Combat weight: | 6,400 kg |
| Crew: | 3 |
| Dimensions in mm (length, width, height): | 4,420/1,850/2,250 |
| Engine: | Maybach NL-38 TRKM inline 6-cylinder petrol, water-cooled, 3,790 cc, 100 hp |
| Power/weight ratio: | 15.6 hp/tonne |
| Max. speed: | 40 km/h road |
| Range: | 180 km road, 130 km cross-country |
| Armament: | 4.7 cm Pak 36(t) L43 anti-tank gun |
| Armour: | 6–14.5 mm |
| Fording depth: | 0.6 m |

The 4.7 cm Pak (t) self-propelled gun – Panzerjäger I – was the first in a long series of self-propelled guns designed specifically for use against tanks. It had become clear as early as 1939 that the Panzer I was ineffective in this role. In order to be able to continue using its chassis, the Czech 4.7 cm Pak L/43, an outstanding anti-tank gun for its day, was mounted on the hull of the Pz.Kpfw. I

Ausf. B. The gun was protected on three sides by an armour-plated superstructure up to 14.5 mm thick but was left open at the back. Alkett in Berlin converted 132 Panzer I Ausf. Bs into tank destroyers. There was no question of converting Ausf. A because of its inadequate engine performance and small size. The Panzerjäger I proved extremely effective on the battlefields of France and North

Africa, and during the first phase of the Russian campaign. Before long, however, its deficiencies became apparent. Against the newer Soviet T-34 and KV-1 the 4.7 cm Pak was simply too weak. It was unable to provide protection for German tanks and therefore began to be withdrawn in 1942. The Panzerjäger I continued to be highly successful in Africa, however, until 1943.

# BISON HEAVY INFANTRY GUN SD.KFZ 138/1

| | Bison Ausführung H |
|---|---|
| Combat weight: | 12,700 kg |
| Crew: | 5 |
| Dimensions in mm (length, width, height): | 4,870/2,150/2,470; length with barrel: 5,600 |
| Engine: | Praga inline 6-cylinder petrol, water-cooled, 7,754 cc, 125 hp |
| Power/weight ratio: | 9.8 hp/tonne |
| Max. speed: | 35 km/h road |
| Range: | 210 km road, 140 km cross-country |
| Armament: | 15 cm SIG-33 |
| Armour: | 10–40 mm |
| Fording depth: | 0.9 m |

Another vehicle built on the chassis of the reliable and resilient Panzer 38 (t) was the Bison self-propelled 15 cm heavy infantry gun. These vehicles were not intended as tank destroyers but were designed to provide mobile artillery

support. There were two versions of the Bison (also known as the 'Grille'). Like the Marder III, the engine was positioned either at the back (Ausf. H) or in the middle (Ausf. M). In total 370 units were built between 1942 and 1944.

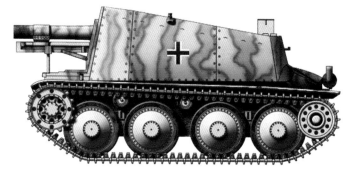

*A Bison Ausf. H from an unknown unit, Russia, 1944.*

## MARDER I, II AND III TANK DESTROYERS

Germany's invasion of the Soviet Union in 1941 and in particular the appearance of the T-34 highlighted the Wehrmacht's urgent need for anti-tank vehicles. As production was already running at capacity and it took time to develop new vehicles, a decision was taken to follow the example of the Panzerjäger I and equip a quantity of out-of-date chassis with high-performance, heavy anti-tank guns. The Marder tank destroyers used three different chassis and were designated Marder I, II and III. When they had invaded France in 1940, German troops had captured around 300 so-called Lorraine tractors, small supply vehicles with a front-mounted engine. Little attention was paid to them initially. It was only with developments in the East that their existence was remembered. On his own initiative, one Hauptmann Becker, an artillery captain and engineer stationed in France, had equipped his battery with self-propelled guns made by members of the unit from British Mark VIs. Hitler had been so impressed that a production unit named 'Baukommando Becker' was formed with the task of developing an appropriate use for the captured French vehicles. An order was duly issued on 25 August 1942 for the construction of a light tank destroyer to be named Marder I. It was initially planned to convert around 160 of the French tractors. Sixty were to be turned

|  | Marder II Sd.Kfz. 132 | Marder III Sd.Kfz. 139 |
|---|---|---|
| Combat weight: | 11,500 kg | 10,800 kg |
| Crew: | 4 | 4 |
| Dimensions in mm (length, width, height): | 4,640/2,300/2,600; length with barrel: 5,650 | 4,870/2,150/2,500; length with barrel: 5,850 |
| Engine: | Maybach HL 62 TRM, inline 6-cylinder petrol, water-cooled, 6,190 cc, 140 hp | Praga inline 6-cylinder petrol, water-cooled, 7,754 cc, 125 hp |
| Power/weight ratio: | 12.2 hp/tonne | 11.6 hp/tonne |
| Max. speed: | 55 km/h road | 42 km/h road |
| Range: | 150 km road, 100 km cross-country | 240 km road, 160 km cross-country |
| Armament: | 7.62 cm Pak 36(r) L/51.1 | 7.62 cm Pak 36(r) L/51.1 |
| Armour: | 14.5–30 mm | 10–50 mm |
| Fording depth: | 0.85 m | 0.9 m |

*A Marder I, based on the chassis of the Lorraine tractor, with 7.5 cm Pak 40.*

into anti-tank vehicles with a 7.5 cm Pak 40/1 L/46 and the rest into self-propelled artillery guns with 10.5 cm and 15 cm howitzers. When other Lorraine tractors became available, they too were fed into the programme. The vehicle's running gear proved to be highly durable.

*A Marder II with 7.5 cm Pak 40.*

*811 Marder IIs were built. They performed their role as tank destroyers extremely well thanks to their excellent firepower.*

Both the tank destroyers and the artillery vehicles were fitted with a box-shaped superstructure made of armour plating up to 12 mm thick. The anti-tank vehicle weighed 8.3 tonnes. Its Delahaye 103TT inline 6-cylinder engine was capable of powering it to a top speed of 38 km/h and it had a range of 150 km. From 1942 onwards 184 vehicles were converted, almost all of which remained in France. Only a few found their way to Italy or the Eastern Front as and when their units were redeployed. Together with other improvised armoured anti-tank vehicles based on captured French models, these self-propelled guns were named Marder I. Most Marder Is were involved in the Battle of Normandy from mid-1944 onwards and were lost in the fighting.

The Marder II was based on the chassis of the Panzer II. Initially it was equipped mainly with the 7.62 cm Pak 36(r) or a 7.62 cm field gun captured in Russia; later with the German Pak 40 L/46. To start with, versions D and E of the Panzer II, the so-called 'Schnellkampfwagen' ('fast fighting vehicle') were converted – 185 in total – including 30 that had previously been converted to Flamingo (Flammpanzer II) flamethrowers. The turret and the rest of the Panzer II's superstructure were removed in order to make room for the centrally positioned anti-tank gun, which was then surrounded

*Marder III Ausf. H with 7.5 cm Pak 40 (seen from above).*

by a box-like guard up to 14.5 mm thick (Sd.Kfz. 132). Once all the available Panzer II Ausf. Ds and Es had been converted, it was the turn of Ausf. F, which meant a further 50 Marder IIs could then be produced. Following the great success of the weapon on the Eastern Front, new orders were received and versions A, B, C and F of the Panzer II were also converted. These differed slightly in appearance to the earlier Marder II model and were designated Sd.Kfz. 131.

The Marder III self-propelled gun was based on the Panzer 38(t) chassis and was produced in greater numbers (1,143) than either of the other two Marders. The first version (Panzerjäger 38(t) Sd.Kfz. 139, Marder III), of which 344 units were eventually produced, appeared in March 1942 and was equipped with the Russian 7.62 cm anti-tank gun mounted on the upper part of the hull and protected only by a small guard. The next version (Sd.Kfz. 138, Marder III Ausf. H) had a 7.5 cm Pak 40 with a special 10 mm-thick guard that was far more substantial than that of the first version. These first models were slightly top-heavy, however, and therefore in the next version (Sd.Kfz. 138, Marder III Ausf. M) the engine was shifted to the middle of the vehicle and the fighting compartment moved to the back. This resulted in a far better-balanced vehicle with a larger fighting compartment. The main armament and the thickness of the armour remained the same. Modifications made to the engine, however, boosted output to 150 hp. Between 1942 and 1944, 418 Ausf. Hs and 381 Ausf. Ms were manufactured.

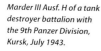

*Marder III Ausf. H of a tank destroyer battalion with the 9th Panzer Division, Kursk, July 1943.*

# STUG III ASSAULT GUN SD.KFZ. 142

The German Blitzkrieg concept was based on rapid advances by Panzer divisions accompanied by mechanized infantry. As tanks were not generally available to them, the infantry needed to have their own armoured vehicles. Back in 1935, General Erich von Manstein had therefore called for an infantry support vehicle. In June 1936 Daimler-Benz was awarded the contract to develop a vehicle of this type incorporating a 7.5 cm gun. Daimler based its designs on the Panzer III, which was already in production. In order to reduce height, the vehicle was given a fixed superstructure (in place of a turret)

|  | StuG III Ausf. D Sd.Kfz. 142 | StuG 40 Ausf. G Sd.Kfz. 142/1 |
|---|---|---|
| Combat weight: | 22,200 kg | 23,900 kg |
| Crew: | 4 | 4 |
| Dimensions in mm (length, width, height): | 5,400/2,950/1,960 | 5,560/2,950/2,150; with barrel and skirts: 6,770/3,410/2,150 |
| Engine: | Maybach HL 120 TRM, V12 petrol, water-cooled, 11,870 cc, 300 hp | Maybach HL 120 TRM V12 petrol, water-cooled, 11,870 cc, 300 hp |
| Power/weight ratio: | 13.5 hp/tonne | 12.5 hp/tonne |
| Max. speed: | 40 km/h road, 19 km/h cross-country | 40 km/h road, 19 km/h cross-country |
| Range: | 140 km road, 90 km cross-country | 130 km road, 80 km cross-country |
| Armament: | 7.5 cm StuK L/24 | 7.5 cm StuK 40 L/48, 1 x 7.92 mm MG 34 |
| Armour: | 18–50 mm | 18–80 mm; skirts: 5 mm |
| Fording depth: | 0.8 m | 0.8 m |

*A StuG III Ausf. G with 'Saukopf' gun mantlet.*

accommodating a 7.5 cm L/24 assault gun. This was based on the almost unchanged chassis of the Panzer III. The first prototypes were built by Alkett in 1937 and were extensively tested. Production of the StuG III Ausf. A (Sd.Kfz. 142), based on Pz.Kpfw III Ausf. F, began in January 1940. The Panzer III hull was adapted and the frontal armour was increased in thickness from 30 mm to 50 mm. The engine and running gear remained identical to those of the Panzer II Ausf. F, however. The first StuGs were tested in combat in France and proved extremely successful, whereupon they went into large-scale production.

Versions B to E differed only in small details, and altogether 734 units were built. Originally intended simply to provide support for infantry attacks, StuGs began to be used in increasing

numbers in a tank destroyer role. Due to its low muzzle velocity, however, the 7.5 cm StuK L/24 was not powerful enough to fight tanks effectively and so Ausf. F was upgunned to the StuK 40 L/43. This significantly improved its firepower and gave it the capability to knock out

targets at a greater distance. With Ausf. F, the vehicle's code number changed to Sd.Kfz. 142/1 and the StuG III was often referred to as the StuG 40 after its new gun. Once 300 or so Ausf. F vehicles had been built, this version was upgraded again and renamed the F/8. In addition to changes to the upper part of the body, the vehicle was also equipped with the 7.5 cm StuK 40 L/48, which was capable of penetrating 85 mm of armour plating at a distance of 1,000 m with a 60° angle of impact. The thickness of the frontal armour was increased from 50 mm to 80 mm. Many vehicles of the earlier versions were later refitted with the long-barrelled StuK 40. From 1943 onwards the StuG III was equipped with side skirts as protection against anti-tank rifles and hollow charge projectiles. The last version of the StuG III, and also the one manufactured in the largest numbers, Ausf. G, went into production in December

*A StuG III Ausf. D of the 243rd StuG Battalion.*

*StuG 40, SS StuG Battalion, 'Leibstandarte Adolf Hitler' Division.*

to be produced right up to the end of the war, long after manufacture of the Panzer III had ceased. The StuG III proved exceptionally successful and by the end of the war had become the Wehrmacht's most important armoured fighting vehicle despite its origins as a compromise solution. Its main advantages were its low cost due to its lack of a turret and the fact that unlike the Panzer III it was able to accommodate the long-barrelled 75 mm gun. In addition to the Wehrmacht, some of Germany's allies also used StuG IIIs and Finland was still using them several years after the war. The Soviets also used captured StuG IIIs and converted a number of them to take their 7.62 cm gun. In total, 7,900 StuG III versions F and G were built.

1942. Its armour was strengthened again and it was equipped with a new cylindrical hatch. A folding machine gun shield now became standard. In February 1944 a cast pig's head mantlet, designed to provide better protection, was introduced, replacing the previous bolted-on box mantlet. Early StuG Ausf. Gs were also equipped with three smoke grenade launchers on either side. Protective track skirts also became standard, as did Zimmerit paste coating. In 1942, the 10.5 cm assault howitzer was also successfully combined with the StuG III and went into production as the 'Sturmhaubitze 42'. By the end of 1944, 1,114 of these vehicles had been built. StuG III Ausf. G continued

## STUIG 33 INFANTRY ASSAULT GUN ON PANZER III CHASSIS

The StuIG 33 was at the planning stage by mid-1941 but the first task was to develop an armoured superstructure capable of accommodating the 15 cm SIG-33 heavy infantry gun. This was the third attempt to produce a mobile version of the SIG-33 as the gun had already been mounted on Panzer I and II chassis. In mid-September 1942 an order was issued to fit a number of existing assault guns with the new superstructure and SIG-33. Different sources place the number of StuIGs produced at either 12 or 24. These vehicles incorporating a heavy infantry gun and therefore belonging to the armoured artillery were used in direct combat against fixed targets such as bunkers or buildings. Their guns were set up for direct fire and could only be raised by 25°. All the vehicles produced were sent to the Eastern Front in 1942 and most are thought to have been lost at Stalingrad.

| Combat weight: | 22,000 kg |
|---|---|
| Crew: | 5 |
| Dimensions in mm (length, width, height): | 5,500/2,950/2,300 |
| Engine: | Maybach HL 120 TRM V12 petrol, water-cooled, 11,870 cc, 300 hp |
| Power/weight ratio: | 13.5 hp/tonne |
| Max. speed: | 38 km/h road, 19 km/h cross-country |
| Range: | 140 km road, 90 km cross-country |
| Armament: | 15 cm SIG-33 L/11, 1 x 7.92 mm MG 34 machine gun |
| Armour: | 18–80 mm |
| Fording depth: | 0.8 m |

*A SIG-33 on a Pz.Kpfw. III chassis, Russia, autumn 1942.*

## STUG IV ASSAULT GUN SD.KFZ. 163

|  | Pz.Kpfw. IV Ausf. H |
| --- | --- |
| Combat weight: | 23,000 kg |
| Crew: | 5 |
| Dimensions in mm (length, width, height) | 5,930/2,900/2,200 without barrel or skirts 6,700/3,350/2,200 with barrel and skirts |
| Engine: | Maybach HL 120 TRM V12 petrol, water-cooled, 11,870 cc, 300 hp |
| Power/weight ratio: | 12 hp/tonne |
| Max. speed: | 38 km/h road, 16 km/h cross-country |
| Range: | 180 km road, 120 km cross-country |
| Armament: | 7.5 cm StuK 40 L/48, 2 x 7.92 mm MG 34 machine guns |
| Armour: | 10–80 mm; skirts 5 mm |
| Fording depth: | 1.2 m |

*A StuG IV photographed at the Krupp works in Essen in September 1944.*

The StuG IV was basically a StuG III mounted on a Panzer IV chassis, albeit with somewhat improved armour. The first experiments with this combination took place in 1943, when it was intended as an interim solution pending the development of a dedicated tank destroyer – the Jagdpanzer IV. At the end of 1943, however, the factory where the Panzer III chassis (on which the StuG III was based) was being built was so badly bombed that production ground almost completely to a halt. Hitler personally ordered part of the Panzer IV production to be switched to the manufacture of assault guns and Krupp converted its Panzer IV production line accordingly. Like the StuG III, the StuG IV proved extremely successful and in total 1,500 were built.

## STURMPANZER IV ASSAULT TANK SD.KFZ. 166 (BRUMMBÄR)

|  | Brummbär – early model |
| --- | --- |
| Combat weight: | 28,200 kg |
| Crew: | 5 |
| Dimensions in mm (length, width, height) | 5,930/2,880/2,520 without skirts; 3,350 width with skirts |
| Engine: | Maybach HL 120 TRM V12 petrol, water-cooled, 11,870 cc, 300 hp |
| Power/weight ratio: | 10.6 hp/tonne |
| Max. speed: | 38 km/h road, 16 km/h cross-country |
| Range: | 180 km road, 120 km cross-country |
| Armament: | 15 cm StuH 43 L/12 |
| Armour: | 10–100 mm; skirts 5 mm |
| Fording depth: | 1.2 m |

*An early version of the Sturmpanzer IV Brummbär.*

This vehicle was developed jointly by Alkett and Krupp in mid-1942. Alkett manufactured the superstructure while Krupp's role was to modify its Panzer IV chassis. Like the StuG III, the Brummbär was intended mainly for urban combat and use against fortifications. It was based on the Panzer IV chassis and incorporated a 15 cm assault howitzer set in a heavily armoured superstructure 100 mm thick at the front and 50 mm at the sides). At first this was its only armament but combat experience revealed that a machine gun was essential against infantry attack. Subsequent vehicles were therefore equipped with an MG 34 on a ball mount. Skirts and Zimmerit coating were standard. The Panzer IV chassis was put under excessive strain by the vehicle's considerable weight, however. The first vehicles were delivered in 1943 to the 216th Sturmpanzer Battalion and 17 were lost at Kursk during Operation Citadel in July 1943. By the end of 1944 around 300 Sturmpanzer IVs had been built.

# JAGDPANZER IV TANK DESTROYER SD.KFZ. 162

*A Jagdpanzer IV/70
of the 116th Panzer
Division, Wesel,
spring 1945.*

| | Jagdpanzer IV Ausf. F |
|---|---|
| Combat weight: | 24,000 kg |
| Crew: | 4–5 |
| Dimensions in mm (length, width, height): | 5,900/2,900/1,860; 6,850/3,170/1,860 with barrel and skirts |
| Engine: | Maybach HL 120 TRM V12 petrol, water-cooled, 11,870 cc, 300 hp |
| Power/weight ratio: | 12.5 hp/tonne |
| Max. speed: | 38 km/h road, 16 km/h cross-country |
| Range: | 190 km road, 130 km cross-country |
| Armament: | 7.5 cm Pak L/48 anti-tank gun, 1 x 7.92 mm MG 34 machine gun |
| Armour: | 10–80 mm; skirts 5 mm |
| Fording depth: | 1 m |

From 1941, assault guns started being used increasingly as tank destroyers, a role for which they had not been intended. Even though they were very low-slung, their angular superstructures presented ample opportunities to enemy gunners. In 1943, Vomag in Plauen began designing a purpose-built tank destroyer to replace the StuG III. The new vehicle was to have as low a silhouette as possible as well as a ballistically optimized shape. Hitler was shown a wooden model in May 1943 and was greatly impressed by the vehicle's low profile. The first production vehicles left the factory five months later.

The Jagdpanzer IV was a modified StuG IV with sloping, shot-deflecting sides and a 7.5 cm Pak L/48 with 'pig's head' mantlet. The original 80 mm-thick frontal armour had to be reduced to 60 mm to improve handling (this version was named the Panzer 39). Another variant, the

Jagdpanzer IV/70 (V) was equipped with the 7.5 cm Pak L/70 (similar to the Panther's main armament). This gun possessed enormous penetrating power but also made the vehicle very top-heavy and therefore hard to steer. As a result it acquired the nickname 'Guderian's Duck'. Alkett also manufactured a Jagdpanzer IV with the L/70 gun. This was a stopgap solution and unlike the Vomag-produced vehicles its superstructure looked improvised, as if it had simply been dropped on to the lower half. This is because unmodified Panzer IV chassis were used. This vehicle was delivered to the Wehrmacht as the Jagdpanzer IV/70 (A). By the time production ceased, around 1,800 Jagdpanzer IVs had been built.

*The Jagdpanzer
IV/70 seen from
above.*

*Prototype of the Jagdpanzer IV/70 (A).*

# JAGDPANZER 38(T) TANK DESTROYER (HETZER)

Although the Marder tank destroyers were very successful, they also had a number of disadvantages such as their extremely thin frontal and side armour and complete lack of armour plating on top and behind, which made them highly vulnerable to artillery and air attack. General Guderian is credited with the idea of developing a tank destroyer based on the Panzer 38(t) that would be completely enclosed like the assault guns. The Army Ordnance Office awarded contracts for the development of such a vehicle in May 1943. A modified version of the 7.5 cm Pak 39 L/48 was chosen to be the main armament. This version had an advanced recoil brake that rendered a muzzle brake superfluous. In order to cope better with the weight of the vehicle, which had increased to 16 tonnes, broader, stronger tracks were fitted and every last bit of power squeezed out of what was originally a 125 hp engine. To secure the vehicle against infantry attack, a remote-controlled machine gun, which could swivel through 360°, was mounted on the roof. The Hetzer's shape was outstanding from a ballistics point of view as the all-round sloping sides ensured maximum shot deflection. The dimensions of the tank were also extremely advantageous – to the chagrin of its crews, who literally had to squeeze themselves into it. The first vehicles were delivered in May 1944. Initially BMM was

the sole manufacturer but in September 1944 it was joined by Škoda.

The Hetzer was one of the best German tank destroyers of the war. It was small and therefore easy to conceal and benefited from good firepower and armour. In actual fact the Hetzer was supposed to replace the Marder but due to production delays and high losses, this objective was never achieved. On 1 April 1945, 627 Hetzers were still operational, making it Germany's most important armoured vehicle after the StuG III during the final months of the war. Even during the very last month of the

| | |
|---|---|
| Combat weight: | 16,000 kg |
| Crew: | 4 |
| Dimensions in mm (length, width, height): | 4,870/2,630/2,170; length with barrel: 6,270 |
| Engine: | Praga inline 6-cylinder petrol, water-cooled, 7,754 cc, 160 hp |
| Power/weight ratio: | 10 hp/tonne |
| Max. speed: | 42 km/h road |
| Range: | 260 km road, 170 km cross-country |
| Armament: | 7.5 cm Pak 39 L/48 anti-tank gun, 1 x 7.92 mm MG 42 machine gun |
| Armour: | 8–60 mm |
| Fording depth: | 1 m |

*A Hetzer with an independent tank destroyer unit, Western Front, winter 1944–45.*

conflict, 121 Hetzers were built and delivered to the Wehrmacht and a few were even delivered to the Hungarian Army. In total, 1,500 vehicles were manufactured including flamethrower and recovery variants. After the war,

Škoda continued making Hetzers for the Czech Army. Switzerland bought 158 vehicles, which remained in service under the name G13 until 1970.

*The front view shows how far to the right of centre the main 7.5 cm gun was set.*

*Rear view of the same vehicle. Both pictures taken at the BMM works, late summer 1944.*

# WESPE MOTORIZED HOWITZER SD.KFZ.124

*Wespe motorized
howitzer, 10th Panzer
Division ('Frundsberg'),
France, 1944.*

| Combat weight: | 11,800 kg |
|---|---|
| Crew: | 5 |
| Dimensions in mm (length, width, height): | 4,810/2,280/2,320 |
| Engine: | Maybach HL 62 TRM inline 6-cylinder petrol, water-cooled, 6,190 cc, 140 hp |
| Power/weight ratio: | 13 hp/tonne |
| Max. speed: | 40 km/h road |
| Range: | 140 km road, 90 km cross-country |
| Armament: | 10.5 cm light FH 18/2 L/28, 1 x 7.92 mm MG 34 or 42 machine gun |
| Armour: | 10–20 mm |
| Fording depth: | 0.8 m |

The German Blitzkrieg strategy was predicated upon rapid tank advances accompanied by artillery support. In order to provide this, the Wehrmacht developed a series of self-propelled artillery guns that proved successful to differing degrees. One of the best known of these guns, and the one produced in the greatest numbers, was the Wespe, which was based on the chassis of the Panzer II and incorporated a 10.5 cm light field howitzer. Alkett, MAN and Rheinmetall-Borsig began work on its development in 1942 and soon after it went into full-scale production at the Famo factory in Warsaw. The Wespe was based on new as well as refitted Panzer II chassis. Famo built 683 of these guns up to 1944. The Wespe's ammunition storage capacity was very small (40 rounds) and so a further 158 weaponless ammunition carriers were built that were capable of carrying a further 90 rounds. If a Wespe were lost, its howitzer could be removed and mounted on to an ammunition carrier, creating a 'new' Wespe. The armour plating of the Wespe's superstructure was only 10–12 mm thick and open-topped while its hull armour was between 15 mm and 20 mm thick. As the vehicle was not generally deployed directly on the front, this was not normally a problem. The Wespe was used by the armoured artillery battalions of the Panzer and mechanized infantry divisions. Units generally consisted of two Wespe batteries made up of six Wespe self-propelled guns and an ammunition carrier.

# HUMMEL MOTORIZED HOWITZER SD.KFZ. 165

The strategy of mobile tank warfare pursued by the Wehrmacht during the early years of the war meant that the artillery had to be able to keep pace with the tank units. This led to the development of self-propelled guns based on more or less suitable chassis. The Geschützwagen III/IV, based on the Panzer IV chassis, was an attempt to create a common base vehicle for a range of self-propelled artillery guns. The engine was moved forward in order to make room for a large fighting compartment at the rear. On top and at the rear the vehicle's armour was poor, but it should be remembered that the designs were completed at a time when the Luftwaffe still possessed air superiority and attacks from enemy bombers were relatively uncommon. During the first few years of the war, troops sometimes even found open-topped vehicles an advantage because of the better all-round vision they afforded. The version of the Geschützwagen III/IV with the heavy 18-calibre 15 cm field howitzer was named the 'Hummel' ('Bumblebee'). As it could only carry 18 rounds of spare ammunition, an unarmed ammunition transporter was also developed. The Hummel first saw action in mid-1943 on the Eastern Front and remained in service with the artillery battalions of the Panzer divisions through to the end of the war. The Hummel proved extremely successful and 666 self-propelled howitzers and 150 ammunition transporters were built in total.

| Combat weight: | 23,500 kg |
|---|---|
| Crew: | 6–7 |
| Dimensions in mm (length, width, height): | 6,200/2,950/2,940; length with barrel: 6,670 |
| Engine: | Maybach HL 120 TRM V12 petrol, water-cooled, 11,870 cc, 300 hp |
| Power/weight ratio: | 12.8 hp/tonne |
| Max. speed: | 40 km/h road, 20 km/h cross-country |
| Range: | 250 km road, 160 km cross-country |
| Armament: | 15 cm heavy FH 18 L/30, 1 x 7.92 mm MG 34 machine gun |
| Armour: | 10–20 mm |
| Fording depth: | 0.8 m |

*Hummel
motorized
howitzer with
the artillery
regiment of the
Grossdeutschland
Division, Eastern
Front, 1944.*

## NASHORN TANK DESTROYER SD.KFZ. 164

The tremendously powerful 8.8 cmPak 43 suffered from the major disadvantage of being highly immobile on the battlefield. Its weight of around 4 tonnes meant that changes of position could only be effected with the help of a towing vehicle. The idea arose at a relatively early stage, therefore, of turning the weapon into a self-propelled unit. The vehicle on to which it was mountedwas the Geschützwagen III/IV, a Panzer IV with the engine shifted to the front, which was intended as the basis for a range of artillery guns including the Hummel motorized howitzer. Alkett was contracted to develop a prototype in February 1942. Chassis and superstructure (493 units)

were manufactured by Deutsche Eisenwerke. Deliveries of the new vehicle, whose official designation was the '8.8 cm Pak 43 L/71 auf Fahrgestell Panzerkampfwagen III/IV(Sf)', started in November 1942. After the first few units had rolled off the production line, the main gun was replaced by the improved Pak 43/1. In February 1944, Hitler ordered that the name of all vehicles equipped with the Pak 43/1 be changed from 'Hörnisse' ('Hornet') to 'Nashorn' ('Rhinoceros') because he considered that the one originally chosen did not sound sufficiently threatening.

Although the vehicle was highly effective on the battlefield and was considered a successful design, it

| Combat weight: | 24,000 kg |
|---|---|
| Crew: | 4–5 |
| Dimensions in mm (length, width, height): | 6,200/2,950/2,940; length with barrel: 8,440 |
| Engine: | Maybach HL 120 TRM V12 petrol, water-cooled, 11,870 cc, 300 hp |
| Power/weight ratio: | 12.5 hp/tonne |
| Max. speed: | 40 km/h road, 20 km/h cross-country |
| Range: | 250 km road, 160 km cross-country |
| Armament: | 8.8 cm Pak 43/1 L/71 anti-tank gun, 1 x 7.92 mm MG 34 machine gun |
| Armour: | 10–30 mm |
| Fording depth: | 0.8 m |

presented a number of disadvantages, among them its thin armour and high silhouette. Furthermore it was open to the top and rear and offered no protection against air or infantry attack. Units equipped with Nashorn tank destroyers nonetheless achieved astounding successes – especially when operating from well-prepared positions and when they were able to rely on the power and range of the Pak 43/1. There are reports of Nashorns hitting Soviet T-34s from a distance of more than 1.5 km with such force that the entire turret was torn from the hull. Nashorn tank destroyers remained in service right up until the end of the war. Shortly before hostilities ceased, a Nashorn became the only German fighting vehicle to knock out a US M26 Pershing tank.

*A Nashorn from an unknown unit, Eastern Front, March 1945.*

*Note the long-barrelled 8.8 cm Pak 43/1, which gave the Nashorn enormous firepower.*

# FLAKPANZER IV ANTI-AIRCRAFT TANKS (MÖBELWAGEN, WIRBELWIND AND OSTWIND)

|  | Flakpanzer IV Wirbelwind |
| --- | --- |
| Combat weight: | 22,000 kg |
| Crew: | 5 |
| Dimensions in mm (length, width, height): | 5,920/2,900/2,760 |
| Engine: | Maybach HL 120 TRM/112 V12 petrol, water-cooled, 11,870 cc, 310 hp |
| Power/weight ratio: | 14.1 hp/tonne |
| Max. speed: | 40 km/h road, 20 km/h cross-country |
| Range: | 180 km road, 120 km cross-country |
| Armament: | 2 cm Flak Vierling anti-aircraft gun, 1 x 7.92 mm MG 34 machine gun |
| Armour: | Hull 10–80 mm, turret 16 mm all round |
| Fording depth: | 0.8 m |

*A Wirbelwind Flakpanzer equipped with a quadruple 2 cm Vierling 38.*

*An Ostwind Flakpanzer IV.*

*A Flakpanzer I of the 614th Flak Battalion, Stalingrad, January 1943.*

As air superiority increasingly slipped away from the Luftwaffe, another method had to be found of protecting the Panzer forces from air attack. While elite troops such as the Waffen-SS, Grossdeutschland Division and others already had self-propelled flak guns at their disposal during the early years of the war, these were mostly part-armoured or unarmoured vehicles. The first, highly provisional, anti-aircraft tanks (based on the Panzer I) had appeared shortly after the Battle of France, albeit without all-round protection. They took the form of a 2 cm Flak 38 gun mounted on the hull of a withdrawn Panzer I. Twenty-four of these vehicles were built and proved successful in spite of appearances. The last of them were lost at the Battle of Stalingrad. Further conversions were not undertaken until October 1943, when Hitler approved the

conversion of 150 Panzer 38(t)s into anti-aircraft tanks with a 2 cm Flak 38. It soon transpired that their firepower was inadequate. In order to accommodate a 2 cm Flak Vierling (quadruple) or 3.7 cm Flak, a bigger chassis was needed and attention turned to the Panzer IV. The early prototypes were equipped with a 2 cm Vierling but the version that went into production, in March 1944, had a 3.7 cm Flak 43 (240 units). The anti-aircraft gun was mounted on the hull of the tank and surrounded by high side walls made of 20 mm-thick steel which had to be folded down when in operation, thereby exposing the crew to enemy fire. The 'Wirbelwind' was an improved version with a 2 cm Vierling in a turret made of 16 mm plates. As a precaution in the event of fire, however, the turret was left open at the top. One hundred and five

Wirbelwinds were created from damaged Panzer IVs. The version named 'Ostwind' mounted a 3.7 cm Flak 43 in a turret similar to that of the Wirbelwind. Forty-three of these were obtained through conversion. During the last few months of the war a number of other prototypes and variants were developed. These included an Ostwind variant with the 3.7 cm Zwilling (double) anti-aircraft gun, a model named the 'Kugelblitz' ('Ball Lightning') based on the Panzer IV or Panzer 38(t) which carried a 3 cm Flak Zwilling 103/38 in a fully enclosed turret, and the 'Zerstörer 45' which was equipped with a 3 cm Flak Vierling 103/38 in a Wirbelwind turret. The armaments ranged from a 2 cm Flak Vierling 151/20 via a 3.7 cm Flak Zwilling 44 to a 5.5 cm Zwilling.

## AB 40 AND 41 ARMOURED SCOUT CARS

The AB 40 and 41 armoured cars came into being as the result of an invitation for tenders to build an armoured vehicle that could be used both by the Italian police in the African colonies and by the Italian cavalry units. The requirements were: four-wheel drive and steering, steering wheels fore and aft to enable the vehicle to be driven in both directions, and good cross-country capability. It was initially intended that the vehicle should carry a machine gun only. All these criteria were met by the AB 40, which appeared in mid-1940. After a small number of units had rolled off the production line, experiments were conducted with a new turret and a 2 cm cannon in place of the twin 8 mm machine guns in order to increase firepower. These experiments proved successful and production was switched to the new version, which was named the AB 41. Many AB 40s were converted. This armoured car was a high-performance vehicle that was very

*An Autoblinda AB 41 in North Africa.*

| Combat weight: | 7,500 kg |
|---|---|
| Crew: | 4 |
| Dimensions in mm (length, width, height): | 5,200/1,920/2,480 |
| Engine: | SPA inline 6-cylinder petrol, water-cooled, 4,995 cc, 88 hp |
| Power/weight ratio: | 11.7 hp/tonne |
| Max. speed: | 78 km/h road |
| Range: | 400 km road |
| Armament: | 2 cm Breda M 35 cannon, 2 x 7.92 mm Breda machine guns |
| Armour: | hull: 6–9 mm; turret: max. 18 mm |
| Fording depth: | 0.6 m |

advanced for its day but plagued by steering problems that were never rectified. A number of vehicles also had an anti-aircraft machine gun mounted on the turret. A special conversion kit enabled the AB 41 to travel on rails, a feature used in the Balkans. The AB 41 was also employed extensively by Italian troops in North

Africa. A command and reconnaissance version was produced in small numbers. Models AB 42 and 43 had a new, flatter turret and L/32 cannon but had only been produced in small numbers by the time Italy surrendered in September 1943. The Wehrmacht also used captured vehicles of this type.

## LIGHT TANKS CV 33 AND CV 35

| | CV 33 |
|---|---|
| Combat weight: | 3,435 kg |
| Crew: | 2 |
| Dimensions in mm (length, width, height): | 3,160/1,400/1,280 |
| Engine: | SPA CV 3 inline 4-cylinder petrol, water-cooled, 43 hp |
| Power/weight ratio: | 12.5 hp/tonne |
| Max. speed: | 42 km/h road |
| Range: | 125 km road |
| Armament: | 8 mm Fiat M18/35 twin MG |
| Armour: | 6.5–13.5 mm |

*A CV 33 of the 67th Bersaglieri Regiment, North Africa, 1940.*

During the late 1920s and early 1930s, the two-man light tank made by British firm Carden-Loyd had been extremely popular due to its reasonable price. Italy also acquired two Carden-Loyd Mk VIs, along with the rights to manufacture them under licence. Following a number of alterations, the outcome was the CV 33. Series I was equipped with a water-cooled 6.5 mm machine gun that proved so catastrophic

that it was soon replaced by a 88 mm Fiat 18/35 twin machine gun (Series II). Other changes subsequently made included modifications to the superstructure and upgrading to a 13.2 mm machine gun. This new version was named the CV 35. CV 33s and 35s were used in the Spanish Civil War and later in Greece, Africa and the Soviet Union and turned into death traps for their crews wherever they came up

against serious opposition. Although this had already become apparent in Spain, the vehicles were only withdrawn after the disastrous experiences in Russia. After 1943 the Wehrmacht also deployed a number of captured vehicles of this type.

# TYPE 2 KA-MI

*Type 2 Ka-Mi.*

| | |
|---|---|
| Combat weight (with pontoons): | 11,300 kg |
| Crew: | 4–5 |
| Dimensions in mm (length, width, height): | 7,420/2,790/2,340 |
| Engine: | Mitsubishi inline 6-cylinder diesel, air-cooled, 120 hp |
| Power/weight ratio: | 10.6 hp/tonne |
| Max. speed: | 37 km/h road 9.6 km/h water |
| Range: | 200 km road, 100 km water |
| Armament: | 3.7 cm Type 94 cannon, 2 x 7.7 mm MG |
| Armour: | 9–13 mm |
| Fording depth: | amphibious |

The Imperial Japanese Army started conducting experiments with amphibious tanks as early as 1928. In 1940 the programme was taken over by the Navy as the tanks were intended for use by the Marines. A whole series of amphibious vehicles was developed, of which Type 2 was produced in the largest numbers. Entering service in 1942, Type 2 had many components in common with Type 95 but was equipped with a brand new watertight hull. Buoyancy was provided by two large pontoons attached to the front and rear which were discarded on dry land. In the water the vehicle was powered by two propellers and steered by two rudders controlled from the turret by the tank commander. These vehicles were ideal for attacking small islands and atolls in the Pacific and were initially successful. When Japan was forced on to the defensive, however, and heavy US tanks were brought into play, these lightly armed and armoured tanks stood no chance. Japanese sources place the number of Type 2s built at 184.

# TYPE 97 TE-KE

This light tank was unveiled in 1937 and went into large-scale production for the Japanese Army in 1938. The Te-Ke was initially intended as a reconnaissance vehicle but was also frequently used in an infantry support role, which was only successful if the enemy had few or ideally no anti-tank weapons. As with Type 95, the commander of this tank was the sole occupant of the turret and was overstretched as a result. In spite of these disadvantages, Type 97 was one of Japan's most important tanks and remained in service throughout the war. Although it was used successfully in China, it stood no chance against the US Army's M3s and M4s. It is interesting to note that US tanks switched during the course of the war from using anti-tank shells to using high explosive shells against Japanese fighting vehicles. Because of the tanks' very thin armour, anti-tank shells generally passed straight through them causing little damage unless they happened to hit a vital component or crew member. There was also an armoured ammunition transporter (with armoured trailer) based on the Type 97.

| | |
|---|---|
| Combat weight: | 4,748 kg |
| Crew: | 2 |
| Dimensions in mm (length, width, height): | 3,680/1,800/1,770 |
| Engine: | Ikega inline 4-cylinder diesel, air-cooled, 65 hp |
| Power/weight ratio: | 13.7 hp/tonne |
| Max. speed: | 42 km/h road |
| Range: | 250 km road |
| Armament: | 3.7 cm Type 94 cannon or 1 x 7.7 mm MG in turret |
| Armour: | 6–16 mm |

*Type 97 Te-Ke.*

# TYPE 95 HA-GO

| | |
|---|---|
| Combat weight: | 7,400 kg |
| Crew: | 3 |
| Dimensions in mm (length, width, height): | 4,380/2,060/2,180 |
| Engine: | Mitsubishi inline 6-cylinder diesel, air-cooled, 120 hp |
| Power/weight ratio: | 16.2 hp/tonne |
| Max. speed: | 45 km/h road |
| Range: | 250 km road |
| Armament: | 3.7 cm Type 94 cannon, 1 x 6.5 mm MG or 2 x 7.7 mm MG |
| Armour: | 6–13 mm |

*Type 95 Ha-Go.*

The prototype of this light tank was built by Mitsubishi in 1934. At that time it was at least as good as the tanks of any other country but by the time Japan entered the war in December 1941 it was completely out of date. The driver and machine gunner sat at the front of the hull while the tank commander occupied the turret alone. He had to command the vehicle and aim, load and fire the main gun. In a later model he also had to operate a turret machine gun, which was asking too much even of the most capable tank commanders. Type 95 tanks first saw combat in the war against China and remained in service throughout the Second World War. The Japanese tactic was to use them solely for infantry support and from the end of 1941 they were deployed mostly in small groups on the numerous occupied islands of the Pacific. Their armour only provided protection against hand-held weapons, with the result that they were an easy target for Allied anti-tank guns and fighting vehicles. On the plus side, they were agile and reliable. By 1945, 2,375 of these tanks had been built, making Type 95 Japan's most important tank of the war.

*Type 95s of the 16th Tank Regiment of the Japanese Army captured by the US Navy on Marcus Island.*

*A Type 95 Ha-Go captured by the US Marines on Guam.*

## TYPE 89B OTSU

Although not much heavier and barely any larger than Type 95, Type 89B qualified as a medium tank because of its 5.7 cm gun. The design of its predecessor, the Type 89, introduced in 1929, had been based on imported British Vickers Mark C tanks. When Type 89's petrol engine was replaced by a Mitsubishi diesel engine in 1934, this new version was named Type 89B. In this form the vehicle became Japan's standard medium tank during the late 1930s and was still in service in 1941–42. By this time, though, it was completely out of date. Like all Japanese tanks, Type 89B had been intended merely to provide infantry

| Combat weight: | 11,500 kg |
|---|---|
| Crew: | 4 |
| Dimensions in mm (length, width, height): | 4,300/2,150/2,200 |
| Engine: | Mitsubishi inline 6-cylinder diesel, air-cooled, 120 hp |
| Power/weight ratio: | 10.5 hp/tonne |
| Max. speed: | 27 km/h road |
| Range: | 200 km road |
| Armament: | 5.7 cm Type 90 cannon, 2 x 6.5 mm MG |
| Armour: | 9–17 mm |

*Type 89 Otsu.*

support but even this was only possible against poorly equipped opponents. Its thin armour made it extremely vulnerable and in addition it was slow and not especially manoeuvrable. After 1942, Type 89B tanks were no longer used at the front. Around 400 Type 89 and 89B tanks were built.

## TYPE 97 CHI-HA

| Combat weight: | 15,000 kg |
|---|---|
| Crew: | 4 |
| Dimensions in mm (length, width, height): | 5,520/2,330/2,230 |
| Engine: | Mitsubishi V12 diesel, air-cooled, 170 hp |
| Power/weight ratio: | 11.3 hp/tonne |
| Max. speed: | 38 km/h road |
| Range: | 210 km road |
| Armament: | 5.7 cm Type 90 cannon, 2 x 7.7 mm MG |
| Armour: | 8–25 mm |

commander occupied the turret. The running gear was well designed and performed respectably. Although more modern than other Japanese tanks, Type 97, like its predecessors, was intended primarily for an infantry support role. Its short-barrelled 5.7 cm cannon was not particularly effective against tanks and its armour was still too thin, a fact that came to light during the 1939 border incidents with Soviet troops in Manchuria. A special version of the Type 97 Shinhoto Chi-Ha

was therefore developed specifically for an anti-tank role. This variant had a new turret equipped with a long 4.7 cm gun with good penetrating power but did not enter service until 1942. Also based on Type 97 were recovery and bridgelaying tanks as well as self-propelled guns with weapons of up to 15 cm calibre. Taking into account all the variants, 2,208 Type 97s were built.

The Type 97 Chi-Ha was the Japanese Army's standard medium tank during the Second World War. Its predecessor, Type 89, had shown as early as 1936 that it was no longer a match for enemy tanks. The armaments industry was therefore invited to draw up proposals for a successor. Mitsubishi won the contract and its tank went into large-scale production (in which other companies were later involved) in 1938. The driver and machine gunner sat at the front of the hull while the main gunner and tank

*Type 97 Shinhoto Chi-Ha with the long 4.7 cm cannon.*

POLAND

## TK3 TANKETTE

In 1929 Poland bought a British Carden-Loyd Mk. IV tank and used it to develop a series of 'tankettes' or light tanks. These vehicles, which generally had a crew of two, were small, manoeuvrable and normally armed with no more than a machine gun. Following various open-topped versions such as the TK1 and TK2, production began in 1931 of a fully enclosed model, the TK3, of which around 300 were made. When it became clear in 1939 that this tank was vastly inferior to most others, attempts were made to improve its firepower. Shortly before the

| | |
|---|---|
| Combat weight: | 2,435 kg |
| Crew: | 2 |
| Dimensions in mm (length, width, height): | 2,580/1,780/1,310 |
| Engine: | Ford Model A, inline 4-cylinder, water-cooled, 40 hp |
| Power/weight ratio: | 16.4 hp/tonne |
| Max. speed: | 45 km/h road |
| Range: | 200 km road |
| Armament: | 1 x 7.92 mm MG |
| Armour: | 4–10 mm |
| Fording depth: | 0.4 m |

war a number of vehicles were upgraded to a 2 cm anti-tank gun but this did little to improve their chances against the Wehrmacht. All surviving TK3s were re-equipped by the Wehrmacht with the French Hotchkiss 9 mm M/1914 and used for security duties.

*A Polish TK3.*

## 7TP

| | |
|---|---|
| Combat weight: | 9,900 kg |
| Crew: | 3 |
| Dimensions in mm (length, width, height): | 5,020/2,410/2,160 |
| Engine: | Saurer diesel, air-cooled, 110 hp |
| Power/weight ratio: | 11.1 hp/tonne |
| Max. speed: | 32 km/h |
| Range: | 160 km road, 120 km cross-country |
| Armament: | 3.7 cm Bofors cannon, 1 x 7.92 mm MG |
| Armour: | 5–18 mm (some up to 40 mm) |
| Fording depth: | 0.7 m |

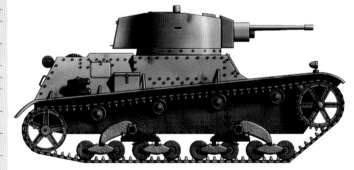

*The 7TP was a match for German tanks in 1939 but was defeated by their superior numbers.*

At the beginning of the 1930s, Poland bought 50 Vickers 6-tonners, in its day a highly modern and successful tank, from British armaments manufacturer Vickers-Armstrong. From this it developed the 7TP, 169 of which were built between 1934 and 1939. The 7TP was the first European tank to be given a diesel engine and was a respectable enough machine for its day. The first versions (7TP dw) had twin turrets each equipped with a 7.92 mm Browning machine gun while later models had a single turret with a Swedish 3.7 cm Bofors cannon and coaxial 7.92 mm machine gun. Unusual for the time was not only the diesel engine but also the fact that most of the tanks were equipped with radio. Shortly before the outbreak of war a more heavily armoured version was designed (up to 40 mm at the front) but it did not progress beyond prototype stage. The 7TP fought bravely against the German invaders and was only overwhelmed by the Wehrmacht's superior numbers. The Wehrmacht used the surviving vehicles as training vehicles and for security duties under the designation Kampfpanzer 7TP(p).

# PANHARD AMD 178 ARMOURED CAR

In 1940, France's main armoured vehicle was the Panhard AMD 178. Work began on its design in the mid-1930s and it was a first-class vehicle in its day. Although its armour was riveted, which meant that, in the event of a hit, rivets would fly through the fighting compartment like bullets, the AMD 178 had many interesting and innovative features, for example a second, rear-facing driver who could take control in the event of danger in order to avoid the vehicle having to turn round. The engine was an unusual two-stroke model with rotary rather than poppet valves. In addition to a version armed with a 2.5 cm cannon, there was also an unarmed radio car and a version armed with only 7.5 mm twin machine guns. Around 300 AMD 178s had been built by the time of France's defeat. The Wehrmacht re-equipped 190 or so with German radios and in some cases frame antennae for use as reconnaissance vehicles with the designation P 204(f). Others were fitted with railway wheels for use as rail patrol vehicles. A few AMD 178s escaped capture by the enemy and were taken to the unoccupied zone, but when the Germans also occupied Vichy France in 1943, they were commandeered by the Wehrmacht. The German Army valued the Panhard highly and regarded it as a very worthwhile addition to its reconnaissance units. Following liberation in 1944, production of the AMD 178 was immediately resumed by Panhard.

| | |
|---|---|
| Combat weight: | 8,500 kg |
| Crew: | 4 |
| Dimensions in mm (length, width, height): | 4,790/2,010/2,290 |
| Engine: | Panhard inline 4-cylinder petrol, water-cooled, 6,330 cc, 105 hp |
| Power/weight ratio: | 12.4 hp/tonne |
| Max. speed: | 72 km/h road |
| Range: | 330 km road, 120 km cross-country |
| Armament: | 2.5 cm cannon, 1 x 7.5 mm MG |
| Armour: | 7–20 mm |
| Fording depth: | 0.6 m |

*Panhard AMD 178.*

# RENAULT UE CHENILLETTE

The Renault UE was an armoured supply vehicle. During the early 1930s the French Army pursued a vigorous policy of mechanization which included the introduction of armoured vehicles to supply troops at the front. Renault took the Carden-Loyd running gear as the starting point for the UE, which went into large-scale production in 1931. The two-man crew sat next to each other under a hemispherical headguard with observation slits which could be folded away. The engine was positioned between the driver and co-driver. At the rear was a tilting loading platform that enabled the cargo to be unloaded without the crew having to leave the vehicle. Renault also developed an armoured tracked trailer that could also run on wheels. UE supply tractors were sometimes used to tow light anti-tank and anti-aircraft guns but were generally unarmed themselves. The Wehrmacht captured around 1,200 of these vehicles and used some of them as supply vehicles and towing machines (for the 3.7 cm Pak, for example) but also turned a number of them into self-propelled guns and weapon carriers. With the 3.7 cm Pak mounted on the vehicle, the only protection available to the gunner was the gun shield. Many other vehicles were converted for security duties through the addition of a machine gun. In 1944, Rommel ordered the remaining UE supply tractors to be fitted with platforms for 28 calibre or 32 cm grenade launchers positioned on the sides of the vehicle or mounted on the hull.

| | |
|---|---|
| Empty weight: | 2,700 kg |
| Crew: | 2 |
| Useful load: | 400 kg |
| Trailer load: | 500 kg |
| Dimensions in mm (length, width, height): | 2,690/1,700/1,040 |
| Engine: | Renault inline 4-cylinder petrol, water-cooled, 2,120 cc, 38 hp |
| Max. speed: | 33.5 km/h road |
| Range: | 125 km road, 60 km cross-country |
| Armament: | see text |
| Armour: | 9 mm all round |
| Fording depth: | 0.4 m |

*Renault UE Chenillette.*

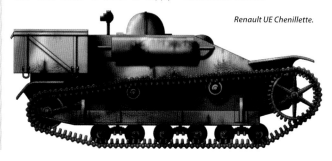

## LORRAINE 37 L

| Empty weight: | 5,650 kg |
|---|---|
| Crew: | 2 |
| Useful load: | 810 kg |
| Trailer load: | 800 kg |
| Dimensions in mm (length, width, height): | 4,200/1,570/1,250 |
| Engine: | Delahaye 135 inline 6-cylinder petrol, water-cooled, 3,556 cc, 70 hp |
| Max. speed: | 35 km/h road |
| Range: | 135 km road |
| Armament: | see text |
| Armour: | 16–12 mm |
| Fording depth: | 0.7 m |

The crew of the 37 L sat at the front, the engine compartment was located in the middle, and at the rear there was a relatively large load area. As with the UE, the vehicle could be unloaded without the crew having to leave it. The 37 L also had an armoured trailer that could be used for transporting fuel. By the time of France's defeat, 432 37 Ls had been built. The Wehrmacht took over some 300 of them, quickly realizing that their rear load area and centrally positioned engine made them ideal for conversion into self-propelled guns, first with the 7.5 cm Pak 40 (see p.78) and later with the 10.5 cm and 15 cm howitzers. Although these conversions strained the 37 L's chassis to its limits, its basic construction was so solid that these self-propelled guns were still highly successful.

*A Lorraine 37 tracked tractor with armoured trailer.*

**T**his vehicle went into production in 1937 as a successor to the Renault UE. By 1940 it had still by no means replaced its predecessor in the supply vehicle role, however.

## RENAULT FT-17

**I**n 1917, after France's first tanks had failed to deliver the anticipated results, Renault unveiled a new light tank whose design was to become the model for all later armoured vehicles. The driver sat at the front of the hull, the turret and commander were located in the middle, and the engine compartment was at the back. The FT-17 also had the distinction of being the first tank whose main armament was housed in a turret with 360° traverse. Despite these features it was a child of its time and essentially just an armour-plated box and feeble engine mounted on an underdeveloped chassis. In 1918, however (by which time some 3,000 units had

been built by Renault and a number of other manufacturers), it was one of the best tanks around and production continued after the war in order to satisfy the demand from abroad. Numerous countries bought the FT-17 after 1918 and used it to build up tank divisions. Accordingly there was a wide range of variants from models with a 7.5 cm anti-tank gun to radio vehicles, bridge-laying tanks and searchlight tanks. In France there were 2,500 FT-17s in service as late as May 1940, although only 500 were with front-

| Combat weight: | 7,000 kg |
|---|---|
| Crew: | 2 |
| Dimensions in mm (length, width, height): | 4,100/1,740/2,300 |
| Engine: | Renault inline 4-cylinder petrol, water-cooled, 4,500 cc, 35 hp |
| Power/weight ratio: | 5 hp/tonne |
| Max. speed: | 7.5 km/h road |
| Range: | 38 km road |
| Armament: | 3.7 cm cannon or 2 x 8 mm MG (numerous variants) |
| Armour: | 6–22 mm |
| Fording depth: | 0.5 m |

line units. By this time, however, the Renaults were completely antiquated and stood no chance against the Wehrmacht's tanks. A large number of captured tanks were redesignated 17/18 R(f) and used by the Germans for security duties. Several FT-17 turrets were also incorporated into German fortifications on the Atlantic coast. The deployment of FT-17s by the Germans during the Battle of Paris in 1944 should probably be seen as an act of desperation.

*An F-17 captured by the Wehrmacht.*

FRANCE

# RENAULT R-35

*R-35.*

In 1934 the French Army called upon a number of manufacturers to develop a successor to the Renault FT-17. The winning design was Renault's R-35 and in May 1935 an order was placed for 300 vehicles. By June 1940 a total of 1,600 R-35s had been built. Like its predecessor the FT-17, the R-35 was intended mainly to provide infantry support. The hull was reasonably well armoured for its day (up to 40 mm at the front) and constructed of cast sections screwed together. The driver sat at the front and the commander occupied the turret by himself. The main armament, a short 3.7 cm M 1918 cannon, was almost completely ineffectual against tanks. A number of R-35s were therefore equipped with the longer-barrelled 3.7 cm L/33. Although the running gear was thoroughly efficient, the poor power/weight ratio (just 8.4 hp/tonne) meant the tank was too slow. The first vehicles lacked radio. A variant named the AMX-40 or R-40 boasted new running gear with 12 small road wheels and tracks of the type used on the Char B (see p.98) but it was only produced in small numbers. It is interesting to note that the turret of the R-35 was identical to that of the H-35/38/39. The R-35 was well suited to its role as an infantry support vehicle but by 1940 this whole strategy was out of date. Large numbers of R-35s were overwhelmed and captured by the German forces. The 800 or so captured vehicles were designated Pz.Kpfw. 35 R(f) and used for security duties, for fighting partisans, as towing machines and as the basis for a range of self-propelled guns.

| Combat weight: | 9,800 kg |
| --- | --- |
| Crew: | 2 |
| Dimensions in mm (length, width, height): | 4,200/1,850/2,100 |
| Engine: | Renault inline 4-cylinder petrol, water-cooled, 5,878 cc, 82 hp |
| Power/weight ratio: | 8.4 hp/tonne |
| Max. speed: | 20 km/h road |
| Range: | 140 km road |
| Armament: | 3.7 cm M 1918 L/21 cannon, 1 x 7.5 mm coaxial MG |
| Armour: | max. 45 mm |
| Fording depth: | 0.5 m |

# HOTCHKISS H-35, H-38, AND H-39

The Hotchkiss H-35 resulted from the same call for tenders for an infantry tank as that which led to the building of the R-35. The H-35 was rejected by the infantry, however, as its mobility was even worse than the R-35's. Weighing 11.5 tonnes, the H-35 had only a 75 hp engine.

Ironically, the armoured cavalry showed an interest in the tank and so it found a use after all. Its armour was 34 mm thick and it was equipped with the same gun as the R-35. The armour at the front of its turret was up to 45 mm thick. Around 400 H-35s were built before production switched to the H-38 in 1938. The new version had a modified hull and was equipped with a 120 hp engine producing a maximum speed of 36.5 km/h. The version equipped with the longer-barrelled 3.7 cm L/33 cannon, which was better suited for use against German tanks, was called the H-39. By June 1940 a total of 1,080 of the three versions had been built. The H-38 and H-39 (and with certain reservations the H-35) were good tanks for the time but the two-man crews greatly restricted their combat effectiveness. Tanks of this type were captured by the Wehrmacht in large numbers and designated Panzerkampfwagen 35, 38 and 39 H(f). In addition to the occupation forces in France, most Panzer units in the Balkans and Norway also used Hotchkiss tanks.

|  | H-39 |
| --- | --- |
| Combat weight: | 12,100 kg |
| Crew: | 2 |
| Dimensions in mm (length, width, height): | 4,220/1,850/2,140 |
| Engine: | Hotchkiss inline 6-cylinder petrol, water-cooled, 5,976 cc, 120 hp |
| Power/weight ratio: | 8.4 hp/tonne |
| Max. speed: | 36.5 km/h road, 16 km/h cross-country |
| Range: | 150 km road, 90 km cross-country |
| Armament: | 3.7 cm SA 38 L/33 cannon, 1 x 7.5 mm coaxial MG |
| Armour: | max. 45 mm |
| Fording depth: | 0.5 m |

*An H-39 with 3.7 cm L/33 from an unknown unit.*

## SOMUA S-35

In 1940 the S-35 was undoubtedly France's best tank. A disadvantage was its one-man turret, which considerably reduced its combat effectiveness. Another factor that prevented the S-35 from fulfilling its potential was the French doctrine of only using tanks in small groups for infantry support. At the beginning of the 1930s the French armoured cavalry called for a new medium tank and in 1935 chose the prototype developed by Somua, which went into production the following year. The S-35 was a well-armoured vehicle (hull max. 35 mm, turret max. 55 mm) equipped with an outstanding gun, the 4.7 cm SA 35 L/32. Its hull consisted of three cast steel sections screwed together. The driver and

*In 1940 the S-35 was one of the best tanks in existence.*

radio operator sat together at the front of the hull while the commander occupied the turret. The engine was located at the rear. An improved version with a 220 hp engine was ready in 1940 but was only built in small numbers. The prototype of an assault gun with a 7.5 cm cannon mounted in its hull was developed the same year but France's defeat put an end to the experiment. At the beginning of the

Battle of France in May 1940 over 418 S-35s were in service with the French Army. The Wehrmacht adopted 297 of them, which were used mainly in secondary theatres of war.

| | S-35 |
|---|---|
| Combat weight: | 19,500 kg |
| Crew: | 3 |
| Dimensions in mm (length, width, height): | 5,380/2,120/2,624 |
| Engine: | Somua V8 petrol, water-cooled, 12,700 cc, 190 hp |
| Power/weight ratio: | 9.7 hp/tonne |
| Max. speed: | 45 km/h road, 37 km/h cross-country |
| Range: | 260 km road, 130 km cross-country |
| Armament: | 4.7 cm SA 35 L/32 cannon, 1 x 7.5 mm coaxial MG |
| Armour: | max. 55 mm |
| Fording depth: | 0.7 m |

## CHAR B-1 BIS

| Combat weight: | 32,000 kg |
|---|---|
| Crew: | 4 |
| Dimensions in mm (length, width, height): | 6,370/2,500/2,790 |
| Engine: | Renault inline 6-cylinder petrol, water-cooled, 16,500 cc, 300 hp |
| Power/weight ratio: | 9.4 hp/tonne |
| Max. speed: | 25 km/h road |
| Range: | 140 km road, 100 km cross-country |
| Armament: | 1 x 4.7 cm SA 34 L/32 cannon (turret), 1 x 7.5 mm coaxial MG 1 x 7.5 cm cannon and 1 x 7.5 mm MG in the hull |
| Armour: | max. 60 mm |
| Fording depth: | 0.75 m |

*The B-1 could withstand all German anti-tank weapons. Only the 8.8 cm*

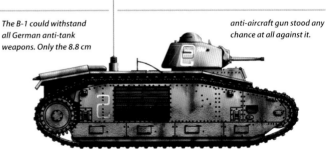

*anti-aircraft gun stood any chance at all against it.*

The Char B-1 bis, whose armour was 60 mm in places, could not be penetrated by the German 3.7 cm Pak and even German tanks had to hope for lucky hits. Only the 8.8 cm anti-aircraft gun was capable of piercing its steel plates. In 1940 around 400 B-1s were in service on the

French side. The origins of the vehicle go back to the late 1920s when the French Army commissioned a heavy tank. The Char B was equipped with a short-barrelled 7.5 cm L/17 cannon and twin machine guns all mounted in the hull. The cannon had no horizontal traverse capability and had to be aimed by adjusting the position of the entire vehicle. To assist with this process, the Char B was equipped with a hydrostatic steering mechanism. Another set of twin machine guns was mounted in the turret. After just 35 vehicles, production switched to version B-1 bis, which was equipped

with a more powerful engine, thicker armour and a turret-mounted 4.7 cm cannon in addition to the hull-mounted 7.5 cm gun. The Wehrmacht used large numbers of captured tanks of this type as training vehicles. In 1941–42 around 60 vehicles were converted to flamethrower tanks and deployed on the Eastern Front. The conversion involved replacing the hull-mounted 7.5 cm gun with a fire tube. The turret, with its 4.7 cm cannon, was retained. A tank containing enough flamethrower oil for up to 200 jets of flame was located at the rear of the hull.

# DAIMLER DINGO SCOUT CAR

This Daimler armoured car was designed by BSA in 1937 and went into production as the Daimler Dingo in 1939 following Daimler's takeover of BSA. The Dingo was a small, relatively lightly armoured four-wheel drive vehicle whose only armament was a Bren machine gun mounted in front of the driver. It was, however, very fast and manoeuvrable and furthermore relatively inconspicuous thanks to its compact form – not bad qualities for a reconnaissance vehicle. The Dingo experienced considerable success with the armed forces of the Commonwealth countries and was manufactured in large numbers. By 1945, Daimler/BSA and Humber had built a total of 6,626 Dingos. In Canada the

| | |
|---|---|
| Combat weight: | 3,048 kg |
| Crew: | 2 |
| Dimensions in mm (length, width, height): | 3,180/1,710/1,500 |
| Engine: | Daimler inline 6-cylinder petrol, water-cooled, 2,500 cc, 60 hp |
| Power/weight ratio: | 19.7 hp/tonne |
| Max. speed: | 88 km/h road |
| Range: | 325 km road |
| Armament: | 1 x 7.7 mm MG |
| Armour: | max. 30 mm |
| Fording depth: | 0.6 m |

*The Daimler Dingo's compact form is seen clearly here.*

design was adopted and reworked by Ford, resulting in the Lynx, which was heavier and more strongly armoured as well as being fitted with a more powerful Ford engine. Ford's Canadian production ran to some 3,255 vehicles. The Dingo remained in service until the 1950s. The Italians captured a few Dingos in North Africa and were so impressed that an almost identical copy, called the Lince, was produced by Lancia.

# DAIMLER MK. 1 ARMOURED CAR

There was no concealing the Daimler Mk. 1's kinship with the Dingo: both were short vehicles with an almost quadratic wheel arrangement and an angular superstructure. What was new in the Mk. 1 was its monocoque hull that helped to save weight and reduce the height of the car. The vehicle was equipped with a radio, servo-steering, and a pre-selector gearbox. The original plan was to mount either two 7.7 mm machine guns or one 12.7 mm and one 7.7 mm machine gun in the turret. Initial combat experience led to the fitting of a 2-pounder and a 7.92 mm machine gun on a parallel axis. The first vehicles were delivered to the British Army in 1941 and were used in all the main theatres of the Second World War. The Daimler Mk. 1 was a reliable and manoeuvrable vehicle and was popular as a result. During the final phase of the war, however, its 2-pounder gun was no longer adequate as it could only shoot anti-tank shells. Taking into account all the different variants, 2,700 vehicles were built. After the war the Daimler Mk. 1 continued to be used until the late 1950s.

*Daimler Mk. 1.*

| | |
|---|---|
| Combat weight: | 7,610 kg |
| Crew: | 3 |
| Dimensions in mm (length, width, height): | 3,960/2,440/2,230 |
| Engine: | Daimler inline 6-cylinder petrol, water-cooled, 4,500 cc, 95 hp |
| Power/weight ratio: | 12.5 hp/tonne |
| Max. speed: | 80 km/h road |
| Range: | 330 km road |
| Armament: | 2-pounder cannon in turret, 1 x 7.92 mm coaxial Besa MG |
| Armour: | max. 30 mm |
| Fording depth: | 0.6 m |

# HUMBER MK. 1 ARMOURED CAR

In terms of numbers (5,600 built), the Humber was one of the British Army's most important fighting vehicles of the Second World War. Its design was derived from a vehicle built by Guy in 1939 based on the chassis of the Guy artillery tractor. Most of these earlier vehicles, of which 101 had been produced, had been lost in France in 1940. As Guy was operating at full capacity producing tractors, Humber took over the design and developed it further. The Humber Mk.1 was based on the 4 x 4 chassis of Rootes' carrier tractor and its superstructure was a modified version of the original design constructed of welded steel plate. The crew compartment was organized in the traditional way with the driver at the front, the gunner and commander in the turret, and the engine, separated from the crew by a fireproof bulkhead, at the rear. The armament was relatively

*Humber Mk. 1.*

| Combat weight: | 6,846 kg |
|---|---|
| Crew: | 3 |
| Dimensions in mm (length, width, height): | 4,570/2,180/2,390 |
| Engine: | Rootes inline 6-cylinder petrol, water-cooled, 90 hp |
| Power/weight ratio: | 13.1 hp/tonne |
| Max. speed: | 72 km/h road |
| Range: | 400 km road |
| Armament: | 1 x 15 mm Besa MG in turret, 1 x 7.92 mm coaxial Besa MG, 1 x 7.7 mm Bren anti-aircraft MG |
| Armour: | max. 15 mm |
| Fording depth: | 0.75 m |

light and so later models were upgunned to a 3.7 cm cannon mounted in a three-man turret. An anti-aircraft version with a 7.92 mm quadruple machine gun entered service in 1943–44 but was unsuccessful due to its small calibre. Humber armoured cars were used by nearly all the Commonwealth armies and a slightly modified version known

as the 'Fox' was built in Canada by General Motors. Humber armoured cars continued to be used by the British Army until the late 1950s.

# UNIVERSAL CARRIER (BREN CARRIER)

| Combat weight: | 4,013 kg |
|---|---|
| Crew: | 2 + 3 |
| Dimensions in mm (length, width, height): | 3,750/2,100/1,600 |
| Engine: | Ford inline V8 petrol, water-cooled, 85 hp |
| Power/weight ratio: | 21.2 hp/tonne |
| Max. speed: | 51 km/h road |
| Range: | 260 km road |
| Armament: | 1 x 7.7 mm Bren MG and/or a 14 mm Boys anti-tank rifle |
| Armour: | 7–12 mm |
| Fording depth: | 0.5 m |

*The Bren Carrier was used extensively by Allied troops.*

These vehicles were a development of the Mk. VI Vickers/Carden-Loyd light tank of the late 1920s. The Universal Carrier was designed to transport a machine gun unit along with its weapons and ammunition safely through enemy infantry fire to its intended position. It was essentially an open-topped sheet-steel box with engine and running gear, and was extremely robust as a result. The driver sat at the front with a machine gunner by his side. The engine was positioned behind

them, in the middle of the vehicle, and to either side of the engine were the load areas (for soldiers, weapons, ammunition or supplies). As the vehicle was frequently used to transport units with Bren machine guns, it came to be known popularly as the Bren Carrier. The first Universal Carrier entered service in 1939. The most common version had three road wheels on each side but there was also a larger version with four wheels on each side that could transport up to nine men. Universal Carriers proved to be extremely flexible. There were countless adaptations

and modifications, some of them executed by the field troops themselves. The Universal Carrier was built by numerous manufacturers throughout the Commonwealth and by 1945 over 84,000 (including all variants) had been produced. Many vehicles were also supplied to Russia under the Lend-Lease programme. In 1940 the Wehrmacht captured large numbers of Universal Carriers in France and adopted them as the Br 731(e) armoured machine gun carrier as well as using them as anti-tank and supply vehicles and for security duties.

# VICKERS MARK VI

During the late 1920s and early 1930s, Vickers built a whole series of light tanks using Carden-Loyd or Horstmann running gear. The Vickers Mark VI, which first appeared in 1941, was the last of the series. It was equipped with a radio and a new, larger turret. The driver sat at the front of the hull on the left next to an 88 hp engine that made the light vehicle extremely nimble. The turret, containing the gunner and 12.7 mm and 7.7 mm machine guns, was located at the rear. At the outbreak of the Second World War the Vickers Mark VI B was the standard light tank of the British Army and remained in service until 1941.

Model VI C was equipped with the more powerful 15 mm Besa machine gun but this could not alter the simple fact that the tank was underarmed. The Wehrmacht captured a large number of Vickers Mark VI tanks in France in 1940 and also encountered them in North Africa, Greece and Crete. In France,

Baukommando Becker (see p.78) converted 20 of the captured vehicles into 10.5 cm and 15 cm self-propelled howitzers and a similar number into armoured ammunition carriers and observation tanks which proved successful on the Eastern Front.

*A Vickers Mk. VI, Tobruk, spring 1942.*

| | Mark VI B |
|---|---|
| Combat weight: | 5,283 kg |
| Crew: | 3 |
| Dimensions in mm (length, width, height): | 3,990/2,050/2,230 |
| Engine: | Meadows inline 6-cylinder petrol, water-cooled, 88 hp |
| Power/weight ratio: | 16.7 hp/tonne |
| Max. speed: | 56 km/h road |
| Range: | 200 km road |
| Armament: | 1 x 12.7 mm MG and 1 x 7.7 mm MG in turret |
| Armour: | 4–14 mm |

# INFANTRY TANK MK. I MATILDA

| Combat weight: | 11,161 kg |
|---|---|
| Crew: | 2 |
| Dimensions in mm (length, width, height): | 4,850/2,280/1,860 |
| Engine: | Ford V8 petrol, water-cooled, 3,600 cc, 70 hp |
| Power/weight ratio: | 6.3 hp/tonne |
| Max. speed: | 13 km/h road |
| Range: | 130 km road |
| Armament: | 1 x 12.7 mm MG or 1 x 7.7 mm MG in turret |
| Armour: | 12–60 mm |
| Fording depth | 0.7 m |

*Mk. I Matilda.*

The British doctrine regarding the use of tanks before and during the war provided for two main types: slow, heavily armoured infantry tanks and fast, relatively lightly armoured cruisers. The Mk. I Matilda was the first infantry support tank to be built under this approach – and proved a complete failure. In order to keep costs down, designer Sir John Carden was forced to limit the tank to the bare essentials. The result was a two-man vehicle with a top road speed of just 13 km/h, which meant it could be overtaken by a runner. The insubstantial armament, consisting of one turret-mounted machine gun, was completely useless. Nevertheless the General Staff accepted the vehicle in April 1937 and it went into production. The tank's shortcomings had been noted, however, and it was therefore regarded as a temporary solution. By 1940 a total of 139 Matildas had been produced, all of which were lost in France. Their sole plus point was their heavy armour of up to 60 mm at the front, which could not be penetrated by Germany's 3.7 cm Pak. The Wehrmacht, which used all other captured tanks for its own purposes, could find no use for these.

# INFANTRY TANK MK. II MATILDA II A12

| | Matilda II Mk. III |
|---|---|
| Combat weight: | 26,926 kg |
| Crew: | 4 |
| Dimensions in mm (length, width, height): | 5,610/2,590/2,510 |
| Engine: | 2 Leyland 6-cylinder diesel, water-cooled, combined 190 hp |
| Power/weight ratio: | 7 hp/tonne |
| Max. speed: | 24 km/h road, 13 km/h cross-country |
| Range: | 145 km road, 90 km cross-country |
| Armament: | 2-pounder cannon in turret, 1 x 7.92 mm coaxial Besa MG |
| Armour: | 20–78 mm |
| Fording depth | 0.91 m |

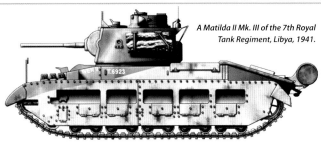

*A Matilda II Mk. III of the 7th Royal Tank Regiment, Libya, 1941.*

*These vehicles are painted in a typical camouflage scheme of dark grey, sky blue and sand colours.*

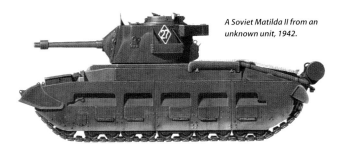

*A Soviet Matilda II from an unknown unit, 1942.*

It had become clear to the British General Staff, even before completion of the trials of the Matilda I prototype, that a better vehicle was needed for the infantry tank role and contracts were therefore awarded for the development of a new machine. This resulted in the Matilda II, whose prototype was unveiled in 1938. This tank was unusually heavily armoured for its day (nose up to 78 mm, sides 65 mm, turret 75 mm all round) and was equipped with a turret-mounted 2-pounder with coaxial machine gun. Although still not particularly fast, it was twice as fast as the Matilda I. The vehicle's cast steel construction was problematic, however, as production had to be entrusted to foundries and locomotive builders with little experience of manufacturing fighting vehicles and the

required production levels were never able to be achieved.

As a result there were only 24 Matilda IIs in operation in France in 1940, although even this small number posed enormous problems to the German troops. Their armour could not be penetrated by German tanks or anti-tank guns and only the 8.8 cm anti-aircraft gun stood any chance against them. The Matilda's 2-pounder, on the other hand, was capable of piercing the armour of any enemy tank from some distance. In North Africa too the Matilda (the tank's popular name) initially notched up a number of major successes against the Italians, acquiring the nickname 'Queen of the Desert' in the process. When Rommel's Afrikakorps turned up in Libya with the 8.8 cm anti-aircraft gun in mid-1941,

however, the tables were turned. Attempts to equip the Matilda with a 6-pounder failed because of the small diameter of the turret ring. The Matilda was last used as a battle tank in the Western European/North African theatre at the second Battle of El Alamein in July 1942. After that it was converted for special tasks such as mine-clearing. No major modifications were undertaken during the lifetime of the tank. The engine output was increased slightly from 174 hp to 190 hp and one variant was given a 7.8 cm turret-mounted howitzer. As part of the Lend-Lease programme, the Soviet Union received around 1,000 of the 3,000 or so Matilda tanks built by the time production ceased in mid-1943 and these played an important role on the Eastern Front.

# INFANTRY TANK MK. III VALENTINE

Between 1939 and 1944 8,275 Valentines were built in the United Kingdom and Canada, which meant that it was manufactured in greater numbers than any other British tank in the Second World War. It was designed by Vickers and shared many components with the A10 cruiser. The prototype was shown to the War Office on 14 February 1938, Valentine's Day, hence the tank's name. Large-scale production began in 1939 and the first vehicles were delivered to the Army in May 1940.

The Valentine had good defensive armour for an infantry tank but was slow and armed with only a 2-pounder. The tank entered service with the British Army in North Africa in 1941 and remained in service until 1945, earning itself a good reputation for its robustness and reliability. The main problem with it was its small turret, which provided just enough room for two men and a 2-pounder. When the vehicle was upgunned to a 5.7 cm and then to a 7.5 cm cannon, however, space became extremely tight. Many tank commanders preferred the confinement of a three-man turret because there was simply too much to do in a two-man turret: command the tank, operate the radio, load the main weapon and maintain an overview of the battlefield. They were not helped in the latter by the fact that they only had a single periscope. The Valentine was extremely adaptable and went through 11 versions with guns ranging from 4 cm to 7.5 cm and a number of different engines. In addition there were also various self-propelled guns and special variants such as bridgelayers and amphibious tanks. The best-known self-propelled gun based on the Valentine was without doubt the 'Archer' tank destroyer, which mounted a 17-pounder anti-tank gun. Interestingly this gun, which had a limited traverse and was mounted on an armoured superstructure, did not point forwards but faced the rear. As the Archer was designed to make surprise attacks and then withdraw, this orientation meant it was already facing in the right direction for its retreat. Canada and the United Kingdom supplied the Soviet Union with 2,690 Valentine tanks under the Lend-Lease programme. The Soviets valued the tanks highly and praised their reliable engines and robust running gear. Nevertheless they found the 2-pounders of the early models too weak and equipped some of the vehicles with Russian-made 7.62 cm cannon. Germany's Afrikakorps captured a number of Valentines in North Africa and used them until the lack of spare parts meant they could no longer be repaired.

| | Valentine Mk. I |
|---|---|
| Combat weight: | 16,257 kg |
| Crew: | 3 |
| Dimensions in mm (length, width, height): | 5,410/2,630/2,270 |
| Engine: | AEC inline 6-cylinder, water-cooled, 9,600 cc, 135 hp |
| Power/weight ratio: | 8.3 hp/tonne |
| Max. speed: | 24 km/h road, 15 km/h cross-country |
| Range: | 140 km road, 80 km cross-country |
| Armament: | 2-pounder cannon in turret, 1 x 7.92 mm coaxial Besa MG |
| Armour: | 8–65 mm |
| Fording depth | 0.9 m |

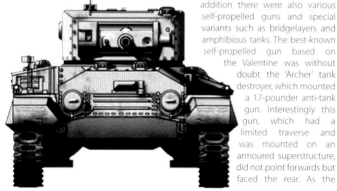

*A Valentine Mk. I of the 8th Royal Tank Regiment, Bardia, Libya, January 1942.*

## INFANTRY TANK MK. IV CHURCHILL A22

*A Churchill Mk. IV.*

| | Churchill Mk. VII |
|---|---|
| Combat weight: | 40,600 kg |
| Crew: | 5 |
| Dimensions in mm (length, width, height): | 7,540/3,250/2,490 |
| Engine: | Bedford twin-six, water-cooled, 21,100 cc, 350 hp |
| Power/weight ratio: | 8.6 hp/tonne |
| Max. speed: | 25 km/h road, 13 km/h cross-country |
| Range: | 145 km road, 80 km cross-country |
| Armament: | 1 x 7.5 cm cannon in turret, 2 x 7.92 mm Besa MGs (one coaxial and one in the hull), 1 x 7.7 mm Bren anti-aircraft MG |
| Armour: | 19–152 mm |
| Fording depth | 1.02 m |

Work on the design of a successor to the Matilda II (designated the A22) was begun by Vauxhall in mid-1940. The war was raging, most British tanks had been lost in France, and replacements were urgently needed. Design time was in short supply and Vauxhall therefore turned to the designs for the A20, which had been developed on the assumption that the war would be fought in a similar way to the First World War, in other words positionally with trenches and fortifications. The Churchill therefore possessed tracks that ran around the entire height of the hull in order to enable it to cross wide trenches. The first prototypes rolled out of the factory barely a year later, in July 1941, and large-scale production began shortly afterwards. The time pressure under which the Churchill was produced meant problems were inevitable. The engine, in essence two linked side-mounted Bedford truck engines, gave continual trouble and neither the steering nor the gearbox had been adequately developed. Furthermore a 2-pounder (4 cm) gun capable of firing only anti-tank shells (not high explosive shells) was inadequate, but at the time it was all that was available. For this reason some of the early vehicles were also fitted with a hull-mounted 7.62 cm howitzer although this was of only limited use because of its minimal traverse. The Mk. III, however, was equipped with the more effective 6-pounder (5.7 cm) gun,

significantly improving the Churchill's combat effectiveness. In North Africa a number of Mk. IVs were fitted with Sherman tank's 5.7 cm gun (Mk IV NA 75). From Mk VI onwards, Churchill tanks carried a 7.5 cm gun as standard. The Churchill was first deployed at the Dieppe landings in August 1942 and was used widely and with considerable

success in North Africa, Italy and later France. Its heavy armour and robust running gear helped it to survive even severe damage and rough terrain. Because of its wide, roomy hull and strong running gear, the tank was ideal for a range of special uses (see p.109). By 1945 a total of 5,460 Churchills had been built.

*A Churchill Mk. VII of the British 34th Armoured Brigade in northern France, September 1944.*

*A Churchill Mk. IV in Tunisia, 1943.*

# CRUISER MARK I A9

*An A9 captured by the Italians in October 1940.*

| Combat weight: | 13,013 kg |
|---|---|
| Crew: | 6 |
| Dimensions in mm (length, width, height): | 5,790/2,490/2,640 |
| Engine: | AEC inline 6-cylinder, water-cooled, 9,600 cc, 150 hp |
| Power/weight ratio: | 11.5 hp/tonne |
| Max. speed: | 40 km/h road, 24 km/h cross-country |
| Range: | 240 km road |
| Armament: | 2-pounder cannon in turret, 1 x 7.7 mm coaxial Vickers MG, 2 x 7.7 mm Vickers MG in small turrets |
| Armour: | 6–14 mm |
| Fording depth | 0.8 m |

The first in Britain's series of fast cruisers was the Mark 1 A9. This vehicle was designed by Vickers-Armstrong under tight financial constraints in the mid-1930s and was far too lightly armoured to be effective in combat. Unusually, it had two machine gun turrets to the left and right of the driver, each housing a 7.7 mm machine gun. Because they were so cramped, however, these turrets often became death traps for the gunners. At the time the Mark I went into production, its hydraulic turret traversing gear was extremely advanced, as was a ventilation system for the fighting compartment. The running gear was robust and capable of coping with rough terrain and was later used in slightly modified form on the Valentine. The A9 was not a success, however, and production was cancelled after just 125 had been manufactured. The last A9 was used in North Africa.

*France, June 1940: a destroyed A9.*

# CRUISER MARK II A10

| Combat weight: | 14,400 kg |
|---|---|
| Crew: | 5 |
| Dimensions in mm (length, width, height): | 5,590/2,530/2,640 |
| Engine: | AEC inline 6-cylinder, water-cooled, 9,600 cc, 150 hp |
| Power/weight ratio: | 10.4 hp/tonne |
| Max. speed: | 26 km/h road, 13 km/h cross-country |
| Range: | 240 km road |
| Armament: | 2-pounder cannon in turret, 1 x 7.7 mm coaxial Vickers MG |
| Armour: | 8–30 mm |
| Fording depth | 0.8 m |

*Mark II A10.*

The A10 was originally intended as an infantry tank version of the A9 but was too lightly armoured for that role. Instead it was reclassified as a heavy cruiser, a role for which it was also unsuited as it was too slow. Expectations were therefore that the A10 would meet with no more success than the A9. Although the two pointless machine gun turrets had been removed, the upper part of the tank still presented too many shell traps. The A10 – of which 175 units were produced – first saw combat in France in 1940, where a number of them fell into German hands. The remainder were used in North Africa, where they achieved initial success against the Italians but were completely outclassed when the Afrikakorps arrived.

# CRUISER MARK VI CRUSADER

*A Crusader Mk. I of the British 7th Armoured Division, North Africa, 1941.*

| | Crusader Mk. III |
|---|---|
| Combat weight: | 20,067 kg |
| Crew: | 3 |
| Dimensions in mm (length, width, height): | 5,990/2,640/2,230 |
| Engine: | Nuffield Liberty V12 water-cooled, 340 hp |
| Power/weight ratio: | 16.9 hp/tonne |
| Max. speed: | 43 km/h road, 24 km/h cross-country |
| Range: | 322 km road |
| Armament: | 6-pounder cannon in turret, 1 x 7.92 mm coaxial Besa MG |
| Armour: | 7–51 mm |
| Fording depth | 1 m |

*A Crusader Mk. III of the British 6th Armoured Division, Tunisia, early 1943.*

It having soon become clear that the running gear of types A9 and A10 could not cope with the speed required of a cruiser tank, alternatives were sought. In the USA, engineer Walter Christie had been experimenting during the 1920s and 1930s with a new kind of running gear that allowed for high speeds while delivering excellent all-terrain capability. 'Christie suspension' used large, rubber-rimmed road wheels and a suspension system housed in the hull. Of the first tank produced using this system (the Mark III A13 cruiser), only 65 were built. Far more successful was the Mark VI cruiser, the Crusader, which went on to become the most important British tank of the desert war. The newly founded Nuffield Mechanization and Aero began to develop a cruiser tank with Christie suspension and powered by its Liberty aeroplane engine. Dating back to the First World War, this engine had proved

its worth and most importantly was extremely powerful. Even though its output was cut back from 400 to 340 hp, this was enough to make the vehicle extremely fast. The Crusader's armament consisted initially of a turret-mounted 2-pounder with coaxial machine gun and a second machine gun in a separate turret located at the front of the tank next to the driver. This machine gun turret was often removed in the field and was dropped altogether for Mk. II. Mk. III, meanwhile, was equipped with the outstanding 6-pounder (5.7 cm) gun.

The new tank received its baptism of fire in North Africa in June 1941 but more tanks were lost to mechanical failure than to enemy fire. The problems were caused not by the engine or running gear but by the cooling system and air filter. The engine was often restored to its original 400 hp by the troops, enabling the tank to reach 64 km/h. The Christie suspension

was able to cope well with speeds of this kind but the lifespan of the engine was shortened. Crusader III, equipped with the 6-pounder, which required a larger but flatter turret, came on the scene in mid-1942. Crusaders remained the most important British tank until the end of the North African campaign, after which they were quickly replaced by US vehicles as their thin armour and inability to take a gun any bigger than the 6-pounder meant they rapidly became obsolete from 1943. Special versions such as anti-aircraft guns and artillery tractors remained in service until the end of the war, however. Taking into account all the different versions, around 5,300 Crusaders were built.

# CRUISER MARK VIII CROMWELL

| | Cromwell Mk. IV |
|---|---|
| Combat weight: | 27,942 kg |
| Crew: | 5 |
| Dimensions in mm (length, width, height): | 6,420/3,040/2,840 |
| Engine: | Rolls-Royce Meteor V12, water-cooled, 27,000 cc, 600 hp |
| Power/weight ratio: | 21.5 hp/tonne |
| Max. speed: | 52 km/h road, 29 km/h cross-country |
| Range: | 280 km road |
| Armament: | 7.5 cm cannon in turret, 1 x 7.92 mm coaxial Besa MG, 1 x 7.92 mm MG in hull (some vehicles) |
| Armour: | 8–76 mm |
| Fording depth | 1.22 m |

In 1941 the British General Staff drew up a list of specifications for a heavy tank as previous models had failed to convince in terms of protection and firepower. Among other things, the new tank was to have 70 mm-thick armour and a 5.7 cm gun. Nuffield and Leyland each submitted a design. Nuffield's design was to be powered by a Liberty engine, Leyland's by a Meteor. The Meteor was a variant of the famous Rolls-Royce Merlin engine that powered the Royal Air Force's Spitfires, Hurricanes and Lancasters. Nuffield was awarded the contract without having built a prototype. Its 'Cavalier' was a complete failure, however, and could only be used for training

purposes. As a result, Leyland's design was resurrected and went into production as the 'Centaur', initially with a Liberty power plant as no Meteor engines had yet been delivered. When the Meteor engines finally arrived, the tank's name was changed to 'Cromwell'. As the British Army had had unfortunate experiences regarding the reliability of its tanks, the Cromwell was intensively tested before being issued. As a result, the first production models were not available until the beginning of 1943. In the meantime the General Staff demanded a 7.5 cm gun instead of a 5.7 cm gun, resulting in further delays. The Rolls-Royce Meteor engine and Merrit-Brown gearbox proved an outstanding choice as the engine was both powerful and reliable. Its 600 hp made the vehicle extremely fast with a top speed of 64 km/h. However, this put the running gear under such strain (in open country in particular) that, when the Mk. IV came out, its

maximum speed was restricted to 52 km/h. In 1943 and early 1944 the Cromwell was only used for training, and it first saw combat at the D-Day landings in June 1944.

The Cromwell proved its worth and remained Britain's most important tank up to the end of the war. Above all it was exceptionally fast and manoeuvrable. Compared to German tanks, however, it was still too lightly armed and armoured, despite the armour of later models being increased to a maximum 102 mm. Furthermore, although the tank did not appear until 1943, its shape was far less sophisticated than that of the T-34 or the Panther. Had the Cromwell been available in the North African desert in 1942, it would no doubt have achieved a better record of success. As things were, it was slightly behind the times, yet remained in service with the British Army until 1950. In total, 4,500 vehicles of all variants were built.

*A Cromwell Mk. IV of the British 7th Armoured Division, Normandy, July 1944.*

*The Cromwell was fast and manoeuvrable but still undergunned.*

# HOBART'S FUNNIES

*M4 Sherman
Duplex Drive DD.*

### Sherman Duplex Drive DD

This was a set of equipment to convert a Sherman tank into an amphibious tank. Buoyancy was provided by a collapsible canvas skirt while forward thrust was provided by two propellers connected to the engine. However, rough seas on 8 June 1944 caused some of the converted tanks to fill with water and sink with the loss of their crews.

### Sherman Amphibian Exhaust Device

The US Army went down a different route, making its Shermans watertight and equipping them with long air supply/exhaust shafts designed to enable them to wade ashore through deep water.

It was clear to the Allied planners that the success of the Normandy invasion would depend on the speed with which the coastal fortifications and obstacles could be overcome. As a result of the Dieppe experience, the British and Canadians in particular had been forced to recognize that the first wave of assault troops would require the support of armoured vehicles to eliminate bunkers and pockets of resistance but also to provide covering fire while the troops overcame the defensive structures erected by the Germans. A whole menagerie of extremely curious but effective armoured vehicles was developed from the ideas of Major-General Percy Hobart. These vehicles came to be known as 'Hobart's Funnies'.

*M4 Sherman AED (Sherman Amphibian Exhaust Device).*

*Sherman Dozer.*

### Sherman Dozer

A much-used piece of equipment was a Sherman tank fitted with a bulldozer blade, which proved particularly useful in clearing hedges in Normandy.

### Churchill Special Vehicles

A whole series of sappers' vehicles (Armoured Vehicle Royal Engineers or AVRE) was developed around the Churchill tank, including a tank armed with a 29 cm mortar for use against bunkers plus explosive charge layers, assault bridges, mine-clearing tanks and fascine carriers whose function was to fill in anti-tank ditches.

### Sherman Crab

A Sherman mine-clearing tank. This vehicle was equipped with a mine flail, a rotating cylinder to which weighted chains were attached that thrashed the ground, detonating any unexploded mines.

### AVRE Bobbin

The purpose of this device mounted on a Churchill chassis was to lay a canvas strip 3 m wide over the beach in order to prevent heavy vehicles from sinking into soft sand.

### AVRE Bridgelayer

This bridgelaying tank carried a bridge 9 m long with a load-bearing capacity of 60 tonnes that could be laid hydraulically.

*Churchill Bobbin.*

*Churchill Bridgelayer.*

*Sherman Crab mine-clearing tank.*

# BISHOP

| | |
|---|---|
| Combat weight: | 17,500 kg |
| Crew: | 4 |
| Dimensions in mm (length, width, height): | 5,530/2,630/2,870 |
| Engine: | AEC inline 6-cylinder diesel, water-cooled, 9,600 cc, 131 hp |
| Power/weight ratio: | 7.4 hp/tonne |
| Max. speed: | 24 km/h road, 15 km/h cross-country |
| Range: | 145 km road, 90 km cross-country |
| Armament: | 25-pounder cannon, 1 x 7.7 mm Bren MG |
| Armour: | 8–60 mm in hull, superstructure 13–51 mm |
| Fording depth | 0.9 m |

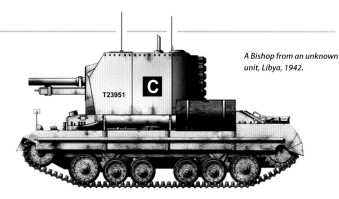

*A Bishop from an unknown unit, Libya, 1942.*

The fast and fluid style of warfare that was being conducted in North Africa highlighted Britain's need for a self-propelled artillery gun capable of following quickly behind the tank units. Such a vehicle, based on the Valentine infantry tank, was designed at great haste and given the name 'Bishop'. A large, angular superstructure housed a 25-pound gun, the standard weapon of the British field artillery. A major disadvantage was that the barrel could only be raised a maximum of 15° – a disastrously small angle for an anti-tank howitzer because it reduced the maximum range by half! To counteract this, the vehicles were often driven on to earth ramps in an attempt to achieve a greater angle of elevation. The Bishop was first used at the second Battle of El Alamein in 1942 and only remained in service until the end of 1943. Due to its low speed (typical of the Valentine) and the narrow vertical traverse capability of the 25-pounder, the Bishop was unable to perform its intended role and was replaced by better self-propelled guns such as the Sexton and the Priest. Sources place the number of Bishops produced at either 100 or 150.

# SEXTON

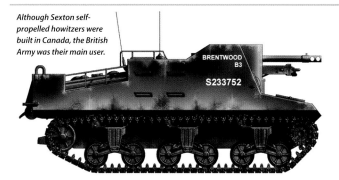

*Although Sexton self-propelled howitzers were built in Canada, the British Army was their main user.*

| | |
|---|---|
| Combat weight: | 25,855 kg |
| Crew: | 6 |
| Dimensions in mm (length, width, height): | 6,120/2,720/2,440 |
| Engine: | Continental R975-4 9-cylinder radial engine, air-cooled, 484 hp |
| Power/weight ratio: | 18.7 hp/tonne |
| Max. speed: | 40 km/h road |
| Range: | 290 km road |
| Armament: | 25-pounder cannon, 2 x 7.7 mm Bren MG |
| Armour: | max. 26 mm |
| Fording depth | 1 m |

In 1942, Great Britain received its first delivery of equipment from the USA including the M7 Priest self-propelled gun. The M7 proved highly effective in North Africa and was vastly superior to the Bishop. The only disadvantage of the US vehicle was that it was equipped with a 10.5 cm howitzer whereas the standard calibre of the Commonwealth field artillery was 8.8 mm (the 25-pounder). In order to avoid supply problems arising from the use of non-standard ammunition, the British General Staff called for a similar vehicle fitted with a 25-pounder. The M7 was based on the hull and running gear of the M3 medium battle tank, a modified version of which (with a turret-mounted 4 cm gun instead of a 7.5 cm weapon housed in a casemate on one side) was built in Canada as the Ram. The Canadians therefore used the Ram as the basis for a self-propelled gun similar to the M7 but incorporating a 25-pounder. This vehicle was named the Sexton. Between 1943 and 1945 Montreal Locomotive Works produced a total of 2,150 Sextons, an extremely useful self-propelled howitzer that remained in service in the British Army into the 1950s.

# BA-10 ARMOURED CAR

*A BA-10 from an unknown unit, Maikop, early 1942.*

| Combat weight: | 5,140 kg |
| --- | --- |
| Crew: | 4 |
| Dimensions in mm (length, width, height): | 4,650/2,070/2,210 |
| Engine: | GAZ M1 inline 4-cylinder, water-cooled, 3,300 cc, 50 hp |
| Power/weight ratio: | 9.7 hp/tonne |
| Max. speed: | 55 km/h road |
| Range: | 300 km road |
| Armament: | 4.5 cm cannon, 1 x 7.62 mm coaxial MG, 1 x hull-mounted 7.62 mm MG |
| Armour: | 6–15 mm |
| Fording depth | 0.6 m |

The BA-10 was the last in a long line of Soviet six-wheel armoured cars whose development had begun in 1930 and which were based on the regular GAZ truck chassis. The BA-10 entered service in 1938 and was heavily armed for an armoured car of the day. Its 4.5 cm cannon was more powerful than the armament of most German tanks of that time. This car, which remained in production until 1941, was the standard vehicle of the Russian reconnaissance units at the time of the German attack on the Soviet Union and was also used by independent tank brigades. In addition to an amphibious variant, there were also ammunition transporters and an ambulance version. The BA-10 remained in service with the Red Army until the beginning of 1943, when it was finally withdrawn. In 1941 the Wehrmacht captured a large number of BA-10s which were renamed the BA-10(r) and used for security duties and in an anti-resistance role.

# BA-64 ARMOURED CAR

| Combat weight: | 2,400 kg |
| --- | --- |
| Crew: | 2 |
| Dimensions in mm (length, width, height): | 3,660/1,530/1,900 |
| Engine: | GAZ MM inline 4-cylinder, water-cooled, 3,300 cc, 54 hp |
| Power/weight ratio: | 22.5 hp/tonne |
| Max. speed: | 80 km/h road |
| Range: | 600 km road |
| Armament: | generally 1 x turret-mounted 7.62 mm DT MG, |
| Armour: | 4–12 mm |

*BA-64 armoured car.*

This small, light scout and liaison car entered service with the reconnaissance units of the Red Army in 1942. It was based on the chassis of the GAZ-64 jeep and its angular superstructure was strongly influenced by the design of Germany's light armoured cars. There were versions with and without radio as well as a variant armed with a 12.7 mm machine gun. In the field, 14.5 mm anti-tank rifles or captured German 2 cm autocannon were sometimes fitted. The BA-64ZhD was a special railcar version for patrolling the railways. Taking into account all the variants, 3,500 BA-64s were built. The vehicle continued to be used after the war, for example by the North Koreans in the Korean War. The Volkspolizei and NVA (People's Army) of the newly created German Democratic Republic were also issued with second-hand BA-64s as start-up equipment.

# T-60

|  | T-60 Model 1941 |
|---|---|
| Combat weight: | 5,500 kg |
| Crew: | 2 |
| Dimensions in mm (length, width, height): | 4,100/2,350/1,750 |
| Engine: | GAZ 202 inline 6-cylinder, water-cooled, 3,300 cc, 70 hp |
| Power/weight ratio: | 12.7 hp/tonne |
| Max. speed: | 45 km/h road, 19 km/h cross-country |
| Range: | 615 km road, 315 km cross-country |
| Armament: | 2 cm ShVAK cannon, 1 x 7.62 mm coaxial MG |
| Armour: | 7–33 mm |
| Fording depth | 0.87 m |

*A T-60 M 1941 of the 3rd Guards Tank Brigade, Kalinin Front, 1942.*

In the summer of 1941 the Red Army lost a vast number of armoured vehicles and was forced to acknowledge that some models were simply not up to the task. A means of producing large numbers of tanks quickly was sought and attention was focused on the light tank. As the T-40 (a light amphibious tank armed with only a machine gun) stood little chance of survival in combat due to its minimal armour, it was decided to use the same basic model to create a new and better tank. The new tank was to be more strongly armed and armoured than its predecessor and it was decided it no longer needed to be amphibious. The resulting T-60 was intended initially to be equipped with a 3.7 cm cannon but its turret proved too small. A powerful 2 cm weapon was therefore developed that would have the same penetrating power as the 3.7 cm gun. Under the pressure of war, this all happened extremely quickly and the T-60 went into production in November 1941. The following year saw the introduction of an improved version with thicker armour. Most T-60s were issued to reconnaissance units or used to provide direct infantry support. As soon as the T-70 became available, the T-60s were converted for use as tractors or carriers for the Katyusha BM-8 rocket launcher (Stalin's Organ). In total, 6,292 T-60s were built.

# T-70

*T-70 M 1942 from an unknown unit, winter 1942–43.*

|  | T-70 Model 1942 |
|---|---|
| Combat weight: | 9,950 kg |
| Crew: | 2 |
| Dimensions in mm (length, width, height): | 4,660/2,470/2,040 |
| Engine: | 2 GAZ 202 inline 6-cylinder, water-cooled, 3,300 cc, combined 140 hp |
| Power/weight ratio: | 12.7 hp/tonne |
| Max. speed: | 51 km/h road, 19 km/h cross-country |
| Range: | 450 km road, 180 km cross-country |
| Armament: | 1 x 4.5 cm L/46 cannon, 1 x 7.62 mm coaxial MG in turret |
| Armour: | 10–60 mm |
| Fording depth | 0.9 m |

Just a few months after the T-60 was delivered to the Red Army, production began of the T-70, intended as its replacement, and for almost a year production of the two models ran in parallel. The T-70 was better armoured and was equipped with a gun based on the 45 mm anti-tank gun. As the weight had nearly doubled, the new tank was powered by two heavy truck engines. While the T-70 could be seen as an advance, its combat effectiveness was limited, not least because of its two-man crew. As the Soviets could not afford to be too fussy in 1942, the T-70 went ahead; it enabled units that would otherwise have had no fighting vehicles at all to be equipped with light tanks. In September 1943 a new version was introduced with stronger armour and a modified turret design, but production of the T-70 nevertheless ceased in the following month. The T-70's running gear continued to be used in modified form on the SU-76 assault gun.

SOVIET UNION

# T-26

*Thousands of T-26s were destroyed in summer 1941.   An earlier T-26 with two machine gun turrets.*

| | T-26 C |
|---|---|
| Combat weight: | 9,600 kg |
| Crew: | 3 |
| Dimensions in mm (length, width, height): | 4,880/2,410/2,010 |
| Engine: | GAZ T-26 inline 6-cylinder, water-cooled, 90 hp |
| Power/weight ratio: | 9.4 hp/tonne |
| Max. speed: | 32 km/h road, 12 km/h cross-country |
| Range: | 345 km road, 175 km cross-country |
| Armament: | 1 x turret-mounted 4.5 cm L/46 cannon with coaxial 7.62 mm MG, 1 x hull-mounted 7.62 mm MG |
| Armour: | 6–15 mm |
| Fording depth | 0.8 m |

After acquiring two Vickers 6 tonne tanks along with a licence to manufacture them, the Soviet Union initiated production of the T-26 in 1931. The first version, the T-26 A, had two adjacent machine gun turrets. Following experiments with a 3.7 cm weapon, a new version (the T-26 B), fitted with a 4.5 cm L/46 cannon, was introduced in 1933. In 1937 production began of the T-26 C, which had a new, slightly conical turret and was equipped with radio. Two flamethrowers (OT-130 and OT-133) were also developed and produced in large numbers. Many other variants (including bridgelaying tanks, command tanks and self-propelled guns) were manufactured in small volumes. The T-26 was intended mainly for infantry support and reconnaissance roles. Following combat experience many vehicles were fitted with additional armour. At the time of the German invasion, the T-26 fleet, though still comparatively well armed, was ageing and had inadequate armour. Thousands were destroyed by the Germans, abandoned by their crews and then either commandeered or blown up by the Wehrmacht. As PzKpfw. T-26(r) they were reused only for security and anti-resistance duties. Between 1931 and 1941 around 14,000 T-26s of all versions were produced.

# T-28

| | T-28 M |
|---|---|
| Combat weight: | 32,000 kg |
| Crew: | 6 |
| Dimensions in mm (length, width, height): | 7,440/2,810/2,820 |
| Engine: | M 17L V12 petrol, water-cooled, 46,900 cc, 500 hp |
| Power/weight ratio: | 15.6 hp/tonne |
| Max. speed: | 37 km/h road, 12.5 km/h cross-country |
| Range: | 240 km road |
| Armament: | 7.62 cm L/26 cannon and 1–2 x 7.62 mm MG in main turret, 2 x 7.62 mm MG in small turrets to the left and right of the driver |
| Armour: | 15–80 mm |
| Fording depth | 0.8 m |

*T-28 M 1934.*

In August 1933, the prototype of the T-28 was presented as a defence-busting tank. It possessed good climbing and trench-crossing capability and was equipped with two machine gun turrets positioned towards the front of the hull. All vehicles had radio and were fitted with a smokescreen device. The first models mounted a short 7.62 cm L/16.5 cannon that was later replaced by the longer L/26. In Manchuria and during the Winter War against Finland, it became clear that the T-28's armour (up to 40 mm thick) was inadequate. A new version was therefore developed (the T-28 M) with 80 mm armour at the front and 40 mm armour at the sides and rear. Although this increased its weight by a good 4 tonnes, it did not affect the tank's mobility and the T-28 acquired a reputation when it was involved in breaking through the Mannerheim Line in Finland in 1940. Around 600 T-28s were built in total.

# T-34

The Russian T-34 was without doubt one of the best and most effective tanks of the Second World War. It successfully combined the three main requirements of a tank – mobility, protection (armour) and firepower. The story of the T-34 began in 1937 with the systematic development of the BT series. The seldom used option of driving on road wheels was dispensed with and all-round sloped armour was introduced for maximum shot deflection. The T-34 was arrived at in spring 1940 via

*Disposable spare fuel tanks gave the T-34/85 an extensive range.*

*A T-34 M 1943 captured and reused by the Wehrmacht.*

|  | T-34/76 Model 1943 | T-34/85 |
|---|---|---|
| Combat weight: | 26,500 kg | 32,000 kg |
| Crew: | 4 | 4–5 |
| Dimensions in mm (length, width, height): | 6,100/3,000/2,650; length with barrel: 6,750 | 6,100/3,000/2,650; length with barrel: 8,100 |
| Engine: | V-2 43 V12 diesel, water-cooled, 38,900 cc, 500 hp | V-2 34 V12 diesel, water-cooled, 38,900 cc, 500 hp |
| Power/weight ratio: | 18.7 hp/tonne | 15.6 hp/tonne |
| Max. speed: | 55 km/h road, 25 km/h cross-country | 50 km/h road, 19 km/h cross-country |
| Range: | 270 km road, 210 km cross-country | 300 km road, 240 km cross-country |
| Armament: | 7.62 cm F-34 L/41 cannon in turret, 1 x 7.62 mm coaxial MG, 1 x hull-mounted 7.62 mm MG | 8.5 cm L/51.5 cannon in turret, 1 x coaxial 7.62 mm MG, 1 x hull-mounted 7.62 mm MG |
| Armour: | 14–70 mm | 22–90 mm |
| Fording depth: | 1.3 m | 1.3 m |

the prototype A-20 and the T-32. Its broad tracks ensured low ground pressure, allowing the vehicle to cope well with mud and snow. A powerful 500 hp diesel engine and improved Christie suspension increased mobility and reduced the risk of fire as diesel is less inflammable than petrol. The vehicles built in 1940 still featured a short 7.62 cm L-11 L/30 cannon while the 1941 model was equipped with the more powerful F-34 L/41.

When the Wehrmacht encountered the T-34 for the first time in summer 1941, it had a massive shock. All its anti-tank weapons and tank guns were rendered ineffectual at a stroke. The only German gun that could beat the new Soviet tank was the 8.8 cm anti-aircraft gun. As a result the 3.7 cm 35/36 Pak earned itself the derisory nickname 'das Heeresanklopfgerät' (meaning roughly 'the Army's door-knocking device'). Naturally the T-34 was not without its weak points. Its transmission, for example, caused continual problems and many of the T-34s that fell into German hands had simply been abandoned because of gearbox damage. The tank only had a two-man turret, which increased the burden on the commander and restricted combat effectiveness, particularly during the early part of the war in the Soviet Union when crews were relatively inexperienced. To start with, the T-34 had no radio and was therefore at a tactical disadvantage to the Wehrmacht.

As production progressed, numerous modifications were made. The most

*T-34/76 M 1942 of the
129th Motorized Brigade.*

important was
carried out in
autumn 1943, when
an anti-tank gun based
on the outstanding 8.5 cm
anti-aircraft gun and housed in a
new cast-steel turret was successfully
mounted on the tank.
This was necessary if
the T-34 was to match the
German Panther or Tiger tanks, which had
revealed themselves to be superior to the
T-34/76. The new version benefited
from thicker armour and its
8.5 cm gun could penetrate tank
armour 100 mm thick at 1,000 m.
There was also, at last, space for
three men in the turret, albeit in almost
unbearably cramped conditions. The T-34
became the standard tank of the Red
Army and was produced in vast numbers.
It is thought that by the end of 1945,
55,000 vehicles had been built, of which
19,430 were T-34/85s.

*The T-34/76 M 1943 had a modified turret with
command hatch.*

At the beginning of the war in the east,
the Wehrmacht captured a large number
of T-34s and thereafter continued to get
its hands on a few examples here and
there. Whenever the German anti-tank
units saw a T-34 they tended to fire
first and only look later to see whether
the tank bore a German cross; thus
these captured vehicles were never
systematically incorporated into the
Wehrmacht's equipment as deployment
on the battlefield was fraught with
danger. Often the turrets were removed
and the vehicles were used as improvised
recovery tanks. Production continued for a
while after 1945 and for a long time the
T-34 remained the standard tank of
the Soviet Union and its allies. It was also
exported in large numbers to third world
countries, where it was often used in
combat, e.g. in Korea, Vietnam, the wars of
the Middle East and many African
conflicts. T-34s were even used in the
fighting in Yugoslavia in the 1990s.

*The T-34/85 had a cast-steel turret and an 8.5 cm L/51 gun.*

# T-35

On paper and on parade, the T-35 appeared a mighty, unbeatable weapon. With its five turrets, three cannon, six machine guns and enormous size, it looked more like a battleship than a tank. In reality, it was a complete failure as it was too slow, mechanically unreliable and too thinly armoured. Furthermore, T-35 tank commanders were completely overstretched, having five turrets and ten men to coordinate. The first prototype of the T-35 was unveiled in 1933 and, like the T-28, was intended as a heavy defence-busting tank. The vehicle's weaknesses had become apparent during the Winter War against Finland in 1939–40 yet this did not prevent it being sent into battle in 1941. Most T-35s either failed to reach the front due to mechanical failure or were very quickly destroyed due to the enormous target they presented to the enemy. They were last used during the Battle of Moscow in winter 1941, by which time the Red Army had long had significantly better heavy tanks at its disposal. Only 60 or so T-35s were built.

| | T-35 M |
|---|---|
| Combat weight: | 49,985 kg |
| Crew: | 11 |
| Dimensions in mm (length, width, height): | 9,720/3,200/3,430 |
| Engine: | M 17M V12 petrol, water-cooled, 46,900 cc, 500 hp |
| Power/weight ratio: | 10 hp/tonne |
| Max. speed: | 30 km/h road, 12.5 km/h cross-country |
| Range: | 150 km road |
| Armament: | 7.62 cm L/16 cannon and 2 x 7.62 mm MG in main turret, 1 x 4.5 cm L/46 cannon in each secondary turret, 1 x 7.62 mm MG in two MG turrets |
| Armour: | 10–30 mm |
| Fording depth: | 1.2 m |

*A T-35 Model 1935.*

*A T-35 abandoned due to mechanical failure.*

*A destroyed T-35 always attracted interest because of its size.*

# BT-5 AND BT-7

*Although highly mobile, BT-7s were thinly armoured and therefore vulnerable.*

BT is the abbreviation of the Russian for 'fast tank'. The BT-7 was the last of a long line of fast tanks designed during the 1930s. Each of the tanks in the series had Christie suspension (the Soviets had purchased a tank of this kind in the USA in 1930) and could be driven either on tracks or on its road wheels (carrying its tracks with it). The rear set of road wheels was powered and the front set was steerable, which gave the vehicle the appearance of a conventional wheeled vehicle. The removing and replacing of the tracks was, however, a laborious, time-consuming process and high speeds without tracks were in any case only possible on roads. As a result, this option was often neglected. The BT-5 went into production at the end of 1932 and, in addition to good mobility, possessed a first-class gun, the 4.5 cm L/46 cannon. Unfortunately it was thinly armoured with riveted plates and the rivets had a tendency to fly around under fire. Externally the BT-7 bore a strong resemblance to the BT-5 but had a new turret, new transmission, a more powerful (500 hp) engine and stronger, welded armour. These tanks were intended to push forward swiftly and break through or circumvent enemy lines, spreading confusion in their wake. For this they needed mobile covering fire, which the BT-5A was designed to provide with its 7.62 mm howitzer. Vehicles of the BT series were deployed in the Spanish Civil War, Manchuria, Finland and the Second World War. Large numbers were lost in 1941. The Wehrmacht did not incorporate captured BT into their tank divisions; instead they were used only for security duties behind the line of advance. About 5,000 BT-5s and 2,700 BT-7s were built.

*Summer 1941: Wehrmacht soldiers inspect a BT-5.*

| | BT-7 |
|---|---|
| Combat weight: | 13,900 kg |
| Crew: | 3 |
| Dimensions in mm (length, width, height): | 5,600/2,290/2,420 |
| Engine: | M 17T V12 petrol, water-cooled, 46,900 cc, 500 hp |
| Power/weight ratio: | 36 hp/tonne |
| Max. speed: on wheels: | 73 km/h |
| on tracks: | 53 km/h |
| Range: road (wheels): | 730 km |
| road (tracks): | 430 km |
| Armament: | 4.5 cm L/46 cannon and 1 x 7.62 mm coaxial MG in turret, 1 x 7.62 mm MG in rear of turret (some vehicles) |
| Armour: | 10–22 mm |
| Fording depth | 1.2 m |

## KV-1 AND KV-2

Development of the KV-1 (named after the Soviet defence minister of the day, Kliment Voroshilov) started at the beginning of 1939. It was intended to replace the heavy multi-turreted tanks T-28 and T-35. In order to save weight, it was of more conventional design than its predecessors and yet had thicker armour. Indeed its front and side armour of 110 mm and 75 mm respectively was sensational for 1939. Its armament consisted of the same 7.62 mm cannon as the T-34. The KV-1 went into production in February 1940 and was immediately put through its paces in the Winter War against Finland. When the Red Army broke through the Mannerheim Line not a single KV-1 was destroyed while numerous T-28s and T-35s were knocked out. There were, however, a number of mechanical problems that required a reworking of the design. The political situation in Europe did not permit this, however, and so large-scale production went ahead in spite of the mechanical defects.

By the time of the German invasion of the Soviet Union in June 1941, 636 KV-1s had already entered service and gave the Wehrmacht an unpleasant surprise. Tanks and anti-tank guns were helpless against them and even the 8.8 cm anti-aircraft gun experienced the occasional difficulty

| | KV-1 Model 1941 | KV-2 |
|---|---|---|
| Combat weight: | 47,500 kg | 52,000 kg |
| Crew: | 5 | 6 |
| Dimensions in mm (length, width, height): | 6,250/3,300/2,710 | 6,250/3,300/3,500; length with barrel: 7,310 |
| engine: | V-2-K V12 diesel, water-cooled, 38,900 cc, 600 hp | V-2-K V12 diesel, water-cooled, 38,900 cc, 600 hp |
| Power/weight ratio: | 12.6 hp/tonne | 11.5 hp/tonne |
| Max. speed: | 30 km/h road, 19 km/h cross-country | 26 km/h road, 15 km/h cross-country |
| Range: | 250 km road | 250 km road |
| Armament: | 7.62 cm F-34 L/41 cannon in turret, 1 x 7.62 mm coaxial MG 2 x 7.62 mm MG (rear of turret and hull-mounted) | 15.2 cm M 1938/40 L/20 howitzer in turret, 1 x 7.62 mm, coaxial MG, 2 x 7.62 mm MG (rear of turret and hull-mounted) |
| Armour: | 30–110 mm | 30–110 mm |
| Fording depth: | 1.5 m | 1.5 m |

in overcoming this colossus. Until the arrival of the Tiger in 1942, the KV-1 remained the best-protected and probably the most powerful tank that the world had seen.

To support the KV-1 units, a version was developed that housed a 15.2 cm howitzer in an enormous, ungainly turret: the KV-2. Although this version was also extremely effective in combat, its turret presented the enemy with an easy target and the vehicle itself was not fast enough. Production was not resumed after the Wehrmacht captured the factory where the KV-2 was made.

Although it was still comparatively well armoured, the KV-1 faced problems when the Panther and Tiger arrived on the scene as its 7.62 cm gun was not powerful enough to penetrate their armour. From mid-1943, therefore, the 8.5 cm anti-aircraft gun was set in a cast-steel turret and mounted on the hull of the KV-1. This version, known as the KV-85, in turn became obsolete with the introduction of the T-34/85, which carried the same armament. Development then continued with the JS-1 and JS-2. By autumn 1943 around 3,000 KV-1s and KV-2s had been built, and 130 KV-85s.

*The design of the KV-1 proved less successful than that of the T-34.*

*A KV-1 of the 235th Motorized Brigade, Stalingrad, September 1942.*

*A KV-2 M 1940.*

*The high turret of the KV-2 provided the enemy with an easy target.*

## JS-2

| Combat weight: | 46,250 kg |
|---|---|
| Crew: | 4 |
| Dimensions in mm (length, width, height): | 6,770/3,360/2,730 |
| Engine: | V-2-IS V12 diesel, water-cooled, 38,900 cc, 600 hp |
| Power/weight ratio: | 11.3 hp/tonne |
| Max. speed: | 37 km/h road, 19 km/h cross-country |
| Range: | 250 km road, 150 km cross-country |
| Armament: | 12.2 cm D-25 L/43 cannon in turret and coaxial 7.62 mm MG, 1 x 7.62 mm MG at rear of turret, 1 x 12.7 mm DShK anti-aircraft MG |
| Armour: | 19–132 mm |
| Fording depth | 1.3 m |

*An IS-2 from an unknown unit, Berlin, May 1945.*

The IS heavy battle tanks, named after Joseph (Iosif) Stalin, were based on the KV series. The IS-1 was introduced in autumn 1943 and incorporated the same 8.5 cm gun as the T-34/85 and SU-85. It did not make sense to equip a heavy tank with the same weapon as a medium tank, so some prototypes were fitted with a 10 cm cannon. When a means of equipping the tank with a 12.2 cm weapon was finally found, this became the preferred variant. Production of the IS-1 ended after only 100 vehicles and the new, more heavily armed model with a larger turret went into production at the end of 1943. Many IS-1s were later converted to IS-2s. The new tank was first used in combat in February 1944. Its 12.2 cm gun was able to destroy Panthers and Tigers with ease but the tank was not without certain drawbacks. The crew compartment was extremely cramped and, as shot and cartridges had to be loaded separately, the rate of fire was slow. Another problem was that, because it was very light for a heavy tank, its armour was far from invulnerable. The next stage of development was the IS-3, a mighty weapon of which only a very small number had entered service by the end of the war. Approximately 3,800 IS-2s were built altogether.

## SU-76

| Combat weight: | 11,200 kg |
|---|---|
| Crew: | 4 |
| Dimensions in mm (length, width, height): | 4,990/2,740/2,200 |
| Engine: | two GAZ 202 inline 6-cylinder engines, water-cooled, 3,300 cc, 140 hp |
| Power/weight ratio: | 12.5 hp/tonne |
| Max. speed: | 44 km/h road, 19 km/h cross-country |
| Range: | 265 km road, 140 km cross-country |
| Armament: | 7.62 cm ZIS-3 cannon |
| Armour: | 10–35 mm |
| Fording depth | 0.9 m |

*SU-76M.*

The SU-76 was a highly successful attempt to find an alternative use for the chassis of the T-70 light tank, which was ageing rapidly. The hull was widened and the running gear lengthened through the addition of one wheel. The engine was located in the middle and an open-topped fighting compartment, housing the renowned ZIS-3 7.6 cm field gun, positioned at the back. These vehicles were first issued to the troops at the end of 1942 but were highly prone to mechanical breakdown, which meant the design had to be reworked. The new version went into production as the SU-76M in May 1943 and large numbers (12,671 SU-76s in total) were built. The vehicle was extremely flexible and was used in a mobile artillery support role both as a tank destroyer and as a self-propelled howitzer. It was also frequently used as an assault gun for direct infantry support despite being inadequately armoured for this function. The ZSU-37 anti-aircraft tank, on which was mounted a 3.7 cm gun, shared the same chassis but was built in smaller numbers.

SOVIET UNION

# SU-122

*SU-122.*

| Combat weight: | 30,900 kg |
|---|---|
| Crew: | 4–5 |
| Dimensions in mm (length, width, height): | 5,950/3,000/2,300; length with barrel: 6,950 |
| Engine: | V-2 34 V12 diesel, water-cooled, 38,900 cc, 500 hp |
| Power/weight ratio: | 16.2 hp/tonne |
| Max. speed: | 55 km/h road, 25 km/h cross-country |
| Range: | 300 km road, 200 km cross-country |
| Armament: | 12.2 cm M-30 L/23 howitzer |
| Armour: | 14–45 mm, mantlet up to 70 mm |
| Fording depth: | 1.3 m |

The SU-122 was the Soviet Union's first assault gun of the Second World War. Its development began in summer 1942 under the name SU-35, when a solid box-shaped superstructure with all-round sloped armour was mounted on the chassis of the T-34. Its armament was a front-mounted 12.2 cm M-30 howitzer with limited traverse. Due to its low muzzle velocity, the howitzer was not particularly well suited to fighting enemy tanks and even a specially developed hollow charge failed to convince. The vehicle was effective in an infantry support role, however, and useful for bombarding fortifications. From the end of 1943 its role was increasingly taken over by the even more effective SU-152. As the Red Army particularly wanted a tank destroyer, development continued with the SU-85 and SU-100. By March 1945 a total of 1,148 SU-122s had been built.

# SU-85 AND SU-100

In 1943 the Soviets needed to find a way of destroying the new German Panther and Tiger tanks, which neither the T-34/76 nor the SU-122 was capable of defeating. In order to save time, they took the hull of the SU-122 and equipped it with the 8.5 cm anti-aircraft gun. The use of existing components speeded up the development time and reduced costs. The first prototype was ready in August 1943 and by the end of the year 750 SU-85s had rolled off the production line. The introduction of the T-34/85 with the same 8.5 cm weapon rendered the SU-85 superfluous, however, and production only ran until September 1944. By that time, 2,000 SU-85s had been built. Its successor was the SU-100, which was introduced the same month. The main difference between the two was the SU-100's new and powerful 10 cm gun. This had originally been a naval weapon and its size meant the command hatch had to jut out over the sloped right-hand side of the superstructure. The mantlet was also different from that of the SU-85. The

|  | SU-85 | SU-100 |
|---|---|---|
| Combat weight: | 29,600 kg | 31,600 kg |
| Crew: | 4 | 4 |
| Dimensions in mm (length, width, height): | 5,950/3,000/2,450; length with barrel: 8,150 | 5,950/3,000/2,250; length with barrel: 9,450 |
| Engine: | V-2 34 V12 diesel, water-cooled, 38,900 cc, 500 hp | V-2 34 V12 diesel, water-cooled, 38,900 cc, 500 hp |
| Power/weight ratio: | 16.9 hp/tonne | 15.8 hp/tonne |
| Max. speed: | 55 km/h road, 25 km/h cross-country | 50 km/h road, 19 km/h cross-country |
| Range: | 300 km road, 200 km cross-country | 300 km road, 200 km cross-country |
| Armament: | 8.5 cm D-5S L/53 cannon | 10 cm D-10S L/56 cannon |
| Armour: | 14–45 mm, mantlet up to 75 mm | 20–54 mm, mantlet up to 75 mm |
| Fording depth: | 1.3 m | 1.3 m |

*An SU-85 from an unknown unit, Berlin, 1945.*

first vehicles went into service at the beginning of 1945 and proved extremely successful. Production ceased in June 1945, by which time 1,675 SU-100s had been built.

# SU-152

| Combat weight: | 45,500 kg |
|---|---|
| Crew: | 5 |
| Dimensions in mm (length, width, height): | 6,250/3,300/2,450; length with barrel: 8,950 |
| Engine: | V-2 K V12 diesel, water-cooled, 38,900 cc, 600 hp |
| Power/weight ratio: | 13.2 hp/tonne |
| Max. speed: | 40 km/h road, 19 km/h cross-country |
| Range: | 250 km road |
| Armament: | 15.2 cm ML-20 L/32.3 cannon-howitzer |
| Armour: | 20–75 mm |
| Fording depth | 1.5 m |

*SU-152.*

At the end of 1942, the Soviet high command called for a powerfully armed and armoured self-propelled gun for use against fortifications and heavy tanks. The first prototype, which was based on the KV-1, was ready in February 1943. The designers had mounted a 15.2 cm ML-20 cannon-howitzer in an angular fixed superstructure. This gun fired a 48.8 kg anti-tank shell which was thought capable of destroying any tank in existence. The SU-152 had its first major combat deployment at the Battle of Kursk in July 1943, where it was believed to have destroyed 12 Tigers and seven Ferdinands. Production ceased after production of the KV-1 chassis ended, by which time 704 SU-152s had been built.

*The SU-152 was based on the chassis of the KV-1.*

# ISU-122 AND ISU-152

*ISU-122.*

*ISU-152.*

As the SU-152 had proved so successful in combat, it was decided to build a similar vehicle based on the IS-2 chassis. Although the superstructure of the ISU-152 was higher and more angular, it bore a strong resemblance to the SU-152. As production of the ML-20 howitzer could not keep up with demand, a further version was produced. The ISU-122 was intended mainly as a tank destroyer and incorporated the 12.2 cm A-19 and later the D-25. In other respects there was hardly any difference between the two models. The main drawback of all three versions (SU-152,

ISU-152 and ISU-122) was the extremely scarce storage space for shells and the low rate of fire of two or three shots per minute dictated by the two-part ammunition. Spare ammunition would often be carried on the engine cover – which was potentially highly dangerous in combat situations. These vehicles were nevertheless extremely effective thanks to their enormous firepower and remained in service with the Red Army long after the end of the war. By the time production ceased in 1945, 4,075 ISU-122s and ISU-152s had been built.

| | ISU-152 |
|---|---|
| Combat weight: | 41,800 kg |
| Crew: | 4 |
| Dimensions in mm (length, width, height): | 6,770/3,360/2,680; |
| length with barrel: | 9,050 |
| Engine: | V-2 IS V12 diesel, water-cooled, 38,900 cc, 600 hp |
| Power/weight ratio: | 14.4 hp/tonne |
| Max. speed: | 37 km/h road, 19 km/h cross-country |
| Range: | 220 km road, 100 km cross-country |
| Armament: | 15.2 cm ML-20 L/32.3 cannon-howitzer, 1 x 12.7 mm DShK anti-aircraft MG |
| Armour: | 19–110 mm |
| Fording depth | 1.3 m |

## M3A1 SCOUT CAR

*General Patton's M3 command vehicle.*

| Combat weight: | 5,624 kg |
|---|---|
| Crew: | 8 |
| Dimensions in mm (length, width, height): | 5,620/2,030/2,110 |
| Engine: | Hercules JXD inline 6-cylinder petrol, water-cooled, 87 hp |
| Power/weight ratio: | 15.7 hp/tonne |
| Max. speed: | 88 km/h road |
| Range: | 400 km road |
| Armament: | 1 x 12.7 mm Browning M2HB MG (sometimes supplemented by 1 x 7.62 cm M1919A4 MG) |
| Armour: | 6–12.7 |
| Fording depth | 0.7 m |

The M3 was developed by the White Motor Company in 1938 and was adopted by the US Army as the M3A1 in 1939. The M3A1 was based on a commercial truck chassis and was open-topped. A Browning M2 machine gun was mounted on a rail which ran around the open fighting compartment and a cylindrical roller was fitted to the front of the vehicle to prevent it getting bogged down in difficult terrain. The bullet-proof windscreen could be covered by a 12.7 mm-thick armour plate. The M3A1 was used only rarely by the US Army and British forces as a scout car, serving more commonly as a personnel transporter or command vehicle (General Patton's, for example) or being used for patrol duties in conquered territory. There was also an ambulance variant. Many of the 20,918 vehicles built by 1944 went to the Soviet Union and to the French units that were reconstituted after June 1944.

## M8 GREYHOUND ARMOURED CAR

| Combat weight: | 7,711 kg |
|---|---|
| Crew: | 4 |
| Dimensions in mm (length, width, height): | 5,010/2,540/2,230 |
| Engine: | Hercules JXD inline 6-cylinder petrol, water-cooled, 110 hp |
| Power/weight ratio: | 14.5 hp/tonne |
| Max. speed: | 88 km/h road |
| Range: | 460 km road |
| Armament: | 1 x 3.7 cm M6 L/56 cannon, 1 x 7.62 mm M1919A4 coaxial MG, 1 x 12.7 mm Browning M2HB anti-aircraft MG |
| Armour: | 3–19 mm |
| Fording depth | 0.6 m |

*An M8 of the 2nd Cavalry Division, Belgium, winter 1944–45.*

*The M8.*

This vehicle was originally developed as a tank destroyer. By the time it was ready for production in 1942, however, its 3.7 cm cannon was no longer effective against tanks and so it was adopted by the US Army as the M8 armoured car. The open-topped turret was manually operated. A 12.7 mm anti-aircraft gun was often mounted on a rail that ran around the perimeter of the turret. The first M8s had no floor armour and later vehicles were fitted with only 3 mm-thick steel plate. This inadequate floor armour was the most significant drawback of a vehicle that otherwise convinced with its reliability, good off-road capability and robustness. The M8 had its baptism of fire in Italy in 1943. The British also used it and gave it the nickname 'Greyhound'. The same year a personnel transporter and command vehicle (the M20) was based on the M8 with the turret removed and with benches fitted in the open fighting compartment. By 1945 Ford had manufactured 11,667 M8s and 3,791 M20s.

# M24 CHAFFEE

| Combat weight: | 18,370 kg |
| --- | --- |
| Crew: | 4–5 |
| Dimensions in mm (length, width, height): | 4,990/2,950/2,450; length with barrel: 5,490 |
| Engine: | Cadillac Twin, comprising two V8 water-cooled petrol engines, combined 220 hp |
| Power/weight ratio: | 12.2 hp/tonne |
| Max. speed: | 56 km/h road, 38 km/h cross-country |
| Range: | 160 km road |
| Armament: | 7.5 cm M6 cannon in turret, 1 x 7.62 mm coaxial M1919A4 MG and 1 x hull-mounted M1919A4 MG, 1 x 12.7 mm anti-aircraft MG |
| Armour: | 12–38 mm |
| Fording depth: | 2 m with waterproofing; 1 m without |

*The M24 remained in service in a number of countries (including Norway and Portugal) until recently – albeit in modernized form.*

In April 1943, work began on the designs for a new light tank to replace the M3 and M5. The first prototypes were ready by October of that year and the US Department of Defense placed an initial order for 1,000 vehicles and then another 5,000 even before testing had finished. The first tanks, named the M24 Chaffee (after US General Adna R. Chaffee), were delivered to Europe in November 1944. The Chaffee was probably the first modern light tank and had a well-designed hull with sloped surfaces all round for maximum shot deflection. Four years before this, its 7.5 cm gun would have been used to arm a heavy tank. The M24 was, however, fast and relatively small – good characteristics for a reconnaissance vehicle. Although around 4,400 tanks were built by 1945, only a fraction of them entered service. Most were still with training units in Europe at the end of the war; after 1945 the Chaffee was exported to many different countries and was used in the wars in Korea and Indochina.

*An M24 of the US 8th Armored Division, Rheinberg, March 1945.*

## HALF-TRACK VEHICLES M2, M3, M5 AND VARIANTS

By the beginning of 1940, a range of half-track vehicles had been designed and tested in the USA, most importantly by the White Motor Company. Two main types emerged. Both were based on a commercial truck chassis and the slightly modified armoured superstructure of the White M3A1 scout car. The M2 was intended as a reconnaissance and towing vehicle and had no rear doors. The M3, which had a slightly elongated superstructure and rear doors, was designed mainly as a personnel carrier. Version M4 was built to carry an 81 mm mortar along with crew and ammunition. All the vehicles were open-topped and were equipped with one or two 7.62 mm or 12.7 mm machine

guns. In bad weather the fighting compartment could be covered by a hood but there was no protection against artillery fire or air attack. Shortly after the US Army placed its order, it became clear that White would not be able to manufacture the necessary number of vehicles itself and so the Autocar and Diamond T companies were brought in to help. Later they were joined by International Harvester, which manufactured what were essentially the same half-tracks with minor modifications under the names M5 and M9. To all intents and purposes, these vehicles represented the Allied counterpart to the German Sd.Kfz. 251 and found a similarly diverse range of uses. They also formed

|  | M3 |
|---|---|
| Combat weight: | 9,072 kg |
| Crew: | 3 + 10–12 |
| Dimensions in mm (length, width, height): | 6,170/2,220/2,260 |
| Engine: | White 160AX inline 6-cylinder petrol, water-cooled, 147 hp |
| Power/weight ratio: | 16.5 hp/tonne |
| Max. speed: | 72 km/h road |
| Range: | 310 km road |
| Armament: | 1 x 12.7 mm Browning M2HB MG and/or 1 x 7.62 mm M1919A4 MG |
| Armour: | 6–16 mm |
| Fording depth | 0.7 m |

*A half-track vehicle of the 1st Infantry Division.*

the basis for a number of self-propelled artillery and anti-aircraft guns for which weapons ranging from 5.7 cm to 10.5 cm were mounted behind guards or on the open fighting compartment or special anti-aircraft mounts fitted that held twin or quadruple 12.7 mm machine guns. US half-track vehicles were extensively used not only by the USA but by all the other Allies as well. Under the Lend-Lease agreement, thousands were also supplied to the Soviet Union, which developed its own variants. The career of these vehicles did not end in 1945 as excess US stocks were exported all over the world.

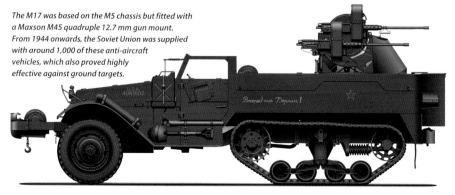

*The M17 was based on the M5 chassis but fitted with a Maxson M45 quadruple 12.7 mm gun mount. From 1944 onwards, the Soviet Union was supplied with around 1,000 of these anti-aircraft vehicles, which also proved highly effective against ground targets.*

*An M3 half-track.*

The M2 is easy to identify from its slightly shortened superstructure.
The Soviet Union received its first consignment of US half-tracks,
most of which were used on the Southern Front as reconnaissance
vehicles or artillery tractors, in winter 1943/44.

USA

# M3 AND M5 STUART

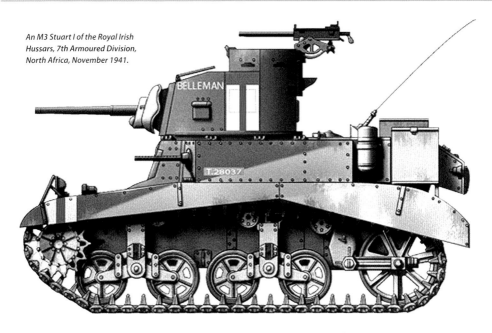

*An M3 Stuart I of the Royal Irish Hussars, 7th Armoured Division, North Africa, November 1941.*

In 1940, events in Europe forced the US Army to recognize that its light tanks were out of date and a decision was taken to modernize the M2. In July 1940 the designs for an improved model with heavier armour were accepted and large-scale production began of what now became the M3 in mid-1941. Initially the tank was only riveted (it was later welded) and had a 250 hp radial aero engine that made the light M3 wonderfully fast for the time. This engine was always in short supply, however, as it was also used by the aircraft industry and some M3s were given a diesel engine instead. Also highly innovative was the main armament's gyroscopic stabilization system designed to improve accuracy, the first use of such technology anywhere in the world. By contrast, the two machine guns mounted on the side of the hull seemed rather anachronistic. During the course of production, modifications were undertaken to the turret and hull and these side-mounted machine guns were dropped. From version M3A3 onwards,

the tank was fitted with a continuous sloped (rather than stepped) glacis plate. The M3 underwent its baptism of fire against Rommel in North Africa. The British had been supplied with a number

of M3s under the Lend-Lease agreement and valued the reliability and speed of this tank (whose official British Army name was the 'Stuart') so highly that they nicknamed it 'Honey'.

| | M3 | M5 |
|---|---|---|
| Combat weight: | 12,430 kg | 14,969 kg |
| Crew: | 4 | 4 |
| Dimensions in mm (length, width, height): | 4,530/2,230/2,510 | 4,340/2,300/2,250 |
| Engine: | Continental W-670 7-cylinder radial, petrol, air-cooled, 250 hp | Cadillac Twin, comprising two V8 petrol engines, water-cooled, combined 242 hp |
| Power/weight ratio: | 20.4 hp/tonne | 16.1 hp/tonne |
| Max. speed: | 58 km/h road, 32 km/h cross-country | 58 km/h road, 30 km/h cross-country |
| Range: | 120 km road | 160 km road |
| Armament: | 37 cm M6 L/56 cannon (turret), 1 x 7.62 mm coaxial M1919A4 MG 2 x 7.62 mm hull-mounted MG 1 x 7.62 mm MG on turret | 3.7 cm M6 L/56 cannon, 1 x 7.62 mm coaxial M1919A4 MG 1 x 7.62 mm M1919A4 MG on turret |
| Armour: | 10–44.5 mm | 12–67 mm |
| Fording depth: | 0.9 m | 0.9 m |

USA

The ongoing shortage of Continental engines led to the M3 being fitted with a new power plant comprising twin auto-engines and a commercially available automatic gearbox. The new drive system worked well and, after further modifications to the turret and hull, the new version went into production in spring 1942 as the M5. Large-scale production, however, only began with the end of the M3 programme in the autumn of the following year.

The M5 Stuart remained in service with the Allies until the end of the war, proving highly effective as a reconnaissance vehicle and with the US cavalry units. Although undergunned and extremely lightly armoured, it was nevertheless reliable and fast. A variant of the M5

known as the M8 carried a short 7.5 cm howitzer in an open turret. Soviet and French units were supplied with large numbers of the 24,522 Stuart tanks of all versions that were built.

*Although its official British designation was the 'Stuart', the troops were so smitten with the M3 that they nicknamed it 'Honey'.*

*An M5A1 Stuart in the Yad la-Shiryon Museum, Israel.*

# M3 LEE AND GRANT

| M3 Grant Mk I | |
|---|---|
| Combat weight: | 27,900 kg |
| Crew: | 6 |
| Dimensions in mm (length, width, height): | 5,640/2,720/3,020 |
| Engine: | Continental R-975 EC2, 9-cylinder radial, petrol, air-cooled, 340 hp |
| Power/weight ratio: | 12.6 hp/tonne |
| Max. speed: | 42 km/h road, 26 km/h cross-country |
| Range: | 170 km road |
| Armament: | 7.5 cm M2 or M3 L/31 in a sponson on the right of the hull, 3.7 cm M5 or M6 L/56 cannon in the turret, 1 x 7.62 mm M1919A4 coaxial MG, 2 x 7.62 mm MGs in the hull |
| Armour: | 12–51 mm |
| Fording depth | 1 m |

*An M3A1 Lee from an unknown Red Army unit, Caucasus, mid-1942.*

In 1940 it became clear that the US medium M2 tank, armed with only a 3.7 cm turret-mounted gun, was out of date. In order to save time, its replacement was based on the same chassis. It had a modified hull with a 7.5 cm gun with limited traverse mounted in the front right of the superstructure. There was also a turret housing a 3.7 cm cannon and coaxial machine gun and in addition the commander had his own small turret and 7.62 mm machine gun. The M3 was intended as an interim solution pending the introduction of the M4, which was yet to be designed. Large-scale production of the M3 began in August 1941 and continued until December 1942, during which time 6,258 M3s of all types were built. Most M3s had riveted hulls and a 9-cylinder radial aero engine. The M3 was built by a number of manufacturers, however, and so there was a variety of finishes. The machine gun turret was dropped in later models. As its own industry was at full stretch, the British government purchased US tanks including the M3 medium tank, which was fitted at its request with a new, larger turret equipped with radio (the machine gun turret was removed). This vehicle was designated the M3 Grant I and was shipped to the British Army in North Africa from early 1942 onwards. Standard M3s, named the M3 Lee (Grant and Lee were American Civil War generals) were shipped direct to the United Kingdom.

Both models earned themselves a good reputation in the desert in 1942 and proved popular with the troops. They were not without certain shortcomings, however, including the limited field of fire of the main gun, their height and their awkward design with vertical sides and numerous shell traps. From 1943 the M3 rapidly began to show its age and was replaced in North Africa and Europe by the M4. In Asia and the Pacific, meanwhile, the M3 remained in service until the end of the war. Around 1,400 M3s were supplied to the Soviet Union under the Lend-Lease agreement. The robust chassis of the M3 also served as a basis for a number of self-propelled guns including the M7, M12 and British-Canadian Sexton.

*GIs of the 1st Armored Division taking a break in front of their M3 in Tunisia, 23 November 1942.*

*An M3 Grant Mk. I of the British 7th Armoured Division, El Alamein, 1942.*

*An M3 at a US Army training ground in 1942.*

# M12

| | |
|---|---|
| Combat weight: | 26,650 kg |
| Crew: | 6 |
| Dimensions in mm (length, width, height): | 6,730/2,670/2,700 |
| Engine: | Continental R-975 EC2, 9-cylinder radial, petrol, air-cooled, 340 hp |
| Power/weight ratio: | 12.6 hp/tonne |
| Max. speed: | 38 km/h road, 26 km/h cross-country |
| Range: | 220 km road |
| Armament: | 15.5 cm M1918M1 howitzer |
| Armour: | 12–63.5 mm |
| Fording depth | 1.2 m |

In June 1941, contracts were awarded for development of a self-propelled carriage for the 15.5 cm M1918 gun based on the M3. The resulting prototype (the T6 GMC) was subsequently rejected, though, as the US Army saw no need for a weapon of its type. The Ordnance Department nevertheless ordered 100 vehicles for evaluation purposes and production of the M12 began in August 1942. The reorganization of the M3 hull involved the engine being moved to the middle and the fighting compartment being shifted to the rear. As a result the gun crew were unprotected, although at least in theory this was not a problem as the M12 was intended as a long-distance artillery piece. It was not until 1944, after the Normandy landings, that the Army showed any further interest in the M12 and 75 units were overhauled and shipped to Europe, where they performed extremely well as artillery weapons. The M12 could only carry ten rounds and had to be accompanied at all times by an M30 transporter (an unarmed M12) that carried the gun crew and spare ammunition.

*An M12 with the apposite name 'Adolph's Assassin'.*

USA

# M4 SHERMAN

The M4 Sherman was probably the most important and versatile Allied tank of the Second World War. Work started on the designs for a successor to the medium M3 in August 1940, just a short while after the M3's designs were approved. The fundamental requirement for the new tank was a 7.5 cm gun with gyroscopic stabilization in a turret with a 360° traverse. In order to save time, the M4 was designed in such a way that as many M3 components as possible could be used in it. Thus the running gear, lower hull, tracks and initially the power plant were the same. The first prototype was unveiled in autumn 1941 and production (which continued until the end of the war) started at the beginning of 1942. No fewer than 12 different manufacturers produced a bewildering number of versions and special variants. The main difference could be observed in the hull, which was either cast steel, displaying a rounded shape, or welded and more angular. A wide range of different engines was also fitted after it transpired that the radial engine of the first few vehicles would not be available in the required numbers. The arming of the tank with the 7.5 cm M3 gun gave rise to a lot of criticism and from 1944 a 7.6 cm weapon was fitted in a new turret. The British, who also used large numbers of Shermans, created their own, better-armed version of the tank named the Firefly, by equipping it with their outstanding 17-pounder (7.62 cm) gun. These two versions finally enabled the Allies to fight Germany's heavy tanks at long range. On the negative side, early M4s had a reputation of catching fire easily and, to remedy this, the ammunition in later models was stowed in special water-jacketed bins. The M4's armour was also steadily improved during the course of the tank's production.

The main version during the final months of the war was the M4A3E8 (HVSS), which had the long-barrelled 7.6 cm cannon and a new suspension system with horizontal instead of the previous vertical volute springs. For direct infantry support there was a variant armed with a 10.5 cm howitzer while the M4A3E2 Jumbo was an assault tank with armour up to 152 mm thick. There was also a large number of special versions including flamethrower, recovery, bridgelaying and mine-clearing tanks, a rocket launcher, artillery tractors, flail tanks and even amphibious tanks.

The M4 was first used in combat at El Alamein in North Africa in 1942. From then on it could be found wherever Allied troops were deployed. Around 2,000 Shermans were also supplied to the Soviet Union under the Lend-Lease programme, although the Red Army was far from happy with the tank and considered its own T-34 far superior.

|  | M4A2 |
| --- | --- |
| Combat weight: | 31,350 kg |
| Crew: | 5 |
| Dimensions in mm (length, width, height): | 5,890/2,670/2,740 |
| Engine: | GM 6-71 6046 V12 diesel, water-cooled, 420 hp |
| Power/weight ratio: | 13.4 hp/tonne |
| Max. speed: | 40 km/h road, 28 km/h cross-country |
| Range: | 250 km road |
| Armament: | 7.5 cm M3 L/40 cannon (turret), coaxial and hull-mounted M1919A4 machine guns, 1 x 12.7 mm anti-aircraft machine gun |
| Armour: | 12.7–1.05 mm |
| Fording depth | 1 m |

*An M4A3E8 (HVSS) Sherman of the US 11th Armored Division, Rhine, March 1945.*

*The M4A3E8 with the long-barrelled 7.62 cm cannon was substantially more powerful than the version with the short 7.5 cm gun.*

Indeed the M4 is widely underestimated and often compared unfavourably with Germany's Panther. It should be remembered, however, that the Panther was around 15 tonnes heavier and that the Sherman possessed three qualities that the Panther lacked: it was extremely reliable, it was robust and it was available in vast quantities. By May 1945 a total of 49,243 M4s of all versions had been built. After the war the tank was sold for a song from excess US stocks to the armed forces of numerous countries and remained in service for many years, undergoing continual improvement. In the 1960s the Israelis created their own version armed with a 10.5 cm gun.

*The Soviet Union was supplied with around 2,000 M4 Shermans. This M4A2 bears the Russian inscription 'Vpered na Berlin!' ('Forward to Berlin!').*

*M4 Shermans preparing to attack, Western Front, early 1945.*

*US Army Shermans going ashore, Sicily, 1943.*

USA

# M26 PERSHING

| Combat weight: | 41,891 kg |
|---|---|
| Crew: | 5 |
| Dimensions in mm (length, width, height): | 6,510/3,510/2,780; length with barrel: 8,650 |
| Engine: | Ford GAF V8 petrol, water-cooled, 500 hp |
| Power/weight ratio: | 10.9 hp/tonne |
| Max. speed: | 40 km/h road, 18 km/h cross-country |
| Range: | 160 km road |
| Armament: | 9 cm M3 cannon (turret), coaxial and hull-mounted M1919A4 machine guns, 1 x 12.7 mm anti-tank MG |
| Armour: | 12.7–114 mm |
| Fording depth: | 1.22 m |

No sooner had the M4 Sherman gone into production than the search for a successor began. The design and development work for the new tank proved both difficult and complicated, however, as the specifications were continually being changed. At one point the US Army even declared that the new tank was no longer needed. At the end of 1944 the Ardennes offensive (Battle of the Bulge) finally pressed home the need for a tank that would match the Panther and Tiger and the M26 went into production but by the end of the war only 310 M26 Pershing tanks had arrived in Europe. The few that were used in battle acquitted themselves extremely well and the new 9 cm gun proved to be extraordinarily powerful. The front armour of the M26 also lived up to expectations, withstanding the Panther's 7.5 cm KwK at battle range. In the Pacific, a few Pershings were used at the Battle of Okinawa in May 1945.

*An M26 Pershing of the US 2nd Armored Division, Germany, May 1945.*

# M18 HELLCAT

| Combat weight: | 17,036 kg |
|---|---|
| Crew: | 5 |
| Dimensions in mm (length, width, height): | 6,140/3,050/2,710; length with barrel: 7,460 |
| Engine: | Continental R-975 C4 9-cylinder radial, petrol, air-cooled, 400 hp |
| Power/weight ratio: | 23.5 hp/tonne |
| Max. speed: | 80 km/h road, 32 km/h cross-country |
| Range: | 170 km road |
| Armament: | 7.62 cm M1A1 cannon (turret), 1 x 12.7 mm anti-aircraft MG |
| Armour: | 8–25.4 mm |
| Fording depth: | 1.22 m |

The M18 was developed in response to the US Army's call for a fast tank destroyer with a 7.62 cm cannon and went into production in mid-1943. In order to save weight, the turret was open-topped. With a maximum speed of 80 km/h, the M18 was the fastest tank of the war and a perfect exponent of the tactic known as 'shoot and scoot'. While its 7.62 cm weapon was incapable of penetrating the frontal armour of a Panther or Tiger and its own armour was minimal, the M18 was fast and manoeuvrable enough to find the best attacking position or retreat to safety when necessary. M18 units achieved astonishing kill statistics. In July 1944, the 630th Tank Destroyer Battalion reported knocking out 53 Tigers and Panthers and 15 StuG IIIs with a loss of just 17 M18s. Altogether 2,507 M18s were manufactured and after the war surplus vehicles were exported to a number of countries including Austria, Argentina and Yugoslavia. An armoured transport vehicle (the M39) based on the M18 was supplied to the Federal Republic of Germany's new armed forces, the Bundeswehr, in 1956.

*An M18 Hellcat of the 701st Tank Destroyer Battalion, Po Valley, Italy, spring 1945.*

# M10 WOLVERINE

| | |
|---|---|
| Combat weight: | 29,937 kg |
| Crew: | 5 |
| Dimensions in mm (length, width, height): | 5,970/3,050/2,480; length with barrel: 6,530 |
| Engine: | GM 6-71 6046 V12 diesel, water-cooled, 420 hp |
| Power/weight ratio: | 14 hp/tonne |
| Max. speed: | 48 km/h road, 28 km/h cross-country |
| Range: | 320 km road |
| Armament: | 7.62 cm M7 cannon (turret), 1 x 12.7 mm anti-aircraft MG |
| Armour: | 12.7–51 mm |
| Fording depth | 1 m |

In 1942 a tank destroyer was introduced that was modelled on the M4A2 with a 7.62 cm cannon based on an anti-aircraft gun. The upper hull of the M4A2 was modified and the vehicle equipped with an open-topped turret with a large counterweight to balance the weight of the long barrel. In total, 6,346 M10s were built. The tank underwent its baptism of fire at the end of 1942 in North Africa and thereafter was widely deployed in Italy and France. Large numbers of M10s were also supplied to the British Army and Free French forces. In Britain some of the guns were replaced by the 17-pounder (7.62 cm). These vehicles were named the 'Achilles' and made extremely effective tank destroyers. The M10's main weakness was its open turret, which left the crew unprotected against artillery fire and air attack, so armoured roofs were often improvised in the field.

*M10 GM.*

# M36

| | |
|---|---|
| Combat weight: | 28,123 kg |
| Crew: | 5 |
| Dimensions in mm (length, width, height): | 6,140/3,050/2,710; length with barrel: 7,460 |
| Engine: | Ford GAF V8 petrol, water-cooled, 500 hp |
| Power/weight ratio: | 17.8 hp/tonne |
| Max. speed: | 40 km/h road, 32 km/h cross-country |
| Range: | 240 km road |
| Armament: | 9 cm M3 cannon (turret), 1 x 12.7 mm anti-tank MG |
| Armour: | 12.7–102 mm |
| Fording depth | 1 m |

While the M10's 7.62 cm gun was considered perfectly satisfactory in 1942, by the middle of 1943 it was no longer adequate as it was incapable of piercing the frontal armour of the Panther and Tiger. A new tank destroyer equipped with the 9 cm M3 gun was therefore developed. This new vehicle, the M36, adopted the M10's hull almost unchanged while the turret was completely new. Its chassis, however,

was based on that of the M4A3, which is why a more powerful Ford engine was fitted. The M36 first saw combat in Europe in July 1944 and proved a potent tank destroyer as its 9 cm weapon penetrated the armour of Panthers and Tigers with ease. By 1945, 1,949 had been built. The M36 remained in service for a long time after the war and the last of them were still being deployed in Yugoslavia in the 1990s.

*An M36 of the 701st Tank Destroyer Battalion, Italy, 1945.*

## M7 PRIEST

The M7 self-propelled howitzer, based on the M3 medium tank, was intended to provide mobile supporting fire for tank units. The upper hull of the M3 was modified accordingly and a 10.5 cm howitzer mounted in an open-topped fighting compartment. To defend itself against air attack and close-range threats, the vehicle was equipped on the right-hand side with a 12.7 mm machine gun mounted in a round structure that looked similar to a pulpit – hence the name 'Priest'.

The M7 went into production in April 1942 and initially served with the British Army in North Africa, where it performed

well. These British M7s were gradually replaced by the Sexton and were converted for use in other roles, including the Kangaroo armoured personnel carrier, which could hold up to 20 soldiers. In the US Army, however, the M7 remained the standard self-propelled howitzer up to the end of the war. When production of the M3 ceased, the M4A3 chassis was used instead, and the new version was designated the M7B1. In total, 4,267 M7s of all versions were built and they remained in use after the war. The Bundeswehr, the new armed forces of the Federal Republic of Germany, was also supplied with the vehicle in 1956.

| | |
|---|---|
| Combat weight: | 22,967 kg |
| Crew: | 7 |
| Dimensions in mm (length, width, height): | 6,020/2,870/2,920 |
| Engine: | Continental R-975 EC2 9-cylinder radial, petrol, air-cooled, 340 hp |
| Power/weight ratio: | 12.6 hp/tonne |
| Max. speed: | 42 km/h road, 26 km/h cross-country |
| Range: | 200 km road |
| Armament: | 1 x 10.5 cm M1A2 howitzer, 1 x 12.7 mm anti-aircraft MG |
| Armour: | 12–63.5 mm |
| Fording depth | 1.2 m |

An M7 of the US
7th Armored
Division, Ardennes,
December 1944.

The same tank seen
from above.

An M7 in action during
the Korean War.

USA

# LVT (A) TRACKED LANDING VEHICLE

During the Second World War the USA developed a whole series of armoured and unarmoured amphibious transporters and fighting vehicles known as LVTs ('Landing Vehicles Tracked'). They were based on a pre-war design for an amphibious tracked vehicle for use in disaster areas which was to be propelled in the water by its tracks.

The first vehicles (LVT1) deployed by the US Marine Corps were unarmoured, which soon proved impractical in a combat zone. An armed and armoured version, the LVT1 (A), was thus developed (the 'A' standing for 'armoured'). The LVT2 (A) was an armoured personnel carrier that could hold up to 25 marines or the equivalent load. One disadvantage was the centrally positioned engine. Models LTV3 and LTV4 were equipped with engines positioned to the side and at the front respectively, which kept the rear free for a loading ramp. There was also a variant of each model equipped with a tank turret and a 3.7 cm cannon or 7.5 cm howitzer that was designed to provide supporting fire. LTVs in service with the British Army were used in the crossing of the Rhine in 1945. Including all the different versions, 18,322 LVTs were built.

| | LVT2 (A) |
|---|---|
| Combat weight: | 14,528 kg |
| Crew: | 3 + 25 |
| Dimensions in mm (length, width, height): | 7,950/3,250/2,500 |
| Engine: | Wright W-670 7-cylinder radial, petrol, air-cooled, 250 hp |
| Power/weight ratio: | 17.5 hp/tonne |
| Max. speed: | 32 km/h road, 12 km/h water |
| Range: | 240 km road, 160 km water |
| Armament: | 1 x 12.7 mm M2HB MG, 2 x 7.62 mm M1919A4 MGs |
| Armour: | max. 12.7 mm |
| Fording depth | amphibious |

A US Marine Corps LVT4.

A US Marines LVT4 (A), Iwo Jima, 1945.

*LVT2 (A): Kwajalein Atoll, February 1945.*

*LVT4 (A) with the turret of an M3 (37 mm cannon).*

ARTILLERY

# 3.7 CM PAK ANTI-TANK CANNON 35/36

| Calibre: | 37 mm |
|---|---|
| Combat weight: | 435 kg |
| Barrel length: | L/45 (1,665 mm) |
| Elevation: | −5° to +25° |
| Traverse: | 60° |
| Ammunition type and weight: | Armour piercing (AP): 0.69 kg; High velocity armour piercing/Armour piercing composite rigid (HVAP/APCR): 0.35 kg; High explosive (HE): 0.65 kg; Super calibre hollow charge (SCHC): 8.5 kg |
| Muzzle velocity: | AP: 760 m/s; HVAP/APCR: 1,030 m/s |
| Effective range: | 600 m |
| Maximum penetration (armour steel): | AP: 48 mm/500 m/90°; HVAP/APCR: 55 mm/500 m/360° |

*A 3.7 cm Pak 36 in an Afrikakorps anti-tank unit.*

At the beginning of the war in September 1939, the Pak ('Panzer-AbwehrKanone') 35/36 was the standard anti-tank cannon of the Wehrmacht. The cannon, developed by Rheinmetall (Rhine Metal), had been tried and tested in the Spanish Civil War (1936–39) and it was introduced into the anti-tank companies of the Wehrmacht in large numbers. At the start of September 1939 there were 11,200 of them. As it was small, the weapon was easy to disguise and to manoeuvre, two important attributes for an anti-tank cannon. Yet as early as the 1940 campaign on the Western Front, the troops had dubbed it the 'Heeresanklopfgerät', literally, 'the Army door-knocker', since it was no longer effective against the medium-sized and heavy French and British tanks. The 8.8 cm anti-aircraft gun frequently had to be deployed for anti-tank fire instead of the anti-tank cannon. Although it was clear by the end of 1940 at the latest that the 35/36 anti-tank cannon was outdated, a large number were still in service for the invasion of the Soviet Union in June 1941, where their inadequacy was again dramatically exposed. The 3.5 cm weapon was still effective against the Russian T-26 or BT-7 tanks, but against the new T-34, KW-1 and KW-2 it made no impact at all. The introduction of a new type of ammunition with a wolfram core (the Panzergranate 40) increased its armour-piercing effectiveness, but this was still insufficient. Consequently the Stielgranate 41, a high-calibre shell with a stabilizing tailpiece, was introduced in February 1942. These shells were 738 mm long and 159 mm in diameter and carried a hollow charge with 2.3 kg of explosive. The shell was inserted in the muzzle and could penetrate up to 180 mm of armour steel, but because of the cannon's limited muzzle velocity of 110 m/s, the enemy tank had to be within 200 m. Production was finally halted in March 1942, after 14,459 anti-tank cannon had been manufactured, but it was still deployed, for example, as an auxiliary weapon on Sd.Kfz. 250 and 251 half-track vehicles, until 1945.

*The 3.7 cm Pak being deployed in Russia. It became obsolete when the T-34 tank was introduced.*

# 5 CM PAK 38 ANTI-TANK CANNON

| Calibre: | 50 mm |
|---|---|
| Combat weight: | 986 kg |
| Barrel length: | L/60 (2,975 mm) |
| Elevation: | −8° to +27° |
| Traverse: | 65° |
| Ammunition type and weight: | AP: 2.06 kg; HVAP/APCR: 0.975 kg; HE: 1.96 kg; |
| Muzzle velocity: | AP: 823 m/s; HVAP/APCR: 1,198 m/s |
| Effective range: | 2,500 m |
| Maximum penetration (armour steel): | AP: 78 mm/500 m/90°; HVAP/APCR: 120 mm/500 m/90° |

*A 5 cm Pak 38 of the Afrikakorps.*

As early as 1935, Rheinmetall began developing a 5 cm anti-tank cannon, but the Pak 37 version was unconvincing. To improve its muzzle velocity, it was fitted with a longer barrel (L/60) and called the Pak 38. After the end of the 1940 campaign on the Western Front, the new anti-tank cannon was put into action, where it was deployed by individual anti-tank platoons, and its maximum range was around 9,400 m. Its protective plate was interestingly constructed, consisting of two 4 mm armour plates 25 mm apart. Firing ammunition with a hard wolfram core (APCR) the Pak 38 was an effective weapon, but the lack of wolfram severely restricted its use, and with normal armour-piercing ammunition the cannon was not always effective against the new Soviet tanks. So a shell with a stabilizing tailpiece was also developed and in March 1943 it was approved by the Army Ordnance Office as the Stielgranate 42. The shell weighed around 13.5 kg and had a hollow charge of 2.3 kg, which could penetrate 180 mm of armour steel. Because the Pak 38 was very heavy, it was usually towed by a 1 tonne tractor or actually mounted on it, making a makeshift but effective self-propelled anti-tank cannon. Variants of the Pak 38 were even installed in aircraft, and in total over 9,500 were produced.

*A 5 cm Pak 38 on a 1 tonne artillery tractor.*

*An artillery tractor towing a 5 cm Pak 38 in the Russian winter.*

GERMANY

## 7.5 CM PAK 40 ANTI-TANK CANNON

The 7.5 cm Pak was introduced in February 1942. Initially, only 15 were produced per month, although at the time a cannon that was effective against the T-34, KW-1 and KW-2 was badly needed. The Pak 40 was an effective weapon, but its excessive weight was one of the reasons why towed artillery was eventually withdrawn from the battlefield. Weighing just under 1,425 kg, the cannon could only be moved with difficulty by teams of men, so they had to be placed on vehicles. In addition, on account of its weight, it had a tendency to get stuck in Russian mud, and as

a result many were left behind when the Wehrmacht retreated from 1943 onwards. Nevertheless, increased weight was the price that had to be paid to manufacture cannon that could penetrate ever tougher tank armour. Consequently, the Pak 40 was often deployed as a self-propelled cannon, for example, on various Marder anti-tank vehicles, and was also installed in eight-wheel scout cars, half-track vehicles and even aircraft.

| | |
|---|---|
| Calibre: | 75 mm |
| Combat weight: | 1,425 kg |
| Barrel length: | L/46 (3,450 mmn) |
| Elevation: | −5° to +22° |
| Traverse: | 65° |
| Ammunition type and weight: | AP: 6.8 kg; |
| | HVAP/APCR: 4.1 kg; HE: 5.74 kg |
| Muzzle velocity: | AP: 790 m/s; |
| | HVAP/APCR: 990 m/s; |
| | HE: 550 m/s |
| Effective range: | AP: 2,500 m; |
| | HE: 7,600 m |
| Maximum penetration | AP: 132 mm/ |
| (armour steel): | 500 m/90°; HVAP/ |
| | APCR: 154 mm/500 m/90° |

*The Pak 40 was the most deployed anti-tank cannon in the Wehrmacht in the latter half of the Second World War.*

*The Pak 40 was also deployed in Italy and the rest of the Mediterranean region.*

*It was an effective weapon right to the end of the war, as it could penetrate the armour on most enemy tanks. In total, more than 23,300 Pak 40s were manufactured (including 11,728 in 1944 alone).*

# 8.8 CM PAK 43 AND 43/41 ANTI-TANK CANNON

*The 8.8 cm Pak 43.*

| Calibre: | 88 mm |
|---|---|
| Combat weight: | Pak 43: 3,650 kg; |
| | Pak 43/41: 4,380 kg |
| Barrel length: | L/71 (6,610 mm) |
| Elevation: | −8° to +40° (Pak 43); |
| | −8° to +38° |
| Traverse: | 360° (Pak 43); 56° (Pak 43/41) |
| Ammunition type and weight: | AP: 10.2 kg; |
| | HVAP/APCR: 7.3 kg; |
| | HE: 9.3 kg |
| Muzzle velocity: | AP: 1,000 mt/s; HVAP/ |
| | APCR: 1,130 m/s; HE: 750 m/s |
| Effective range: | AP: 4,000 m; |
| | HE: 15,300 m |
| Maximum penetration | AP: 190 mm/ |
| (armour steel): | 1,000 m/90°; HVAP/APCR: |
| | 241 mm/1,000 m/90° |

The Pak 43 was designed by Krupp and was actually conceived as a prototype in competition with Rheinmetall's 8.8 cm Flak 41. Nevertheless, it was accepted by the Army Ordnance Office as an anti-tank cannon. The weapon had a new type of cross-shaped gun mount, which meant that the cannon could be rotated 360°. But it was also expensive and complicated, which meant that it was not put into service until February 1944. The barrels of the 8.8 cm Pak 43 were also mounted on the gun carriage of the light Feldhaubitze 18 howitzer to make a less expensive and more readily available cannon: the 8.8 cm Pak 43/41. The first of these cannon were ready in February 1943, and they were manufactured until April 1944. Because the cannon was so tall, it was known as the 'Scheunentor', or barn door. The exceptionally large gun mount made the cannon very unwieldy, but it was extremely effective at penetrating tank armour and was feared by enemy tank personnel. The cannon was also deployed as a self-propelled weapon, as in

Nashorn and Elefant anti-tank vehicles. The KwK 43 L/71, which was installed in the Königstiger and Jagdpanther, for example, was a variant of the Pak 43. In total, 3,500 Pak 43s were produced.

# LEIG 18 7.5 CM LIGHT INFANTRY CANNON

*The 7.5 cm LeIG 18 infantry support cannon on the Eastern Front.*

| Calibre: | 75 mm |
|---|---|
| Combat weight: | 400 kg |
| Barrel length: | L/11.2 (884 mm) |
| Elevation: | −10° to +35° |
| Traverse: | 12° |
| Ammunition type and weight: | HE: 6 kg |
| Muzzle velocity: | HE: 220 m/s |
| Maximum range: | 3,375 m |

The LeIG 18 7.5 cm light infantry cannon was developed as early as 1927. It had a tipping breechblock and a simple box trail gun mount, and it was meant to be horse-drawn. So it initially had wooden wheels, which were later replaced by steel wheels with rubber tyres. The weapon was introduced in 1932, and at the beginning of the war 2,933 were available. Two different versions, which could be broken down into manageable loads, were also developed for mountain divisions and paratroops. In total, almost 12,000 of all the different versions of the LeIG were produced for the Wehrmacht.

## LEFH 18 AND LEFH 18M 10.5 CM LIGHT FIELD HOWITZER

The LeFH 18 light field howitzer was the Wehrmacht artillery divisions' standard weapon. Rheinmetall had designed it as early as 1929, but it was not introduced until 1935. Although it was solidly constructed, with modern elements such as a split-trail gun mount and a hydropneumatic reloading system, the LeFH 18 still had old-fashioned wooden or steel wheels, as it was designed to be horse-drawn. The modernized version, the LeFH 18M, which was designed to be transported by a motorized vehicle, had a muzzle brake, and with better ammunition its range was increased to 12,325 m. Both models were deployed right to the end of the war and were always bound together in batteries of four cannon apiece. The LeFH 18 was effective when aimed directly at tanks and other moving targets, and this howitzer could also be found on self-propelled gun carriages like the Wasp. In total, 6,986 LeFH 18 howitzers were manufactured, and it was in service in some countries' armies even after

1945 (Yugoslavia, Czechoslovakia, Chile, Argentina, Austria, Sweden and Portugal).

*A 10.5 cm LeFH 18 light field howitzer in the Afrikakorps.*

| Calibre: | 105 mm |
| --- | --- |
| Combat weight: | 1,985 kg |
| Barrel length: | L/28 (2,941 mm) |
| Elevation: | −5° to +42° |
| Traverse: | 56° |
| Ammunition type and weight: | HE: 14.81 kg; AP: 14 kg; HC: 12.3 kg |
| Muzzle velocity: | HE: 470 m/s |
| Maximum range: | 10,675 m |

## SIG 33 5.9 INCH (15 CM) INFANTRY HEAVY FIELD CANNON

| Calibre: | 150 mm |
| --- | --- |
| Combat weight: | 1,750 kg |
| Barrel length: | L/11.3 (1,688 mm) |
| Elevation: | −0° to +75° |
| Traverse: | 11° |
| Ammunition type and weight: | HE: 28.8 kg; HC: 24.6 kg; SCHC: 54 kg |
| Muzzle velocity: | HE: 240 m/s; SCHC: 105 m/s |
| Maximum range: | HE: 4,700 m; SCHC: 1,000 m |

*A SIG heavy infantry support cannon with 15 cm calibre.*

The Rheinmetall company had begun developing a 15 cm infantry support gun as early as 1927. The result, a 149.1 mm calibre weapon, was introduced in 1933 as the SIG 33 infantry heavy field cannon. In 1939, 410 of these cannon were in service. From July 1942 onwards, 300 mm super-calibre shells containing 27 kg of explosive were produced for the SIG 33. Overall, this cannon's design was robust and effective, but it was really too heavy for the infantry. In total, 4,565 SIG 33 cannon were manufactured before production ceased in March 1945.

# SFH 18 AND SFH 18M 15 CM HEAVY FIELD HOWITZER

| Calibre: | 150 mm |
|---|---|
| Combat weight: | 5,512 kg |
| Barrel length: | L/29.6 (4,440 mm) |
| Elevation: | −3° to +45° |
| Traverse: | 64° |
| Ammunition type and weight: | HE: 43.5 kg; AP: 14.6 kg; HL: 25 kg |
| Muzzle velocity: | HE: 620 m/s |
| Maximum range: | 13,325 m |

*The 15 cm SFH 18 heavy infantry support cannon.*

The SFH 18 15 cm heavy field howitzer was manufactured jointly by Krupp, who made the gun mount, and Rheinmetall, who made the barrel, and was introduced in 1934. In 1939, the Wehrmacht had 1,353 SFH 18s. A new version with a muzzle brake, called the SFH 18M, was introduced in 1943. This howitzer was too heavy to be horse-drawn and it had a limited range – especially compared to the Russian ML-20 15.2 cm howitzer, which had a range of 17,300 m. So the world's first rocket-propelled shells were developed for the SFH 18; these had a range of up to 19,000 m but were not very accurate and rapidly wore out the barrel. After the war, some of these howitzers were put into service and partially modernized by Albania, Bulgaria, Portugal and Czechoslovakia.

# MRS 18 21 CM MORTAR

| Calibre: | 210 mm |
|---|---|
| Combat weight: | 16,700 kg |
| Barrel length: | L/29.3 (6,150 mm) |
| Elevation: | 0° to +70° |
| Traverse: | 16° |
| Ammunition types and weights: | HE: 43.5 kg; HP: 14.6 kg; AC: 25 kg |
| Muzzle velocity: | HE: 565 m/s |
| Maximum effective range: | HE: 16,700 m |
| Maximum penetration (CP): | 2,200 mm |

Introduced in 1939, the MRS 18 21 cm mortar was intended to replace a 21 cm mortar that dated back to 1916, but the latter remained in service until 1942. When the war broke out, 27 MRS 18 mortars were in service, with 8,300 rounds of ammunition. Because it was designed as siege artillery, it had concrete piercing shells, called Röchling shells, to destroy bunkers. It was also extremely heavy and had to be transported in two parts. In total, 711 of these mortars were manufactured.

*The MRS 18 21 cm mortar.*

## 2 CM FLAK 30 ANTI-AIRCRAFT GUN

The 2 cm Flak 30 was developed by Rheinmetall and introduced in 1934 as an improved version of the 2 cm MG C/30 L machine gun. Ammunition was inserted on the left side from a 20-cartridge anti-aircraft magazine. The lower gun mount consisted of a triangular steel frame that could be mounted on the 51 special trailer. In theory it could fire 280 rounds per minute, but in practice it managed closer to 120 rounds per minute. It took a team of eight men to operate this weapon: one to move it into place, one to aim it, one to find the range, and five gunners who constantly had to supply more ammunition and change overheated barrels. The 2 cm Flak 30 was first deployed in the Spanish Civil War, where two batteries were in service from 1936. During the Second World War, it was deployed mostly in light anti-aircraft companies, which had 12 guns each on the front line and 16 each in Germany. To make the gun more mobile, it was mounted on various self-propelled gun carriages, such as the Sd.Kfz. 10/4. It was also mounted on Maultier half-track vehicles or, as a makeshift measure, on trucks or large cars. Until production ceased in March 1945, more than 147,000 Flak 30 and 38 guns were manufactured.

*A 2 cm Flak 30 anti-aircraft gun on its trailer.*

| Calibre: | 20 mm |
|---|---|
| Combat weight: | 463 kg |
| Barrel length: | 2,300 mm |
| Elevation: | −12° to +90° |
| Traverse: | 360° |
| Ammunition type and weight: | HE-I: 0.12 kg |
| Muzzle velocity: | 900 m/s |
| Rate of fire: | 280 rpm (theoretically) |
| Maximum range: | 4,800 m |
| Maximum effective range (vertical): | 3,700 m |

## 2 CM FLAK 38 ANTI-AIRCRAFT GUN

| Calibre: | 20 mm |
|---|---|
| Combat weight: | 405 kg |
| Barrel length: | 2,252.5 m |
| Elevation: | −20° to +90° |
| Traverse: | 360° |
| Ammunition type and weight: | HE-I: 0.12 kg |
| Muzzle velocity: | 900 m/s |
| Rate of fire: | 450 rpm (theoretically) |
| Maximum range: | 4,800 m |
| Maximum effective range (vertical): | 3,700 m |

The Flak 38 was introduced in 1938 as an improved version of the Flak 30 – it weighed less at 450 kg, and had a higher theoretical rate of fire, 450 rpm (rounds per minute). A net was set up around the weapon to catch empty cartridges and protect those standing nearby, and it was transported on the 51 special trailer. It is also worth mentioning the 2 cm Flak 38 four-gun mount, theoretically capable of firing 1,800 rpm, which was conceived by the German Navy (Kriegsmarine) but was frequently deployed also by the Army and the Luftwaffe. Its ballistic effectiveness was the same as that of the 2 cm Flak 38. The first of the four-gun mounts was delivered in May 1940, with two foot pedals to select which guns to fire. When one of the levers was operated, only two guns (one left and one right) could fire while the others could be reloaded, and if both pedals were pressed, all four guns would fire. A shield could be attached to protect the soldiers operating the gun. Flak 38s were either transported on the 52 special trailer or motorized, mounted on various half-track vehicles (the Sd.Kfz 6/1 and Sd. Kfz. 7/1) or tank chassis. The single-gun and four-gun mounts were also deployed by the Army in tank platoons.

*A 2 cm Flak 38 four-gun mount being moved into position.*

GERMANY

# 3.7 CM FLAK 36 ANTI-AIRCRAFT GUN

| Calibre: | 37 mm |
|---|---|
| Combat weight: | 1,552 kg |
| Barrel length: | 3,626 mm |
| Elevation: | −8° to +85° |
| Traverse: | 360° |
| Ammunition type and weight: | HE-I: 0.635 kg |
| Muzzle velocity: | 820 m/s |
| Rate of fire: | 160 rpm (theoretically) |
| Maximum range: | 6,500 m |
| Maximum effective range (vertical): | 4,800 m |

*The 3.7 cm Flak 36 anti-aircraft gun on a Maultier (Mule) half-track vehicle.*

The 3.7 cm Flak 18 that had originally been introduced in the Wehrmacht used a complicated and expensive four-wheel gun carriage, but, most importantly, it was too heavy. To overcome this problem, it was mounted instead on a single-axle trailer, which reduced its weight by around 200 kg, with no loss of ballistic effectiveness. The new weapon was called the 3.7 cm Flak 36 which first used a simple Type 36 visor. Weapons using the Flak 40 visor were designated Flak 37s. Like the 3.7 cm Flak, 3.7 cm anti-aircraft guns were frequently mounted on self-propelled gun carriages to increase their mobility. Guns of this type were deployed throughout the war in all branches of the services, and they proved their effectiveness not only as anti-aircraft guns, but also in combat on the ground. By the end of the war, 15,170 Flak 36s and 37s had been manufactured.

# 3.7 CM FLAK 43 ANTI-AIRCRAFT GUN

| Calibre: | 37 mm |
|---|---|
| Combat weight: | 1,392 kg |
| Barrel length: | 3,300 mm |
| Elevation: | −7.5° to +90° |
| Traverse: | 360° |
| Ammunition type and weight: | HE-I: 0.635 kg |
| Muzzle velocity: | 820 m/s |
| Rate of fire: | 150 rpm (theoretically) |
| Maximum range: | 6,500 m |
| Maximum effective range (vertical): | 4,800 m |

and its actual rate of fire was around 300 rpm. For use on ships, the Flak 43 was mounted on a LM-42 triple-axle double gun carriage. By the time that production ceased in 1945, 6,103 Flak 43s had been built.

*A 3.7 cm Flak 43 two-gun mount.*

The 3.7 cm Flak 43 was another improved anti-aircraft gun: its weight was reduced to 1,392 kg, yet its rate of fire was increased. The soldiers operating the gun were protected by a splinter-proof shield, and the gun's ballistic effectiveness matched that of the 3.7 cm Flak 36. The first of these guns were delivered in February 1944. There was also a twin-gun unit whose barrels were, unusually, arranged one above the other, rather than next to each other. This version weighed about 2,780 kg

# 8.8 CM FLAK 18 AND 36 ANTI-AIRCRAFT GUNS

The legendary 'Eight-Eight' was introduced as the Flak 18 in the Wehrmacht in 1933. The terms of the 1919 Treaty of Versailles prevented Germany from developing or manufacturing her own heavy anti-aircraft gun, so engineers from Krupp went to Bofors, the Swedish arms manufacturer, to use their expertise, and the preliminary designs for the Flak 18 were produced in Sweden. As a rule, Wehrmacht weapons were designated according to the year in which they were first manufactured, or the year in which they were introduced into the Army. To maintain secrecy, however, all weapons developed after the 1919 ban had the model number 18. The original Flak 18 had a barrel made up of one part, but because barrel wear was particularly severe near the chamber, a three-part barrel was introduced for the Flak 36, which could only be replaced with the same specific parts. A version with improved communication between the controls and the gun was designated the Flak 37.

The 'Eight-Eight' was first deployed in the Spanish Civil War, and was later deployed in every branch of the German military and on every front in the Second World War. It did not gain its legendary reputation in its intended role as an anti-aircraft gun, but mostly in combat on the ground, particularly in anti-tank deployment. In the early years of the war, the 8.8 cm Flak was often the only weapon to make any impact against heavy tanks, and the Allies were afraid

| Calibre: | 88 mm |
|---|---|
| Combat weight: | 4,983 kg |
| Barrel length: | L/56 (4,930 mm) |
| Elevation: | –3° to +85° |
| Traverse: | 360° |
| Ammunition type and weight: | HE: 9.4 kg; AP: 10.2 kg |
| Muzzle velocity: | 820 m/s |
| Maximum penetration (armour steel): | 106 mm/ 1,000 m/360° |
| Maximum range: | 14,600 m |
| Effective range (vertical): | 8,000 m – Max: 10,000 m |

of its firepower: the 'Eight-Eight' could easily destroy armoured targets from around 1,800 m away. Nevertheless, it had two disadvantages: it was tall and relatively heavy.

*An 8.8 cm Flak 18 anti-aircraft gun being prepared for deployment.*

*An 8.8 cm Flak 36 anti-aircraft gun being deployed to protect an industrial site in the Ruhr.*

*The legendary 'Eight-Eight' being reloaded.*

*In the summer of 1944, more than 10,000 8.8 cm anti-aircraft guns were in service. In October that year alone, these guns fired more than 3.1 million rounds. Their importance is also reflected in the fact that one-third of all gun barrels manufactured in Germany in 1944 were made for 'Eight-Eights'. The British and Americans also deployed 'Eight-Eights' which they had seized from the Germans. A total of 20,754 8.8 cm anti-aircraft guns in this series were manufactured.*

# 8.8 CM FLAK 41 ANTI-AIRCRAFT GUN

| Calibre: | 88 mm |
|---|---|
| Combat weight: | 7,800 kg |
| Barrel length: | L/74 (6,545 mm) |
| Elevation: | −3° to +90° |
| Traverse: | 360° |
| Ammunition type and weight: | HE: 9.4 kg |
| Muzzle velocity: | 1,000 m/s |
| Maximum penetration (armour steel): | |
| | 192 mm/1,000 m/90°; |
| | 127 mm/2,000 mm/90° |
| Max effective range: | 10,675 m |

To cope with the increasing flying altitudes of enemy aircraft, the Luftwaffe invited tenders for a new 8.8 cm calibre anti-aircraft gun, and Rheinmetall's bid was successful. Much of the Flak 41 was completely new: it used a different kind of ammunition from previous models (though the calibre was the same), and it had a longer barrel, a different gun mount and an electronic detonation device. It was unveiled in 1941 but was not deployed until two years later.

The Flak 41 was even more effective than the 18, 36 or 37. Not only could it shoot higher; it could also shoot faster: up to 25 rpm. Yet it was also much more complicated and expensive to manufacture and maintain, and the ammunition cartridges used to jam

*Krupp built an experimental self-propelled anti-aircraft gun carriage in 1941, the 'experimental heavy anti-aircraft car' with the 8.8 cm Flak 41 anti-aircraft gun.*

the barrel continually. There were significantly fewer Flak 41s manufactured than earlier models.

*An 8.8 cm Flak 41 in firing position.*

*An 8.8 cm Flak 41 on a special platform.*

*The 8.8 cm Flak 41 anti-aircraft gun.*

*An early 8.8 cm Flak 41 with a cross-shaped gun mount.*

## 10.5 CM FLAK 38 ANTI-AIRCRAFT GUN

The 10.5 cm Flak 38 was originally developed for the German Navy, but in 1933 the order came from the Army Ordnance Office to convert it for use in the Army and the Luftwaffe. It was very advanced for its time, with many new features, including a pivoting gun mount, an electrically powered aiming device and an automatic reloading facility. Until 1939, four of these guns were delivered per month. They had some technical glitches, as the electrical systems did not work perfectly. So in 1939 various aspects of the gun, especially the electrical installations, were changed, and the improved weapons were called

| Calibre: | 105 mm |
|---|---|
| Combat weight: | 10,224 kg |
| Barrel length: | L/63.3 (6,648 mm) |
| Elevation: | −3° to +85° |
| Traverse: | 360° |
| Ammunition type and weight: | HE: 14.8 kg |
| Muzzle velocity: | 881 m/s |
| Maximum range: | 17,500 m |
| Effective range: | 9,450 m – Max: 12,100 m |

the 10.5 cm Flak 39. In 1944, 2,068 versions of both types were deployed by the Wehrmacht, and 3,755 were manufactured in total.

*A 10.5 cm Flak 38 anti-aircraft gun.*

## 12.8 CM FLAK 40 ANTI-AIRCRAFT GUN

| Calibre: | 128 mm |
|---|---|
| Combat weight: | 18,000 kg |
| Barrel length: | L/61.2 (7,835 mm) |
| Elevation: | −3° to +88° |
| Traverse: | 360° |
| Ammunition type and weight: | HE: 26.02 kg |
| Muzzle velocity: | 800 m/s |
| Maximum range: | 20,900 m |
| Effective range: | 10,675 m – Max: 14,800 m |

In 1936 Rheinmetall received the order to develop the 12.8 cm Flak 40, but it was not introduced into the Wehrmacht until 1941. It was equipped with an electric aiming device and an automatic reloading facility. Early versions could be transported in two parts, and later versions were transported in one piece on the 220 special trailer. However, because of the gun's weight, it was generally installed in one place or transported on rail gun carriages. Thus in 1944 there were six mobile Flak 40s, 242 Flak 40 installations and 201 Flak 40s deployed on rail gun carriages. The 12.8 cm anti-aircraft gun proved to be an excellent weapon, but its limitations were exposed in the heavy Allied attacks of late 1944. It was manufactured until the end of the war, and in total 1,129 were produced.

*Each ring round the barrel of this 12.8 cm Flak 40 anti-aircraft gun stands for one aircraft shot down.*

GERMANY

# 21 CM K 12 (E) RAIL CANNON

*The 8.3 inch (21 cm) K 12 (E) rail cannon.*

The Wehrmacht deployed a number of different rail cannon with calibres varying from 17 cm to 80 cm, but only in very small numbers, and they had a limited impact on the course of the war. Technically, however, some of them were real masterpieces. One of them, based on the famous Paris cannon of the First World War, was the 21 cm K 12 (E) cannon, with a maximum range of over 115,000 m; this was the greatest of all the guns of the Second World War and still retains its reputation today. The first

of these cannon types was put into service in March 1939, and a second, the 12 cm K 12 N, was produced in July 1940. Since neither cannon had any traverse (they could only be pointed straight ahead), either they had to be mounted on revolving platforms, or the gun carriage had to be placed on a circular track. In the entire Second World War, the 701st Artillery Battery, which deployed these cannon, fired precisely 83 shots! Certainly, the money and effort that went into the construction,

production and deployment of these cannon could have been spent more wisely in other areas. But in spite of their limited practical use, they are still masterpieces of engineering.

| Calibre: | 210 mm |
|---|---|
| Combat weight: | 308,000 kg |
| Barrel length: | L/158.5 (33,300 mm) |
| Elevation: | −25° to +55° |
| Traverse: | 0° |
| Ammunition type and weight: | HE: 107.5 kg |
| Muzzle velocity: | 1,500 m/s |
| Maximum range: | HE: 115,000 m |

*A 21 cm rail cannon on the French coast fires at a target on the other side of the English Channel. Photo taken from the German Army magazine, Signal.*

## 80 CM DORA AND GUSTAV RAIL CANNON

These two giant 80 cm cannon were ordered by the Wehrmacht high command in 1937, with a view to destroying the fortifications on the Maginot Line in Alsace. Gustav was named after Gustav Krupp von Bohlen und Halbach, senior partner in the Krupp company, while Dora was named after the wife of the engineer in charge of the project. Both of these cannon were completed too late for their intended purposes, so they were deployed on the Eastern Front instead. They were the largest cannon the world had ever (or has ever) seen, and had to be transported in several pieces, then assembled and mounted on a prepared emplacement. To assemble and disassemble each cannon, its emplacement and all the necessary tracks took around 4,000 men! Each cannon was defended against air strikes by an entire anti-aircraft regiment, as well as being protected against attacks from Soviet partisans by a guard regiment. Because neither cannon had any traverse, the tracks had to be laid down in a circle, and the cannon had to be aimed by shunting it round the track. To do so, Krupp developed two purpose-built V188 diesel locomotives, and the cannon could

be aimed while in motion by electric motors built into the gun carriage. As with all German rail cannon since the First World War Paris cannon, the shell cartridges were stored in a specially acclimatized car to keep the temperature of the nitroglycerine powder explosive at around 15°C. This was to optimize its combustion, and to make the latter as controllable as possible.

Of the two cannon, Gustav was the only one to see active service. It was deployed in the siege of Sebastopol in the Soviet Union in 1942, where it fired a total of 48 shots. The penetrative power of its huge 80 cm shells, which weighed 7.1 kg each, was enough to destroy an ammunitions dump protected by 30 m of rock. Dora was never deployed, and at the end of the war a third cannon was still being built. There were also plans for rocket-propelled shells that could reach targets more than 150 km away. After the end of the war, the US Army found the remains of two of the three cannon in Grafenwöhr, Bavaria: they had been exploded so that they would not fall into enemy hands intact. The other cannon fell into Soviet hands in Auerswalde, Saxony, also partially destroyed. The parts

| Calibre: | 800 mm |
| --- | --- |
| Combat weight: | 1,350,000 kg |
| Barrel length: | L/41 (32,800 mm) |
| Elevation: | −10° to +65° |
| Traverse: | 0° |
| Ammunition type and weight: | HE: 4,800 kg; CP: 7,100 kg |
| Muzzle velocity: | HE: 820 m/s; CP: 710 m/s |
| Maximum range: | HE: 47,000 m; CP: 38,000 m |
| Maximum penetration (concrete): | 10,000 mm |

that had remained intact and some of the wreckage were analysed by Soviet experts – it is not known what happened to the rest of the cannon. Again, Dora and Gustav were technical masterpieces, but they were basically a waste of materials, technological expertise and manpower.

*Dora, the 80cm rail cannon.*

# 4.7 CM M 35 ANTI-TANK CANNON

This 4.7 cm anti-tank cannon was originally designed by the Austrian firm Böhler and sold on the international market, so the Italians and the Dutch also had this weapon. The Italians manufactured it under licence as the 47/32 M 35 and deployed it as both an anti-tank and an infantry cannon. In fact, so many were manufactured in Italy that in effect it was an Italian weapon, though it

was produced in Austria until September 1940. After the German annexation of Austria in 1938, the Wehrmacht took charge of all 330 Pak M 35 cannon manufactured until 1940, calling it the Pak 35/36 (ö), but almost all were sold to Italy in February 1941. The Italians mounted it on self-propelled gun carriages based on the Sahariana all-terrain vehicle, and it was also adapted as a tank weapon.

| Calibre: | 47 mm |
| --- | --- |
| Combat weight: | 277 kg |
| Barrel length: | L/32 (1,525 mm) |
| Elevation: | −15° to +56° |
| Traverse: | 62° |
| Ammunition type and weight: | AP: 1.44 kg; HEAT: 2.37 kg |
| Muzzle velocity: | AP: 630 m/s; 250 m/s |
| Maximum range: | HE: 7,000 m |
| Maximum penetration (armour steel): | AP: 43 mm/ 500 m/90° |

*A 4.7 cm M 35 anti-tank cannon.*

# 7.5 CM 75/18 M 35 HOWITZER

| Calibre: | 75 mm |
| --- | --- |
| Combat weight: | 1,100 kg |
| Barrel length: | L/18.3 (1,572 mm) |
| Elevation: | −10° to +45° |
| Traverse: | 50° |
| Ammunition type and weight: | HE: 6.3 kg |
| Muzzle velocity: | HE: 400 m/s |
| Maximum range: | HE: 9,400 m |

The Italians always emphasized the importance of equipping their Alpini (mountain divisions) with good modern equipment. So in 1934, to replace the old Škoda weapons of the First World War, they produced the 75/18 M 34 mountain

howitzer. It could be disassembled quickly and easily, which meant that it could be transported by the 'Mule' half track in the mountains. A new howitzer based on this model was produced for the field divisions in 1935. It was easier to assemble, while having the same ballistic properties as the earlier model. The newer version was also exported to Portugal in 1940, and a number of these howitzers

were exchanged for raw materials with some South American states. The M 35 proved to be a good modern weapon, and it was also acquired and deployed by the Wehrmacht in 1943 as the 7.5 cm LeFH 255 (i).

*The 7.5 cm 75/18 howitzer.*

## 2 CM BREDA MODEL 35 ANTI-AIRCRAFT GUN

As indicated by its name, this anti-aircraft gun was introduced into the Italian Army in 1935. It was intended both as an anti-aircraft gun and for combat on the ground, and it had visors for both applications. It had a particularly interesting loading mechanism: a metal strip with 12 rounds was inserted in one side and came out of the other with the spent cartridges. Anti-aircraft guns of this kind were also

| Calibre: | 20 mm |
|---|---|
| Combat weight: | 307 kg |
| Barrel length: | L/65 (1,300 mm) |
| Elevation: | −5° to +80° |
| Traverse: | 360° |
| Ammunition type and weight: | HE: 0.135 kg |
| Muzzle velocity: | HE: 840 m/s |
| Rate of fire: | 230 rpm |
| Maximum effective range (vertical): | HE: 2,600 m |

*The 2 cm Breda M 35 anti-aircraft gun.*

deployed in all-terrain vehicles such as the Sahariana. From 1943 until the end of the war, the Wehrmacht deployed the 2 cm Model 35; initially they were acquired from the Italians, while later they were produced by Breda under German supervision.

## 9 CM 90/53 ANTI-AIRCRAFT GUN

| Calibre: | 90 mm |
|---|---|
| Combat weight: | 6,240 kg |
| Barrel length: | L/52.6 (4,736 mm) |
| Elevation: | −2° to +85° |
| Traverse: | 360° |
| Ammunition type and weight: | HE: 10.33 kg |
| Muzzle velocity: | HE: 830 m/s |
| Maximum effective range (vertical): | HE: 10,500 m |

also installed in trucks and tanks to create self-propelled artillery weapons. In total, 1,087 guns of this type were ordered, but by July 1943 only 539 had been delivered. Then the Ansaldo factories were taken over by the Germans and all 9 cm anti-aircraft guns subsequently manufactured were for the Wehrmacht. These guns were mostly used to defend northern Italian industrial sites against bombing raids and were known as the 9 cm Flak 309/I (i). British forces also seized a number of these guns on their advance through Italy and deployed them in defence of the ports they occupied.

The 9 cm anti-aircraft gun was solidly and intelligently constructed, and it was the most effective of all the Italian anti-aircraft guns in the Second World War, comparing favourably with any of its contemporary counterparts. It was developed and produced by Ansaldo, and the first guns of this kind were ready for deployment in 1939. It was used by the Italian Army not only as an anti-aircraft gun, but also as an anti-tank cannon and in coast batteries. As an anti-aircraft gun and an anti-tank cannon, it was in the same league as the legendary German 8.8 cm anti-aircraft gun. A number of 9 cm anti-aircraft guns were

*The Italian 9 cm 90/53 anti-aircraft gun.*

# 7 CM TYPE 92 INFANTRY CANNON

| Calibre: | 70 mm |
|---|---|
| Combat weight: | 212.25 kg |
| Barrel length: | L/11.3 (790 mm) |
| Elevation: | −8° to +70° |
| Traverse: | 45° |
| Ammunition type and weight: | HE: 3.97 kg |
| Muzzle velocity: | HE: 197 m/s |
| Maximum range | HE: 2,800 m |

*A Japanese 7 cm Type 92 cannon subsequently deployed by the Chinese in the Korean War.*

This cannon, introduced in 1932, was the Japanese Army's standard infantry support cannon during the Second World War, and each infantry battalion had two of them. Because it could be aimed so high, it could be used both as a cannon with a straight trajectory and as a mortar with a curved trajectory. Because it was very light and could be broken down into small parts, it was easy to transport, which was a significant advantage in Asian jungle warfare. After 1945 weapons of this kind were used by Chinese and Korean troops well into the 1950s.

# 15 CM TYPE 96 HOWITZER

| Calibre: | 149.1 mm |
|---|---|
| Combat weight: | 4,140 kg |
| Barrel length: | L/23.6 (3,523 mm) |
| Elevation: | −5° to +65° |
| Traverse: | 30° |
| Ammunition type and weight: | HE: 31.3 kg |
| Muzzle velocity: | HE: 540 m/s |
| Maximum range | HE: 11,900 m |

Although only a small number of weapons of this type (440) were produced compared to Western equivalents, it was the main weapon deployed by Japanese heavy artillery batteries from 1941 to 1945. Relative to other Japanese artillery cannon, this was a very modern weapon, and it was always meant to be transported by motor vehicles. It was first deployed in the Second Sino-Japanese War from 1937 onwards, and was immensely popular with the Japanese artillery troops, who rated it very highly.

*The 15 cm Type 96 howitzer.*

## 7.5 CM MODEL 1897 CANNON

This was the predecessor of all modern rapid fire cannon, and it was a world leader when introduced in the French Army in the late 19th century. In the First World War, it was the French artillery's standard cannon and was exported in large numbers after 1918 to Poland, Romania, Portugal and Greece, among other countries. More than 17,000 of these cannon are thought to have been manufactured, and in 1940 the French still had a large number of them. After its first encounters with the Russian T-34 and KW-1 tanks, the Wehrmacht based its makeshift 7.5 cm Pak 97/38 on the Model 1897 cannon it had seized in France and Poland, adding muzzle brakes to the original barrels and placing them on the gun mount of the 5 cm Pak 38. It is believed that around 700 of these cannon were assembled. At first, the Wehrmacht loaded them with ammunition left over by the French and the Poles, but this proved to be ineffective. Only special hollow charge shells (known as HEAT) made sufficient impact.

|  | Model 1897 | 97/38 anti-tank gun |
|---|---|---|
| Calibre: | 75 mm | 75 mm |
| Combat weight: | 1,160 kg | 1,190 kg |
| Barrel length: | L/36 (2,700 mm) | L/36 (2,700 mm) |
| Elevation: | −11° to +18° | −8° to +18° |
| Traverse: | 6° | 60° |
| Ammunition type and weight: | HE: 5.2 kg; FRAG: 7.24 kg | AP: 6.8 kg; HEAT: 4.8 kg |
| Muzzle velocity: | HE: 584 m/s; FRAG: 529 m/s | AP: 570 m/s; HEAT: 450 m/s |
| Maximum effective range (vertical): | HE: 8,500 m | 8,500 m |
| Maximum penetration (armour steel): | N/A | AP: 58 mm/1,000 mm/60°; HEAT: 90 mm/any distance/60° |

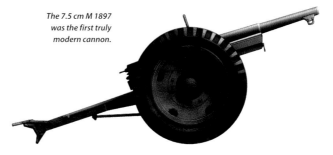

*The 7.5 cm M 1897 was the first truly modern cannon.*

## 2.5 CM HOTCHKISS MODEL 38/39 ANTI-AIRCRAFT GUN

| Calibre: | 25 mm |
|---|---|
| Combat weight: | 805 kg |
| Barrel length: | L/60 (1,500 mm) |
| Elevation: | −3° to +110° |
| Traverse: | 360° |
| Ammunition type and weight: | HE: 0.25 kg; AP: 0.3 kg |
| Muzzle velocity: | HE: 900 m/s |
| Maximum effective range (vertical): | HE: 2,500 m |
| Maximum penetration (armour steel): | AP: 35 mm/ 500 m/90° |

*A 2.5 cm Hotchkiss M 39 anti-aircraft gun in firing position.*

This anti-aircraft gun was produced by Hotchkiss, the French arms manufacturer, from 1938 onwards, and a later model with an improved gun mount was known as the M 39. It was used both as an anti-aircraft gun and as an anti-tank cannon, and its armour-piercing shells were effective for their time. Only around 1,000 anti-aircraft guns of this type were produced, and after France had been defeated in June 1940 the Wehrmacht seized and deployed most of them, renaming them the 2.5 cm Flak Hotchkiss 38/39 (f).

# 3 INCH (7.5 CM) MODEL 1930 AND 1936 ANTI-AIRCRAFT GUN

|  | Model 1930 | Model 1936 |
|---|---|---|
| Calibre: | 75 mm | 75 mm |
| Combat weight: | 3,800 kg | 4,100 kg |
| Barrel length: | L/45 (3,375 mm) | L/45 (3,675 mm) |
| Elevation: | +1° to +70° | +1° to +70° |
| Traverse: | 360° | 360° |
| Ammunition type and weight: | N/A | N/A |
| Muzzle velocity: | 700 m/s | 810 m/s |
| Maximum effective range (vertical): | 8,000 m | 8,200 m |

*A 7.5 cm M 30 anti-aircraft gun.*

Before 1940 France produced a number of different types of 7.5 cm anti-aircraft gun. Just three types of First World War anti-aircraft gun were still in service after 1918, but they were extensively modified to create a number of different new models. Most of them had their barrels modernized by Schneider, but at least five completely new types were manufactured and put into service before 1940. Because there were many different sorts of anti-aircraft gun but only a modest number of each, the French anti-aircraft divisions were relatively disorganized, so the cannon were not very wisely deployed. Nevertheless, because they were equally effective, these two relatively modern models were selected for further deployment by the Wehrmacht, which renamed them the 7.5 cm Flak M 30 (f) and M 36 (f).

*A German anti-aircraft battery with French 7.5 cm M 36 anti-aircraft cannon on the northern French coast.*

# 4 CM 2-POUNDER ANTI-TANK CANNON

When it first appeared in 1936, the British 2-pounder anti-tank cannon was undoubtedly the best of its kind. It had an innovative gun mount which gave it 360° traverse (it could be aimed in all directions), a useful property in anti-tank combat. It did, however, have one disadvantage: it did not have any high explosive (HE) ammunition. Since most British tanks were equipped with this weapon until 1942, this was a serious problem. Nevertheless, when it was first deployed, in the campaign on the Western Front in 1940, it had no trouble dealing with the German tanks. From 1941, to make up for the huge material

| Calibre: | 40 mm |
|---|---|
| Combat weight: | 797 kg |
| Barrel length: | L/52 (2,082 mm) |
| Elevation: | −5° to +23° |
| Traverse: | 360° |
| Ammunition type and weight: | AP: 0.907 kg |
| Muzzle velocity: | AP: 808 m/s |
| Maximum effective range: | AP: 1,000 m |
| Maximum penetration (armour steel): | |
| | AP: 42 mm/1,000 mm/60° |

losses of the British retreat from France in the previous year, including 500 of this weapon alone, a modified 2-pounder cannon was built, even though a 6-pounder anti-tank cannon was already being developed. When the British encountered Rommel's Afrikakorps in North Africa in 1941 and 1942, this decision was vindicated.

*The British 2-pounder anti-tank cannon with its crew.*

# 5.7 CM 6-POUNDER ANTI-TANK CANNON

| Calibre: | 57 mm |
|---|---|
| Combat weight: | 1,144 kg |
| Barrel length: | L/45 (2,564 mm) |
| Elevation: | −5° to +15° |
| Traverse: | 90° |
| Ammunition type and weight: | AP: 2.72 kg; |
| | APDS: 1.47 kg |
| Muzzle velocity: | AP: 821 m/s; |
| | APDS: 1,235 m/s |
| Effective range: | AP: 1,500 m – |
| | Maximum: 4,600 m |
| Maximum penetration (armour steel): | |
| | AP: 74 mm/1,000 m/60°/ |
| | APDS: 146 mm/1,000 m/60° |

Although it was at the design stage in 1938, the 6-pounder anti-tank cannon was not ready for production until late 1941. Nevertheless, it was a great success, and highly rated by the troops. It was not only produced under licence in the USA, but also used by some British tanks. The 6-pounder cannon fired high-explosive shells (which had finally been developed) and high-velocity armour-piercing (HVAP) shells (known in Britain as APCR, or 'armour-piercing composite rigid' shells), and in 1944 it was the first cannon in the world to fire armour-piercing, discarding sabot (APDS) shells, which greatly increased its penetrative power. Although towards the end of the war, the 6-pounder anti-tank cannon had trouble destroying German Panther and King Tiger tanks head-on, even with this new ammunition, it remained in the arsenal of the British Army until the mid-1960s. As well as various models with or without a muzzle brake, and with different barrel lengths, there was an interesting version with an automatic reloading facility installed in the De Havilland Mosquito fighter aircraft. The American M1 anti-tank cannon was based on the British 6-pounder cannon and was the US Army's standard anti-tank weapon from late 1943 onwards. The most significant difference between the two cannon was that the US version had a slightly longer barrel, yet it was rather less effective than its British counterpart.

*The 6-pounder anti-tank cannon.*

# 7.62 CM 17-POUNDER ANTI-TANK CANNON

| | |
|---|---|
| Calibre: | 76.2 mm |
| Combat weight: | 2,097 kg |
| Barrel length: | L/60 (4,580 mm) |
| Elevation: | −6° to +16.5° |
| Traverse: | 60° |
| Ammunition type and weight: | AP: 7.26 kg; |
| | APDS: 3.45 kg; HE: 6.98 kg |
| Muzzle velocity: | AP: 884 m/s; |
| | APDS: 1,203 m/s; |
| | HE: 876 m/s |
| Maximum range: | HE: 9,145 m |
| Maximum penetration (armour steel): | |
| | AP: 109 mm/1,000 m/60°; |
| | APDS: 231 mm/1,000 m/60° |

The British 17-pounder anti-tank cannon proved to be one of the best cannon of its kind, capable of dealing with practically every type of tank, not least because of its newly designed armour-piercing, discarding sabot (APDS) ammunition. In 1942 the first models were provisionally mounted on the same gun carriages as the 25-pounder howitzers, so that they could be deployed as soon as possible in the North African campaign against the German Tiger tanks, but standard models were mounted on heavy split trail gun mounts, which represented this weapon's only disadvantage, as it was almost impossible to move it without a motor vehicle. The 17-pounder cannon was also used as a self-propelled weapon (the Archer), and was deployed both as an anti-tank weapon (on the Wolverine) and on the Sherman Firefly and Centurion tanks.

*The 17-pounder anti-tank cannon.*

# 3.4 INCH (8.76 CM) 25-POUNDER FIELD CANNON

Built from 1938 onwards, the 25-pounder was the standard field cannon of all the Commonwealth forces in the war. Around 12,000 of these cannon were manufactured up to the end of hostilities, and it was still in many states' arsenals after 1945. It was called the '25-pounder' because of the approximate weight of its ammunition, and was extremely successful. It was also very popular with the troops, as it was reliable and did not suffer from technical glitches. In his memoirs, one Canadian artillerist describes how in 1944 his battery of 25-pounders in Normandy would often keep firing for so long that the barrels would start glowing red! This cannon had different models (or 'marks') of gun mount, barrel and barrel cradle, arranged in various configurations, and was one of the first weapons that could be deployed both as a cannon and as a

| | |
|---|---|
| Calibre: | 87.6 mm |
| Combat weight: | 1,800 kg |
| Barrel length: | L/31 (2,716 mm) |
| Elevation: | −5° to +45° |
| Traverse: | 360° |
| Ammunition type and weight: | HE: 7.36 kg; |
| | AP: 9 kg |
| Muzzle velocity: | HE: 518 m/s |
| Maximum range | HE: 12,250 m |

howitzer. The box trail gun mount looked conservative but was well designed. It allowed the cannon to be aimed high as a howitzer, and it had a disc at the base that could be lowered to the ground, which enabled gunners quickly to turn the cannon round 360°, a very useful property in anti-tank combat. The versatility of the 25-pounder also made it an excellent self-propelled weapon. It was deployed by the British in the North African campaign on special truck loading platforms and was fired over the driver's cab. It was also installed in the Bishop and Sexton self-propelled artillery weapons. The latter, which was open-topped, was built in larger numbers than any other British self-propelled artillery weapon.

*The British 25-pounder field cannon.*

## 14 CM MK. 2 FIELD CANNON

| Calibre: | 140 mm |
|---|---|
| Combat weight: | 6,190 kg |
| Barrel length: | L/31 (2,716 mm) |
| Elevation: | −5° to +45° |
| Traverse: | 60° |
| Ammunition type and weight: | HE: 45.36 kg |
| Muzzle velocity: | HE: 517 m/s |
| Maximum range | HE: 14,813 m |

**A**s it became increasingly likely that war would break out in Europe, the British Army came under pressure to replace its outdated 11.4 cm and 12.7 cm cannon and howitzers. In early 1939 a

new cannon in the same class was ordered. It was first introduced in May 1942, and it was deployed in the African campaign against Rommel's troops. At first, its range was disappointing, and only the introduction of a new shell, which

was around 9 kg lighter, improved this to an acceptable level. Yet it remained in the British Army armoury until the 1980s, and is still part of the arsenals of South Africa, Pakistan and New Zealand.

*The 14 cm Mark 2 field cannon.*

## 9.4 CM MK.1 ANTI-AIRCRAFT GUN

| Calibre: | 94 mm |
|---|---|
| Combat weight: | 9,316 kg |
| Barrel length: | L/50 (4,700 mm) |
| Elevation: | −6° to +80° |
| Traverse: | 360° |
| Ammunition type and weight: | HE: 12.7 kg |
| Muzzle velocity: | HE: 792 m/s |
| Maximum range | HE: 18,800 m |
| Maximum effective range (vertical): | HE: 9,755 m |

**T**he 9.4 cm gun was the British Army's standard heavy anti-aircraft gun throughout the Second World War. Its development had begun in the early 1930s, but it did not go into production until 1937 – only just in time to produce large numbers for the outbreak of war. This gun had many innovative features, such as remote fire control. Only reloading had to be done manually.

Yet this made it difficult to aim the gun for combat on the ground, which meant that, unlike the German 'Eight-Eight', it was not easy to use the gun to attack tanks. From 1943, an automatic reloading

mechanism was introduced, increasing its rate of fire from 25 to 30 rpm.

*A British 9.4 cm anti-aircraft gun seized by the German Army at Dunkirk in 1940.*

SOVIET UNION

# 4.5 CM MODEL 1937 ANTI-TANK CANNON

When the Red Army was in need of a modern anti-tank weapon in the 1930s, the Soviet Union still enjoyed close economic ties with Germany enabling it to acquire some Rheinmetall 3.7 cm anti-tank cannon. The Russians studied these weapons, made a few alterations (a larger calibre, different sights) and produced the 4.5 cm Model 32, which still had wooden wheels and no suspension. The main variant, the Model 1937, had modern rubber tyres and suspension. During the Winter War against Finland (1939–40), the Finns seized hundreds of these cannon and deployed them themselves. In June 1941 it was the Red Army's standard anti-tank cannon, but, like the German 3.7 cm anti-tank cannon, it was no longer effective. So a new version was introduced in 1942 with a longer barrel (L/68.6, or 3,087 mm). Anti-tank cannon of both types were also acquired by the Wehrmacht, which renamed them the 4.5 cm Pak 184 (r). The Model 1942 remained in the Red Army arsenal after the end of the war, and, according to Russian sources, 56,742 cannon of this type were produced in total.

| Calibre: | 45 mm |
|---|---|
| Combat weight: | 425 kg |
| Barrel length: | L/46 (2,070 mm) |
| Elevation: | −5° to +25° |
| Traverse: | 60° |
| Ammunition type and weight: | AP: 1.43 kg; HE: 2.15 kg |
| Muzzle velocity: | AP: 760 m/s; HE: 340 m/s |
| Effective range | AP: 500 m (max. 4,400 m) |
| Maximum penetration (armour steel): | AP: 35 mm/500 m/60° |

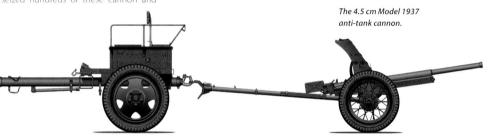

*The 4.5 cm Model 1937 anti-tank cannon.*

# 5.7 CM ZIS-2 MODEL 1943 ANTI-TANK CANNON

Because they could foresee that the 4.5 cm anti-tank cannon would soon become obsolete, the Russians began developing a new 5.7 cm anti-tank cannon in 1940, but technical difficulties halted its introduction into the Red Army until 15 June 1943. Production was halted in 1949, after 13,400 had been manufactured. They were very effective weapons, and could penetrate the armour of most German combat vehicles, particularly when they started firing high-velocity armour-piercing (HVAP) ammunition. The ZIS-2 was also installed

| Calibre: | 57 mm |
|---|---|
| Combat weight: | 1,250 kg |
| Barrel length: | L/73 (4,159 mm) |
| Elevation: | −5° to +25° |
| Traverse: | 54° |
| Ammunition type and weight: | AP: 1.43 kg; APCR: 1.79 kg |
| Muzzle velocity: | AP: 990 m/s; APCR: 1,270 m/s |
| Maximum effective range | AP: 2,000 m |
| Maximum penetration (armour steel): | AP: 80 mm/1,000 m/90° APCR: 105 mm/1,000 m/90° |

in the M-3 half-track vehicle, creating the SU-57 self-propelled artillery weapon, and in some T-34 tanks, creating the T-34/57 variant. Some cannon of this type were seized by the Wehrmacht, which renamed them the Pak 208 (r) and deployed them with some success.

*A Russian 5.7 cm ZIS-2 anti-tank cannon.*

# 7.62 CM ZIS-3 MODEL 1936, 1939 AND 1942 FIELD CANNON

The Red Army artillery's standard weapons were 7.62 cm field cannon, which were deployed both as anti-tank cannon and for a variety of other uses. The original Model 1936 (of which a total of 2,844 were manufactured) was judged by the Red Army to be too heavy, so a lighter version with a shortened barrel and altered recoil system went into production in 1939. In total, 9,812 new variant weapons were manufactured. Because the cannon had a relatively high muzzle velocity and produced a distinctive sound when fired, the German soldiers nicknamed it the 'Ratsch-Bumm'. After invading Russia, the Wehrmacht seized huge numbers of these cannon and their ammunition, renaming them the 7.62 cm Pak 36 (r) and Pak 39 (r). Because the Germans did not have a comparable anti-tank weapon, they produced their own ammunition for the captured cannon, achieving even

|  | Model 1936 | Model 1939 | Model 1942 |
|---|---|---|---|
| Calibre: | 76.2 mm | 76.2 mm | 76.2 mm |
| Combat weight: | 1,620 kg | 1,470 kg | 1,116 kg |
| Barrel length: | L/51.1 | L/42 | L/42.6 |
|  | (3,894 mm) | (3,200 mm) | (3,240 mm) |
| Elevation: | −6° to +43° | −6° to +45° | −5° to +37° |
| Traverse: | 57° | 57° | 54° |
| Ammunition type and weight: | HE: 6.3 kg; AP: 6.3 kg | HE: 6.23 kg; AP: 6.3 kg | HE: 6.3 kg; AP: 6.3 kg; HEAT: 3.94 kg |
| Muzzle velocity: | HE: 700 m/s | HE: 662 m/s | HE: 680 m/s |
| Maximum effective range: | HE: 13,620 m | HE: 13,290 m | HE: 13,290 m |

better results than the Russians. They also armed the Marder self-propelled artillery weapon with both types of Russian cannon. In order to offset their enormous losses of cannon in the first months of the German invasion, the Russians put the 7.6 cm ZIS-3 field cannon into production in 1942. It was far lighter than previous models, and could be produced quickly and cost-effectively. Hence, there were a lot of similarities between the

ZIS-2 and ZIS-3 gun carriages. The ZIS-3 was one of the main artillery weapons of the Soviet Union and its allies in the Second World War, and it was also installed in the SU-76 as a self-propelled artillery weapon. Up to 1945 49,016 units of this versatile and effective weapon had been produced, and it remained in production after the war, being manufactured both in the Soviet Union and under licence in other countries, including China. Large numbers of ZIS-3 cannon were also exported, and a number of countries in the developing world still have them in their arsenals.

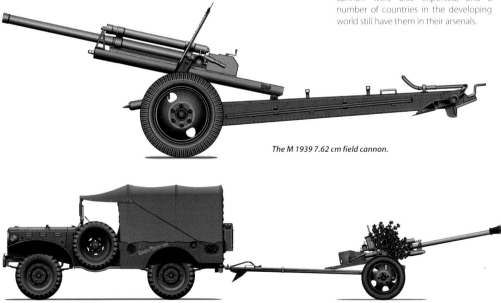

*The M 1939 7.62 cm field cannon.*

*A 7.62 cm ZIS-3 being towed by a Dodge WC-51, which the Soviet Union received as part of its Lend-Lease agreement with the USA.*

# 12.2 CM M-30 MODEL 1938 HOWITZER

The M-30 howitzer was produced from 1938 onwards, hence its designation. Like most other Soviet cannon, it was noted for being very resilient. It was mounted on the T-34 tank chassis to create the SU-122 self-propelled artillery weapon. Because of its own shortage of similar weapons, the Wehrmacht also deployed this howitzer, renaming it the 12.2 cm 396 (r) heavy field howitzer. Up to 1945, 17,526 of these howitzers had been manufactured, and cannon of the same sort were still deployed for decades after the war. China also produced large numbers of these weapons under licence after 1945, calling them the 54 and 54-1.

| Calibre: | 122 mm |
|---|---|
| Combat weight: | 2,450 kg |
| Barrel length: | L/23 (2,800 mm) |
| Elevation: | −3° to +65.5° |
| Traverse: | 49° |
| Ammunition type and weight: | HE: 21.76 kg; HEAT: 13.2 kg |
| Muzzle velocity: | HE: 515 m/s |
| Maximum range: | HE: 11,800 m |
| Maximum penetration (armour steel): | |
| | HEAT: 500 mm/200 m/90° |

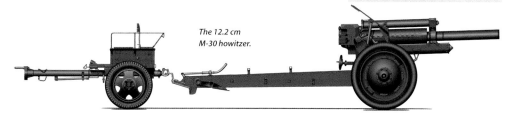

The 12.2 cm M-30 howitzer.

*The ZIS-3 was the Red Army's standard artillery weapon.*

## 15.2 CM D-1 MODEL 1943 HOWITZER

To simplify production and reduce weight, this howitzer was manufactured in a special way, which gained popularity in the Soviet Union during the course of the war. The barrel of the 15.2 cm Model 1938 was connected to the strengthened split trail gun mount of the 12.2 cm M-30 howitzer. To function properly, this combination needed a large muzzle brake to reduce recoil and avoid

| Calibre: | 152.4 mm |
|---|---|
| Combat weight: | 3,600 kg |
| Barrel length: | L/24.6 (4,201 mm) |
| Elevation: | −3° to +65.5° |
| Traverse: | 35° |
| Ammunition type and weight: | HE: 40 kg |
| Muzzle velocity: | HE: 508 m/s |
| Maximum range | HE: 12,400 m/s |

overstretching the smaller gun mount, but it made an effective howitzer, which weighed more than half a tonne less than its predecessor. From 1943 to 1945, 1,404 D-1 type howitzers were manufactured, and production continued after the war. In fact, it was still a common weapon in Eastern Bloc countries and among Soviet allies in the developing world until the 1990s.

*The 15.2 cm D-1 howitzer.*

## 15.2 CM ML-20 MODEL 1937 CANNON-HOWITZER

| Calibre: | 152.4 mm |
|---|---|
| Combat weight: | 7,128 kg |
| Barrel length: | L/32.3 (4,925 mm) |
| Elevation: | −2° to +65.5° |
| Traverse: | 58° |
| Ammunition type | HE: 43.56 kg; |
| and weight: | AP: 48.8 kg |
| Muzzle velocity: | HE: 655 m/s |
| Maximum range | HE: 17,250 m |
| Maximum penetration (armour steel): | |
| | AP: 124 mm/1,000 m/90° |

This weapon was designed in the mid-1930s to replace outdated cannon. It was one of the first cannon-howitzers, in that it could fire ammunition in a straight or a curved trajectory. The earliest version of this weapon was first produced in 1937, and although it had metal wheels it did not yet have rubber tyres. Further alterations were made over time – for example, the barrel was lengthened from L/29 to L/32.3. Among this howitzer's distinctive features were its 'horns', coil springs on either side of the barrel to offset its weight. The cannon-howitzer was the Red Army artillery corps' standard

weapon and was produced in large numbers (around 7,000 up to 1945) for a heavy cannon. At the beginning of the campaign on the Eastern Front in June 1941, 2,800 of these cannon were ready for deployment, but the Wehrmacht seized 974 of these highly rated weapons, renaming them 15.2 cm 433/1 (r) cannon-howitzers. In fact, they were deployed

so often that the Germans manufactured special ammunition for them. The ML-20 was also installed in the SU-152 and JSU-152 self-propelled artillery weapons, and in the Eastern Bloc the last examples of these cannon-howitzers were only taken out of service in the 1980s.

*The 15.2 cm ML-20 cannon-howitzer.*

# 20.3 CM B-4 M 1931 HOWITZER

| Calibre: | 203 mm |
|---|---|
| Combat weight: | 15,800 kg |
| Barrel length: | L/22 (4,466 mm) |
| Elevation: | −0° to +60° |
| Traverse: | 8° |
| Ammunition type and weight: | HE: 100 kg; CP: 146 kg |
| Muzzle velocity: | HE: 573 m/s |
| Maximum range | HE: 16,000 m |
| Maximum penetration (concrete): | CP: 1,000 mm |

*The 20.3 cm B-4 M 1931 howitzer.*

More units of this 20.3 cm howitzer were manufactured by the Soviet Union than of any other heavy artillery cannon in the entire Second World War. While no more than a few dozen other weapons with calibres ranging from 20.3 cm to 30.5 cm were produced before 1941, 944 of the two main variants of this howitzer, the B-4 and B-4 M (which had a new four-wheel gun carriage), were manufactured. Howitzers of this type were used by front-line artillery, and they were designed especially for sieges, so they had special concrete-piercing (CP) shells. So that it could move more easily over Russian roads in typically difficult conditions, the gun carriage had chain tracks around its wheels. At the start of the Russian campaign, German troops seized a number of these howitzers, including 27 of both types in Dubno in June 1941, renaming them the 20.3 cm 503/1 (r) and 503/2 (r) howitzers and subsequently deploying them. By March 1944, however, the Wehrmacht only had three left.

# 3.7 CM MODEL 1939 ANTI-AIRCRAFT GUN

| Calibre: | 37 mm |
|---|---|
| Combat weight: | 2,100 kg |
| Barrel length: | L/74 (2,729 mm) |
| Elevation: | −5° to +85° |
| Traverse: | 360° |
| Ammunition type and weight: | HE: 0.732 kg; AP: 0.758 kg |
| Muzzle velocity: | HE: 880 m/s |
| Rate of fire: | 180 rpm (theoretically) |
| Maximum range | 8,400 m |
| Maximum penetration (vertical): | 4,000 m |

The development of this 3.7 cm anti-aircraft gun began in 1938. It was based on designs from the 1930s by the Swedish manufacturer Bofors, as is very clear from its appearance, and the first 15 guns were produced in 1939, the same year in which it was introduced in the Red Army as the 37 mm 61-K Model 1939. Around 19,000 of them were produced from 1939 to 1946, and the gun was one of the earliest weapons of the forces of the German Democratic Republic, where

*A 3.7 cm M 39 (r) anti-aircraft gun being deployed by the German Army.*

it remained in service until the 1960s. A naval version of this gun was also produced in large numbers, and almost all the ships in the Soviet Navy had them until well into the 1950s.

## 7.6 CM MODEL 1931 AND 1938 ANTI-AIRCRAFT GUN

| Calibre: | 76.2 mm |
|---|---|
| Combat weight: | 3,650 kg |
| Barrel length: | L/55 (4,200 mm) |
| Elevation: | −3° to +82° |
| Traverse: | 360° |
| Ammunition type and weight: | HE: 6.3 kg |
| Muzzle velocity: | HE: 815 m/s |
| Maximum effective range (vertical): | HE: 7,500 m |
| Maximum penetration (armour steel): | |
| | AP: 68 mm/1,000 m/90° |

*The 7.62 cm M 1938 anti-aircraft gun.*

The design of this Soviet anti-aircraft gun was based on the Bofors 7.5 cm Model 1925, and Rheinmetall designs for an anti-aircraft gun of the same dimensions. The earliest examples of this gun only had a single-axle, two-wheeled gun carriage, but because this proved to be impractical for a heavy anti-aircraft gun, the Model 1938 was introduced with an improved, four-wheel gun carriage and minor alterations to the gun itself. At the beginning of the German campaign on the Eastern Front, these anti-aircraft guns were one of the mainstays of the Red Army, but large numbers of them were seized by the Germans, who renamed them the Flak 31 (r) and 38 (r). They were frequently deployed as part of Germany's home defence or supplied to Germany's allies. When the Russian ammunition ran out, the guns were converted to fire 8.8 cm ammunition. By the time production was halted in 1939, 4,781 of these guns had been manufactured.

## 8.5 CM MODEL 1939 ANTI-AIRCRAFT GUN

| Calibre: | 85 mm |
|---|---|
| Combat weight: | 3,057 kg |
| Barrel length: | L/52 (4,460 mm) |
| Elevation: | −2° to +82° |
| Traverse: | 360° |
| Ammunition type and weight: | HE: 9.2 kg; AP: 9.2 kg |
| Muzzle velocity: | HE: 800 m/s |
| Maximum effective range (vertical): | HE: 7,600 m |
| Maximum penetration (armour steel): | |
| | AP: 71 mm/1,000 m/60° |

The 8.5 cm anti-aircraft gun was one of the best and most versatile of all the Soviet guns and cannon, which on the whole were generally effective weapons. Although it did not particularly stand out when it first appeared in 1939, it was a neatly and intelligently designed gun. Right from the outset, it was designed for combat on the ground as well as anti-aircraft fire, and was equipped with appropriate ammunition and sights for both. In fact, when the Soviets needed an effective anti-tank weapon during the war, it provided an excellent basis for the weapons in the T-34/85 and the SU-85. The Wehrmacht deployed this gun as the 8.5 cm Flak M 39 (r) until it ran out of Russian ammunition, after which many guns of this type were fitted with new chambers and barrels to fire 3.5 cm ammunition. Some of these guns were given to the Finnish Army. Up to 1945, 13,422 of these anti-aircraft guns had been manufactured, and they remained in the arsenals of almost all the Eastern Bloc countries until the 1970s.

*The 8.5 cm M 1939 anti-aircraft gun.*

USA

## 3.7 CM M3 ANTI-TANK CANNON

| | |
|---|---|
| Calibre: | 37 mm |
| Combat weight: | 413.7 kg |
| Barrel length: | L/56.6 (2,095 mm) |
| Elevation: | −10° to +15° |
| Traverse: | 60° |
| Ammunition type and weight: | AP: 0.87 kg; |
| | HE: 0.87 kg; FRAG: 0.73 kg |
| Muzzle velocity: | AP: 762 m/s |
| Effective range | AP: 500 m − |
| | HE Max: 8,700 m |
| Maximum penetration (armour steel): | |
| | AP: 53 mm/500 m/60° |

The M3 was introduced in 1937, and it was the US armed forces' standard anti-aircraft gun when America entered the war in December 1941. But it was already dated by then, and production stopped in late 1943, when the 5.7 cm M1 anti-aircraft gun was introduced. Nevertheless, the M3 was deployed in the Pacific until the end of the war, as

Japanese tanks were only lightly armoured. The gun's light weight was a major advantage in jungle warfare, as it did not have to be towed by a motor vehicle. M3s were particularly effective when firing fragmenting ammunition (FRAG) against Japanese infantry attacks. They also used the same ammunition as the M5 and M6 tank cannon.

*The 3.7 cm M3 anti-tank cannon...*

## 7.62 CM M5 ANTI-TANK CANNON

Development of this anti-tank cannon began in 1940. It was based on the M3 anti-aircraft gun of the same calibre, and it had the same gun carriage as the 10.5 cm M2 howitzer. The first prototypes were already complete in late 1941, but the US Army decided that, because of the gun's weight, it would be more sensible to deploy it as a self-propelled weapon.

This project (which would finally produce the M-10 anti-tank vehicle) progressed relatively slowly, so the first M5s were not ready for serial production until late 1942. The M5 was a solid design and was deployed until the end of the war, but it could not replace the 5.7 cm anti-tank cannon.

| | |
|---|---|
| Calibre: | 76.2 mm |
| Combat weight: | 2,210 kg |
| Barrel length: | L/50 (3,800 mm) |
| Elevation: | −5° to +20° |
| Traverse: | 45° |
| Ammunition type and weight: | AP: 6.8 kg |
| Muzzle velocity: | 792 m/s |
| Effective range | AP: 2,000 m |
| Maximum penetration (armour steel): | |
| | AP: 71 mm/1,000 m/60° |

*...and the 7.62 cm M5 anti-tank cannon.*

USA

# 9 CM M1 ANTI-AIRCRAFT GUN

The M1 was built to replace the proven but dated 7.6 cm M3 anti-aircraft gun, whose range was no longer sufficient to hit modern fighter aircraft flying at high altitudes. So work began on a design for this 9 cm anti-aircraft gun in 1938 and it was introduced into the US Army in May 1941. It was a well-designed weapon with many modern features, such as remote control for gun elevation and traverse,

| Calibre: | 90 mm |
|---|---|
| Combat weight: | 8,618 kg |
| Barrel length: | L/52.5 (4,728 mm) |
| Elevation: | −0° to +80° |
| Traverse: | 360° |
| Ammunition type and weight: | HE: 10.61 kg |
| Muzzle velocity: | HE: 823 m/s |
| Effective range (vertical): | HE: 10,300 m – Max: 12,050 m |

and a spring-loaded rammer to make reloading easier and increase the firing rate. Unfortunately, the rammer proved to be faulty, and it was often removed by artillerists. Nevertheless, the M1 remained the standard US anti-aircraft gun long after the end of the war.

*A US Army M-1 anti-aircraft installation on Okinawa.*

# 7.5 CM M1A1 AND M8 PACK-HOWITZER

| Calibre: | 75 mm |
|---|---|
| Combat weight: | 607.4 kg |
| Barrel length: | L/16 (1,200 mm) |
| Elevation: | −5° to +45° |
| Traverse: | 6° |
| Ammunition type and weight: | HE: 6.35 kg |
| Muzzle velocity: | HE: 381 m/s |
| Maximum range: | HE: 8,780 m |

This weapon was developed as early as 1927 but not produced in large numbers until the war broke out. It was originally intended for mountain divisions, as well as other divisions which needed a light but effective howitzer which could be transported by teams of men or pack animals (hence the term 'pack-howitzer'). To make transportation easier, it was possible to dismantle the gun and carry it in six separate loads, the heaviest of which weighed just 100 kg, and it took a trained team only three minutes to assemble the gun.

A modern version with metal wheels and rubber tyres, called the M8, was introduced in 1936 especially for

*The 7.5 cm M8 pack-howitzer.*

paratroopers, and in that form it remained in the US and British armed forces' arsenals until the 1960s.

# 10.5 CM M2 A1 HOWITZER

The 10.5 cm M2 A1 howitzer was the US Army artillery divisions' standard weapon in the Second World War and beyond. Although the earliest models of this weapon were produced as early as 1928, large-scale serial production began only in early 1941. This robust, resilient weapon had a split trail gun mount, a hydro-pneumatic recoil system, and single piece ammunition (the shell and its cartridge were loaded together). When deployed as an anti-tank weapon, it was also loaded with hollow charge ammunition.

| | |
|---|---|
| Calibre: | 105 mm |
| Combat weight: | 2,030 kg |
| Barrel length: | L/22 (2,310 mm) |
| Elevation: | −5° to +66° |
| Traverse: | 46° |
| Ammunition type and weight: | HE: 14.97 kg |
| Muzzle velocity: | HE: 472 m/s |
| Maximum range: | HE: 11,200 m |

*The 10.5 cm
M2 A1 howitzer.*

*After 1945 the M2 A1 was renamed the M101 and exported in large numbers. It has been put into service in 67 countries, and it is still in some of their arsenals. Because of this howitzer's widespread use in the West, its ammunition has become almost standard for its calibre.*

*An M2 A1 battery in firing position.*

*An M2 A1 howitzer firing on German positions, France, August 1944.*

# 15.5 CM M1 HOWITZER

| Calibre: | 155 mm |
|---|---|
| Combat weight: | 5,760 kg |
| Barrel length: | L/23.4 (3,620 mm) |
| Elevation: | −2° to +63° |
| Traverse: | 49° |
| Ammunition type and weight: | HE: 42.96 kg |
| Muzzle velocity: | HE: 564 m/s |
| Maximum range: | HE: 14,600 m |

*The 15.5 cm M1 howitzer being deployed.*

The 15.5 cm M1 howitzer was one of a new generation of American artillery weapons introduced in the early 1940s. Work began on its design in 1940, and the first of these howitzers were delivered to the US armed forces in 1941. The M1 howitzer was a very modern design for its time: it was designed to be transported by a motor vehicle, which was by no means the norm in 1940. Even the Wehrmacht, one of the best-equipped armies in the world in 1940, still had a large number of horse-drawn cannon at the time. The split trail gun mount had only a small protective shield, but it was very robust and could take heavy loads, and it had a spring on either side of the barrel to keep it level. Wherever the US Army was fighting in the war, the 15.5 cm M1 howitzer was there, and more than 6,000 were manufactured up to 1945. After the war it was renamed the M114 and exported to over 40 countries. Almost every US ally after 1945 received this howitzer; it is still in frequent use today, and some arms companies are still prepared to modernize it.

# 15.5 CM M2 'LONG TOM' CANNON

The M2 cannon was nicknamed 'Long Tom' on account of its long barrel. It was based on the French 15.5 cm cannon, which the US Army had deployed in the First World War. Impressed by the cannon's effectiveness, the US designed its own version in the 1930s, but it did not go into production until 1941. The M1 was a very powerful and accurate weapon, although it was extremely large and heavy. Moreover, the breech lock did not always close completely, which could cause accidents. The improved M2 became a standard weapon in the US Army and proved to be one of the best of its kind; it was still used by the US Army and its allies after the war. It had an eight-wheel gun mount on account of its weight, but its wheels could be raised while firing, so that the weapon rested directly on the gun carriage, improving its stability and accuracy.

| Calibre: | 155 mm |
|---|---|
| Combat weight: | 13,880 kg |
| Barrel length: | L/45 (6,970 mm) |
| Elevation: | −1.5° to +63° |
| Traverse: | 60° |
| Ammunition type and weight: | HE: 90.72 kg |
| Muzzle velocity: | HE: 853 m/s |
| Maximum range: | HE: 23,220 m |

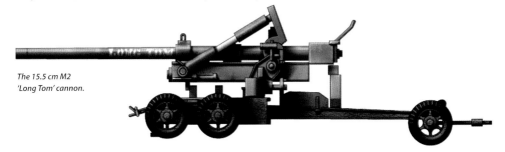

*The 15.5 cm M2 'Long Tom' cannon.*

# 20.3 CM M1 HOWITZER

Along with the 15.5 cm M2 cannon, this was the US Army's standard artillery weapon in the final stages of the war, and both weapons used the same eight-wheel gun carriage and two-wheel limber. Development began as early as 1939 but progressed very slowly because of technical difficulties, and the first howitzers of this type were only delivered to the Army in January 1944. Although its

| Calibre: | 203 mm |
|---|---|
| Combat weight: | 134,380 kg |
| Barrel length: | L/25 (5,080 mm) |
| Elevation: | −2° to +65° |
| Traverse: | 60° |
| Ammunition type and weight: | HE: 90.72 kg |
| Muzzle velocity: | HE: 595 m/s |
| Maximum range: | HE: 17,000 m |

heavy shells, which weighed 90.72 kg each, had a devastating effect on its targets, the 20.3 cm howitzer was never as accurate as the 15.5 cm M2 cannon.

*The 20.3 cm M1 howitzer in firing position.*

*The 20.3 cm M1 howitzer being deployed in Korea.*

*Like the 15.5 cm howitzer, this weapon remained in the arsenals of the USA and its allies for many years after the war. During the Cold War, the Americans even developed nuclear shells for it.*

# 2 CM OERLIKON ANTI-AIRCRAFT GUN

This weapon was similar to the 4 cm Bofors, and it was deployed by practically every country involved in the war. It was originally designed in 1914 by Reinhold Becker, and the Swiss company Semag obtained the patent and the production rights in 1919. Later, Oerlikon took over Semag, developing the weapon further and selling it on the international market. It was manufactured under licence in numerous countries (with some alterations), and was probably produced in larger numbers than any other anti-aircraft gun in the Second World War. The USA alone produced 124,735 and over 1 billion rounds of ammunition. Moreover, while there are no exact figures for the United Kingdom and the Commonwealth, they had over 55,000 of these guns in service in May 1945, although some of these came from the USA.

The Oerlikon was a reliable, robust and simple design, and it was easy to maintain. It was also successful: 32% of all Japanese aircraft shot down by US forces between December 1941 and September 1944 were hit by Oerlikon guns. Nevertheless, from late 1944 onwards the Allies began to replace it with the 4 cm Bofors, which had a more destructive impact on its targets, thus reducing the possibility of lethal kamikaze attacks. The German Army and Navy also deployed the Oerlikon, renaming it the 2 cm Flak 28/29. Different versions were also developed for deployment in aircraft and armoured vehicles, and a very simple, inexpensive version was designed in Poland in 1939. The plans for the Polish gun were brought to England before the Germans occupied Poland, and it went into production as the 'Polsten gun'. Even today the Oerlikon can be found in many countries' arsenals – an astonishing fact for an anti-aircraft gun which originated in 1914.

| Calibre: | 20 mm |
|---|---|
| Combat weight (excluding gun carriage): | 68.04 kg |
| Barrel length: | L/70 (1,400 mm) |
| Elevation: | −10° to +90° |
| Traverse: | 360° |
| Ammunition type and weight: | HE-I: 0.12 kg |
| Muzzle velocity: | 835 m/s |
| Rate of fire: | 450 rpm (theoretically) |
| Maximum range: | 4,400 m |
| Maximum vertical range: | 3,050 m |

*The 2 cm Oerlikon in a two-gun mount with twin drum magazines.*

*An Oerlikon 2 cm anti-aircraft gun mounted on an American Gato-class submarine.*

# 4 CM BOFORS L/60 ANTI-AIRCRAFT GUN

This 4 cm anti-aircraft gun, manufactured by Bofors, the Swedish arms manufacturer, was one of the most produced anti-aircraft weapons of all time, deployed by practically all the countries involved in the Second World War. There was, however, very little relation between the original Bofors design and the weapons actually produced, as they were manufactured under licence with some major alterations. The origins of this weapon can be traced back to a 1918 Bofors design, which Bofors (partly under the auspices of Krupp) significantly altered and improved. The first prototype appeared in 1933, but the 1936 version, which had been altered further, was the first to go into serial production. Before 1939 Bofors exported this weapon to numerous European countries and gave them the rights to manufacture it under licence. The British Army ordered the first 100 Bofors anti-aircraft guns in 1937 and was very satisfied with them, so the British obtained the rights to manufacture them under licence. There are no exact figures for the number of air-cooled Bofors anti-aircraft guns manufactured in the Commonwealth countries up to 1945, but the estimated figure is around 2,800. The British Royal Navy also deployed this gun on almost all its ships, albeit a specially developed water-cooled version. The US Army and Navy also deployed Bofors weapons, but the guns manufactured in the USA were significantly altered to

make them more suitable for rapid mass production. The original design required a lot of hand tooling, and it was expensive and complicated to produce, as was the ammunition. The US Navy installed single-gun, two-gun and four-gun mounts on almost all their ships from mid-1942 onwards. Up to the end of the war, a total of 39,200 water-cooled Bofors guns had been manufactured.

The Bofors anti-aircraft gun proved to be a reliable, robust weapon, but towards

| Calibre: | 40 mm |
|---|---|
| Combat weight (ex gun carriage): | 1,981 kg |
| Barrel length: | L/56.25 (2,250 mm) |
| Elevation: | −5° to +90° |
| Traverse: | 360° |
| Ammunition type and weight: | HE: 0.9 kg; AP: 0.889 kg |
| Muzzle velocity: | HE: 829–881 m/s |
| Rate of fire: | 120 rpm |
| Maximum vertical range: | 6,800–7,200 m, depending on the model |
| Maximum penetration | AP: 30 mm/1,800 m/90° |

*An improvised self-propelled anti-aircraft gun carriage with a 4 cm Bofors gun.*

the end of the war in the Pacific, the explosive power of its 4 cm shells was not always sufficient to prevent determined kamikaze attacks. This is why the US Navy decided to introduce the 7.6 cm anti-aircraft gun after the war. The Wehrmacht and Navy, particularly the latter, also deployed Bofors guns which they had seized in Poland, Norway and the

Netherlands – a large number also fell into German hands after Britain's retreat from Dunkirk – and a limited number were produced for the Wehrmacht under licence by the Norwegian firm Kongsberg. The Japanese also seized some British Bofors guns in early 1942, before using them as the basis for their own 4 cm Type 5 anti-aircraft gun.

*A Bofors gun in a Wehrmacht anti-aircraft division.*

*A light 4 cm Bofors anti-aircraft gun being deployed by the Wehrmacht on the Atlantic coast.*

# SPECIAL WEAPONS

# REMOTE-CONTROLLED DEMOLITION CARRIER

|  | Goliath (Carburettor) | Borgward IV 'A' Version |
|---|---|---|
| Combat weight: | 360 kg | 3,450 kg |
| Crew: | None | None |
| Dimensions (length/width/height): | 1,600 mm/ 850 mm/ 600 mm | 3,350 mm/ 1,800 mm/ 1,250 mm |
| Engine: | Zündapp 2-cylinder, air-cooled petrol engine, 703 cc, 12.5 hp | Borgward 4-cylinder inline petrol engine, 49 hp |
| Maximum speed: | 10 km/h road | 40 km/h road |
| Range: | 7 km road | 120 km road |
| Weaponry: | 75 kg explosive | 450 kg explosive |
| Armour: | N/A | Max. 20 mm |

*The Goliath demolition carrier.*

The Wehrmacht used two types of remote-controlled demolition vehicle: the Borgward IV and the Goliath. The Borgward model was initially designed as an ammunition carrier and was later intended to be a mine detector. But because most of the vehicles were destroyed and were too expensive for this task, they were converted for use as demolition carriers. The first of these were accepted by the Army Ordnance Office in April 1942 and put into service in the following November. The vehicle carried a payload of 450 kg, which it released by remote control as soon as it had reached its target. Then the vehicle was withdrawn by remote control, and the payload exploded. Up to June 1943, when it was replaced by the improved Versions B and

C, a total of 613 Version A vehicles had been produced, and 565 of the later versions were manufactured. There were also attempts to equip Borgward vehicles with cameras to make it easier to control them at longer ranges, but these were still unsuccessful at the end of the war. In early 1945 some Borgward vehicles were converted into remote-controlled anti-tank vehicles and deployed mostly in defence of Berlin.

The Goliath was significantly smaller than the Borgward and was delivered to the Army in April 1942. These vehicles were wire-controlled and exploded on impact with their targets. Their electric motors were too expensive, so a new petrol-powered version was developed, but up to 1944 2,650 of the electric

vehicles were produced nevertheless. The first version to be powered by a Zündapp petrol engine was delivered in April 1943, and in total 4,594 of these were manufactured. A larger model which could carry 100 kg of explosive was first produced in November 1944, and 325 were built in total, but all the Goliaths were vulnerable and difficult to handle, and their payloads were too small. The huge number of both versions in existence on 1 March 1944 – 2,527 with electric motors and 3,797 with petrol engines – shows how ineffectual a weapon it was. Nevertheless, the designs of both the Borgward IV and the Goliath were way ahead of their time – the technology available in the war was just not advanced enough.

*The Borgward IV demolition carrier.*

# NEBELWERFER 41 AND 42 'SMOKE LAUNCHERS'

|  | Model 41 | Model 42 |
|---|---|---|
| Calibre: | 150 mm | 210 mm |
| Combat weight: | 770 kg | 1,100 kg |
| Barrel length: | 1,300 mm | 1,300 mm |
| Rocket length: | 931 mm | 1,260 mm |
| Rocket weight: | 34.2 kg | 110 kg |
| Warhead: | HE: 2.83 kg | HE: 28.6 kg |
| Muzzle velocity: | 340 m/s | 320 m/s |
| Maximum range: | 6,700 m | 7,8050 m |

*A Nebelwerfer 42 of the Grossdeutschland Division.*

According to the conditions of the Treaty of Versailles, Germany was forbidden to develop heavy artillery weapons, but there was no mention of rockets. So as early as 1931 the Germans began research into rocket technology, including rocket-propelled chemical weapons. This was, of course, top secret, so the weapons were known as Nebelwerfer 'smoke launchers' and the troops deploying them were known as 'smoke troops', which has caused plenty of confusion. During the war the Wehrmacht used a large number of artillery weapons firing rocket-propelled ammunition, but the Nebelwerfer was the best known. The 15 cm weapon had six barrels arranged in a circle, mounted on the same gun carriage as the 3.7 cm anti-tank cannon, and all six barrels could be fired within six seconds. Each projectile had a rocket engine at the front which weighed 6.5 kg, firing through 26 diagonally attached jets which produced the necessary rifling (or spin), and the 2.8 kg payload was located in the rear, achieving a more powerful explosion and increasing fragmentation on impact. The first of these weapons were produced in March 1940.

The launcher was also mounted on armoured half-track vehicles (Sd.Kfz. 4/1 Maultiers, or Mules), its configuration was altered, and the number of barrels was increased to ten. But the 21 cm Nebelwerfer 42 had even greater firepower – in fact, it had considerably more, with five 130 cm barrels bound together and placed on the same gun mount as the 15 cm launcher. All five projectiles could be fired within eight seconds, and 15 cm ammunition could also be fired through removable rails inserted in the barrels. It also had fewer jets (22) to rifle the projectiles than the earlier model. The 21 cm Nebelwerfer 42 was produced from March 1942 until the end of the war, and in total 6,009 of Model 41 and 1,487 of Model 42 were produced for the Army. Also 17,678 launcher barrels and 21,000 projectiles were delivered to the Luftwaffe, which installed the barrels under the wings of twin-engine fighter planes and deployed them to attack bomber groups.

*The Nebelwerfer 42, mounted on the partially armoured chassis of the Maultier (Mule) half-track vehicle.*

# HENSCHEL HS 293

The Henschel Hs 293 was a radio-controlled glider bomb which was mainly deployed against ships from 1939 to 1945. It was based on the SC 500 high-explosive bomb, which had wings, a tail, a navigation system and a Walther rocket engine slung underneath. After the bomb was released from a carrier aircraft (such as the Do 217, the He 177 or the Fw 200), it would be carried by the rocket for ten seconds, then it would glide the rest of the way. At the rear of the missile, a light was installed which made it easier for the gunner to observe it at all times of day. Although the bomb was radio-controlled, work began on a wire control system, which would have made it immune to radio interference, but it was never put into service. A version with a camera installed in its nose to aid navigation was also developed, without ever being put into serial production. In tests it was found to be 90% accurate, but its accuracy fell to around 50% in combat.

The Hs 293 was first deployed on 25 August 1943. Two days later it sank the British corvette HMS *Egret*, and it would prove to be the most effective guided weapon in the war, sinking numerous destroyers and merchant ships, though it

lacked sufficient penetrating power to harm cruisers or battleships. On the Eastern Front and in Normandy it was also deployed against targets on the ground, such as bridges. At least 1,200 Hs 293 bombs were fired up to 1945, but towards the end of the war the Allies discovered the radio frequencies used to steer these weapons, and by causing interference they greatly reduced their effectiveness.

| Launch weight: | 975 kg |
|---|---|
| Length/wingspan: | 3.82 m/ 3.2 m |
| Engine: | Walther HWK 109-507 rocket engine with 590 kp thrust |
| Maximum speed: | 950 km/h |
| Launch altitude: | 400–2,000 m |
| Range: | 3–18 km |
| Weaponry: | 320–500 kg warhead |

*An Hs 293 under a Do 217 E-5 in the 100th German Bomber Wing.*

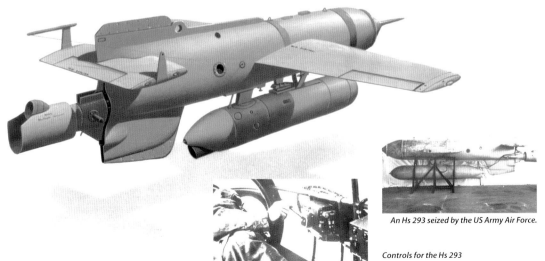

*An Hs 293 seized by the US Army Air Force.*

*Controls for the Hs 293 FuG 203 (Kehl III).*

# RUHRSTAHL SD 1400 'FRITZ X'

| | |
|---|---|
| Launch weight: | 1,570 kg |
| Dimensions (length/wingspan): | 3.62 m/ 1.35 m |
| Engine: | None |
| Maximum falling speed: | 280 m/s |
| Minimum launch altitude: | 4,000 m |
| Range: | 9,000 m |
| Weaponry: | 320 kg warhead |

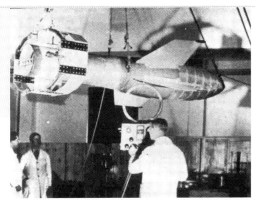

*A 'Fritz X' being tested.*

This radio-controlled bomb, generally known as 'Fritz X' for short, was developed in the early 1940s by Max Kramer at the Ruhrstahl (Ruhr Steel) company, and it was intended primarily to destroy heavily armoured naval targets.

The Fritz X was based on the standard Type SD 1400-piercing bomb, but it had superior aerodynamics, four small wings with a wingspan of 1.35 m and a tail. To control it after it had been fired, the gunner had to be above his target, which meant that, unfortunately, the carrier aircraft often had to fly over it.

The Fritz X was put into service on 29 August 1943, and its greatest success came less than two weeks later, on 9 September. After the truce between the Italians and the Allies, the Italian fleet was on its way to Malta to surrender. To prevent this, 12 Type Do 217 aircraft from the 100th Bomber Wing took off, each carrying a Fritz X. The Italian battleship *Roma* was hit several times, the fires exploded its ammunition, and it sank with 1,455 men on board.

Later in the war, Fritz X bombs sank the British cruiser HMS *Spartan*, the British destroyer HMS *Janus* and the *Newfoundland* hospital ship. It also inflicted severe damage on numerous other ships, including the British battleship HMS *Warspite*, which was hit three times by Fritz X bombs and reached Malta only with great difficulty, and the USS *Savannah* suffered a similar fate. Around 2,000 Fritz X bombs were manufactured, but only around 200 were ever deployed in battle. Because the carrier aircraft had to fly over their targets, and the bombs could not change direction abruptly, bomber groups equipped with Fritz X bombs suffered heavy losses.

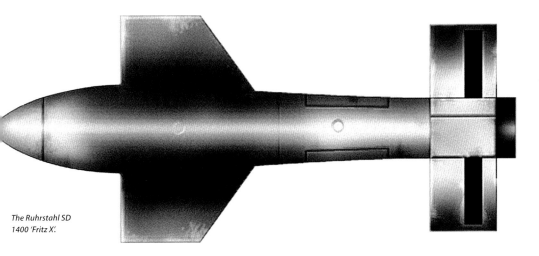

*The Ruhrstahl SD 1400 'Fritz X'.*

# FIESELER FI 103 V1

The V1 – or, to be more precise, the FI 103 – was essentially a primitive cruise missile, with less refined navigation than its modern counterparts. On 25 July 1942, Fieseler received an order for an automatically steered flying bomb. It was to be powered by the newly developed Pulso-Schubrohr, a simple jet engine, and to keep it secret the project was called 'FZG 76', 'FZG' meaning 'Flakzielgerät', or 'flak-aiming device'. For propaganda purposes, it was dubbed the 'V1', or 'Vergeltungswaffe 1', literally 'retaliation weapon 1', shortly before being put into service. The V1 was constructed like an aircraft, and its jet engine was located above the fuselage and achieved a

maximum thrust of 335 kp. It was steered by an autopilot using a weighted pendulum and a gyromagnetic compass, and its range was determined by an unpowered propeller on its nose, which cut off the fuel supply to the engine after a specific number of revolutions. It took only 280 working hours to manufacture a V1, which meant that it could be produced in large numbers. The V1 was launched either from launching ramps on the ground, which each used a 55 m-long catapult with a 6° angle of elevation, or mid-air from carrier aircraft.

The V1 was first deployed on 12 or 13 June 1944, and more than 9,300 V1s were launched within the next 80 days, with London and other southern English cities their primary targets, though Liège and Antwerp in Belgium were also targeted (by 3,141 and 8,696 V1s respectively). Around 2,000 of these launches failed immediately after take-off on account of technical failures, while 25% of the remainder were destroyed by fighter aircraft, and another 25% were shot down by anti-aircraft fire or intercepted by balloon barrages. British fighter pilots used a particularly effective tactic against the V1, aligning one of their wings just beneath one of the V1's wings

| | |
|---|---|
| Launch weight: | 2,810 kg |
| Dimensions (Length/wingspan): | 7.92 mm/ 5.71 m |
| Engine: | Argus As 014 Pulso jet engine with 335 kp thrust |
| Maximum speed: | 625 km/h |
| Minimum altitude: | N/A |
| Range: | 350 km |
| Weaponry: | 850 kg warhead |

then rolling away, thus confusing its navigation system and making it crash.

Towards the end of the war, there were also plans to deploy the V1 as a guided missile against Allied bombers. For these plans, which went under the name 'Reichenberg', it was to be converted into a manned version, the Fi 103/R 3, but none of these suicide bombs was ever deployed. As early as 1945, before Germany's surrender, V1s which had come into British possession, with related technical documents, were shipped to the USA, where Ford and Republic Aircraft produced a V1 copy, called the JB 2, in very little time. Though intended for deployment against Japan, it was only ever used for test purposes.

*The big disadvantage of fixed launching sites was that they were easy for bombers to destroy, and many launching platforms were lost after the Allies landed in Normandy. Hence, carrier aircraft were increasingly deployed instead, and the V1 was launched from the Heinkel He-111 H-22. It was first fired from a Heinkel on 7 July 1944, and the last V1 rocket was fired on 15 January 1945. In total, 80 carrier aircraft were lost, and approximately 1,600 V1s were launched, but only around 50% of them reached London.*

# PEENEMÜNDE AGGREGAT A4 V2

*A V2 is prepared for launch on its Meilerwagen transporter. Up to 27 March 1945, a total of 5,500 A4s were fired, of which around 2,000 struck the Greater London area and 1,600 struck Antwerp. Other targets included Brussels, Liège, Paris and the bridge at Remagen: 11 rockets were fired at the latter, but not one of them hit it.*

| | |
|---|---|
| Launch weight: | 12,825 kg |
| Dimensions (length/wingspan): | 14.026 m/ 3.564 m |
| Engine: | Rocket engine with 27,500 kp |
| Maximum speed: | 1,500 m/s – or Mach 5 |
| Maximum altitude: | 80 km |
| Range: | Initially 320 km, later 380 km |
| Weaponry: | 975 kg warhead |

The V2 was first deployed on 7 September 1944. Its forerunner, the A4, was presented to Hitler in March 1939 at the Peenemünde Rocket Research Institute on the German island of Usedom, and he ordered the institute to develop the prototype into a deployable long-range rocket. The A4 was not, however, ready for production until July 1943. After bombing raids on the institute, production continued in an underground factory in Nordhausen. Both to create the tunnel system for this factory and to build the V2, the Germans relied heavily on forced labour from concentration camps. Some 60,000 prisoners, many of whom died of starvation, cold, or disease, were used.

Production of the weapon now known as the V2 began in October 1943, and in January 1944 the first rockets could be delivered, but almost none were of sufficient quality to be deployed. It was impossible to steer the rocket, its range could only be roughly determined, and it was often several miles off target. This meant that it could only be deployed as a terror weapon. Initially, around 500 V2 rockets were produced per month, but the intention was to increase this figure to 900. When considering these figures, however, we must bear in mind that around 6% of all V2s exploded immediately upon being launched, and a further 60% were too defective to be deployed without further improvements.

After the fixed launch installations were hit by Allied air strikes, the V2s were launched from mobile ramps. Each mobile launch group consisted of 25 special vehicles, which travelled only by night to avoid being attacked from the air, and the rockets were launched in wooded areas, protecting them from both the wind and enemy aircraft.

There were many projects based on the V2, such as a two-stage version, with a range of 5,500 km, and a manned kamikaze model. There were also plans to attack New York, firing a V2 from an underwater container that was towed by a submarine.

JAPAN/SOVIET UNION

## MXY-7 OHKA

The Yokosuka MXY-7 Ohka was a rocket-propelled aircraft designed especially for kamikaze attacks. The prototype's maiden flight took place in September 1944, and serial production began in the same month. To build these machines, the Japanese used as little important raw material as possible, and the aircraft's construction was very simple. There were four different models in total, the main difference between them being their propulsion. Normally the Ohka was carried under the fuselage of a Mitsubishi G4M until the target was within close range, when it was released. The pilot would then try to glide as close to the target as possible, before firing the rockets and striking the target. Because of its high terminal velocity, it was almost impossible to intercept the Ohka once it had been fired, but the weapon enjoyed little success, as the carrier aircraft could easily be attacked, as could the Ohka when it was gliding. In addition, to steer the Ohka once the rockets had been

fired, the pilot needed to be relatively experienced. Nevertheless, at least one US destroyer was sunk by this weapon, which the American soldiers nicknamed the 'Baka', which means something like 'idiot' in Japanese.

| Crew: | 1 |
|---|---|
| Launch weight: | 2,142 kg |
| Length/wingspan: | 6.04 m/ 5.3 m |
| Engine: | Solid propulsion charge rocket engine with 800 kp thrust |
| Maximum speed: | Launched at 660 km/h; terminal velocity 920 km/h |
| Maximum altitude: | N/A |
| Maximum range: | 80 km |
| Weaponry: | 1,200 kg warhead |

*A Yokosuka MXY-7 seized by the US Army.*

## 'KATYUSHA' BM-8 AND BM-13 MULTIPLE ROCKET LAUNCHER

| | BM-8 | BM-13 | BM-31 |
|---|---|---|---|
| Calibre: | 82 mm | 132 mm | 300 mm |
| Combat weight: | N/A | N/A | N/A |
| Elevation: | +4° to +45° | +4° to 45° | +4° to 45° |
| Traverse: | 20° | 20° | 20° |
| Rocket length: | 714 mm | 1,415 mm | 1,760 mm |
| Rocket weight: | 8 kg | 42.5 kg | 92.4 kg |
| Warhead: | HE: 0.6 kg | HE: 4.9 kg | HE: 28.8 kg |
| Muzzle velocity: | 315 m/s | 355 m/s | 255 m/s |
| Maximum range: | 5,500 m | 8,500 m | 4,300 m |

This Soviet rocket launcher was nicknamed 'Stalin's Organ' by the German infantry, because of the launching rails, which were arranged next to and on top of each other like organ pipes, as well as the wailing noise it made when fired. The Red Army soldiers, on the other hand, called it 'Katyusha', an affectionate diminutive of Katya.

'Stalin's Organ' was one of the best-known weapons of the Second World War. There were numerous different

versions with a wide range of different chassis, but essentially, they all had several rocket-launching pipes (between 16 and 48) with limited traverse, mounted on a truck or a tank, which could all be fired in a matter of seconds. They had a devastating impact on targets on the ground, in spite of their limited accuracy. The shrill noise they made when fired also proved to be an extremely powerful psychological weapon.

*Loading 'Stalin's Organ'.*

The development of the Rs-82 and Rs-132 rockets began in the 1930s, but they were originally intended as aircraft weapons – in fact, they were used in this capacity by almost all Soviet ground attack aircraft and fighter bombers for a long time. In 1938 the Russians began testing ground launchers, and in May 1941 the first of the serial production models, called the BM-13, were finally delivered. They were first deployed on 14 July 1941, against German troops advancing on Smolensk, and seven BM-13s fired 112 rounds into a troop concentration in Orsha, Belarus, inflicting very heavy losses. Nevertheless, the weapon had to remain as well kept a secret as was possible, and only Soviet secret service (NKVD) teams were allowed to use it. During the war, all the different versions of 'Stalin's Organ' were dreaded by the enemy and deployed in large numbers: although the exact number produced cannot be established (the only available sources are contradictory), it is clear that over 10,000 of all the different versions were manufactured.

*A Studebaker 2.5-tonner with a BM-31.*

*A Studebaker 2.5-tonner with a BM-13.*

*A BM-13 fires a salvo of rockets.*

USA

# LITTLE BOY AND FAT MAN: THE ATOMIC BOMBS OF HIROSHIMA AND NAGASAKI

|  | Little Boy | Fat Man |
|---|---|---|
| Weight | 4,040 kg | 4,670 kg |
| Length | 3,200 mm | 3,660 mm |
| Diameter | 710 mm | 1,520 mm |
| Explosive power: | c.13,000 tonnes TNT | c. 20,000 tonnes TNT |

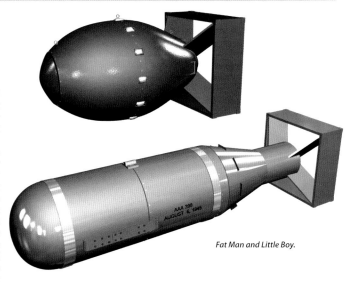

When these bombs were dropped on Japan on 6 August and 9 August 1945, respectively, they heralded not only a new era of weapons technology, but also a new age in history.

Development of these weapons began in 1942, and they were originally intended for use against Germany rather than Japan. The Americans feared that German physicists, who were among the best in the world, would build an atomic bomb for Hitler, and they did not want to be defenceless if the Germans succeeded. So in 1942 in the New Mexico desert, they established a huge secret research complex, which they called Los Alamos, an important part of the Manhattan Project to build an atomic bomb. From 1943 the physicist Robert Oppenheimer led and coordinated thousands of physicists, engineers and technicians, and within a couple of years they achieved their objective. On 16 July 1945, the Trinity Test took place, and the world's first atomic weapon was successfully tested above ground.

*Fat Man and Little Boy.*

The war in Europe had ended on 8 May 1945, but war was still raging in the Pacific, so the Americans decided to deploy the first of these new weapons against Japan. Although by this time the Japanese troops already had their backs to the wall, and defeating them would only have been a matter of time, the Americans wanted to avoid a land invasion of Japan. High casualties would have been unavoidable on both sides, and conventional bombing raids would have continued to inflict terrible devastation without necessarily forcing Japan to surrender. But after two B-29 bombers, 'Enola Gay' and 'Bocks Car', devastated Hiroshima and Nagasaki respectively with one atomic bomb apiece, killing hundreds of thousands of people, the Japanese Government realized that continuing the war would be pointless, and it acceded to the Allies' conditions of surrender.

Undoubtedly, if the Manhattan Project had succeeded earlier, or the war in Europe had lasted longer, Germany would also have been hit by an atomic bomb.

*Hiroshima after the atomic bomb was dropped.*

*The crew of 'Enola Gay' standing in front of their B-29 bomber.*

AIRCRAFT

## MESSERSCHMITT BF 109

The Bf 109 was manufactured in larger numbers than any other military aircraft – around 35,000 were produced – and was the standard plane in the Luftwaffe's fighter squadrons throughout the war. In 1935 the Luftwaffe had only been established relatively recently and was still in need of a single-seat fighter. Four designs were examined, and those from Messerschmitt and Heinkel were short-listed. The first Bf 109 prototype had its maiden flight on 28 May 1935, powered by a Rolls-Royce engine, and the second prototype had a Jumo 210 engine. Other pre-production models had a variety of different weaponry and engines.

The first production model was the Bf 109B-1, which was delivered in early 1937 and soon deployed in the Spanish Civil War. It proved to be the best fighter aircraft in that war, and the German pilots in the Condor Legion, in which fighter aces like Mölders and Galland honed their expertise, experimented with both new aircraft and new tactics. In November 1937 a modified Bf 109 also broke the world speed record for land-based aircraft and won a race around the Alps. As with all Luftwaffe aircraft manufactured in large numbers, very many different versions of the Bf 109 were manufactured, so it is impossible to cover all of them in detail here. But the main model in the

| | Bf 109E-7 | Bf 109G-10 |
|---|---|---|
| Type: | Fighter | Fighter |
| Crew: | 1 | 1 |
| Weight when empty/ max weight at takeoff: | 2,014 kg/2,767 kg | 1,970 kg/3,500 kg |
| Length/wingspan/ height: | 8.75 m/9.86 m/3.4 m | 8.95 m/9.97 m/3.4 m |
| Engine(s): | One Daimler-Benz DB 601N hanging V12 engine with 1,200 hp | One Daimler-Benz DB 605 hanging V12 engine with 1,475 hp normal performance, and 1,800 hp emergency performance with methanol/water injection |
| Maximum speed: | 578 km/h at 3,750 m | 685 km/h at 7,400 m |
| Service ceiling: | 11,125 m | 12,500 m |
| Range: | 1,094 km | 560 km |
| Weaponry: | 1 x 20 mm MGFF machine gun firing through propeller hub, and 4 x 7.92 mm MG17 fixed forward-firing machine guns in the fuselage and wings | 1 x 20 mm MG151/20 machine gun or 1 x 30 mm MK automatic cannon firing through propeller hub, 2 x 13 mm MG131 fixed forward-firing machine guns in the fuselage, and various configurations with MG151/20 machine guns or MK108 automatic cannon or an external payload of max. 500 kg |

autumn of 1939 was the Bf 109 E, known as 'Emil', whose main advantage compared to the British Spitfires and Hurricanes was that it had a fuel injection pump rather than a carburettor, meaning that fuel could be conserved even with negative G-forces. The Bf 109 F appeared in 1941 and its variants (the F-0 to F-6) are generally regarded as the most attractive of all the Bf 109 models. With a larger

propeller, a new engine cowling, a cantilever tail and a retractable tail wheel, the Bf 109 F had superior aerodynamics and performance to previous models. The version of the Bf 109 that was manufactured in the greatest numbers was the Model G, which was put into service late in the summer of 1942. It had a more powerful DB (Daimler-Benz) 605 engine and was better armed, with

*A restored Bf 109 G-6 from the Messerschmitt Foundation.*

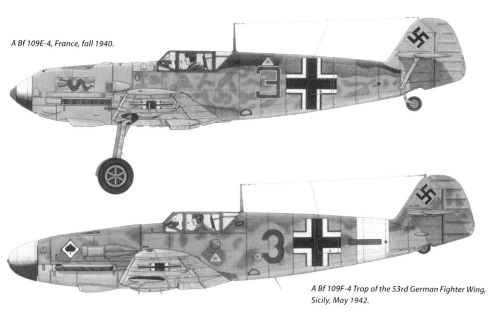

*A Bf 109E-4, France, fall 1940.*

*A Bf 109F-4 Trop of the 53rd German Fighter Wing, Sicily, May 1942.*

two 13 mm MG131 machine guns above the engine (its large gun cowls were known as 'bumps'). Because there were so many different Bf 109 G configurations, it could be used for a wide variety of missions. The next version, the Model H, had a longer wingspan and was only produced in very small numbers. The Model K, based on the Model G, appeared shortly before

*A Bf 109G.*

the end of the war, and a few dozen Bf 109T-1s with tail hooks were built for deployment on the *Graf Zeppelin* aircraft carrier, which was never completed. After this project was abandoned, the planes had their special equipment removed and were put into service as T-2 aircraft. There were other projects, such as the Bf 109 Z, which consisted of two Bf 109 F frames with

a new wing layout, but this version was never put into service.

The Bf 109 was deployed variously as an interceptor, a fighter bomber and a reconnaissance aircraft. In the early years of the war, it was second only to the Spitfire, but it was later superseded, particularly by the P-51 and the P-47. Its aerodynamics dated back to the 1930s, and it did not have a high-performance engine, so it could not be developed any further. In addition, although its performance easily surpassed that of the Fw 190, it was less robust than the latter. Its landing gear was also very narrow, which led to a number of accidents and could be very dangerous for inexperienced pilots. Nevertheless, production of the Bf 109 was continued after the war. In Spain from 1942 Hispano manufactured it under licence as the Ha-1109, Ha-1110, or Ha-1112, installing Hispano-Suiza and, later, Rolls-Royce Merlin engines. The Czech firm Avia also manufactured the Bf 109 under licence after 1945, initially installing the original DB 605 engine (Avia 99) and, later, the Jumo 211 F (Avia 199). The Israeli Air Force's first aircraft were Avia 199s donated by Czechoslovakia.

# MESSERSCHMITT BF 110

The German Air Ministry (Reichs-luftministerium – RLM) ordered the development of a heavy fighter aircraft, and the Bf 110, whose maiden flight took place on 12 May 1936, was the result. After initial problems with the DB 600, this model was fitted with the Jumo 210 engine, which made for a disappointing performance. Consequently, its development was slow, and the first mass-produced model, the C version with twin DB 601 engines, was not delivered to the Luftwaffe until 1939. The D and E versions differed from the C version only in minor respects, while the Bf 110E was fitted with improved DB 610 engines, producing 1,350 hp, and the last models, the G and H, were powered by DB 605 engines.

In the early months of the war, the Bf 110 aircraft were very successful, gaining many aerial victories, but in the late summer and autumn of 1940, when they were deployed to escort bombers over England and encountered Hurricanes and Spitfires, they suffered such heavy losses that it seemed they needed a Bf 109 escort themselves. Nevertheless, on account of their firepower and range, they proved to be valuable aircraft in the Mediterranean area and in the East. They were also very successful as reconnaissance aircraft and fighter bombers, but they were used primarily as night fighters. The earliest tests took place in the winter of 1940–41, but because the aircraft did not yet have radar, they were less than convincing. They fared better when fitted with simple infrared sensors and guided by radar stations on the ground, but the Bf 110 night fighters only really became successful after the installation of on-board radar devices, easily recognizable with their 'stag's antlers'. Until the very end of the war, the British Royal Air Force and Luftwaffe fought dramatic battles above Germany, in which electronic warfare played an important role for the first time. The Bf 110 was also deployed in daylight against USAAF (United States Army Air Force) bombers in 1943 and 1944, but they suffered heavy losses primarily because of the P-47 and P-51 fighters accompanying the bombers. When production was halted in March 1945, a total of around 6,050 Bf 110s had been built.

|  | Bf 110C-4 | Bf 110G-4/R3 |
|---|---|---|
| Type: | Heavy fighter/destroyer | Night fighter |
| Crew: | 2 | 3 |
| Weight when empty/ max weight at takeoff: | 4,500 kg/6,750 kg | 5,090 kg/9,890 kg |
| Length/wingspan/ height: | 12.11 m/16.29 m/4.18 m | 13.05 m/16.29 m/4.18 m |
| Engine(s): | Two Daimler-Benz DB 601B-1 hanging V12 engines with 1,020 hp | Two Daimler-Benz DB605B hanging V12 engines with 1,475 hp |
| Maximum speed: | 560 km/h at 3,750 m | 550 km/h at 6,980 m |
| Service ceiling: | 10,000 m | 8,000 m |
| Range: | 1,300 km | 2,100 km with 2 additional fuel tanks |
| Weaponry: | 2 x 20 mm MG/FF and 4 x 7.92 mm MG17 machine guns fixed in the nose, 1 x 7.92 mm MG15 machine gun in the rear of the cockpit, and an external payload of max. 500 kg | 2 x 20 mm MG151/20 machine guns and 2 x 30 mm automatic cannon fixed in the nose, 1 x MG81Z machine gun in the rear of the cockpit, and 2 x 20 mm MG/FF machine guns firing diagonally upward from the fuselage. Also fitted with radar |

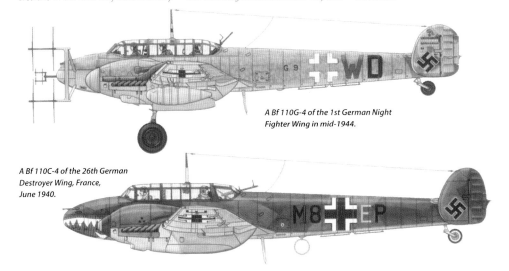

A Bf 110G-4 of the 1st German Night Fighter Wing in mid-1944.

A Bf 110C-4 of the 26th German Destroyer Wing, France, June 1940.

# FOCKE-WULF FW 190 (SHRIKE)

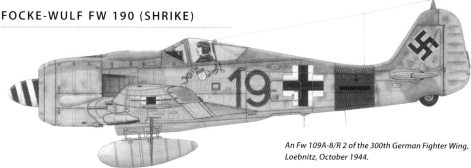

*An Fw 109A-8/R 2 of the 300th German Fighter Wing, Loebnitz, October 1944.*

The Focke-Wulf Fw 190 was the best and most versatile piston-engine German fighter aircraft of the Second World War, and it was deployed as a fighter, a fighter-bomber, a ground attack aircraft, a reconnaissance aircraft, a torpedo bomber and a flight instruction aircraft. The Fw 190 prototype had its maiden flight on 1 July 1939, but at first there were major problems with the new BMW 801 radial engine. This delayed the Fw 190's development, and it was not ready to be put into service until the summer of 1941, when the Fw 190A-1 was delivered to the Luftwaffe. As soon as it was first deployed, the new aircraft proved to be more powerful and versatile than the Me 109; it had superior firepower, but it was less manoeuvrable than the latter, and could not climb as fast or as high – the BMW 801 engine had been designed for optimum performance at low and medium altitudes. The Fw 190 was dogged by this problem until the introduction in 1944 of the D version with the Jumo 213 V12 engine, which was intended as a high-altitude fighter. When it was introduced, the Fw 109A was vastly superior in terms of performance to its Allied counterparts, but, as the war progressed, the Allies caught up with and then overtook the Fw 190. The P 51 and P41 in particular clearly outperformed even the D version at altitudes in excess of 7 km.

Numerous variants and sub-variants of the Fw 190 were produced. The A version was a fighter which could also be deployed as a fighter bomber, and the F and G versions were fighter bombers and ground attack aircraft with an increased payload and enhanced armour, while the S version was a two-seater flight instruction aircraft. The D version, which was fitted with a liquid-cooled Jumo 213 V12 engine to attain higher altitudes than the other models, is the easiest to distinguish from the rest. The airframe underwent various alterations so that the engine could be installed, and the Jumo's ring-shaped cooler made it look like a radial-engine aircraft. The wings

and tail were no different from the A version, though the horizontal stabilizer was widened, but the fuselage was lengthened to 10.2 m. As in the later radial-engine models, it was possible to inject the engine with a methanol-water mixture (called MW-50), greatly enhancing the machine's performance.

When production was halted, around 20,000 of all Fw 190 variants had been manufactured. The Jumo-powered D series was developed further and called the Ta 152, but very few were built.

| | Fw 190A-8/R2 | Fw 190D-9 |
|---|---|---|
| Type: | Fighter bomber | Fighter bomber |
| Crew: | 1 | 1 |
| Weight when empty/ max weight at takeoff: | 3,170 kg/4,900 kg | 3,490 kg/4,840 kg |
| Length/wingspan/ height: | 8.84 m/10.5 m/3.96 m | 10.2 m/10.5 m/3.35 m |
| Engine(s): | One BMW 901D-2 14 cylinder radial engine with 1,730 hp normal performance and 2,100 hp emergency performance with MW-50 injection | One Junkers Jumo 213A-1 hanging V12 engine with 1,775 hp normal performance and 2,100 hp emergency performance with MW-50 injection |
| Maximum speed: | 655 km/h; 685 km/h with MW-50 injection | 676 km/h; 705 km/h with MW-50 injection |
| Service ceiling: | 11,400 m | 12,000 m |
| Range: | 805 km | 835 km |
| Weaponry: | 2 x 7.92 mm MG17 engines fixed above the engine, 4 x 20 mm MG151/20 machine guns fixed in the wings, and an external payload of up to 1,000 kg | 2 x 13 mm MG131 machine guns fixed above the engine, 2 x 20 mm MG151/20 machine guns fixed in the wings, and an external payload of up to 500 kg |

*An Fw 190A-5 of the 51st German Fighter Wing, Eastern Front, July 1943.*

# MESSERSCHMITT ME 210 AND 410 HORNISSE (HORNET)

The Me 210 was developed as the successor to the Bf 110 and flew for the first time as early as 5 September 1939, but suffered from severe stability and manoeuvrability problems. Nevertheless, it went into production after a few modifications, though without great success: production was halted after just 200 models had been manufactured, and the design was completely revised. With the installation of automatic leading-edge slats, a longer fuselage and more powerful DB 603A engines, its problems were solved. The new model was called the Me 410, and the first aircraft of this kind were delivered in 1943. It was deployed as a fighter (the A-1), a high-speed bomber (the A-2) and a reconnaissance aircraft (the A-3). The B series versions were deployed in the same way, but they were fitted with slightly more powerful DB 603G engines and 13 mm MG131 machine guns in the nose, instead of the 7.92 mm MG17. Up to September

| | Me 410B-1 |
|---|---|
| Type: | Heavy fighter/reconnaissance aircraft/high-speed bomber |
| Crew: | 2 |
| Weight when empty/ max weight at takeoff: | 7,930 kg/11,237 kg |
| Length/wingspan/height: | 12.48 m/16.35 m/4.28 m |
| Engine(s): | Two Daimler-Benz DB 603G hanging V12 engines with 1,900 hp each |
| Maximum speed: | 630 km/h |
| Service ceiling: | 9,500 m |
| Range: | 1,690 km |
| Weaponry: | 2 x 20 mm MG151/20 and 2 x 13 mm machine guns fixed in the nose, 2 x 13 mm MG131 machine guns in remote-controlled installations (FDSL.131) on the sides of the fuselage, and a payload of up to 1,000 kg in the internal bomb bay; or 2 x 20 mm MG151/20 machine guns or 1 x 50 mm BK5 in the internal bomb bay |

1944, a total of 1,160 Me 410s had been manufactured, including around 30 different series with different weapon configurations. The Me 410 was used in the bombardment of the English coast and defensively against Allied bombers, but it could never entirely replace the Bf 110, which remained in service as a night fighter until the end of the war. There were plans for an Me 410 C with an increased wingspan and a supercharger for the DB 603 engine, but the project never got past the planning stage.

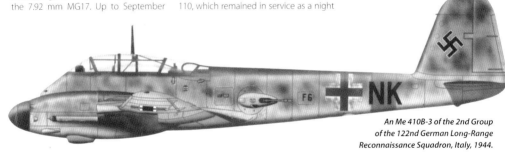

An Me 410B-3 of the 2nd Group of the 122nd German Long-Range Reconnaissance Squadron, Italy, 1944.

*The Me 262B-2a night fighter.*

*General Adolf Galland was so impressed by the Me 262 that after its maiden flight he likened it to a jet-powered angel. He reckoned that one Me 262 was as effective in combat as five Bf 109s.*

# MESSERSCHMITT ME 262 SCHWALBE (SWALBE)

The Me 262 was the first jet-powered combat aircraft to be put into serial production. Its development began in 1938, when Messerschmitt was contracted by the German Air Ministry to develop a jet-powered fighter aircraft. The airframe had already been designed, but the BMW jet engines were still at the experimental stage. So for its maiden flight on 18 April 1941, the Me 262 had to be fitted with a conventional Junkers piston engine in the nose, but it was already clear that it handled well. Development of the BMW jet engines was still progressing slowly, so the plane was converted to be fitted with Junkers jet engines instead, and the modified version's maiden flight took place on 18 July 1942. It is often claimed that Hitler's wish to use the Me 262 as a high-speed bomber slowed down its development, but the main reason for this was that it was difficult to develop jet engines that were both powerful and reliable. Consequently, the Me 262A-1a was not put into service until July 1944. The A-2 was the high-speed bomber which Hitler wanted, the A-5 was a reconnaissance aircraft, the B-1a was a two-seater flight instruction aircraft (B-1a) and the B-2a was a night fighter fitted with radar. In total, 1,433 Me 262s were manufactured, but there were never more than 250 in service at any given time. Many crashed into the ground, and

*An Me 262A-1a Swallow.*

|  | Me 262A-1a |
| --- | --- |
| Type: | Fighter/fighter bomber |
| Crew: | 1 |
| Weight when empty/ max weight at takeoff: | 3,800 kg/6,400 kg |
| Length/wingspan/height: | 10.6 m/12.48 m/3.84 m |
| Engine(s): | Two Junkers Jumo 004B-1/2/3 jet engines with 900 kp thrust each at takeoff |
| Maximum speed: | 870 km/h at 6,000 m |
| Service ceiling: | 11,450 m |
| Range: | 1,050 km |
| Weaponry: | 4 x 30 mm MK108 machine guns in the nose; 24 R4M 55 mm rockets could also be carried under the wings |

many more simply could not be flown, as there was not enough fuel, and too few pilots were available.

Although they were able to attain exceptionally high speeds for the era, many Me 262s were shot down – they were especially vulnerable when landing – so units with Bf 109 and Fw 190 aircraft were stationed at Me 262 airbases. In spite of its limitations, the Me 262 was

heavily armed, with four 30 mm MK108 guns in its nose and rocket launchers with 24 rockets under its wings, and it destroyed a number of enemy targets. There were projects to develop it further, but Germany's fortunes in the war meant that these were abandoned.

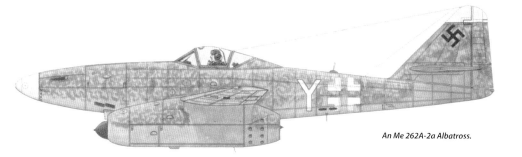

*An Me 262A-2a Albatross.*

# HEINKEL HE 219 UHU (EAGLE OWL)

| He 219A-7/R-4 | |
|---|---|
| Type: | Night fighter |
| Crew: | 2 |
| Weight when empty/ max weight at takeoff: | 11,200 kg/15,300 kg |
| Length/wingspan/height: | 15.54 m/18.5 m/4.1 m |
| Engine(s): | Two DB 603G hanging V12 engines with 1,900 hp each |
| Maximum speed: | 615 km/h |
| Service ceiling: | 9,800 m |
| Range: | 1,850 km |
| Weaponry: | 2 x 20 mm MG151/20 machine guns fixed at the wing roots, 2 x 20 mm MG151/20 machine guns fixed in the underside of the fuselage, 2 x 30 mm MK108 automatic cannon firing diagonally upwards from the fuselage ('diagonal music'). Also fitted with radar |

*An He 219A-7/R 4 of the 1st German Night Fighter Wing, Westerland (Sylt), early 1945.*

The Heinkel He 219 was a Luftwaffe night fighter and, in many respects, a very advanced aircraft. It was the first Luftwaffe aircraft with a three-wheel undercarriage and an ejector seat, and it was fitted with radar as standard, which was apparent from the twin antennae on its nose. This model was originally based on a design for a bomber, which Heinkel altered to meet the requirements of the night fighter, as ordered by the German Air Ministry. The original prototype flew for the first time in November 1942, and in simulated battles with the Do 217N and Ju 88S it proved to be far superior to both. Yet for no apparent reason, and in spite of its performance, the He 219 was never prioritized, although British RAF bombers were devastating Germany. In mid-1943 the first A-O pre-production models were deployed in the 1st NJG (Night Fighter Wing) in Venlo, Netherlands, and within a few days they had shot down 20 enemy aircraft, including six Mosquito high-speed bombers. Yet they were never delivered to the Night Fighter Wings rapidly enough or in sufficient numbers. Eventually, the He 219 was outperformed by new versions of the Mosquito, so a limited series was produced of aircraft with high-performance engines and less weaponry, which could reach 650 km/h at 12,000m. Only 294 He 219s, including prototypes and pre-production models, were built in total, before production was halted in November 1944 as part of the German Fighter Emergency Programme.

# MESSERSCHMITT ME 163 COMET

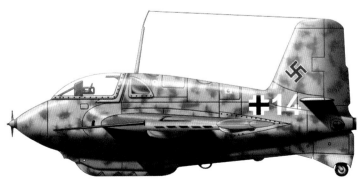

*An Me 163B.*

The Me 163 was the world's first rocket-propelled fighter aircraft, and the first machine to fly faster than 1,000 km/h. It was designed by Dr Alexander Martin Lippisch, who worked on tailless gliders in the 1930s and joined Messerschmitt in 1939, along with his research team. The first prototype of the Me 163a flew as early as 1941, but its problems were so severe that the improved Me 163B was not delivered until 1944. It shed its undercarriage after takeoff and landed on a skid below its fuselage, but before landing it had to have spent all, or nearly all, its fuel, because severe shocks could cause rocket fuel to explode. The Me 163 had a minimal wingspan and was intended to target bombers, picking off

| | Me 163B-1a |
|---|---|
| Type: | Fighter |
| Crew: | 1 |
| Weight when empty/ max weight at takeoff: | 1,905 kg/4,110 kg |
| Length/wingspan/height: | 5.84 m/9.32 m/2.77 m |
| Engine(s): | One Walther HWK-509A-2 R rocket engine with 1,700 kp thrust |
| Maximum speed: | 1,002 km/h at 9,150 m |
| Service ceiling: | 12,100 m |
| Flight duration: | Around 8 minutes with rocket propulsion |
| Weaponry: | 2 x 30 mm MK108 machine guns in the wing roots |

target before the Me 163 had shot past it. In fact, the main Me 163 wing, the 400th Fighter Wing (JG 400), had shot down only nine US bombers by March 1945. Because it flew without an undercarriage, lacked quality and had such volatile fuel, the Me 163 posed a greater threat to its own crew than to the enemy, so production was halted in February 1945 after only 400 had been built.

only the bombers that were within very close range. With a climbing speed of 4,800m/min, it had no difficulty in finding its targets, but its speed was also its greatest weakness, as the pilot had only a few seconds to aim and fire at the

## HEINKEL HE 162 SALAMANDER

The He 162 Salamander – also known as the Volksjäger, or 'People's Fighter' – was developed and prepared for serial production by Heinkel in a very short time. Heinkel received the contract to build it on 15 September 1944, and just 69 days later, on 6 December, the first prototype took off on its maiden flight. However, it crashed because of construction deficiencies. It was designed to be built using the minimum of scarce raw materials (such as aluminium), and sections of the fuselage and wings were made of wood. In fact, the lack of appropriate construction materials would always be the He 162's main problem and resulted in the imposition of a 600 km/h speed limit, which could only be broken to elude enemy aircraft. Like the Ar 234 (see p.205), the He 162 was equipped with an ejector seat – and because of the aircraft's limitations He 162 pilots often used it. It is claimed that it shot down an enemy aircraft on 26 April 1945, the day it was put into service. Around 270 He 162s were manufactured up to May 1945, and 800 were still under construction at the end of the war. Because the war ended so soon after it was first manufactured, only very few He 162s were actually deployed, and 50 of those in the 1st Fighter Wing were seized by the British at Leck/Schleswig air base.

| | He 162A |
|---|---|
| Type: | Fighter |
| Crew: | 1 |
| Weight when empty/ max weight at takeoff: | 2,050 kg/2,690 kg |
| Length/wingspan/height: | 9.05 m/7.2 m/2.55 m |
| Engine(s): | One BMW-003A-1 jet engine with 800 kp thrust at takeoff and 920 kp emergency thrust (deployable for max. 30s) |
| Maximum speed: | 840 km/h with normal thrust and 905 km/h at 6,000 m |
| Service ceiling: | 12,000 m |
| Range: | 900 km |
| Weaponry: | 2 x 20 mm MG151/20 machine guns in the fuselage |

*This He 162A-2 was tested intensively by the US Air Force after the war.*

# HENSCHEL HS 123

As early as 1933 the Germans wanted a dive-bomber for their air force, which was still being formed. Henschel won the contract with its Hs 123, and the first prototypes were flying in 1935. After two aircraft were destroyed in test dives, the design was completely revised, and the result was an extremely robust aircraft which fulfilled its role superbly. The first serial production machines (Hs 123 A-1) were put into service in 1936 and were first deployed by the Condor Legion in the Spanish Civil War. Production ceased as early as November 1938, as biplanes were considered old-fashioned, yet the Hs 123's deployment in the Second World War belies this evaluation, as it performed very well indeed. Its robust build proved especially valuable for its role as a ground attack aircraft on the Eastern Front, where it was deployed until early 1944.

| | Hs 123A-1 |
|---|---|
| Type: | Dive-bomber and ground attack aircraft |
| Crew: | 1 |
| Weight when empty/ max weight at takeoff: | 1,500 kg/2,215 kg |
| Length/wingspan/height: | 8.33 m/10.5 m/3.2 m |
| Engine(s): | One BMW 132Dc 9-cylinder radial engine with 880 hp |
| Maximum speed: | 340 km/h |
| Service ceiling: | 9,000 m |
| Range: | 855 km |
| Weaponry: | 2 x 7.92 mm MG17 machine guns fixed in the fuselage, and an external payload of up to 450 kg – 1 x 250 kg and 4 x 50 kg bombs |

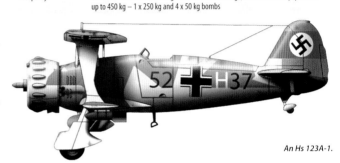

*An Hs 123A-1.*

# JUNKERS JU 87 STUKA

| | Ju 87D-1 |
|---|---|
| Type: | Dive-bomber and ground attack aircraft |
| Crew: | 2 |
| Weight when empty/ max weight at takeoff: | 3,900 kg/6,600 kg |
| Length/wingspan/height: | 11.5 m/13.8 m/3.9 m |
| Engine(s): | One Junkers Jumo 211J-1 hanging V12 engine with 1,410 hp |
| Maximum speed: | 410 km/h at 3,840 m |
| Service ceiling: | 7,300 m |
| Range: | 1,535 km |
| Weaponry: | 2 x 7.92 mm MG 17 machine guns fixed in the wings, 1 x 7.92 mm MG81Z machine gun in rear of cockpit, and an external payload of max. 1,800 kg |

The Junkers Ju 87 Stuka (Sturz-kampfbomber, or dive-bomber) is one of the best-known aircraft of the Second World War, both because it was a symbol of the Blitzkrieg (literally, 'lightning war') of 1939–41, and because of its striking appearance. It was made entirely out of metal, and it had distinctive inverted gull wings and a fixed undercarriage. In 1934, in Dessau, Junkers presented the first prototypes, which still had a twin-tail. The first production aircraft (Ju 87 B-1) were delivered to the German Dive-Bomber Wing in 1937 and were soon tested by the Condor Legion in Spain. As long as the Luftwaffe dominated the skies, the Ju 87 proved to be a highly effective weapon, which could attack specific targets in mid-dive. Its intimidating appearance and the wail of its 'Jericho sirens' were enough to spread terror and panic on their own. But when it came up against Hurricanes and Spitfires in the Battle of Britain, the tables were turned, and many Stukas were

*A Ju 87D-5 of the 3rd Group of the 2nd German Ground Attack Wing, Eastern Front, July 1943.*

*A Ju 87B-2 during the French campaign in 1940.*

destroyed. Consequently, it was no longer deployed on the Western Front, but it continued to enjoy some success in Africa, the Mediterranean and Russia. At the beginning of the war, the main version was the Ju 87B, but a new model, the Ju 87R, which could carry two additional 300 litre fuel tanks under its wings, was introduced especially for anti-ship operations in the Mediterranean. The Ju 87C was to be deployed on the *Graf Zeppelin* aircraft carrier, but the latter was never finished. The most frequently produced version was the Ju 87D, which had a more powerful engine, superior aerodynamics (thanks to the removal of the large cooler on the front of the fuselage, new engine cowling and a new cockpit hood), and a heavy bomb load of 1,800 kg. There was also a training version with two sets of controls, called the Ju 87H. The final production model was the Ju 87G, which had two 3.7 cm guns beneath its wings to fire at tanks, and was the brainchild of Colonel Hans-Ulrich Rudel, who destroyed 519 tanks during the war and is said to have survived being shot down

30 times. From 1944 onwards the Ju 87 was frequently deployed at night, as it was too dangerous to fly it during the day.

*A Ju 87G-1 with two 3.7 cm on-board cannon under its wings.*

*In total, 5,709 Stukas were manufactured. In spite of its drawbacks,* *the Ju 87 was one of the most successful dive-bombers and ground attack aircraft in the war, though its legendary reputation owes more than a little to skilful propaganda.*

# HENSCHEL HS 129

| | Hs 129B-1/R-2 |
|---|---|
| Type: | Ground attack aircraft |
| Crew: | 1 |
| Weight when empty/max weight at takeoff: | 3,810 kg/5,110 kg |
| Length/wingspan/height: | 9.75 m/14.2 m/3.25 m |
| Engine(s): | Two Gnome-Rhône 14M-4/5 14-cylinder radial engines with 700 hp each |
| Maximum speed: | 407 km/h at 3,800 m |
| Service ceiling: | 9,000 m |
| Range: | 560 km |
| Weaponry: | 2 x 7.92 mm MG17 and 2 x 20 mm MG151/20 machine guns fixed in the fuselage, and 1 x 30 mm MK-101 automatic cannon in a container under the fuselage or four 50 kg bombs under the wings |

The Hs 129 was a ground attack aircraft designed especially to support the ground troops. The first prototypes were presented in 1939, but among other problems they were underpowered, and the aircraft had to be completely redesigned. In fact, the B-1 version, with a French 700 hp radial engine and front section, was not put into production until late 1941, and Hs 129s did not enter service until mid-1942. They were deployed mostly on the Eastern Front, but also in North Africa and Italy. Because of the nature of its deployment, it was heavily armoured (with a cockpit screen

*An Hs 129B-2R1 in a Stabskette (a flight of three aircraft) of the 2nd Group of the 1st German Ground Attack Wing, Eastern Front, November 1942.*

made of 75 mm reinforced glass) and armed, but its Gnome-Rhône engines were constantly beset with problems, which limited its effectiveness. As well as infantry support, the Hs 129 was also used as an anti-tank aircraft, which earned it the nickname 'the Flying Can

Opener'. It came with many different weapons configurations, capable of carrying 30 mm, 37 mm or 75 mm guns under its fuselage, and more than 800 were manufactured in total.

# DORNIER DO 17

Like the He 111 (p.201), the Do 17 was ordered in 1932. A twin-engine shoulder-wing metal aircraft with an electrically retractable tail wheel, it had a very elegant, slim design which earned it the nickname 'the Flying Pencil'. In the Zurich-Dübendorf Air Race in 1937, it easily outstripped fighter aircraft from other countries. Nevertheless, relatively few of the earliest combat and reconnaissance models were built. Only the Z version was produced in large numbers (506 in total), but in the early months of the war it was the predominant aircraft in both combat and reconnaissance wings. To give its crew more room, the front section of the Do 17's fuselage was completely redesigned, but the four-seat cockpit spoiled the aircraft's slim appearance. It was also

| | Do 17Z-2 |
|---|---|
| Type: | Bomber |
| Crew: | 4 |
| Weight when empty/max weight at takeoff: | 5,210 kg/8,590 kg |
| Length/wingspan/height: | 15.8 m/18 m/4.55 m |
| Engine(s): | Two BMW Bramo 323P 9-cylinder radial engines with 1,000 hp each |
| Maximum speed: | 410 km/h at 1,220 m |
| Service ceiling: | 8,200 m |
| Range: | 1,160 km |
| Weaponry: | 6–7 x 7.92 mm MG15 mobile machine guns, with a payload of max. 1,000 kg in the internal bomb bay |

deployed as a night fighter, for which it was fitted with an infrared device and fixed weapons – four MG17 and four 20mm MGFF guns – towards the front. The Do 17's performance was phenomenal in 1937, but by the time of the Battle of Britain it was no longer sufficient. Thereafter, the remaining

aircraft were increasingly used for flight instruction, donated to Germany's allies, such as Croatia, or – especially in the case of the E and F versions – put into service as glider tugs.

*A Do 17Z.*

# HEINKEL HE 111

The He 111 prototype flew for the first time in February 1935, and at the outset it was officially a high-speed commercial aircraft (like the Do 17). Some He 111s were indeed put into service by Lufthansa, but the military variant was more important. Because the version with BMW engines was initially a disappointment, a variant with 1,000 hp DB 600A engines was tested in 1936 and performed far better. The first He 111 B-1 aircraft were delivered to the Luftwaffe in late 1936, and very soon they were deployed by the Condor Legion in the Spanish Civil War. The E version and later models were fitted with Junkers Jumo engines, as the Daimler-Benz engines were required for fighter aircraft. The He 111 had elliptical wings, which gave it excellent lift, but they were difficult to manufacture, so the G version had new wings with straight edges front and rear. The most important alteration in its appearance, however, came with the introduction of the P series in 1938, which had a glazed dome rather than a 'stepped' cockpit, increasing visibility. This model was replaced by the H series in September 1939, and the latter was the predominant He 111 model throughout the war.

| | He 111H-6 |
|---|---|
| Type: | Bomber |
| Crew: | 5 |
| Weight when empty/ max weight at takeoff: | 8,680 kg/14,000 kg |
| Length/wingspan/height: | 16.4 m/22.5 m/3.4 m |
| Engine(s): | Two Junkers Jumo 211F-2 hanging V12 engines with 1,350 hp each |
| Maximum speed: | 435 km/h at 6,000 m |
| Service ceiling: | 6,700 m |
| Range: | 2,900 km |
| Weaponry: | 1 x 20 mm MG/FF machine gun in the nose, 1 x 13 mm MG131 or 1 x 7.92 mm MG81Z machine gun on the back of the fuselage, 2 x 7.92 mm MG81 machine guns in the ventral gondola, 2 x 7.92 mm machine guns on the sides, and a combined external and internal payload of max. 3,000 kg |

When Germany invaded Poland, 808 He 111s (including all the variants) were deployed. In fact, during the early months of the war, the majority of bombing raids were carried out by He 111s, and they were constantly in service. In May 1940, they were flown in the campaign on the Western Front, and throughout the Battle of Britain later that year, the He 111 was the Luftwaffe's standard bomber. But it was during the Battle of Britain that its vulnerability to determined fighter attacks was exposed, and many were shot down. Thereafter, the He 111 was deployed as a night bomber and for other specialist tasks

– for example, as a torpedo bomber, reconnaissance aircraft, transporter and glider tug. But it still served as a bomber during the day on the Eastern Front.

When production was halted in the autumn of 1944, around 7,300 He 111s had been manufactured, and there was a bewildering array of different versions, converted models and weapons configurations. Another 26 He 111Hs were manufactured under licence in Spain and called the CASA 2.111. Ironically, when the supply of Junkers engines had run out, these aircraft were fitted with Rolls-Royce Merlin engines.

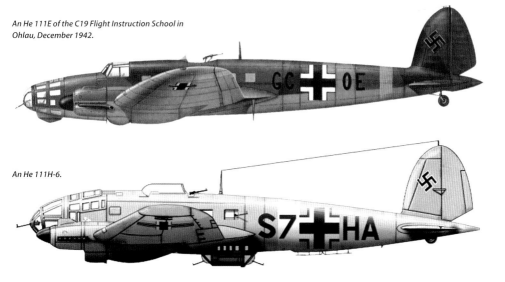

*An He 111E of the C19 Flight Instruction School in Ohlau, December 1942.*

*An He 111H-6.*

## JUNKERS JU 88

*A Ju 88G-1.*

The Junkers Ju 88 was certainly the most versatile aircraft in the Luftwaffe. Numerous different versions were produced throughout the war, and around 15,000 of all versions were manufactured in total. The first prototype, which was conceived as a high-speed medium range bomber, had its maiden flight in December 1936, the fifth prototype set a few world records in March 1939, and soon afterwards the first Ju 88A-1s were delivered to the Luftwaffe. Even when it was first deployed, it soon became apparent that its defences were inadequate, so they were considerably improved on the A-4. The main version of the Ju 88A was always the A-4, though later variants (up to the A-17) were also produced, and there was a bewildering array of Ju 88 variants and sub-variants.

While the Ju 88A was designed primarily as a bomber, the Ju 88C was used as a heavy fighter and a destroyer. The D series models were reconnaissance bombers with an increased range, and

| | Ju 88A-4 | Ju88G-6c |
|---|---|---|
| Type: | Bomber/dive-bomber | Night fighter |
| Crew: | 4 | 3 |
| Weight when empty/ max weight at takeoff: | 9,860 kg/14,000 kg | 9,081 kg/13,100 kg |
| Length/wingspan/ height: | 14.4 m/20.08 m/4.85 m | 15.55 m/20.08 m/4.85 m |
| Engine(s): | Two Junkers Jumo 211J-1 hanging V12 engines with 1,350 hp each | Two Junkers Jumo 213A-1 hanging V12 engines with 1,750 hp each |
| Maximum speed: | 470 km/h at 5,300 m | 625 km/h |
| Service ceiling: | 8,200 m | 10,000 m |
| Range: | 2,730 km | 2,250 km |
| Weaponry: | 1 x 13 mm MG131 or 1 x 7.92 mm MG81 forward-firing machine gun in the cockpit, 2 x MG81 machine guns in the rear of the ventral gondola, 2 x MG81 machine guns in the rear of the cockpit, and a combined internal and external payload of max. 3,000 kg | 4 x 20 mm MG151/20 machine guns fixed in a ventral gondola, and 2 x MG151/20 machine guns firing diagonally upwards from behind the cockpit ('diagonal music') |

the G series models served as night fighters with radar. The Ju 88H was a long-range reconnaissance aircraft and destroyer, with an extended fuselage for additional fuel tanks. There was also the Ju 88P, with 3.7 cm, 5 cm or

7.5 cm anti-tank guns installed in the underside of the fuselage. The more defensive weaponry and equipment the Ju 88 acquired, the slower it became. So in order for it to fulfil its intended role as a high-speed bomber, the Ju 88's

*A Ju 88A-6U with FuG-200 ship-locating radar, Mediterranean region.*

aerodynamics were improved on later versions, and they were fitted with more powerful engines. They were the Ju 88S and Ju 88T, which were a bomber and a reconnaissance aircraft respectively.

Although the earliest examples were still relatively undeveloped and caused a few problems, in the course of the war the Ju 88 became one of the best and most versatile machines on either side. Towards the end of the war, there were attempts to use ageing Ju 88s as flying bombs: each plane had its nose removed and replaced with a 3,800 kg warhead. An Me 109 or Fw 190 would carry it close to the enemy on a strip on the underside of the fuselage, aim it in the right direction and release it to fly into its target. Although this was a very promising plan, Ju 88s fired in this way actually hit very few enemy targets, as they could not be relied upon to stay on course when released.

*A Ju 88A of the 51st German Bomber Wing (known as 'Edelweiss').*

GERMANY

## DORNIER DO 217

The Dornier Do 217 was best known for firing Hs 293 and Fritz X missiles. The prototype had its maiden flight as early as 1938, having been developed from the Do 17 and fitted with more powerful engines and a greater payload. The A series was conceived as a reconnaissance aircraft, fitted with DB 601 engines, but only eight were ever produced. It was succeeded by the E series, which was fitted with twin 1,600 hp 801 A/B BMW radial engines and used as a bomber, a reconnaissance aircraft and a torpedo bomber. The E-5 was the first to be equipped with the Hs 293. The K-series was introduced in the autumn of 1942, with a completely altered nose – rounded rather than layered, with a glazed cockpit – and more powerful engines: each BMW 801 G/H engine produced 1,730 hp. In addition, the K-2 had a greater wingspan, so that it could carry Fritz X. The M series was fitted with DB 603 engines

*A Do 217E of the 100th German Bomber Wing with Hs 293s (see p.180) under its wings.*

instead of their BMW counterparts, but the two models are virtually identical in every other respect. As well as bombers and reconnaissance aircraft, there were also night fighters based on the Do 217. The E series bomber was converted to produce the J series, which was equipped with four 20 mm MGFF and four 7.92 mm MG17 guns, as well as 'Lichtenstein' radar in the nose. The N series night fighter was also developed from the M series, and as well as its standard weaponry and radar, these planes often had four additional guns,

MG151/20s firing diagonally upwards in the fuselage ('diagonal music'). Because of their long range and stability, the Do 217 J and N excelled as weapons platforms, but were not sufficiently manoeuvrable to serve as night fighters. There was also a P version, a high-altitude reconnaissance aircraft. With a DB 605 engine in the fuselage driving a supercharger, it could reach altitudes in excess of 16 km. Few P series machines were ever produced, but 1,730 Do 217s were manufactured in total.

| | Do 217M-1 |
|---|---|
| Type: | Bomber |
| Crew: | 4 |
| Weight when empty/ max weight at takeoff: | 8,840 kg/16,700 kg |
| Length/wingspan/height: | 16.9 m/19 m/5 m |
| Engine(s): | Two Daimler-Benz DB 603A hanging V12 engines with 1,750 hp each |
| Maximum speed: | 560 km/h at 5,700 m |
| Service ceiling: | 9,500 m |
| Range: | 2,150 km |
| Weaponry: | 2 x 13 mm MG131 and up to 6 x 7.92 mm MG81 mobile machine guns to be fired in various directions in the nose, and a combined internal and external payload of max. 4,000 kg |

## JUNKERS JU 188 RÄCHER (AVENGER)

Junkers began developing a successor to the Ju 88 as early as 1940, but it soon became clear that designing the Ju 288, as it was known, would be hindered by engine trouble, so Junkers decided to produce an interim model. The Ju 88B and E test aircraft had a new fuselage and greater wingspan, and the Ju 188 was developed from them. The prototype of this new model flew for the first time in January 1943, and the first production models were ready just two months later, even though the German Air Ministry had specifically demanded that the new model had to be compatible with both BMW 801 radial and Jumo 213 inline engines. Ju 188s were primarily deployed as reconnaissance aircraft (some of which were equipped with FuG 200 radar to detect ships), bombers and torpedo bombers. They were manoeuvrable and handled well, but they appeared two years too late. A high-altitude model,

the Ju 388, was also developed. Only a handful of the latter were ever built, but 1,076 Ju 188s were manufactured in total.

| | Ju 188E-1 |
|---|---|
| Type: | Bomber and reconnaissance aircraft |
| Crew: | 4 |
| Weight when empty/ max weight at takeoff: | 9,860 kg/15,200 kg |
| Length/wingspan/height: | 14.95 m/22 m/4.44 m |
| Engine(s): | Two BMW 801D-2 14-cylinder radial engines with 1,730 hp each |
| Maximum speed: | 500 km/h at 6,000 m |
| Service ceiling: | 9,345 m |
| Range: | 1,945 km |
| Weaponry: | 1 x 20 mm MG151/20 mobile machine guns in the nose, 1 x 13 mm MG131 machine gun in the rear of the cockpit, 1 x 7.92 mm MG81Z rearward-firing machine gun in the ventral gondola, and a combined internal and external payload of max. 3,000 kg |

*The Ju 188D-2.*

# FOCKE-WULF FW 200 CONDOR

The Fw 200 was originally a long-haul passenger aircraft. The initial design appeared in 1935, and it successfully completed its first long-distance flight in 1937. In fact, the test flight was such a success that the prototype set a few world records, and Lufthansa ordered the first series of production models. In 1940 there were attempts to convert the existing Condors for military purposes, but the test results were unsatisfactory because the engines were not sufficiently powerful. Instead, two prototypes were converted for use as Hitler's personal transport, and another was converted for Goering. As the war progressed, however, it became clear that Germany required a long-range bomber and reconnaissance aircraft, so the German Air Ministry ordered the Fw 200C, which had a reinforced airframe and a ventral gondola with a bomb bay, as well as new 1,200 hp engines. This model was deployed primarily as a sea reconnaissance aircraft and bomber in the Atlantic. Because the sea convoys were poorly defended at first, the Fw 200 enjoyed plenty of success for

a while. They took off from bases in France and Norway, either locating targets for submarines or attacking ships themselves with bombs and Hs 293s. Between

August 1940 and February 1941, Fw 200s sank 85 Allied ships, amounting to 363,000 GRT (gross register tons).

|  | Fw 200C-3 |
|---|---|
| Type: | Sea reconnaissance aircraft and transporter |
| Crew: | 7–8 |
| Weight when empty/ max weight at takeoff: | 17,005 kg/24,520 kg |
| Length/wingspan/height: | 23.46 m/32.84 m/6.3 m |
| Engine(s): | Four BMW-Bramo 323R 9-cylinder radial engines with 1,200 hp each |
| Maximum speed: | 360 km/h at sea level |
| Service ceiling: | 6,000 m |
| Range: | 3,560 km |
| Weaponry: | 1 x 20 mm MG151/20 machine gun in the turret, 1 x 20 mm MG151/20 machine gun in the front and 1 x 7.92 mm MG15 machine gun in the rear of the ventral gondola, 1 x MG15 machine gun on the back of the fuselage, and 1 x MG15 machine gun on each side |

*An Fw 200C-8 of the 40th German Bomber Wing with Hs 293s under its wings for anti-ship combat.*

# ARADO AR 234

|  | Ar 234B-2 |
|---|---|
| Type: | High-speed bomber and reconnaissance aircraft |
| Crew: | 1 |
| Weight when empty/ max weight at takeoff: | 5,200 kg/9,850 kg |
| Length/wingspan/height: | 12.64 m/14.1 m/4.3 m |
| Engine(s): | Two Junkers Jumo 004B jet engines with 890 kp of thrust each |
| Maximum speed: | 740 km/h at 6,000 m |
| Service ceiling: | 10,000 m |
| Range: | 1,630 km |
| Weaponry: | 2 x fixed rearward-firing 20 mm MG151/20 machine guns in the rear, and a payload of up to 2,000 kg under the wings |

*An Ar 234B-2.*

The Arado Ar 234 was the world's first jet-powered bomber to be put into service. From 1941 Arado developed a reconnaissance bomber with two jet engines, and the test model was introduced in 1943. To save weight, it shed its undercarriage after takeoff and landed on skids, but this system did not

work, so the production model had a three-wheel undercarriage. Not only was the jet engine revolutionary but the Ar 234 also had an ejector seat. The reconnaissance version, the Ar 234 B-1, which was fitted with up to four cameras, appeared in 1944, followed by the bomber version, the Ar 234 B-2, which

had a three-axle autopilot and a BZA bomb counter, and which could carry 2,000 kg of bombs externally. The bomber first came into service with the 76th Bomber Wing in the Ardennes offensive of December 1944, but by April 1945 they could no longer be flown because of the shortage of fuel.

## HEINKEL HE 177 GREIF (GRIFFIN)

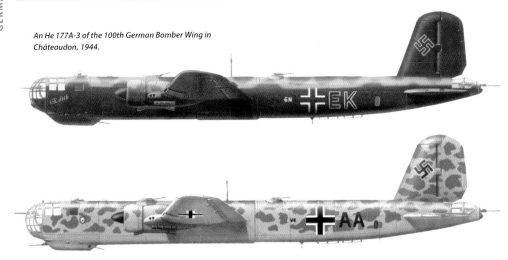

*An He 177A-3 of the 100th German Bomber Wing in Châteaudon, 1944.*

*An He 177A-5 of the 3rd Group of the 1st German Bomber Wing in East Prussia, summer 1944.*

In 1938 the German Air Ministry ordered a heavy bomber with a maximum speed of at least 540 km/h, a maximum payload of at least 2,000 kg, and the capability to dive. The aircraft that Heinkel developed was technically advanced and innovative. The He 177 flew for the first time in November 1939 and looked like a twin-engine aircraft, but in fact it had four engines. To reduce air resistance, it was originally supposed only to have two engines, but because no sufficiently powerful engines were available, Daimler-Benz produced a DB 606 engine from two DB 601 engines, and the He 177 had two of the former. But the DB 606 was never reliable and kept overheating, which earned it the nicknames 'Reichsfeuerzeug' (lighter) and 'Reichsfackel' (torch). Even at the prototype stage, several aircraft crashed because of engine fires or structural failure. The first He 177s were delivered in mid-1942, and the A-3, delivered later in the year, was the first to be called the 'Griffin'. Though the aircraft were still ridden with structural flaws, the He 177's main problems would always be its engines. Most He 177s were deployed in air raids against England or put into service on ships, which made it possible for them to carry Hs 293 or Fritz X flying bombs. The A-5 had a new reinforced structure so that it could carry a heavier payload, and improved DB 610 compound engines, each consisting of two DB 603 engines, but they were still not entirely reliable. The A-7 version was also produced, albeit in small numbers, with a wider wingspan of 36.6 m to attain higher altitudes. Production of the He 177 was halted in the autumn of 1944, by which time fewer than 900 had been built. It had the potential to be an excellent aircraft, but because its engines were so unreliable and its manufacturer was bogged down with so many test models and equipment configurations, its effectiveness was severely limited.

| He 177A-5 | |
|---|---|
| Type: | Heavy bomber |
| Crew: | 6–7 |
| Weight when empty/ max weight at takeoff: | 16,800 kg/31,000 kg |
| Length/wingspan/height: | 20.4 m/31.44 m/6.39 m |
| Engine(s): | Two Daimler-Benz DB 610A/B engines (each consisting of two Daimler-Benz DB603 hanging V12s) with 2,950 hp normal power and 3,100 hp emergency power each |
| Maximum speed: | 490 km/h at 6,000 m |
| Service ceiling: | 8,000 m |
| Range: | 5,500 km with two HS 293s |
| Weaponry: | 1 x 7.92 mm MG81 machine gun in the nose, 1 x 20 mm MG151/20 machine gun towards the front, a remote-controlled installation on the fuselage with 2 x 13 mm MG131 machine guns, 1 x 13 mm MG131 machine gun in a turning turret on the fuselage, 1 x 20 mm MG151/20 machine gun in an installation in the rear, and a combined internal and external payload of 6,000 kg |

# FIESELER FI 156 STORCH (STORK)

| | Fi 156C-2 |
|---|---|
| Type: | Liaison and reconnaissance aircraft |
| Crew: | 2 |
| Weight when empty/ max weight at takeoff: | 930 kg/1,325 kg |
| Length/wingspan/height: | 9.9 m/14.25 m/3.05 m |
| Engine(s): | One Argus As10C-3 hanging V8 engine with 240 hp |
| Maximum speed: | 175 km/h at sea level |
| Service ceiling: | 4,600 m |
| Range: | 385 km |
| Weaponry: | One mobile rearward-firing 7.92 mm MG15 machine gun |

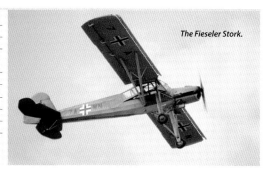

*The Fieseler Stork.*

The Germans required a liaison and observation aircraft that could take off from a very short runway, and the Fieseler Fi 156 was built to meet this need. The first of three test aircraft took off on its maiden flight on 10 May 1936, and it was very clear even at this stage that none of the other models could compete with the Fieseler. A slat along the front and flaps along the entire reverse edge of the wings gave it the required landing and takeoff capabilities, and its glazed cabin allowed for excellent downward visibility. After the production of the limited A and B series, the C series went into serial production, and in total around 2,900 Fi 156s were built. The C-1 was soon replaced by the C-2, which had an MG15 gun in a plexiglass bubble ('Linsenlafette') to defend it against attacks from the rear. The C-3 was manufactured in the largest numbers, with the C-3 Trop being equipped for use in Africa. There was also a D-series (D-0 and D-1), made to transport wounded personnel. Storks were also frequently used for special missions, such as the flight of Hanna Reitsch into Berlin on 26 April 1945, when the city was beleaguered and lay in ruins.

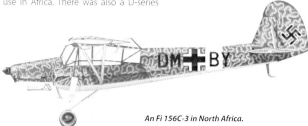

*An Fi 156C-3 in North Africa.*

# HENSCHEL HS 126

*The Hs 126B-1.*

| | Hs 126B-1 |
|---|---|
| Type: | Short-range reconnaissance aircraft |
| Crew: | 2–3 |
| Weight when empty/ max weight at takeoff: | 2,030 kg/3,090 kg |
| Length/wingspan/height: | 10.95 m/14.5 m/3.75 m |
| Engine(s): | One BMW-Bramo 323A-1 9-cylinder radial engine with 850 hp |
| Maximum speed: | 310 km/h |
| Service ceiling: | 8,300 m |
| Range: | 720 km/h |
| Weaponry: | 1 x 7.92 mm MG17 fixed machine gun in the fuselage, 1 x 7.92 mm machine gun in the rear of the cockpit, and an external payload of 1 x 50 kg or 5 x 10 kg bomb(s) |

During the early years of the war, the Henschel Hs 126 was the Luftwaffe's standard short-range reconnaissance aircraft. The earliest prototype was completed in 1936, and in 1937 Henschel built a pre-production series of ten machines. Because these were highly rated, the Hs 126 went into full-scale production, and more than 600 were manufactured. From 1942, however, it was gradually withdrawn from service and replaced by the Fw 189. It was first deployed by the Condor Legion in the Spanish Civil War on the Nationalist side, and the surviving aircraft remained in Spain. The Hs 126 served the Luftwaffe well: it had excellent downward visibility, it was very robust, and there was room for a pilot, a look-out and/or a gunner.

## FOCKE-WULF FW 189 UHU (EAGLE OWL)

In 1937 the German Air Ministry ordered a short-range reconnaissance aircraft with excellent visibility, and Focke-Wulf's bid was successful. The company designed a machine made entirely from metal with a double tail boom, a glazed fuselage and a retractable tail wheel. There was room for three men: a pilot, a gunner or an observer, and an engineer. The main production model was the A version, and the B version was a flight instruction aircraft. There was also a light ground attack prototype called the Fw 189C. The Fw 189's engine reliability was legendary, but it would have

*The Fw 189 was deployed mostly on the Eastern Front and performed extremely well. Because it was so manoeuvrable, it could often elude enemy fighters in spite of its relative lack of speed.*

benefited from more power. Hence, the E version was tested with 700 hp Gnome-Rhône radial engines, though these were unsuccessful, and the F model was fitted with 580 hp Argus As 411MA1 engines,

but was very similar to the Fw 189A-2 in other respects. In total, 864 Eagle Owls were produced.

|  | Fw 189A-1 |
|---|---|
| Type: | Short-range reconnaissance aircraft |
| Crew: | 2–3 |
| Weight when empty/ max weight at takeoff: | 2,805 kg/3,950 kg |
| Length/wingspan/height: | 13.85 m/13.8 m/5 m |
| Engine(s): | 2 Argus As 410A-1E hanging V12 engines with 465 hp each |
| Maximum speed: | 335 km/h at 2,500 m |
| Service ceiling: | 7,000 m |
| Range: | 680 km |
| Weaponry: | 2 x 7.92 mm MG17 machine guns in the wing roots, 2 x 7.92 mm mobile machine guns in the rear of the cockpit, and a payload of up to 4 x 50 kg bombs under the wings |

## MESSERSCHMITT ME 321 AND ME 323 GIGANT (GIANT)

|  | Me 323E-2 |
|---|---|
| Type: | Transporter |
| Crew: | 5 plus gunners |
| Weight when empty/ max weight at takeoff: | 29,060 kg/45,000 kg |
| Length/wingspan/height: | 28.5 m/55 m/9.6 m |
| Engine(s): | Six Gnome-Rhône 14N 14-cylinder radial engines with 1,140 hp each |
| Maximum speed: | 240 km/h at 1,500 m |
| Service ceiling: | 4,500 m |
| Range: | 1,300 km |
| Weaponry: | 2 x 20 mm MG151/20 and up to 7 x 13 mm MG131 mobile machine guns in the fuselage, additional 7.92 mm machine guns in the side windows (optional), and a payload of max. 15,000 kg |

For the planned invasion of the United Kingdom (Operation Sea Lion), a gigantic transport glider that could carry tanks or up to 200 men was ordered. But the Me 321 did not make its maiden flight until February 1941, after the invasion had

been called off. The Me 321 was deployed primarily on the Eastern Front, where it was towed by three Bf 110s or a special He 111 variant. This was a dangerous and laborious procedure, so the Me 321 was motorized. Because German engines

were at a premium, each aircraft was fitted with six French engines (built in occupied France) instead. This new transporter went into production as the Me 323 D-1 in the summer of 1942, and from November that year it was used primarily to transport supplies across the Mediterranean to the troops in North Africa. When the Allies gained the upper hand in that area, the Me 323 was deployed mainly on the Eastern Front. Up to August 1944, 201 Me 323s had been produced. It was the largest transport aircraft of its time, and it was simple to load, thanks to the large trapdoor in its nose, but it was also very ponderous, and its Gnome-Rhône engines were unreliable.

*An Me 323 D-1 of the 5th German Air Transport Wing, winter 1943–44.*

# JUNKERS JU 52

Junkers began designing the single-engine Ju 52/1m as early as 1929; this led to the development of the triple-engine Ju 52/3m transport aircraft, which had its maiden flight in March 1932. It had Junkers double wings to increase its lift, and a characteristic corrugated iron covering on its fuselage and wings. Before long, it formed the backbone of both the Lufthansa (German civil airline) fleet and the Air Force's transport units. The new Luftwaffe had only recently been established, and it urgently needed an auxiliary bomber until there were sufficient numbers of He 111s and Do 17s. To meet this

| | Ju 52/3mg6e |
|---|---|
| Type: | Transporter |
| Crew: | 3–4 |
| Weight when empty/ max weight at takeoff: | 6,560 kg/10,515 kg |
| Length/wingspan/height: | 18.9 m/29.25 m/4.5 m |
| Engine(s): | Three BMW 132T-2 9-cylinder radial engines with 830 hp each |
| Maximum speed: | 295 km/h at sea level |
| Service ceiling: | 5,500 m |
| Range: | 1,290 km |
| Weaponry: | 3 x 7.92 mm MG15 machine guns, up to 17 passengers or an equivalent freight load. |

requirement, the Ju 52/3m was fitted with a machine gun installation at the rear, another (which was retractable) between its wheels, and hanging containers which could carry a payload of 1,500 kg. This version of the Ju 52/3m was deployed in Spain by the Condor Legion and in the early months of the Second World War.

*A Ju 52g6e of the 3rd German Air Transport Wing, winter 1942–43.*

At the beginning of the war, around 1,000 Ju 52/3ms were in service, and it is claimed that more than 4,800 were manufactured before hostilities ended. This model was nicknamed 'Aunt Ju' by the troops, and it was used in almost every capacity, from transport missions to minesweeping (for which a special version was manufactured, with a large aluminium ring which produced a strong magnetic field when electric current was passed through it). Thirteen main versions were manufactured during the war, with improved radios, more powerful engines or heavier weaponry, as well as removable skis, floats or wheels, which showed how many different roles the Luftwaffe had to fulfil. Although the aircraft began to show its age during the war, its reliability and robustness made it very popular. In Spain 170 Ju 52/3ms were built under licence and called the CASA 352, while the French manufactured them as AAC.1 Toucans after the war and kept them in service until the late 1950s.

*A Ju 52 landing. Note the Junkers double wings.*

GERMANY

# ARADO AR 196

The Arado Ar 196 was manufactured in larger numbers than any other German seaplane in the Second World War – around 500 were built in total, including 401 of the A-3 version. The first prototypes flew in 1938, and the first Ar 196s were deployed in 1939. Ar 196s served as a reconnaissance aircraft on the majority of German cruisers and battleships, from which they were launched by catapult, but they landed next to their carriers and had to be hoisted back on board. They were also used in coastal aviation and sea reconnaissance groups, where their agility and very heavy weaponry made them ideal for sea patrols and reconnaissance missions. Although the Ar 196 was made almost entirely out of metal, the back of the fuselage was covered with fabric. It was also manufactured by the French firm SNCA and the Dutch company Fokker under German orders (both countries had been occupied), and the last Ar 196s were delivered in August 1944.

| | Ar 196A-3 |
|---|---|
| Type: | Ship-based and coastal reconnaissance aircraft |
| Crew: | 2 |
| Weight when empty/ max weight at takeoff: | 2,990 kg/ 3,730 kg |
| Length/wingspan/height: | 11 m/12.4 m/4.45 m |
| Engine(s): | One BMW 132K 9-cylinder radial engine with 960 hp |
| Maximum speed: | 310 km/h at 4,000 m |
| Service ceiling: | 7,000 m |
| Range: | 1,070 km |
| Weaponry: | 2 x 20 mm MGFF fixed machine guns in the wings, 1 x 7.92 mm MG17 fixed machine gun in the upper fuselage, and a payload of 2 x 50 kg bombs under the wings |

*An Ar 196A-3.*

# HEINKEL HE 115

| | He 115-C1 |
|---|---|
| Type: | Reconnaissance aircraft and bomber |
| Crew: | 3 |
| Weight when empty/ max weight at takeoff: | 6,861 kg/ 10,665 kg |
| Length/wingspan/height: | 17.3 m/22.26 m/6.57 m |
| Engine(s): | Two BMW 132K 9-cylinder radial engines with 960 hp each |
| Maximum speed: | 288 km/h |
| Service ceiling: | 5,170 m |
| Range: | 2,785 km |
| Weaponry: | 1 x 7.92 mm MG15 mobile machine gun in the nose, 1 x 15 mm fixed machine gun under the nose, 1 x 7.92 mm machine gun in the rear of the cockpit, 2 x 7.92 mm fixed machine guns in the rear of the engine gondolas, and an internal or external payload of max. 750 kg – LTF 5 or LTF 6b torpedoes, mines or 3 x 250 kg bombs |

The Heinkel He 115 was a twin-engine seaplane with wings attached to the middle of the fuselage and two floats. It had its maiden flight in 1936, and the prototype set six seaplane world records. It was deployed as a minelayer in 1940, with a single magnetic 920 kg mine. The 106th and 406th Coastal Aviation Groups regularly flew mine-laying missions on the south and east coasts of the United Kingdom. In late 1940 the 115C-1 was introduced with an additional MG151 machine gun in a gondola under the nose, and two rearward-pointing MG17 machine guns in the engine gondolas. There was also a sub-variant with stronger floats for landing on ice and frozen snow. The C-4 was a variant built especially for torpedo attacks, and it was deployed on numerous occasions against convoys in the North Pole. The He 115 flew in coastal aviation groups until the end of the war.

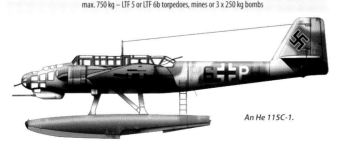

*An He 115C-1.*

# BLOHM UND VOSS BV 138

| | BV 138C-1 |
|---|---|
| Type: | Reconnaissance seaplane |
| Crew: | 5 |
| Weight when empty/ max weight at takeoff: | 8,100 kg/ 14,700 kg |
| Length/wingspan/height: | 19.9 m/27 m/6.6 m |
| Engine(s): | Three Junkers Jumo 205D diesel engines with 880 hp each |
| Maximum speed: | 275 km/h at sea level |
| Service ceiling: | 5,000 m |
| Range: | 5,000 km |
| Weaponry: | 1 x 20 mm MG151/20 machine gun in a turning nose turret, 1 x 20 mm MG151/20 machine gun in a turning tail turret, 1 x 13 mm MG131 machine gun in an open installation behind the central engine gondola, and a payload of up to 6 x 50 kg bombs or 4 x 150 kg depth charges |

*The Bv 138C-1. Because of its somewhat bizarre appearance, this aircraft's crew nicknamed it the 'Flying Clog'.*

In 1933 the German Air Ministry invited bids to produce a diesel-engine sea reconnaissance aircraft, and the successful design was submitted by the Hamburg shipbuilders Blohm und Voss. This model was initially called the Ha 138, then later the BV 138. But it soon became apparent that the engines with which it was supposed to be fitted were not available, so the design was altered to accommodate three Jumo 205 engines – the third engine was mounted in a structure attached to the base of the fuselage. Early test results were disappointing, and the design had to be revised again. The first production model

(the A-1) was delivered in 1939 with 605 hp Jumo 205C engines. The B-1 version had more powerful Jumo 205D engines and a more robust structure, and it was more heavily armoured; the C-1 model also had its structure reinforced and its weapon load increased. The BV 138 was

primarily used as a reconnaissance aircraft during the war, but it was less effective as an air-sea rescue aircraft. There was also a special minesweeping version with an electromagnetic aluminium ring. In total 279 BV 138s were produced, including 127 C-1s.

# DORNIER DO 24

In 1935 the Dutch Government required a replacement for its Dornier Whale in the Dutch East Indies, for which Dornier itself submitted a successful bid. It decided to alter the competition design for the BV 138 in accordance with the wishes of the Dutch Government, equipping it with 875 hp Wright radial engines, and in 1937 the Do 24K was manufactured under licence by the Dutch company Aviolanda. When German troops occupied the Netherlands in 1940, three seaplanes of this type were seized and subsequently tested in Germany. As the Do 24 vastly outperformed both the He 59 and the BV 138, its production continued in the Netherlands under German orders, and it became the standard air-sea rescue aircraft. Do 24s were so urgently needed that 48 were also manufactured in France by SNCA from 1942. The company continued to manufacture this model even after France was liberated, and 40 were delivered to the French Air Force. In June 1944 12 Do 24s were delivered to Spain, serving in Majorca until the mid-1970s. In total, around 240 Do 24s were produced.

| | Do 24T |
|---|---|
| Type: | Reconnaissance and air-sea rescue seaplane |
| Crew: | 5 |
| Weight when empty/max weight at takeoff: | 9,200 kg/18,400 kg |
| Length/wingspan/height: | 19.9 m/27 m/6.6 m |
| Engine(s): | Three BMW Bramo 323-R-2 9-cylinder radial engines with 1,000 hp each |
| Maximum speed: | 340 km/h at sea level |
| Service ceiling: | 5,000 m |
| Range: | 2,900 km |
| Weaponry: | 2 x 7.92 mm MG15 machine guns, one in the nose turret, one in the tail turret, and 1 x 20 mm MG151/20 machine gun in the rear turret |

*A Do 24N-1 from Dutch stocks, fitted with American radial engines. Because Wright radial engines were no longer available, later Do 24s were fitted with 1,000 hp BMW Bramo 323 R 2 engines.*

ITALY

# FIAT C.R.42 FALCO (FALCON)

The Fiat C.R.42 Falcon had its maiden flight on 23 May 1938, but although it was a robust, tidy and attractive design, it was already dated when it was put into production. Nevertheless, 34 were exported to Belgium, 68 to Hungary and 72 to Sweden. From the very beginning of the war, the Falcon's weaknesses were exposed: although it was easy to manoeuvre, it was too lightly armed and too slow, and it was completely out of its depth in the Battle of Britain. It fared rather better, however, in the Mediterranean, where the British also employed outdated aircraft. Once modern fighters such as the M.C. 202 had become available, the Falcon was used as a fighter bomber and a flight instruction aircraft. When the Italians changed sides in 1943, the Luftwaffe took possession of 112 Falcons, and employed them primarily for night raids and anti-partisan missions. In fact, 150 additional C.R.42s specially designed for night raids were manufactured for the Luftwaffe. When production was halted in late 1944, a total of 1,780 Falcons had been produced, and they were still being flown on night missions in May 1945.

| | C.R.42 |
|---|---|
| Type: | Fighter |
| Crew: | 1 |
| Weight when empty/max weight at takeoff: | 1,782 kg/2,295 kg |
| Length/wingspan/height: | 8.27 m/9.7 m/3.59 m |
| Engine(s): | One Fiat A.74-RC-38 14-cylinder radial engine with 840 hp |
| Maximum speed: | 430 km/h at 5,000 m |
| Service ceiling: | 10,200 m |
| Range: | 775 km |
| Weaponry: | 2 x 12.7 mm Type SAFAT fixed machine guns in the nose, and an external payload of up to 200 kg |

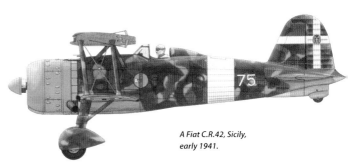

*A Fiat C.R.42, Sicily, early 1941.*

# FIAT G.50 FRECCIA (ARROW)

| | G.50 |
|---|---|
| Type: | Fighter |
| Crew: | 1 |
| Weight when empty/ max weight at takeoff: | 1,975 kg/2,415 kg |
| Length/wingspan/height: | 7.79 m/10.96 m/2.96 m |
| Engine(s): | One Fiat A.74-RC-38 14-cylinder radial engine with 840 hp |
| Maximum speed: | 472 km/h at 5,000 m |
| Service ceiling: | 9,835 m |
| Range: | 670 km |
| Weaponry: | 2 x 12.7 mm Type SAFAT fixed machine guns in the nose |

*A Fiat G.50bis in Libya, summer, 1941.*

The Fiat G.50 Arrow was the first Italian single-wing fighter. It was made of metal, and it had an enclosed cockpit and retractable undercarriage. Work began on its design in 1935, and it made its maiden flight in early 1937. It was tested in combat by the Aviazione Legionaria, the Italian pilots fighting on the side of the Nationalists in the Spanish Civil

War, where it became obvious that it was underpowered. In addition, the Italian pilots greatly disliked the closed cockpit, so it was fitted with an open cockpit based on the 45 version. During the Second World War, the basic G.50sie version was replaced by the G.50bis, which had its maiden flight on 9 September 1940. The latter also

had an open cockpit, and was equipped with larger fuel tanks and stronger armour. The Arrow was very agile, but this could not compensate for its underpowered engine or limited weaponry, weaknesses which were a death sentence for many pilots when they were confronted by the British Hurricanes. At diving speeds in excess of 500 km/h, the aircraft was very difficult to manoeuvre, and on some occasions parts of the wings and fuselage would even come loose. In total, around 774 G.50s, including 108 two-seater G.50B training aircraft, were produced.

# FIAT G.55 CENTAURO (CENTAUR)

| | G.55/I |
|---|---|
| Type: | Fighter and fighter bomber |
| Crew: | 1 |
| Weight when empty/ | 2,630 kg/ |
| max weight at takeoff: | 3,718 kg |
| Length/wingspan/height: | 9.37 m/11.85 m/3.13 m |
| Engine(s): | One Fiat RA-1050-RC-58 Tifone hanging V12 engine with 1,475 hp |
| Maximum speed: | 630 km/h |
| Service ceiling: | 12,300 m |
| Range: | 1,200 km |
| Weaponry: | 1 x 20 mm MG151/20 machine gun firing through the propeller hub, 2 x 20 mm MG151/20 fixed machine guns in the wings, 2 x 12.7 mm Type SAFAT machine guns in the nose, and external payload of max. 320 kg |

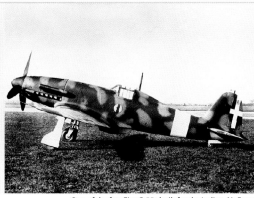

*One of the few Fiat G.55s built for the Italian Air Force.*

The Fiat G.55 Centaur was a massive improvement on its predecessor, the G.50, mostly because of its superior engine, a DB 605 built under licence. It had its maiden flight on 30 April 1942, and it was first tested in combat in March 1943, by which time the Italian Air Ministry had already decided to put it into production. Yet production for the Italian Air Force (Regia Aeronautica) was halted in September 1943, after only 16 G.55/0s and 15 G.55/1s had been completed. All 274 Centaurs produced thereafter were delivered to Mussolini's Fascist forces. Thanks to its robust structure, excellent visibility, speed and good manoeuvrability, the G.55 was very successful and very popular with its pilots. Early in 1944 two prototypes were fitted with the German DB 603A engine. This model, the G.56, was an aircraft as good as, if not better than, any of its German or Allied counterparts, but the severe shortage of DB 603 engines meant that it could not be put into serial production. In 1944 and 1945 the G.55 was also deployed by the Luftwaffe, which rated it very highly. After the cessation of hostilities Fiat used parts left over from the wartime production of the G.55 to produce the G.55A for the Italian and Argentinian Air Forces. In 1948 some of the Argentinian machines were given to the Egyptians, who deployed them against Israeli Avia 199s that same year.

*A Fiat G.55 of the National Republican Air Force (ANR). This was the air force of the northern Italian Fascist republic led by Mussolini after 1943.*

## MACCHI M.C. 200 SAETTA (LIGHTNING)

*A Macchi M.C. 200, Libya, June 1941.*

| | M.C. 200 |
|---|---|
| Type: | Fighter and fighter bomber |
| Crew: | 1 |
| Weight when empty/ | 1,895 kg/ |
| max weight at takeoff: | 2,590 kg |
| Length/wingspan/height: | 8.19 m/10.58 m/3.5 m |
| Engine(s): | One Fiat A.74-RC-38 14-cylinder radial engine with 840 hp |
| Maximum speed: | 502 km/h at 4,500 m |
| Service ceiling: | 8,900 m |
| Range: | 870 km |
| Weaponry: | 2 x 12.7 mm Type SAFAT machine guns in the nose; later models had 2 additional 7.7 mm SAFAT machine guns in the wings |

The M.C. 200 Lightning had an all-metal layered construction. Its low wings and its tail were cantilevered, and it had a retractable rear wheel. In 1936 Macchi started designing a replacement for the Fiat C.R.32 biplane, and the first prototype, which had an enclosed cockpit, flew at Christmas 1937. Because Italian pilots preferred open cockpits, later models were built in accordance with their wishes, but glazed side shutters were added for wind protection. In 1938 the first series of 99 aircraft was ordered, and in October 1939 the first production aircraft were delivered to the Italian Air Force. By the time the Italians entered the war in June 1940, they had 156 M.C. 200s, and they were first flown in combat against Malta in autumn that same year. Although the M.C. 200 handled well, its light weaponry and weak radial engine put it at a disadvantage compared to fighters from other countries. M.C. 200s were deployed in Greece, North Africa, Yugoslavia and later on the Eastern Front, and 23 were flown by free Italian fighter pilots on the side of the Allies after Italy's surrender in September 1943. The M.C. 200AS variant was built for service in Africa, and the M.C. 200CB was a fighter bomber. In total, 1,153 MC 200s were produced.

## MACCHI M.C. 202 FOLGORE (THUNDERBOLT) AND M.C. 205 VELTRO (GREYHOUND)

Mario Castoldi was convinced that the M.C. 200 could be more effective with a more powerful engine, which was why its basic design was altered to accommodate an imported Daimler-Benz DB 601 engine. The new machine had a larger fuselage and an enclosed cockpit, but its undercarriage, wing assembly and tail were practically indistinguishable from the M.C. 200. The M.C. 202 made its maiden flight on 10 August 1940, and Castoldi's convictions were entirely corroborated, so the new model went into production without delay. Nevertheless, because it was not easy to import the DB 601 engine or to manufacture it under licence, the M.C. 200 was produced alongside its intended successor. The M.C. 202 was first used in combat in 1941 in North Africa, but it also served on the Eastern Front. Although it still was not sufficiently well armed, Castoldi's new model performed more than well enough to cope with its enemy counterparts. To improve their weaponry, later models in the series were

| | M.C. 202 | M.C. 205 |
|---|---|---|
| Type: | Fighter and fighter bomber | Fighter and fighter bomber |
| Crew: | 1 | 1 |
| Weight when empty/ | 2,350 kg/ | 2,581 kg/ |
| max weight at takeoff: | 3,010 kg | 3,408 kg |
| Length/wingspan/ | 8.85 m/10.58 m/ | 8.85 m/10.58 m/ |
| height: | 3.04 m | 3.04 m |
| Engine(s): | One Alfa-Romeo RA-1000-RC-41-1 Monsone hanging V12 engine with 1,175 hp | One Fiat RA-1050-RC-58 Tifone hanging V12 engine with 1,475 hp |
| Maximum speed: | 595 km/h at 5,000 m | 642 km/h |
| Service ceiling: | 11,500 m | 11,300 m |
| Range: | 765 km | 1,040 km |
| Weaponry: | 2 x 12.7 mm Type SAFAT fixed machine guns in the nose – later models also had 2 additional 7.7 mm SAFAT machine guns in the wings – and partial gondolas under the wings with 1 x 20 mm MG151/20 machine gun each | 2 x 12.7 mm Type SAFAT fixed machine guns in the nose, 2 x 7.7 mm SAFAT machine guns under the wings – later models had 20 mm MG151/20 instead of the 7.7 mm MG20 machine guns |

*An M.C. 205 from the Italian Co-Belligerent Air Force, which fought on the side of the Allies.*

*An M.C. 202, Sicily, early 1942.*

equipped initially with two extra 7.7 mm machine guns, and later some of them also had gondolas under their wings, each with one 20 mm MG 151/20 machine gun. As with all Italian fighters, there was also a version for the tropics (AS) and a fighter bomber (CB) with a maximum payload of

320 kg. For as long as the M.C. 202 was produced, its engine was difficult to obtain, so only around 1,500 were ever manufactured. The M.C. 205 Greyhound had a more powerful DB 605, producing 1,475 hp, but the body and undercarriage were almost identical. The prototype had

its maiden flight as early as 19 April 1943, but because the DB 605 engine was produced only very slowly under licence, the first production models were not delivered to the Italian Air Force until mid-1943. By the time Italy surrendered in September 1943, just 66 Greyhounds had been manufactured, of which only six were put into service by the Italians. After Italy's surrender, 205 more were manufactured under German supervision in northern Italy, some of which were used by the Luftwaffe. The M.C. 205 was certainly one of Italy's best fighter aircraft, second only to the Fiat G.55.

## C.A.N.T. Z.1007 ALCIONE (KINGFISHER)

The Kingfisher was first put into service by the Italian Air Force under the Fascists, and after 1943 it was flown both by Italians fighting on the side of the Allies and by Mussolini's forces. The first prototype of the Z.1007, fitted with three 825 hp Isotta-Frachini engines, had its maiden flight in March 1937.

Performance was disappointing on account of the underpowered engines, so the Z.1007 was converted to accommodate three Piaggio radial engines, and its fuselage was also made taller and wider in the process. The converted aircraft, called the Z.1007bis, went into production at the C.A.N.T. factory in Monfalcone, Italy, in 1939. The earliest machines had a single tail fin but a twin tail was introduced to give the gunner a better view from his turret. The Z.1007bis was made entirely of wood, which could lead to problems in extreme weather conditions, but it was an excellent bomber, used everywhere from the Sahara to Russia. The Z.1007ter had three 1,150 hp engines and had a maximum speed of 500 km/h, but few were ever built, and only 567 Z.1007s were manufactured altogether.

| | Z.1007bis |
|---|---|
| Type: | Bomber |
| Crew: | 5 |
| Weight when empty/ max weight at takeoff: | 9,395 kg/ 13,620 kg |
| Length/wingspan/height: | 18.35 m/24.8 m/5.22 m |
| Engine(s): | Three Piaggio P.XI-R2C.40 radial engines with 1,000 hp each |
| Maximum speed: | 465 km/h at 4,000 m |
| Service ceiling: | 8,200 m |
| Range: | 1,750 km |
| Weaponry: | 1 x 12.7 mm Type SAFAT or Scotti machine guns in a turning turret on the fuselage, two further 12.7 mm rearward and downward-firing machine guns of the same type, 2 x 7.7 mm Type SAFAT machine guns on the sides, and an internal or external payload of max. 1,200 kg |

*A C.A.N.T. Z.1007bis from the 95th Group of Italian Squadron 230a in Greece, 1940.*

# SAVOIA-MARCHETTI S.M. 79 SPARVIERO (SPARROW HAWK)

In October 1934 Savoia-Marchetti introduced the prototype of an eight-seat transport aircraft, which set six world records in September 1935. So the Italian Air Force ordered a new version modified as a bomber, which flew for the first time in October 1936. It had a machine gun installation on top of the fuselage, a ventral gondola for the bombs and a raised cockpit (hence its nickname, the 'Hunchback Bomber'), but it was not significantly different from the transport version in other respects.

The Sparrow Hawk was first flown in 1937 in the Spanish Civil War, like many other Italian and German aircraft. The Italian Air Force had 594 Sparrow Hawks when the country entered the Second World War, and they were soon in use on all fronts. Because it was slightly underpowered, the torpedo bomber version, the S.M. 79-II, had more powerful Piaggio engines, producing 1,000 hp each, and in this format it was an outstanding machine. The Sparrow Hawk was very versatile, serving as a high-

|  | S.M.79-I |
| --- | --- |
| Type: | Bomber |
| Crew: | 5–6 |
| Weight when empty/ max weight at takeoff: | 6,800 kg/ 10,480 kg |
| Length/wingspan/height: | 15.8 m/21.2 m/4.3 m |
| Engine(s): | Three Alfa-Romeo 126-RC.34 radial engines with 780 hp each |
| Maximum speed: | 430 km/h at 4,000 m |
| Service ceiling: | 6,500 m |
| Range: | 1,900 km |
| Weaponry: | 1 x 12.7 mm Type SAFAT fixed forward-firing machine gun above the cockpit, 1 x 12.7 mm rear machine gun, 1 x 12.7 mm machine gun in the ventral gondola, 1–2 x 7.7 mm Type SAFAT machine guns in the side windows in the central fuselage, and an internal payload of max. 1,250 kg |

altitude and torpedo bomber, a ground attack aircraft and a reconnaissance aircraft. The final version, the S.M. 79-III, appeared in 1943 with higher-performing engines and improved aerodynamics. After the truce between Italy and the Allies in September 1943, the Sparrow Hawk was still used by Mussolini's RSI (Repubblica Sociale Italiana) on Germany's side, while the Italian Co-Belligerent Air Force on the Allied side

used them only as transporters. A twin-engine version (the S.M. 79B) was exported to Romania, Iraq and Brazil. Yugoslavia bought 45 S.M. 79-Is before the war, and between October 1936 and June 1943 around 1,300 S.M. 79s were built.

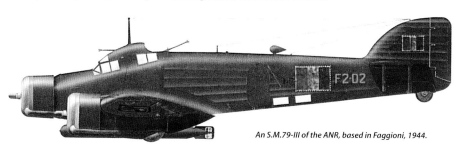

*An S.M.79-III of the ANR, based in Faggioni, 1944.*

*An early S.M.79-I model being deployed by the Spanish Nationalists.*

# FIAT BR.20 CIGOGNA (STORK)

The Fiat BR.20's maiden flight took place on 10 February 1936. It had a retractable tail wheel, all-metal wings and a body made partially out of metal. The first Fiat BR.20s were delivered to the Italian Air Force in autumn 1936, and 233 were manufactured up to 1940. The Japanese took delivery of 85 and deployed them in China, but according to some reports, the Japanese pilots were not very impressed by the Stork. Some were also delivered to Venezuela, and others were flown on the Nationalist side in the Spanish Civil War. In 1940 the new BR.20M version, which had a new nose cone and a smoother outer surface, was delivered to the Italian Air Force. Up to early 1942, 264 BR.20s had been built, and 15 of the final version, the BR.20bis, which had more powerful engines and improved defensive weaponry, were produced in 1943. When Italy entered the war in 1940, the Italian Air Force had 172 BR.20s, which were flown in the French campaign and the Battle of Britain.

|  | BR.20 |
|---|---|
| Type: | Bomber |
| Crew: | 5 |
| Weight when empty/ | 6,400 kg/ |
| max weight at takeoff: | 9,900 kg |
| Length/wingspan/height: | 16.1 m/21.56 m/4.3 m |
| Engine(s): | Two Fiat A.80-RC-41 18-cylinder radial engines with 1,000 hp each |
| Maximum speed: | 432 km/h at 5,000 m |
| Service ceiling: | 9,000 m |
| Range: | 3,000 km |
| Weaponry: | 1 x 12.7 mm Type SAFAT or Scotti machine gun in an installation on the fuselage, 1 x 7.7 mm Type SAFAT machine gun in the nose, 1 x 7.7 mm machine gun in the lower fuselage, and a payload of up to 1,600 kg |

*A BR.20 with the Spanish Nationalist emblem – the Italian Aviation Legion fought on the Nationalist side in the Spanish Civil War.*

# PIAGGIO P.108

The Piaggio P.108 was the only Italian four-engine long-range bomber in the war, making its maiden flight on 24 November 1939. Four different variants were planned, but only the P.108B (Bombardier) was built in significant numbers. There was a civilian transporter version that could carry 32 passengers, but this was later converted into a military transporter that could carry 56 soldiers. The P.108B was put into service in May 1941, but was not deployed in the 274th Long-Range Bomber Squadron for another year, and even then, on account of technical difficulties, there were never more than seven or eight machines ready to be flown at any time. Piaggio bombers carried out night raids on Gibraltar and Algerian ports during the Allied 'Torch'

|  | P.108B |
|---|---|
| Type: | Bomber |
| Crew: | 6–7 |
| Weight when empty/ | 17,325 kg/ |
| max weight at takeoff: | 29,885 kg |
| Length/wingspan/height: | 22.3 m/32 m/6 m |
| Engine(s): | Four Piaggio PXII-RC.35 radial engines with 1,500 hp each |
| Maximum speed: | 430 km/h at 4,200 m |
| Service ceiling: | 8,500 m |
| Range: | 3,520 km |
| Weaponry: | Up to 6 x 12.7 mm Type SAFAT machine guns, 2 x 12.7 mm machine guns in the outer engine gondolas, and an internal payload of max. 3,500 kg |

campaign in November 1942. Its remote-controlled gun installations, each of which had a 12.7 mm machine gun, were situated in the rear of each engine gondola. Production was halted in 1943, after only 163 P.108s had been produced, including all the different variants. The P108B's manoeuvrability was poor, and it suffered from technical problems. By the time Italy surrendered in 1943, more than 95% of P.108s had been destroyed, the remainder serving either in Mussolini's forces or in the Luftwaffe.

*Italy's only four-engine bomber, the Piaggio P.108, enjoyed little real success, though it had numerous innovative details.*

## NAKAJIMA KI-27 SETSU (NATE)

| | Ki-27a |
|---|---|
| Type: | Fighter |
| Crew: | 1 |
| Weight when empty/ max weight at takeoff: | 1,110 kg/ 1,790 kg |
| Length/wingspan/height: | 7.53 m/11.31 m/3.25 m |
| Engine(s): | One Nakajima Ha-1b radial engine with 710 hp |
| Maximum speed: | 470 km/h |
| Service ceiling: | 10,200 m |
| Range: | 625 km |
| Weaponry: | 2 x 7.7 mm Type 97 fixed machine guns in the nose |

*The Ki-27 (Nate).*

The Nakajima Ki-27 was an all-metal low-wing aircraft with a fixed undercarriage, and it was put into serial production in 1937. After a few pre-production models, the first variant to be delivered to the Japanese fighter squadrons was the Ki-27a. It was first deployed over northern China in March 1938, where it proved to be very effective against its Chinese counterparts. It was not surpassed until the introduction of the Polikarpov I-16. When the war in the Pacific broke out, the Ki-27a and Ki-27b (a very slightly modified version) represented a large proportion of the Japanese Imperial Army's fighter aircraft. The Ki-27 was codenamed 'Abdul', then later 'Nate', by the Allies. From early 1943 onwards, the Ki-27 was withdrawn from the front line and served primarily as a flight instruction aircraft, though it was deployed as a kamikaze aircraft towards the end of the war. From 1937 to 1942, 3,399 Ki-27s were built.

## NAKAJIMA KI-43 HAYABUSHA (OSCAR)

| | Ki-43IIa |
|---|---|
| Type: | Fighter/fighter bomber |
| Crew: | 1 |
| Weight when empty/ max weight at takeoff: | 1,910 kg/ 2,590 kg |
| Length/wingspan/height: | 8.92 m/10.84 m/3.27 m |
| Engine(s): | One Nakajima Ha-115 radial engine with 1,150 hp |
| Maximum speed: | 530 km/h at 4,000 m |
| Service ceiling: | 11,200 m |
| Range: | 1,600 m |
| Weaponry: | 2 x 12.7 mm Type 1 fixed machine guns in the nose, and an external payload of max. 500 kg, e.g., two 250 kg bombs under the wings |

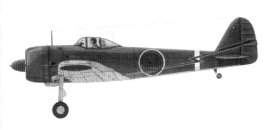

*The Ki-43IIa (Oscar), Burma, mid-1943.*

The Ki-43 prototype was an all-metal low-wing aircraft with retractable undercarriage, and it had its maiden flight in January 1939, when its manoeuvrability was found wanting. So the wings and flaps were altered, and the modified version went into production in early 1941 as the Ki-43Ia, codenamed 'Oscar' by the Allies. It was armed with two 7.7 mm machine guns, and it was powered by a 975 hp Nakajima-Sakae engine. Although its agility made it very effective in the early stages of the war, it had many faults, which its manufacturers tried to correct in different versions. It was equipped with heavier weaponry (the Ki-43Ic had two 12.7 mm machine guns), and the Ki-43II was fitted with a more powerful engine, producing 1,150 hp, protected fuel tanks and armour for the pilot and the engine. It could also carry a maximum payload of 50 kg. Because its successor, the Ki-44, was ineffective, the Ki-43 was kept in production until the end of the war, and 5,919 were produced in total. It was manufactured in larger numbers than any other Japanese fighter aircraft. There was also a Ki-43III, built in 1945, which attained higher altitudes and had a better engine, but it never got past the prototype stage. Like almost all other Japanese aircraft, it was also deployed in kamikaze operations.

# KAWASAKI KI-45 TORYU (NICK)

In early 1937, Kawasaki was ordered by the Imperial Japanese Army to design a twin-engine long-range bomber to be deployed in the Pacific. In 1939 a prototype, which had Nakajima-Ha 25 radial engines and was called the Ki-45 Toryu (Dragon Slayer), flew for the first time, but its performance was disappointing. Consequently, its development was delayed until it could be modified to accommodate the more powerful Mitsubishi Ha-102 engine, but in the event this proved to be beset with technical problems. Thus the first Ki-45 models were not produced until September 1941, and further delays meant that they could not be put into service until August 1942. Once they were in service, however, they proved to be effective fighter aircraft (Ki-45Ia), night fighters (Ki-45 KAIc), and ground-attack and anti-ship aircraft (Ki-45 KAIb and KAId). The Allies gave the Ki-45 the codename 'Nick'. In total, 1,698 Ki-45s were manufactured.

| | Ki-45 KAIc |
|---|---|
| Type: | Heavy fighter/night fighter |
| Crew: | 2 |
| Weight when empty/ max weight at takeoff: | 4,000 kg/5,500 kg |
| Length/wingspan/height: | 11 m/15.05 m/3.7 m |
| Engine(s): | Two Mitsubishi Ha-10s radial engines with 1,080 hp each |
| Maximum speed: | 545 km/h at 7,000 m |
| Service ceiling: | 10,000 m |
| Range: | 2,000 km |
| Weaponry: | 1 x 37 mm fixed automatic cannon in the nose, 2 x 20 mm Type 99 automatic cannon in the fuselage firing diagonally upwards, 1 x 7.7 mm Type 92 machine gun in the rear of the cockpit, and an external payload of max. 500 kg |

*The Kawasaki Ki-45 KAIa (Nick).*

# MITSUBISHI KI-46 HEI (DINAH)

| | Ki-46II |
|---|---|
| Type: | Reconnaissance aircraft |
| Crew: | 2 |
| Weight when empty/ max weight at takeoff: | 3,263 kg/ 5,800 kg |
| Length/wingspan/height: | 11 m/14.7 m/3.88 m |
| Engine(s): | Two Mitsubishi Ha-102 radial engines with 1,080 hp each |
| Maximum speed: | 604 km/h at 5,800 m |
| Service ceiling: | 10,720 m |
| Range: | 2,480 km |
| Weaponry: | 1 x 7.7 mm Type 92 machine gun in the rear of the cockpit |

The Ki-46 Hei was one of the best reconnaissance aircraft of its time: it attained high speeds and altitudes, and had a good range. The prototype had its maiden flight in late November 1939, and its performance proved superior to that of all the other Japanese aircraft, though it did not quite attain the standards originally expected. It went into production as the Ki-46I but was soon replaced by the improved Ki-46II, which actually surpassed the standards originally set. The Ki-46III performed even better, with a maximum speed of 630 km/h and a range of 4,000 km/h; however, the Ha-112II engines could not be delivered reliably, so Mitsubishi had to continue producing the Ki-46II. In the early years of the war, almost nothing could intercept the Ki-46, and it provided the Japanese with valuable intelligence. Towards the end of the war, some Ki-46IIIs were converted into Ki-46III KAI fighter aircraft, and in total 1,742 Ki-46s were produced, including 1,093 Ki-46IIs and 611 Ki-46IIIs. It is claimed that the Luftwaffe was interested in manufacturing the Ki-46 under licence, but these plans were never realized.

*The Mitsubishi Ki-46II (Dinah).*

# KAWASAKI KI-61 HIEN AND KI-100 GOSHIKI (TONY)

The Ki-61 Hien (Swan) was the only Japanese fighter with an inline engine to be deployed in the Second World War. Like Italian models, it depended upon the transfer of German engine technology, in particular, on the delivery of Daimler-Benz DB 601 V12 engines. The first prototype of the Hien had its maiden flight in December 1941 and was immediately put into production. However, problems arose with the DB 601, which was built under licence by Kawasaki as the Ha-40, and this model was not put into service until April 1943, fitted with Ki-61 engines. Nevertheless, it proved a dangerous opponent for Allied aircraft, and the Allies codenamed it 'Tony', initially mistaking it for a German Bf 109 produced under license. Two main variants, the Ki-61 I and II, were built, whose weaponry and maximum altitudes were significantly different, and 2,666 were manufactured in total. When the Ha-40 manufacturing plants were completely destroyed by US bombers in January 1945, a new engine was urgently needed for the existing frames. In an incredible feat of improvisation, in just one month Kawasaki engineers succeeded in converting the Ki-61 to accommodate a radial engine. With a 1,500 hp Mitsubishi Ha-112 II radial engine, the new variant, called the Ki-100 Ia, performed even better than the Ki-61 and was one of the best Japanese fighters. After 275 Ki-61 II airframes were successfully converted, 99 additional converted Ki-100 Ibs, with a new cockpit canopy and rear section, were also produced.

| | Ki-61 Ic | Ki-100 Ib |
|---|---|---|
| Type: | Fighter/fighter bomber | Fighter/fighter bomber |
| Crew: | 1 | 1 |
| Weight when empty/ max weight at takeoff: | 2,640 kg/ 3,470 kg | 2,700 kg/ 3.670 kg |
| Length/wingspan/height: | 8.95 m/12 m/3.7 m | 8.8 m/12 m/3.7 m |
| Engine(s): | One Kawasaki hanging V12 engine with 1,175 hp | One Mitsubishi Ha-112-II radial engine with 1,500 hp |
| Maximum speed: | 560 km/h at 4,000 m | 590 km/h at 10,000 m |
| Service ceiling: | 10,000 m | 10,700 m |
| Range: | 1,900 km | 2,000 km |
| Weaponry: | 2 x 12.7 mm Ho-103 machine guns in the nose, 2 x 20 mm Ho-5 automatic cannon in the wings, and an external payload of up to 500 kg, e.g., two 250 kg bombs or two drop tanks | 2 x 12.7 mm Ho-103 machine guns in the nose, 2 x 20 mm Ho-5 automatic cannon in the wings, and an external payload of up to 500 kg, e.g., two 250 kg bombs or two drop tanks |

*A Ki-100 in the Royal Air Force Museum, Hendon.*

# NAKAJIMA KI-84 HAYATE (FRANK)

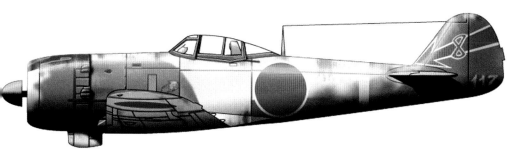

*The Nakajima Ki-84 Ia (Frank).*

The Allies were fortunate that the Nakajima Ki-84 Hayate (Storm) was not put into service until the summer of 1944, as 'Frank' – as the Allies codenamed it – could match the best US fighters at altitudes of up to 9,000 m and was one of the Allies' most feared adversaries in Asia and the Pacific. Its low manifold pressure was only a problem at higher altitudes. The Ki-84 had a higher climbing speed and was more agile than its Allied counterparts, as well as being very heavily armed. Right from the start, all Ki-84s were armoured and equipped with self-sealing fuel tanks. Work on this model's design began in early 1942, and after two prototypes had successful test flights, the Ki 84 Ia was put into production in late 1943. Its successors were even more heavily armed – for example, the Ki-84 Ib had four 20 mm machine guns, and the Ki-84 Ic had two 20 mm and two 30 mm machine guns. The Ki-84 IIa, b and c were similar to the K-84 I series models, apart from being partially made of wood to save precious raw materials. In the course of the war, the Ki-84 suffered from the deteriorating quality of construction materials, as well as the declining number of experienced pilots, and its true potential could not be realized. There were various attempts to develop the Ki-84 further, but the war ended before they could get past the testing stage. In total, 3,514 Ki-84s were built.

| | Ki-84 Ia |
|---|---|
| Type: | Fighter/fighter bomber |
| Crew: | 1 |
| Weight when empty/ max weight at takeoff: | 2,660 kg/ 3,890 kg |
| Length/wingspan/height: | 9.92 m/11.24 m/3.39 m |
| Engine(s): | One Nakajima Ha-45 radial engine with 1,900 hp |
| Maximum speed: | 631 km/h at 6,100 m |
| Service ceiling: | 10,500 m |
| Range: | 2,160 km |
| Weaponry: | 2 x 12.7 mm Type 1 fixed machine guns in the nose, 2 x 20 mm Ho-103 automatic cannon in the wings, and an external payload of max. 500 kg, e.g. two 250 kg bombs under the wings |

*The Ki-84 was one of the best Japanese fighters in the Second World War.*

# MITSUBISHI A6M REI-SEN (ZERO OR ZEKE)

The Mitsubishi A6M Rei-Sen Type Zero was (and still is) the best-known Japanese fighter aircraft of the Second World War. Its Type Zero designation – hence its name 'Zero' – derived from the year that it was introduced into the Imperial Japanese Navy (2600 according to the Japanese calendar, and 1940 according to the Western calendar). The A6M gave the Allies (who codenamed it 'Zeke') an unpleasant surprise in the early stages of the war in the Pacific, although they had received reports from China about a new fighter. It was fast and agile, and it had a considerable range – at first, none of the other aircraft in the Pacific could touch it. The Zero had its maiden flight in April 1940, and it performed so well that an order was immediately submitted for 15 pre-production A6M1s. They were deployed in China, where they

| | A6M5b |
|---|---|
| Type: | Fighter/fighter bomber |
| Crew: | 1 |
| Weight when empty/ max weight at takeoff: | 1,895 kg/ 2,950 kg |
| Length/wingspan/height: | 9.07 m/12 m/3.5 m |
| Engine(s): | One Nakajima NK1F-Sakae-21 radial engine with 1,130 hp |
| Maximum speed: | 560 km/h at 7,000 m |
| Service ceiling: | 10,700 m |
| Range: | 1,800 km |
| Weaponry: | 1 x 13.2 mm Type 3 machine gun in the nose, 2 x 13.2 mm Type 3 and 2 x 20 mm Type 99 automatic cannon in the wings, and an external payload of max. 300 kg, e.g., one 250 kg bomb, or an additional fuel tank, or two 60 kg bombs |

were so successful that the A6M2 was immediately put into production in July 1940. The A6M3 prototype was tested about six months before war broke out in the Pacific. Unlike its predecessors, which only had folding wing tips, the A6M3's entire wings could be folded upwards to save valuable space on aircraft carriers. In the early months of the war, the Zero was the undisputed ruler of the Pacific skies. Naturally, however, it did have some weaknesses: although its performance was excellent, this was partly due to its extremely light construction and

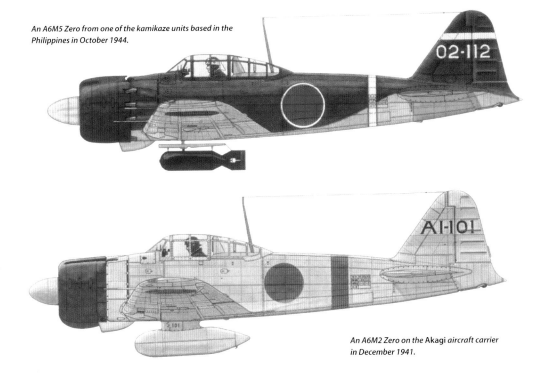

*An A6M5 Zero from one of the kamikaze units based in the Philippines in October 1944.*

*An A6M2 Zero on the Akagi aircraft carrier in December 1941.*

complete lack of defensive weaponry. Moreover, although it was manoeuvrable, it could not cope with high-speed dives. Once the Allied pilots had discovered these weaknesses, the A6M lost its supremacy. And when the Americans introduced new, higher-performance models (the Hellcat, Corsair or P-38 Lightning), the tables turned completely. Under pressure because of increasing losses, Mitsubishi strove to improve the Zero with more powerful engines, stronger armour and heavier weaponry, and the A6M3 was duly replaced in autumn 1943 by the A6M5. Yet, as early as mid-1944, this model proved barely capable of competing with the enemy, and it was deployed as a kamikaze aircraft and a dive-bomber. Although the Zero was clearly past its prime, Japan continued to manufacture it in large numbers, and there were even new models. The A6M6 was fitted with a more powerful engine, and the A6M7 version was a dive-bomber. The A6M8, powered by a 1,560 hp engine, was Japan's last attempt to catch up with the Allies, but it was only ever built as a prototype. In total, including all the different variants, 10,937 Zeros were manufactured.

*The Americans seized numerous A6Ms during the war, some of which (including this one) were subjected to tests in the USA.*

## AICHI D3A KAUBAKU (VAL)

The Aichi D3A was an all-metal single-wing aircraft with a fixed undercarriage; its development began in 1936 and was heavily influenced by Heinkel designs. The first pre-production models were in service with the Japanese Navy from March 1939. The first models to be deployed still had 1,000 hp Mitsubishi engines, whose power was later increased to 1,070 hp. The D3A1 was the standard bomber on board Japanese aircraft carriers and was in the first wave of attacks on Pearl Harbor. Because its pilots were highly trained and it handled well, 'Val' (as it was codenamed by the Allies) was astonishingly successful at first, sinking the British cruisers HMS *Cornwall* and HMS *Dorsetshire* in April 1942 off the coast of Ceylon, followed four days later by the aircraft carrier HMS *Hermes* and the destroyer HMS *Vampire*. The improved D3A2 version had a more powerful 1,300 hp radial engine, a new cockpit and larger fuel tanks, giving it a range of around 2,500 km. But towards the end of the war, the D3A lagged a long way behind its enemy counterparts, and it was used as a flight instruction aircraft and in kamikaze operations. Including both series, around 1,500 D3As were manufactured in total.

| | D3A1 (a later series model) |
| --- | --- |
| Type: | Carrier-borne dive-bomber |
| Crew: | 2 |
| Weight when empty/max weight at takeoff: | 2,408 kg/3,650 kg |
| Length/wingspan/height: | 10.19 m/14.36 m/3.84 m |
| Engine(s): | One Mitsubishi-Kinsei 44 radial engine with 1,070 hp |
| Maximum speed: | 385 km/h at 3,000 m |
| Service ceiling: | 9,300 m |
| Range: | 1,470 km |
| Weaponry: | 2 x 7.7 mm Type 97 fixed machine guns in the nose, 1 x 7.7 mm Type 92 machine gun in the rear of the cockpit, and an external payload of up to 370 kg, e.g., one 250 kg bomb under the fuselage and two 60 kg bombs under the wings |

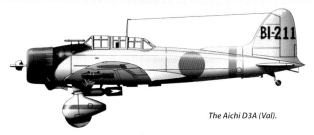

*The Aichi D3A (Val).*

## YOKOSUKA D4Y SUISEI (JUDY)

| | D4Y2 |
| --- | --- |
| Type: | Carrier-borne dive-bomber |
| Crew: | 2 |
| Weight when empty/ max weight at takeoff: | 2,440 kg/ 4,250 kg |
| Length/wingspan/height: | 10.22 m/11.5 m/3.74 m |
| Engine(s): | One Aichi-Atsuta 32 hanging V12 engine with 1,400 hp |
| Maximum speed: | 560 km/h |
| Service ceiling: | 10,700 m |
| Range: | 1,465 km – 3,600 km with additional fuel tanks |
| Weaponry: | 2 x 7.7 mm Type 97 fixed machine guns in the nose, 1 x Type 1 7.7 mm machine gun in the rear of the cockpit, and a combined internal and external payload of max. 560 kg |

*The D4Y was the only Japanese carrier-borne aircraft with an inline engine.*

The Yokosuka D4Y was the only Japanese carrier-borne aircraft with an inline engine. Work began on its design in 1938, and it was fitted with a DB-600 engine, which was built under licence. As with many Japanese aircraft designed before the war, its astounding performance figures were achieved at the expense of solid construction, strong armour, and self-sealing fuel tanks. Thus when it was tested, it became clear that its wing structure was not suitable for dive-bombing, so the first production model, the D4Y-1C, which appeared in late 1942, was flown as a reconnaissance aircraft. In March 1943 a new version, the D4Y1, was introduced with reinforced wings. Various different versions of the D4Y were built either for dive-bombing or for reconnaissance, but they differed only in minor respects. The only exception to this rule was the D4Y3, which was fitted with a 1,580 hp Mitsubishi-Kinsei radial engine. The D4Y2-S version was a night fighter, which had no weaponry in its wings but did have a 20 mm machine gun in the fuselage pointed upwards. Because it lacked defensive weaponry, and the Allies began to dominate the skies, the Suisei suffered very heavy losses. In the final months of the war, it was also used for kamikaze operations. In total, 2,038 Suiseis were built, including all the different variants.

*The D4Y (Judy).*

## NAKAJIMA B5N2 KANKOH (KATE)

*A B5N (Kate) taking off.*

|  | B5N1 |
|---|---|
| Type: | Carrier-borne torpedo bomber/bomber |
| Crew: | 3 |
| Weight when empty/ max weight at takeoff: | 2,279 kg/ 4,100 kg |
| Length/wingspan/height: | 10.3 m/15.52 m/3.7 m |
| Engine(s): | One Nakajima-Sakae 11 radial engine with 1,000 hp |
| Maximum speed: | 370 km/h |
| Service ceiling: | 8,260 m |
| Range: | 1,935 km |
| Weaponry: | 1 x 7.7 mm Type 92 machine gun in the rear of the cockpit, and an external payload of up to 800 kg, e.g., one 800 kg torpedo or three 250 kg bombs |

The Nakajima B5N, codenamed 'Kate', was the only Japanese carrier-borne torpedo bomber when war broke out in the Pacific. But in late 1941 Kate was already rather dated, as its design went back to 1935. Nevertheless, it fared rather better than its American counterpart, the Douglas TBD Devastator, and until the introduction of the Grumman Avenger, the B5N2 was the best torpedo bomber in the Pacific. When Pearl Harbor was attacked, 145 B5N2s, 40 armed with torpedoes and 105 armed with bombs, took part, and this model's greatest successes were sinking the American aircraft carriers USS *Yorktown*, USS *Lexington* and USS *Hornet*. From 1943, however, it was largely superseded by its successor, the B6N, and it was put into service as a flight instruction vehicle, as a target finder and in anti-submarine operations. For the latter role, it was fitted with primitive radar and sensors to detect magnetic disturbances. Kate's last major deployment was in the Battle of the Philippines in October 1944. Around 1,150 B5Ns were manufactured in total.

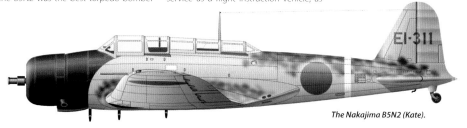

*The Nakajima B5N2 (Kate).*

## NAKAJIMA B6N2 TENZAN (JILL)

The Nakajima B6N was the B5N's successor and was very similar to it, as the Imperial Japanese Navy had stipulated that the new aircraft must not differ in any significant respect from its predecessor because of the size of the lifts on Japanese aircraft carriers. Nakajima began designing the new torpedo bomber as early as 1939, but it did not make its maiden flight until the summer of 1941. Contrary to the demands of the Navy, which had anticipated a Mitsubishi-Kasei radial engine, the Tenzan prototype was fitted with a Nakajima-Momaru radial engine, which was claimed to offer better fuel economy and greater development potential. It was not, however, very successful in flight tests, and alterations to the engine and tail were unavoidable. Consequently, it was not tested on an aircraft carrier until late 1942, and it was still beset with problems with the engine and the tail hook. An altered version, the B6N1, finally went into production in early 1943, but production was halted after only 135 aircraft had been manufactured, as the Navy insisted the model had to be fitted with the Mitsubishi-Kasei engine. So it was converted to accommodate the new engine, and the new model was

| | B6N2 |
|---|---|
| Type: | Carrier-borne torpedo bomber/bomber |
| Crew: | 3 |
| Weight when empty/ max weight at takeoff: | 3,010 kg/ 5,650 kg |
| Length/wingspan/height: | 10.87 m/14.89 m/3.8 m |
| Engine(s): | One Mitsubishi MK 4T Kasei 25 radial engine with 1,850 hp |
| Maximum speed: | 468 km/h |
| Service ceiling: | 9,040 m |
| Range: | 2,960 km |
| Weaponry: | 1 x 7.7 mm Type 92 machine gun in the rear of the cockpit, 1 x 7.7 mm firing rearwards and downwards in the fuselage, and an external payload of max. 800 kg, e.g., one 800 kg torpedo or three 250 kg bombs |

*The Nakajima B6N2 (Jill).*

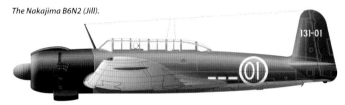

called the B6N2. Even now, however, the Tenzan could only be flown from the largest aircraft carriers, as it required a relatively long runway, and aircraft carriers were not yet equipped with catapults. In fact, by the time it was put into service in mid-1944, most Japanese aircraft carriers had already been sunk, and there was a

serious shortage of pilots. Hence, most B6Ns were flown from land bases. By that time, the Allies had won the struggle for the Pacific skies, and the Tenzan enjoyed no real success, even in kamikaze operations. In total, 1,268 B6Ns were manufactured.

## MITSUBISHI G4M HAMAKI (BETTY)

| | G4M3 |
|---|---|
| Type: | Bomber |
| Crew: | 7 |
| Weight when empty/ max weight at takeoff: | 8,350 kg/12,500 kg |
| Length/wingspan/height: | 19.5 m/25 m/6 m |
| Engine(s): | Two Mitsubishi MK 4T Kasei 25 radial engines with 1,825 hp each |
| Maximum speed: | 470 km/h at 5,000 m |
| Service ceiling: | 9,220 m |
| Range: | 4,350 km |
| Weaponry: | 4 x 20 mm Type 99 automatic cannon – one each in nose, tail, waist and rear installations – 2 x 7.7 mm Type 92 machine guns in the sides, and a combined internal and external payload of max. 1,000 kg, e.g., one 800 kg torpedo or four 250 kg bombs |

The G4M Hamaki, codenamed 'Betty' by the Allies, was the best-known and most deployed heavy bomber in the Japanese Navy during the war. It was an all-metal single-wing aircraft with retractable undercarriage and powerful engines. Because the Imperial Japanese Navy required a long-range bomber,

*The G4M was the standard Japanese twin-engine bomber.*

the G4M had a good range, but again this was achieved, in part, by a light frame, a lack of armour and no protection for the fuel tanks. In 1937 work began on

developing a successor for the G3M, and the G4M had its maiden flight in October 1939, being first deployed in 1941 in the Sino-Japanese War. In the early months of

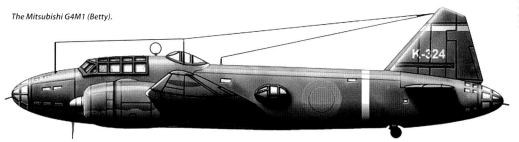

*The Mitsubishi G4M1 (Betty).*

the war in the Pacific, this bomber enjoyed some spectacular success, including playing a major part in the sinking of the British battleships HMS *Prince of Wales* and HMS *Repulse*. It carried the Yokosuka MXYOhka manned bombs, and also, on 19 August 1945, transported the Japanese delegation to Iwo Jima, where they officially surrendered.

Betty had really had its day after the summer of 1942. In the Battle of Guadalcanal in August that year, it became clear that these large, unprotected and ponderous machines would catch fire as soon as they were hit – a consequence of leaving the fuel tanks unprotected – which earned Betty the nickname the 'One-Shot Lighter'. There were four main production models of the G4M: the G4M1 Model 11, the G4M2 Model 22, the G4M3 Model 34 and the G6M1, which differed primarily in their engine specifications and level of defensive weaponry. In addition, there were a few sub-variants, including the GM61-L2 transporter. Altogether, 2,479 machines were built, but by the end of the war only around 160 had survived.

## MITSUBISHI KI-21 (SALLY)

| | Ki-21 IIb |
|---|---|
| Type: | Bomber |
| Crew: | 5–7 |
| Weight when empty/ max weight at takeoff: | 6,070 kg/ 10,610 kg |
| Length/wingspan/height: | 16.6 m/22.5 m/3.7 m |
| Engine(s): | Two Mitsubishi Ha 101 radial engines with 1,500 hp each |
| Maximum speed: | 485 km/h at 7,000 m |
| Service ceiling: | 10,000 m |
| Range: | 2,700 km |
| Weaponry: | 4 x 7.7 mm Type 92 machine guns – one each in the nose, sides and waist – 1 x 7.7 mm Type 92 remote-controlled machine gun in the tail, 1 x 12.7 mm tail machine gun (in the rear of the cockpit), and an internal payload of max. 1,000 kg |

*The Mitsubishi Ki-21 (Sally).*

In the early months of the war in the Pacific, the Ki-21, codenamed 'Sally' by the Allies, was the Japanese Army's standard bomber, and it remained in front-line service until late 1944. Work began on its design in 1936, and in 1938 the first production model (Ki-21 Ia) was put into service in the Sino-Japanese War. It soon became clear that the Ki-21's defensive weaponry was inadequate, so the improved Ki-21 Ib was ordered to replace it. The Ki-21 Ic had additional fuel tanks and was intended to be a long-range bomber, and the next model, the Ki-22 IIa, had more powerful engines and was better armed. The final model, the Ki-22 IIb, differed only in minor respects from the Ki-22 IIa. One interesting feature was the remote-controlled machine gun in the tail. Given that Sally was meant to be a long-range bomber, its defensive weaponry and payload were insufficient.

Like many other Japanese aircraft, the Ki-21 was also very vulnerable when hit, and from 1943 a large number fell victim to Allied fighters. Hence, it was withdrawn from front-line service in late 1944. By the time production was halted, 2,064 Sallys had been manufactured, and they were deployed throughout the Pacific.

## NAKAJIMA KI-49 DONRYU (HELEN)

The Nakajima Ki-49 was the Ki-21's successor, flying for the first time in August 1939, but with two 950 hp Nakajima Ha 5 engines, it failed to attain the desired performance, and the second prototype was converted to accommodate two 1,250 hp Nakajima Ha 41 engines. It went into production in this format as the Ki-49 I, and it was deployed in China and in the early battles in the Pacific. Although the Ki-49's performance was supposed to be so good that it did not require a fighter escort, it became apparent that its payload, speed, protection and range all fell short of the

*The Nakajima Ki-49 (Helen).*

required standards. So in early 1942 the Ki-49 II was fitted with more powerful Nakajima Ha 109 engines, self-sealing fuel tanks, better armour and defensive weaponry. But Helen was still no match for its enemies and suffered heavy losses.

Consequently, production was halted in December 1944, after 819 Ki-49s had been manufactured. In the final stages of the war, it was deployed primarily as a transporter, and for anti-submarine and kamikaze operations.

|  | Ki-49 IIb |
|---|---|
| Type: | Bomber |
| Crew: | 8 |
| Weight when empty/ max weight at takeoff: | 6,530 kg/ 11,400 kg |
| Length/wingspan/height: | 16.5 m/20.42 m/4.25 m |
| Engine(s): | Two Nakajima Ha 109 radial engines with 1,500 hp each |
| Maximum speed: | 492 km/h at 5,000 m |
| Service ceiling: | 9,300 m |
| Range: | 2,950 km |
| Weaponry: | 5 x 12.7 mm Type 1 machine guns – one each in the nose, tail, underside and sides – 1 x 20 mm dorsal automatic cannon, and an internal payload of up to 1,000 kg |

## KAWANISHI H8K (EMILY)

The H8K was the highest-performing Japanese reconnaissance seaplane, and probably the best Japanese seaplane, in the Second World War. It was codenamed 'Emily' by the Allies, and only 167 machines were ever built. The H8K had considerable reserves of power and a high load-carrying capacity, but its wing load was relatively high (200 kg/m²), so only specially trained pilots flew it. The prototype (H8K1) of this four-engine shoulder-wing aircraft flew for the first time on 31 December 1940, which revealed some weaknesses. In particular, it was very unstable on water. After significant alterations to the model's frame, the first H8Ks went into serial production in 1941 and were put into service in March 1942. The model that was manufactured in the largest numbers was the H8K2 (112 were built), and it had radar, protected fuel tanks, heavier weaponry and stronger armour. The H8K2-L (of which 36 were built) was a transporter which accommodated 29–64 passengers, and was less heavily armed than the other models. There were also prototypes (the H8K3 and 4) which never

|  | H8K2 |
|---|---|
| Type: | Reconnaissance seaplane |
| Crew: | 9–10 |
| Weight when empty/ max weight at takeoff: | 18,380 kg/ 32,500 kg |
| Length/wingspan/height: | 28.13 m/38 m/9.15 m |
| Engine(s): | Four Mitsubishi MK 40 Kasei 22 radial engines with 1,850 hp each |
| Maximum speed: | 472 km/h at 5,000 m |
| Service ceiling: | 8,600 m |
| Range: | 7,100 km |
| Weaponry: | 3 x 20 mm Type 99 automatic cannon – one each in the nose, tail and rear turrets – 2 x 20 mm automatic cannon in the sides, up to 6 x 7.7 mm Type 92 machine guns in the portholes, and a payload (internal or external) of max. 2,000 kg, e.g., two 800 kg torpedoes, eight 250 kg bombs or depth charges under the wings |

*The Kawanishi H8K2 (Emily).*

got past the experimental stage. Because it had a considerable range (it could fly for up to 20 hours), was well armed and was

fitted with radar, Emily was a very successful reconnaissance aircraft.

# MORANE-SAULNIER M.S.406

*The Morane-Saulnier M.S.406.*

| | M.S.406C-1 |
|---|---|
| Type: | Fighter |
| Crew: | 1 |
| Weight when empty/ max weight at takeoff: | 1,900 kg/ 2,470 kg |
| Length/wingspan/height: | 8.15 m/10.6 m/2.8 m |
| Engine(s): | One Hispano-Suiza 12Y 31 V12 engine with 860 hp |
| Maximum speed: | 485 km/h at 5,000 m |
| Service ceiling: | 9,400 m |
| Range: | 8,000 km |
| Weaponry: | 1 x 20 mm HS404 automatic cannon firing through the propeller hub, 2 x 7.5 mm MAC 1934 machine guns in the wings |

The M.S.406 was France's first fighter aircraft with an enclosed cockpit and retractable undercarriage, and its prototype flew for the first time in August 1938. The French Air Force ordered 1,000 slightly altered production M.S.406s, intending that it should be their standard fighter, but production in the newly built state factories was so painfully slow (there were serious shortages of replacement parts and Hispano-Suiza engines) that its competitor, the Bloch M.B.151, which had initially been turned down, was put into production to ensure that the Air Force would have modern fighter aircraft. By the beginning of the war, 572 M.S.406 aircraft had been delivered, but they were outclassed by the German Bf 109s and suffered heavy losses. In total, 1,081 M.S.406s were built, including all the different versions. After France had surrendered, the German and Italian Air Forces took possession of all serviceable M.S.406s and used them as training aircraft. Even in this capacity, however, they were found to be unsatisfactory and given to Germany's allies: Finland received 68, Croatia acquired 48, and 20 were given to Bulgaria. The Finns modified 41 of their machines to accommodate the Klimov engines they had taken from the Russians, calling the new machines the Mörkö Morane, which performed better than the French version. Switzerland also bought the rights to produce the M.S.406 under licence in 1938, before renaming it the D-3800 (of which 82 were built) and later replacing it with the improved D-3801, which served as a flight instruction aircraft until 1959.

# DEWOITINE D.520

| | D.520 |
|---|---|
| Type: | Fighter |
| Crew: | 1 |
| Weight when empty/ max weight at takeoff: | 2,036 kg/ 2,677 kg |
| Length/wingspan/height: | 8.6 m/10.2 m/2.57 m |
| Engine(s): | One Hispano-Suiza 12Y 45 V12 engine with 935 hp |
| Maximum speed: | 534 km/h at 5,500 m |
| Service ceiling: | 10,500 m |
| Range: | 1,530 km |
| Weaponry: | 1 x 20 mm HS404 automatic cannon firing through the propeller hub, 4 x 7.5 mm MAC 1934 machine guns in the wings |

*The Dewoitine D.520.*

The D.520 was a modern and potentially very effective French aircraft, but it was put into service too late. It made its maiden flight in October 1938, and although there were a few problems with its cooler, it was obviously the best French combat aircraft and a match even for the Bf 109. But because of political disputes and the restructuring of the French air industry (Dewoitne formed part of the state-owned SNCAM company), mass production began only in 1940. Consequently, only a few squadrons were equipped exclusively with D.520s when the Germans invaded. Many units were still phasing in the new fighter, and, although it enjoyed some success, only 437 had actually been produced, and even fewer (351) had been delivered, so it could not make a difference to the outcome of the campaign. In the last days of the Fall of France, some squadrons escaped to the unoccupied areas of the country or to North Africa. In 1941 production of the D.520 began under the Vichy Government, which ordered 550 aircraft. Most of the D.520s were seized by the Wehrmacht when it occupied southern France, and they were used as flight instruction aircraft or supplied to Romania, Bulgaria and Italy.

## BLOCH M.B.151 AND M.B.152

In July 1934 Marcel Bloch Aircraft competed for a tender from the French Air Force for an all-metal single-wing aircraft, which was won by Morane-Saulnier. During the competition, Bloch's M.B.150 had serious difficulties – in fact, it did not even manage to take off! Nevertheless, Bloch remained undeterred and radically modified the design. The modified version could actually fly and in fact performed very well, but it was completely unsuited for serial production, so the design had to be fundamentally altered again. The new model, called the M.B.151, flew for the first time in August 1938 and was supposed to be put into production immediately, but only four had been delivered by April 1939. In the intervening period, Bloch had become part of the state-owned SNCASO company, and its engineers had developed a new and improved version, the M.B.152. In total, 160 M.B.151s and 340 M.B.152s were ordered, but production remained very sluggish, and only 120 of both types had been delivered by September 1939. By late November, 358 machines had been received by the Air Force, but they were nowhere near ready for deployment. At least half of them had no propeller, no sights, or neither a propeller nor sights.

*Though it was a modern and high-performing aircraft, the Bloch M.B.152 arrived too late to make much difference to France's fortunes in the war.*

| | M.B.152 |
|---|---|
| Type: | Fighter |
| Crew: | 1 |
| Weight when empty/ max weight at takeoff: | 2,020 kg/ 2,680 kg |
| Length/wingspan/height: | 9.1 m/10.55 m/3.95 m |
| Engine(s): | One Gnome-Rhône 14N 25 radial engine with 1,080 hp |
| Maximum speed: | 515 km/h at 4,000 m |
| Service ceiling: | 10,000 m |
| Range: | 600 km |
| Weaponry: | 2 x 7.5 mm MAC 1934 machine guns and 2 x 20 mm HS404 automatic cannon, or 4 x 7.5 mm machine guns |

These problems were not rectified very quickly, and when the Germans invaded, the French pilots were still not sufficiently well acquainted with the new fighters, potentially very effective though they were, to make any significant impact on the enemy. After France's defeat, six squadrons of the Air Force under Vichy continued to use the Bloch fighters, and when the Wehrmacht occupied Vichy France in November 1942, the remaining M.B.151s and 152s were given to Romania or used as training aircraft.

*The Bloch M.B.152.*

# POTEZ 63 SERIES

| | Potez 63.11 |
|---|---|
| Type: | Reconnaissance and liaison aircraft |
| Crew: | 3 |
| Weight when empty/ | 3,135 kg/ |
| max weight at takeoff: | 4,530 kg |
| Length/wingspan/height: | 10.93 m/16 m/3.08 m |
| Engine(s): | Two Gnome-Rhône 14M 6/7 radial engines with 700 hp each |
| Maximum speed: | 425 km/h at 5,000 m |
| Service ceiling: | 8,500 m |
| Range: | 1,500 km |
| Weaponry: | 1 x 7.5 mm MAC 1934 machine gun fixed in the nose, 2 x 7.5 mm machine guns – one in the rear of the cockpit, and one in the fuselage – and a payload of max. 200 kg |

*The reconnaissance and light ground attack version, the Potez 63.11.*

The Potez 63 Series was intended as a stable of heavy twin-engine fighters and reconnaissance aircraft, and the first prototype had its maiden flight on 25 April 1936. Serial production began in 1937, but problems with the delivery of engines, propellers and weapons caused significant delays, and only 291 machines were available when the war broke out. The Potez 630 fighter version was powered by Hispano-Suiza engines, and the Potez 631 by Gnome-Rhône engines, but in every other respect the two versions were virtually identical. Their basic design was similar to that of the Bf 110, and they were deployed both as destroyers and as night fighters. The 632 was a light bomber, as was the 633; the latter was the export version, but it was requisitioned by the French when the war broke out. The Potez 63.11, which had a glazed nose and shortened cabin, was introduced to modernize the reconnaissance squadrons, and 850 were delivered. The Potez had first-class flight characteristics, but it was underpowered for a fighter. After the Fall of France, more than 600 Potez aircraft remained in the unoccupied areas of the country and in Algeria, and they were initially put into service by the Vichy Government. More Potez aircraft were produced under the supervision of the Luftwaffe, who used at least 100 Potez 61.11s as training and liaison aircraft.

# BREGUET 690 SERIES

*The Breguet Bre. 693.*

| | Bre. 693 |
|---|---|
| Type: | Bomber |
| Crew: | 2 |
| Weight when empty/ | 3,010 kg/ |
| max weight at takeoff: | 4,900 kg |
| Length/wingspan/height: | 9.67 m/15.37 m/3.19 m |
| Engine(s): | Two Gnome-Rhône 14M 6/7 radial engines with 700 hp each |
| Maximum speed: | 490 km/h at 5,000 m |
| Service ceiling: | 9,500 m |
| Range: | 1,350 km |
| Weaponry: | 1 x 20 mm HS404 automatic cannon and 2 x MAC 1934 machine guns fixed in the nose, 1 x 7.5 mm machine gun in the cockpit, 1 x 7.5 mm machine gun in the fuselage – later 2 additional 7.5 mm fixed machine guns in the motor gondolas – and an internal payload of max. 400 kg |

Breguet began designing a two-seater fighter in 1935, and the initial prototype, called the Bre. 690, flew for the first time in March 1938. Then the French Air Force wanted an entire stable of aircraft based on this prototype. The first production version, called the Breguet 691, was powered by Hispano-Suiza in-line engines, but because these were at a premium, a decision was made to fit the aircraft with Gnome-Rhône radial engines, and the new version, called the Bre. 693, had its maiden flight in October 1939. This was followed by the 695, which was very similar but was powered by Pratt & Whitney engines. Unfortunately, the combination of a French design and an American engine resulted in inferior performance. The 695 prototype flew for the first time in early 1940, but the Bre. 697 heavy fighter never got past the prototype stage. The first deployment of the 693 took place on 12 May 1940, with catastrophic results: 10 of the 11 aircraft deployed were destroyed or severely damaged. Before France was defeated, half of all the 690 series aircraft were destroyed, but a few were still used by the Vichy regime. In November 1942 the remaining aircraft were confiscated by the Germans and given to the Luftwaffe or the Italians, who used them as training aircraft. Around 300 of the 690 series aircraft were produced in total.

## BLOCH M.B.174 AND M.B.175

| | M.B.175 B.3 |
|---|---|
| Type: | Bomber |
| Crew: | 3 |
| Weight when empty/ max weight at takeoff: | 5,660 kg/ 8,023 kg |
| Length/wingspan/height: | 12.43 m/17.95 m/3.55 m |
| Engine(s): | Two Gnome-Rhône 14N 48/49 radial engines with 1,140 hp each |
| Maximum speed: | 540 km/h at 5,200 m |
| Service ceiling: | 11,000 m |
| Range: | 1,600 km |
| Weaponry: | 2 x 7.5 mm MAC 1934 machine guns fixed in the nose, 2 x 7.5 mm machine guns in the rear of the cockpit, 3 x 7.5 mm waist machine guns, and an internal payload of max. 600 kg |

*Antoine de Saint-Exupéry, author of* The Little Prince, *flew an M.B.174 in early 1940.*

The Bloch M.B.174 and 175, a light bomber and reconnaissance aircraft respectively, were the best aircraft available to the French in 1940. Bloch began work on the design as early as 1936, and the prototype had its maiden flight in February 1938. After a few alterations, the M.B.174 was created, and it took off for the first time in January 1939. Test flights went well at first, but later there were problems with the engine cooling system, so the first production models were not delivered until March 1940. The 174 proved to be a first-class reconnaissance aircraft, but its bomb bay was too small to carry bombs heavier than 50 kg. After 50 machines had been produced, the bomb bay was enlarged, and the new model was called the M.B.175, but only 25 had been delivered when France fell to the Germans. Because the supply of Gnome-Rhône engines dried up, a new version (the M.B.176) was fitted with Pratt & Whitney engines. Most M.B.174s, 175s, and 176s available on 10 June 1940 were destroyed in action, but a few aircraft were withdrawn to the unoccupied area of France. The Luftwaffe took possession of a small number and had a few constructed from existing parts, using them as training aircraft.

## BOULTON PAUL P.82 DEFIANT

| | Defiant Mk. II |
|---|---|
| Type: | Night fighter |
| Crew: | 2 |
| Weight when empty/ max weight at takeoff: | 2,849 kg/ 3,821 kg |
| Length/wingspan/height: | 10.77 m/11.99 m/3.34 m |
| Engine(s): | One Rolls-Royce Merlin XX with 1,280 hp |
| Maximum speed: | 504 km/h at 5,790 m |
| Service ceiling: | 9,250 m |
| Range: | 748 km |
| Weaponry: | 4 x 7.7 mm Browning machine guns in the rear turret |

*A Defiant Mark I of No. 410 Squadron, Scotland, autumn 1941.*

The Defiant was an unusual fighter aircraft, in that it had no fixed forward-firing weaponry, but a motorized gun turret with four 7.7 mm machine guns. The idea was to enable the weaponry to be fired in as many directions as possible, allowing the pilot to concentrate on flying the aircraft. Work on its design began in 1935, the prototype had its maiden flight on 11 August 1937, and the Mark I production model was delivered to the Royal Air Force in the summer of 1939. Although it enjoyed considerable success at first, particularly because German pilots mistook it for the Hurricane and did not expect machine gun fire from the turret, the Defiant proved to be an impractical design, as Luftwaffe pilots just began attacking it head on. So from August 1940 the Defiant was only used as a night fighter. The second series model, the Mark II, which had on-board radar, was put into service in September 1941. Until it was replaced by the Beaufighter, the Defiant was flown in 13 night fighter squadrons, and it also served as a target finder and air-sea rescue aircraft. In total, 1,065 Defiants were built.

# GLOSTER S.S.37 GLADIATOR

The Gloster Gladiator was the last fighter biplane in the Royal Air Force. Its prototype had its maiden flight in September 1934, but the first production models were not completed until early 1937. The RAF took delivery of 151 Gladiator Mark I aircraft, and another 147 machines were built to be exported, although the Gladiator was dated in comparison to contemporary single-wing aircraft. The Mark I was soon replaced by the Mark II, which had a triple-blade propeller, an electric starter motor, a dust filter for the engine and a more powerful engine. Around 100 Mark IIs were converted to create the carrier-borne Sea Gladiator, which served in six squadrons on board British aircraft carriers. When the Second World War broke out, the Gladiator was hopelessly outclassed by modern single-seaters like the Bf 109, so they were only flown by the RAF in less strategically significant areas, such as the Mediterranean. After its involvement in the defence of Norway in 1940, the Sea Gladiator was deployed primarily in the Mediterranean, where both models gave a good account of themselves in defending Malta. In total, 746 Gladiators were produced, taking into account all the different models.

|  | Gladiator Mk. II |
|---|---|
| Type: | Fighter |
| Crew: | 1 |
| Weight when empty/ max weight at takeoff: | 1,562 kg/ 2,206 kg |
| Length/wingspan/height: | 8.36 m/9.83 m/3.53 m |
| Engine(s): | One Bristol-Mercury VIIIA radial engine with 850 hp |
| Maximum speed: | 414 km/h at 4,450 m |
| Service ceiling: | 10,210 m |
| Range: | 708 km |
| Weaponry: | 6 x 7.7 mm Browning fixed machine guns – two in the nose, and two under each lower wing |

*The Gloster Gladiator.*

# HAWKER HURRICANE

The Hurricane was initially used as a fighter (day and night), but later it served primarily as a dive-bomber and ground attack aircraft. Its simple (albeit very robust) design and inferior performance meant that it lived very much in the shadow of the famous Spitfire, although it actually shot down more aircraft than the latter in the Battle of Britain. Its prototype took off for the first time on 6 November 1935. The Hurricane's body and wings were largely made of steel tubing, most of which was covered with fabric, and it was armed with eight 7.7 mm

*A Hurricane Mark IIB with 12 7.7 mm machine guns in the wings.*

*A Hurricane Mark I of No. 1 Squadron, Northolt (Middlesex), August 1940.*

| | Hurricane Mk. IIB |
|---|---|
| Type: | Fighter bomber |
| Crew: | 1 |
| Weight when empty/ | 2,498 kg/ |
| max weight at takeoff: | 3,311 kg |
| Length/wingspan/height: | 9.82 m/12.19 m/4.65 m |
| Engine(s): | One Rolls-Royce Merlin XX V12 engine with 1,280 hp |
| Maximum speed: | 530 km/h at 6,705 m |
| Service ceiling: | 11,125 m |
| Range: | 772 km |
| Weaponry: | 12 x 7.7 mm Browning fixed machine guns in the wings, and an external payload of max. 454 kg, e.g., two 227 kg bombs |

machine guns in its wings. In 1939 a raft of improvements was introduced, including an improved triple-blade propeller, metal covering on the wings, and the installation of a Rolls-Royce Merlin III engine.

The Hurricane squadrons sent to defend France made little impact on the mighty Luftwaffe, but in the Battle of Britain 32 Hurricane squadrons completely thwarted the Germans' attempts to take control of the British

skies. While the 19 Spitfire squadrons concentrated on German fighters, the Hurricanes attacked the German bombers. The Hurricane was also deployed in the Mediterranean and North Africa, and throughout the war its

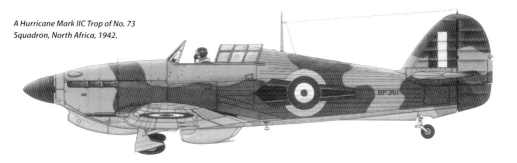

*A Hurricane Mark IIC Trop of No. 73 Squadron, North Africa, 1942.*

*The Hurricane Mark I.*

engines and weaponry were constantly upgraded. In addition, the Hurricane's role as a fighter became less important, and Hawker's priority was to improve its capability as a ground attack aircraft – for example, extra features such as rockets, bombs, additional fuel tanks and gun installations were added. One ground attack model was the Mark IID, which had two 40 mm machine guns and was primarily used in anti-tank operations.

The Hurricane was also manufactured in Canada, where they had different designations and were mainly fitted with Packard-built Merlin engines. To use it in

the Fleet Air Arm (the British Naval Air Force), various versions were converted for use on aircraft carriers. Altogether, 14,231 Hurricanes were produced, and before the war there were plenty of customers for the export version – among others, it was sold to Yugoslavia, Belgium, Turkey and Persia. In fact, Hurricanes were still being exported after the war, to countries such as Portugal, Ireland and Persia. In addition, around 3,000 were delivered to the Soviet Air Force during the Second World War.

*The Mark IIC was armed with four 20 mm machine guns.*

# SUPERMARINE SPITFIRE

The Supermarine Spitfire is undoubtedly the best-known British fighter aircraft, which enjoys almost legendary status in the United Kingdom, entirely because of its key role in the Battle of Britain. Supermarine had plenty of experience producing record-breaking seaplanes to draw upon for the Spitfire, and the designer Reginald J. Mitchell started work on its development in 1935. Its design included a slender, aerodynamic body and elliptical wings, which guaranteed perfect lift, and it was fitted with a Rolls-Royce V12 engine. The prototype's maiden flight took place on 5 March 1940, and its performance was so impressive that the British Air Ministry immediately ordered 370 Mark I Spitfires. By the time of the Battle of Britain, there were 370 Spitfires in 19 squadrons.

The main version then was the Mark Ia, which was not as heavily armed as the Bf 109E but could climb faster and was more agile. Development and production of the Spitfire continued throughout the war, and there were numerous variants and sub-variants. The first mass-produced model, the Mark V (of which 6,664 were built), was the first to be fitted with variable wing weaponry, which was

*The Spitfire's elliptical wings optimized its lift.*

| Spitfire Mk. VB | |
|---|---|
| Type: | Fighter |
| Crew: | 1 |
| Weight when empty/max weight at takeoff: | 2,267 kg/ 2,911 kg |
| Length/wingspan/height: | 9.12 m/11.23 m/3.02 m |
| Engine(s): | One Rolls-Royce Merlin XX with 1,480 hp |
| Maximum speed: | 594 km/h at 5,945 m |
| Service ceiling: | 11,125 m |
| Range: | 1,827 km |
| Weaponry: | 2 x 20 mm Hispano-Suiza automatic cannon and 4 x 7.7 mm Browning machine guns fixed on the wings |

*A Spitfire Mark IXB of No. 421 Squadron, Tangmere (Sussex), June 1944.*

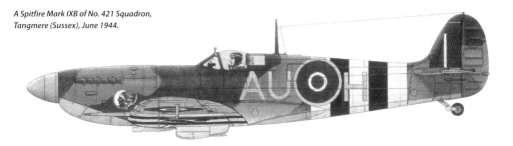

retained on all the following models. For example, the A model had eight 7.7 mm machine guns, the B had two 20 mm and four 7.7 mm machine guns, the C had four 20 mm machine guns, and the E had two 20 mm and two 12.7 mm machine guns, as well as a payload of up to 454 kg. The Mark V was flown across the English Channel in raids against occupied France from early 1941, and by the end of that year 43 squadrons had Mark V Spitfires, though the aircraft lost ground to the Fw 190 from 1942. The version that was most in use in the last three years of the war was the Mark IX, which had a four-blade propeller and a 1,665 hp Merlin engine with a maximum speed of 658 km/h at an altitude of 7,626 m. The Mark XIV appeared towards the end of the war, fitted with a five-blade propeller, teardrop canopy and new 2,050 hp Griffon engine which powered it to a maximum speed of 717 km/h. A Mark XIV earned the distinction of being the first British aircraft to shoot down an Me 262.

For service in North Africa and the Mediterranean, the Spitfire had large sand filters in front of the air intake in the nose, which spoiled its elegant appearance, as with this Mark VC Trop.

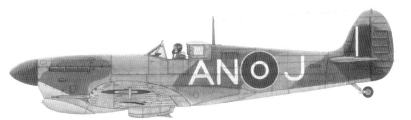

A Spitfire Mark IA of No. 66 Squadron, Kenley (Surrey), September 1940.

The Spitfire Mark VE.

The Spitfire was not only a fighter and a bomber: it was also a photo reconnaissance aircraft (the FR and PR) and took off from aircraft carriers. The latter version, called the Seafire, was first delivered in January 1942, and 2,556 were manufactured, though its narrow gauged, fragile undercarriage was not ideal for service on aircraft carriers. Spitfires flew not only in the RAF, but in practically every Allied air force. By the time production ceased in October 1947, 20,351 Spitfires, comprising 20 different series, had been manufactured.

## HAWKER TYPHOON

To replace the Hurricane, the RAF wanted a fighter powered by the Napier Sabre 24-cylinder H engine or the Rolls-Royce Vulture 24-cylinder X engine, both of which were still being developed. Because the development of the Rolls-Royce engine was halted, the Typhoon prototype which took off for the first time in February 1940 was fitted with a Napier Sabre engine. But there were major problems with the engine, and the airframe and wings were nowhere near secure enough, so the prototype had to be completely re-engineered. By 1943 most of the defects in the airframe and the engine had been ironed out, but the Typhoon failed to impress either as an interceptor against the Fw 190 or as an escort. Because the Spitfire IX, which was also ready to go into service by then, was a first-class fighter, there was no need to use the Typhoon in this role, but the RAF did require an effective dive-bomber, so the existing Typhoons were converted for deployment as low-altitude combat

| Typhoon Mk. IB | |
|---|---|
| Type: | Fighter bomber and ground attack aircraft |
| Crew: | 1 |
| Weight when empty/ max weight at takeoff: | 3,992 kg/ 5,171 kg |
| Length/wingspan/height: | 9.74 m/12.67 m/4.67 m |
| Engine(s): | One Napier Sabre IIA 24 engine in an H-configuration with 2,180 hp |
| Maximum speed: | 652 km/h at 5,500 m |
| Service ceiling: | 10,365 m |
| Range: | 821 km |
| Weaponry: | 4 x 20 mm Hispano-Suiza automatic cannon, and an external payload of max. 908 kg |

*A Typhoon Mark IB of No. 440 Squadron, France, July 1944.*

aircraft. They accompanied Allied troops as they advanced into Germany from France, proving to be excellent dive-bombers and ground attack aircraft. With its four 20 mm machine guns and eight rockets under its wings, as well as carrying bombs, it terrorized the Wehrmacht. In total, 3,300 Typhoons were produced.

## GLOSTER G.41 METEOR

The Gloster Meteor was the Allies' first jet-powered fighter aircraft, and one of only two jet-powered aircraft, along with the Me 262, to be put into service in large numbers in the Second World War. As with German jets, the development of the Meteor was severely hindered by technical difficulties with new jet technology, and although work on its design began in 1940, the first prototype did not fly until March 1943. From July

*The Gloster Meteor Mark III.*

1944 20 pre-production machines (called the Mark 1), fitted with Rolls-Royce Welland turbines which produced 906 kp of thrust, were in use, but the model's performance was disappointing – it had a maximum speed of only 668 km/h and lacked stability – so they remained in Britain, where they were deployed against the V1s. The first serial production models (Mark III) were fitted with more powerful turbines, which enabled them to attain an acceptable speed. Shortly before the end of the war, some Meteors were flown in Holland and Germany. In total, 3,875 Meteors were manufactured.

| Meteor F. Mk. III (early version) | |
|---|---|
| Type: | Fighter |
| Crew: | 1 |
| Weight when empty/max weight at takeoff: | 4,771 kg/6,314 kg |
| Length/wingspan/height: | 12.58 m/13.11 m/3.96 m |
| Engine(s): | Two Rolls-Royce W.2B/23 Welland 1 jet engines with 906 kp thrust each |
| Maximum speed: | 768 km/h at 3,000 m |
| Service ceiling: | 13,100 m |
| Range: | 1,100 km |
| Weaponry: | 4 x 20 mm Hispano-Suiza automatic cannon fixed in the nose |

# BRISTOL TYPE 152 BEAUFORT

The Bristol Beaufort was based on the Blenheim but had significantly more powerful engines and a taller and wider body. It had its maiden flight on 15 October 1938, but was not put into service until January 1940, as the Bristol Taurus engines suffered from problems at first. Even when in service the newly developed engines were always temperamental, as they had sleeve valves rather than valve-trains, and at one point all Beauforts had to be grounded. Some were also produced by the Australians, who decided early on to install more reliable American Pratt & Whitney radial engines, and Australian Beauforts were flown in the Pacific from mid-1942 until the end of the war. In spite of all its faults, from 1940 to 1943 the Beaufort was the RAF's standard land-based torpedo bomber and minelayer.

*The Bristol Beaufort. Beauforts equipped with radar were flown not only in Britain, but also in the Mediterranean. In total, 1,900 Beauforts were manufactured, including all the different versions.*

|  | Beaufort Mk. I |
| --- | --- |
| Type: | Torpedo bomber |
| Crew: | 4 |
| Weight when empty/ max weight at takeoff: | 5,945 kg/ 9,630 kg |
| Length/wingspan/height: | 13.59 m/17.63 m/3.78 m |
| Engine(s): | Two Bristol Taurus radial engines with 1,130 hp each |
| Maximum speed: | 418 km/h at 1,830 m |
| Service ceiling: | 5,030 m |
| Range: | 1,670 km |
| Weaponry: | 4 x 7.7 mm Browning machine guns – two in the turret, two in a remote-controlled installation under the nose – an internal payload of max. 681 kg, and one 728 kg torpedo |

# BRISTOL TYPE 142M, 149 AND 160 BLENHEIM

|  | Blenheim Mk. I |
| --- | --- |
| Type: | Light bomber |
| Crew: | 3 |
| Weight when empty/ max weight at takeoff: | 3,810 kg/ 5,670 kg |
| Length/wingspan/height: | 12.12 m/17.2 m/3 m |
| Engine(s): | Two Bristol Mercury VIII 9-cylinder radial engines with 840 hp each |
| Maximum speed: | 428 km/h at 3,600 m |
| Service ceiling: | 8,320 m |
| Range: | 1,810 km |
| Weaponry: | 1 x 7.7 mm Browning machine gun, 1 x Vickers K 7.7 mm machine gun, and an internal payload of max. 454 kg |

*The Bristol Blenheim Mark I.*

The Blenheim was based on one of the first ever commercial aircraft, and on its first flight in 1935 the Bristol Type 142 exceeded all expectations, as it was around 50 km/h faster than the fastest RAF fighter at the time. The Air Ministry was interested in the Type 142, and Bristol designed a military version, the 142M. With the exception of the fabric-covered control surfaces, the 142M was made entirely of metal, and it was called the Blenheim Mark I. Its maiden flight took place on 25 June 1936, and the first production machines were delivered to the RAF in March 1937. They were used not only as bombers, but also as night fighters, for which they had a ventral gondola with four 7.7 mm guns and were fitted with radar. In July 1940 a Blenheim night fighter became the first aircraft in the world to achieve a radar-guided kill. The Mark I was replaced by the Blenheim Mark IV (the Type 149), which had a longer nose to accommodate the observer and his equipment. At its peak there were 70 Blenheim squadrons in the RAF, and one of its variants, the Bolingbroke, was produced in Canada, though this was used only for training purposes. The final version was the Blenheim Mark V (the Type 160); it had additional armour and weaponry but was fitted with the same engine, which made it very slow and ponderous, so it was soon withdrawn from front-line service. The Blenheim was exported to numerous countries, including Finland, Yugoslavia, Romania and Turkey, and during the war it was flown by the RAF, the RCAF (Royal Canadian Air Force), RSAAF (Royal South African Air Force), the Free French, Portugal and Greece. Altogether, 3,983 Blenheims were produced, including the Canadian-built model.

UNITED KINGDOM

## BRISTOL TYPE 156 BEAUFIGHTER

The Type 156 was actually developed by Bristol as a heavy long-range bomber, based on the Beaufort and called the Beaufighter, but during the war it was used as a night fighter, a torpedo bomber, and an anti-ship and ground attack aircraft. It had its maiden flight on 17 July 1939 and immediately proved to be an outstanding machine. It was initially mainly used as a night fighter (the Mark IF), as its body was large enough to accommodate very bulky radar equipment. The first production models were delivered to the RAF in September 1940 and made a great impact on the Luftwaffe. As soon as there were sufficient numbers of Mosquitoes for night fighting, Beaufighters were mainly used as heavy fighters and anti-ship aircraft; German transport aircraft on their way to North Africa had some

unpleasant encounters with them. Australia also built the Beaufighter under licence and flew it against the Japanese. The different variants differed primarily in their engine specifications and weapon configurations, and numerous models

were fitted with radar. Altogether, 5,562 were manufactured before production was halted in 1945.

|  | Beaufort Mk. X |
|---|---|
| Type: | Heavy (nocturnal) fighter/torpedo bomber/anti-ship aircraft |
| Crew: | 2 |
| Weight when empty/ max weight at takeoff: | 5,945 kg/ 9,630 kg |
| Length/wingspan/height: | 12.71 m/17.63 m/4.83 m |
| Engine(s): | Two Bristol Hercules XVII radial engines with 1,770 hp each |
| Maximum speed: | 488 km/h at 400 m |
| Service ceiling: | 4,570 m |
| Range: | 2,365 km |
| Weaponry: | 4 x 20 mm Hispano-Suiza fixed automatic cannon in the nose, 6 x 7.7 mm Browning machine guns in the wings, 1 x Vickers K 7.7 mm machine gun on the back of the fuselage, and one 728/966 kg torpedo – also, instead of wing guns, this model could carry eight 41 kg air-to-surface rockets or two 113 kg bombs |

*A Beaufighter takes off on an anti-ship mission in July 1942.*

# VICKERS WELLINGTON

The Vickers Wellington was one of the mainstays of British Bomber Command for raids on continental Europe in the first half of the war; it had its maiden flight on 15 June 1936. The

Wellington had an interesting design: its body and wings were fabric-covered, but its geodesic structure, with cantilevered light metal struts like an airship, was pretty well bulletproof, yet the 'Wimpey', as it was nicknamed, suffered heavy losses early on. This inspired RAF Bomber Command to use it for night raids instead. Until 1942 Wellingtons were the main aircraft deployed in bombing raids on Germany, using pioneering electronic target location equipment. In the first 1,000-bomber night raid on Cologne, which took place on 31 March 1941, 600 Wellingtons were involved.

From 1943 the Wellington was withdrawn from bomber squadrons but was still used in the Mediterranean and in Coastal Command as a minesweeper, a torpedo bomber and an anti-submarine aircraft. It was still in service as a training aircraft as late as 1954. Wellingtons flew on 63,977 missions for Bomber Command, and no fewer than 11,461 planes had been manufactured by the time production was halted in October 1945. The various versions mainly differed in their engine specifications (most were powered by Bristol radial engines, but some had Rolls-Royce Merlin or Pratt & Whitney engines), their weapon configurations and their electronics.

*A Wellington B. Mark III of No. 426 Squadron, Dishforth (Yorkshire), early 1943.*

| Wellington B.Mk. III | |
|---|---|
| Type: | Medium range bomber |
| Crew: | 6 |
| Weight when empty/ max weight at takeoff: | 8,417 kg/ 13,381 kg |
| Length/wingspan/height: | 18.54 m/26.26 m/5.31 m |
| Engine(s): | Two Bristol Hercules XI radial engines with 1,500 hp each |
| Maximum speed: | 410 km/h at 3,810 m |
| Service ceiling: | 5,790 m |
| Range: | 2,478 km |
| Weaponry: | 2 x 7.7 mm Browning machine guns in the nose, 4 x 7.7 mm machine guns in the rear turret, 2 x 7.7 mm machine guns in side installations, and an internal payload of max. 2,041 kg |

*The Wellington B. Mark II.*

# DE HAVILLAND D.H. 98 MOSQUITO

The D.H. 98 Mosquito was used in a wide variety of roles: as a bomber, a fighter bomber, a night fighter, a reconnaissance aircraft, an anti-ship aircraft, a carrier-borne combat aircraft and a target finder.

On its own initiative De Havilland began work on a design for a high-speed bomber in 1938, and to save raw materials large parts of the plane's structure consisted of laminated wood. The British Air Ministry initially turned down De Havilland's offer; only when the military situation became more difficult did a bomber that was not made of light metal come to be seen as an attractive proposition.

So the first Mosquito prototype had its maiden flight on 25 November 1940, achieving an astounding maximum speed of over 630 km/h – which, at the time, made it even faster than the Spitfire. In addition, it could carry the same payload as a contemporary medium-range bomber. The Air Ministry had been

*A Mosquito NF Mark II of No. 23 Squadron, Malta, January 1943.*

*A Mosquito FB Mark VI of No. 418 Squadron, Hendon (Hertfordshire), autumn 1944.*

| | Mosquito FB Mk. VI |
|---|---|
| Type: | Fighter bomber |
| Crew: | 2 |
| Weight when empty/ max weight at takeoff: | 6,486 kg/ 10,115 kg |
| Length/wingspan/height: | 12.47 m/16.51 m/4.65 m |
| Engine(s): | Two Rolls-Royce Merlin 25 V12 engines with 1,620 hp each |
| Maximum speed: | 583 km/h at 1,675 m |
| Service ceiling: | 10,070 m |
| Range: | 2,655 km |
| Weaponry: | 4 x 20 mm Hispano-Suiza automatic cannon, 4 x 7.7 mm Browning machine guns fixed in the nose, and a combined internal and external payload of max. 908 kg, e.g., two 113 kg bombs in the internal bomb bay and eight 41 kg air-to-surface rockets under the outer wings |

won over, and ordered three different versions: a photo reconnaissance (PR) model, a bomber (B) and a night fighter (NF). As soon as it was first put in service on 14 July 1941, it lived up to all expectations, and a PR Mark I eluded three Bf 109s over France. From early 1942 the first bomber squadrons with B Mark IV aircraft were ready for service, and they began a series of bombing raids on Germany. The radar-equipped NF Mark II was first deployed in late December 1941.

The Mosquito soon showed that, even with its wooden frame, it was very robust, and it quickly developed into a highly successful aircraft.

As well as the three variants already mentioned, there were numerous other models. The Mosquito manufactured in the largest numbers and the most important version was the FB (fighter bomber) Mark IV, which was heavily armed with automatic cannon and machine guns in its nose and could

also carry bombs and rockets. The Mosquito bombers were increasingly given the role of 'scouts' (target finders), marking out targets for Lancaster and Halifax bombers with 'Christmas Tree' light bombs. Mosquitoes were also manufactured in Canada and Australia, but their performance was not quite as impressive in the Pacific as in Europe: the warm and humid climate was not good for their wooden parts, and some Mosquitoes literally fell apart in mid-air. In total, 7,781 Mosquitoes were built, including all the different versions, of which 1,134 were manufactured in Canada and 212 in Australia.

*German night fighters found the Mosquito night bomber virtually untouchable.*

## SHORT S.29 STIRLING

*The Stirling Mark III.*

The S.29 prototype had its maiden flight on 14 May 1939, and Stirlings flew their first missions for RAF Bomber Command in February 1941. The Mark I was manufactured in large numbers at first, and later the Mark III was used in missions in occupied Europe. In its heyday 11 bomber squadrons were flying the Stirling. It was also deployed as a 'scout', a target finder which dropped light bombs above targets. Once there were sufficient numbers of Halifax and Lancaster bombers, the Stirling was restricted to missions of secondary importance, as it could not reach a satisfactory altitude, and its bomb bay could not carry the new 1,816 kg bombs. From 1944 it served primarily as a glider

tug and a transporter for paratroopers, for which two new versions, the Mark IV and Mark V, were specially built, but in 1946 the Stirling was withdrawn from service even in these capacities. Including all the

different versions, 2,383 Stirlings were produced altogether.

|  | Stirling Mk. III |
|---|---|
| Type: | Heavy bomber |
| Crew: | 7 |
| Weight when empty/ max weight at takeoff: | 19,595 kg/ 31,751 kg |
| Length/wingspan/height: | 26.89 m/30.2 m/6.93 m |
| Engine(s): | Four Bristol Hercules XVI radial engines with 1,650 hp each |
| Maximum speed: | 435 km/h at 4,400 m |
| Service ceiling: | 5,180 m |
| Range: | 3,090 km |
| Weaponry: | 4 x 7.7 mm Browning machine guns – two in the nose turret, two in the rear turret – 4 x 7.7 mm machine guns in the tail turret, and an internal payload of max. 6,350 kg |

# AVRO LANCASTER

The Lancaster was, by quite some way, the most important and the best British bomber in the Second World War, yet it had its roots in the unsuccessful twin-engine Avro Manchester, which struggled with many different problems for the short time it was in service. To overcome these problems, Avro completely revised its design, equipping the new model with four reliable Rolls-Royce Merlin engines, instead of the problematic Vulture engines. The Lancaster prototype had its maiden flight on 9 January 1941, and in September that same year, bomber crews began training with the first production aircraft. Very little in the basic design was changed at any point during the war, showing how effective it was, and though there were versions other than the Mark I (which was manufactured throughout the war), the differences between them were primarily their engine specifications and weapon configurations. The Mark II had Bristol Hercules engines, and the Mark III was powered by the American-built version of the Merlin, while the Mark X was

*The Lancaster's excellent Rolls-Royce Merlin engines contributed significantly to its success.*

| Lancaster Mk. I | |
|---|---|
| Type: | Heavy bomber |
| Crew: | 7 |
| Weight when empty/ max weight at takeoff: | 16,738 kg/ 31,751 kg |
| Length/wingspan/height: | 21.18 m/31.09 m/16.1 m |
| Engine(s): | Four Rolls-Royce Merlin XX V12 engines with 1,280 hp each |
| Maximum speed: | 448 km/h at 3,500 m |
| Service ceiling: | 7,468 m |
| Range: | 4,072 km |
| Weaponry: | 4 x 7.7 mm Browning machine guns – two in the nose turret, two in the rear turret – 4 x 7.7 mm machine guns in the tail turret, and normally an internal payload of max. 6,350 kg |

manufactured in Canada. The Mark VII had a turning gun turret with a 12.7 mm machine gun, but special mention should go to the B version of the Mark I, which was modified to carry the 9,979 kg 'Grand Slam' bomb, which was mainly used against submarine bunkers, and the Mark III B, which carried out the celebrated 'Dambuster' raids in 1943, dropping the famous bouncing bombs, which skimmed over the water like stones to destroy the Möhne, Sorpe and Eder dams in Germany. The 5,396 kg

'Tallboy' bomb was also dropped by Lancasters – among other targets, it struck and sank the German battleship *Tirpitz* in November 1944.

During the war 59 RAF bomber squadrons flew the Lancaster, and it was the main bomber used in night raids on German cities, where a weakness in many Lancasters was exposed which was never eradicated: they lacked defensive weaponry to protect their undercarriages, where many of them carried their ground target-finding radar equipment, which

*A Lancaster Mark II of No. 426 Squadron,*
*Linton-on-Ouse (Yorkshire), late 1943.*

*A Lancaster Mark X of No. 419 Squadron, Durham, June 1944.*

gave them no visibility directly downwards. German night fighters exploited this weakness by approaching the bombers from below, flying directly beneath them, then opening fire diagonally upwards (this was called 'diagonal music'). Nevertheless, the Lancaster was by far the RAF's most successful bomber, playing a major role in the Allies' eventual victory. Lancasters flew on more than 156,000 missions and dropped 618,350 tonnes of explosives, as well as 51 million incendiary bombs. A new version with an increased range was also planned for deployment in the Far East. Lancasters were not only flown by the RAF: the Canadian (RCAF) and Australian (RAAF) Air Forces also flew them, as did the French Navy. The last of a total of 7,377 Lancasters was completed in February 1946.

*The Lancaster was the RAF's most important*
*heavy bomber in the Second World War.*

# HANDLEY PAGE H.P.57 HALIFAX

| | Halifax B. Mk. III |
|---|---|
| Type: | Heavy bomber |
| Crew: | 7 |
| Weight when empty/ max weight at takeoff: | 17,345 kg/ 29,484 kg |
| Length/wingspan/height: | 21.82 m/31.75 m/6.32 m |
| Engine(s): | Four Bristol Hercules XVI radial engines with 1,615 hp each |
| Maximum speed: | 454 km/h at 4,100 m |
| Service ceiling: | 7,315 m |
| Range: | 4,072 km |
| Weaponry: | 8 x 7.7 mm Browning machine guns – two in the rear turret, two in the tail turret – 1 x 7.7 mm machine gun in the nose, and an internal payload of max. 5,897 kg |

*A Halifax Mark II.*

The Handley Page Halifax was one of Britain's foremost heavy bombers in the Second World War, second only to the Lancaster. It was originally meant to be powered by Rolls-Royce Vulture engines, but Handley soon doubted the latter's reliability, so the model was redesigned to take four Rolls-Royce Merlin engines, which resulted in a much larger and heavier machine. The first prototype of the H.P.57 flew on 25 October 1939. So that it could carry a large payload, the all-metal Halifax was built with medium-height wings, and two additional bomb bays were created in the inner wings. The Halifax Mark I, which did not have a machine gun turret on the fuselage, was put into service from November 1940. Because many bombers were lost in daytime raids, in late 1941 the Halifax was used instead as a night bomber and was successful in this capacity. Halifax bombers were the first machines ever to be equipped with new, top-secret H2S radar installations to locate targets on the ground, and eventually 38 RAF bomber wings put them into service. The Mark II had a machine gun turret on its fuselage, but it no longer had a turret in its nose, while the Mark III was powered by Bristol Hercules radial engines instead of Rolls-Royce Merlins. Altogether, 6,178 Halifax bombers were produced in the various versions.

*Although the Halifax was overshadowed by the Lancaster, it was the better multi-purpose aircraft. Up to 1945 it flew 75,532 missions and dropped 231,252 tonnes of bombs. In addition, it was deployed in nine Coastal Command squadrons as a sea reconnaissance and anti-submarine aircraft, towed gliders, carried paratroopers, and flew secret missions to drop agents and parachute weapons and equipment for partisans and resistance fighters.*

# FAIREY SWORDFISH

| | Swordfish Mk. I |
|---|---|
| Type: | Carrier-borne torpedo bomber and reconnaissance aircraft |
| Crew: | 2–3 |
| Weight when empty/ max weight at takeoff: | 2,145 kg/ 3,419 kg |
| Length/wingspan/height: | 10.89 m/13.86 m/3.76 m |
| Engine(s): | One Bristol Pegasus III M.3 radial engine with 690 hp |
| Maximum speed: | 222 km/h |
| Service ceiling: | 3,260 m |
| Range: | 874 km |
| Weaponry: | 2 x 7.7 mm Vickers machine guns (one in the nose, one mobile in the rear of the cockpit), and one 728 kg torpedo, or an external payload of max. 681 kg |

*The Fairey Swordfish Mark I.*

In 1930 the Air Ministry required a torpedo bomber and reconnaissance aircraft which could be flown from an aircraft carrier, and the Swordfish was designed to meet this need. But Fairey's first prototype was far from successful – in fact, it even crashed. But the second prototype lived up to expectations, and the Swordfish Mark I went into serial production in 1935. The Swordfish was a fabric-covered biplane with fixed undercarriage, and its wings could be folded so that it could be accommodated on an aircraft carrier. In November 1940

Swordfishes successfully attacked the Italian fleet anchored at the port of Taranto, and in May 1941 a Swordfish carried out a torpedo attack on the *Bismarck*, the famous German battleship. From 1942 it was mostly flown from aircraft carriers in anti-submarine operations. In 1943 the Mark II was introduced, with a more powerful engine

and metal-reinforced lower wings, from which rockets could be fired. The Mark III, which was put into service in late 1943, had a radar device in a large dome on its underside, and some Swordfishes (called the Mark IV) had enclosed cockpits for use in extremely cold regions. In total, 2,391 machines were produced up to 1944.

# SHORT S.25 SUNDERLAND

The Short Sunderland was mainly used in sea reconnaissance and anti-submarine operations, but was also an air-sea rescue aircraft and a transporter. It was based on the S.23 civil seaplane, making its maiden flight on 16 October 1937, and the first Sunderlands were put into service by British Coastal Command in the autumn of 1938. From 1940 Sunderlands were equipped with ASV (Air to Surface Vessel) radar to protect

| | Stirling Mk. III |
|---|---|
| Type: | Reconnaissance and anti-submarine seaplane |
| Crew: | 10 |
| Weight when empty/ max weight at takeoff: | 14,969 kg/ 26,308 kg |
| Length/wingspan/height: | 26.01 m/34.38 m/9.79 m |
| Engine(s): | Four Bristol Pegasus XVIII radial engines with 1,065 hp each |
| Maximum speed: | 341 km/h at 1,500 m |
| Service ceiling: | 4,570 m |
| Range: | 4,828 km |
| Weaponry: | 4 x 7.7 mm Browning machine guns – two in the tail turret, two in the rear turret – 4 x 7.7 mm machine guns in the tail turret, 2 x 12.7 mm Browning machine guns in side installations, 4 x 7.7 mm machine guns fixed in the nose, and an internal payload of max. 2,250 kg |

*A Short Sunderland Mark III with ASV ship locating radar on the back of the fuselage.*

Allied convoys and detect and destroy enemy submarines, and it was feared by the Luftwaffe on account of its 'porcupine' defensive weaponry. In fact, it is claimed that, when under attack from eight Ju 88s, one Sunderland shot down three enemy planes. Because its undercarriage had to be watertight, its bombs were carried on rails through lateral gaps in the fuselage into the inner wings before being dropped. In total, 749 machines were manufactured in five series which mainly differed in their engine specifications.

## POLIKARPOV I-16

| | I-16 Type 24 |
|---|---|
| Type: | Fighter and fighter bomber |
| Crew: | 1 |
| Weight when empty/<br>max weight at takeoff: | 1,475 kg/<br>2,060 kg |
| Length/wingspan/height: | 6.04 m/8.88 m/2.41 m |
| Engine(s): | One M-62 radial engine with 1,000 hp |
| Maximum speed: | 490 km/h |
| Service ceiling: | 9,470 m |
| Range: | 600 km |
| Weaponry: | 4 x 7.62 mm ShKAS machine guns, or 2 x 7.62 mm machine guns and 2 x 20 mm ShVAK automatic cannon, and an external payload of max 200 kg |

The Polikarpov I-16 was the world's first mass-produced single-wing fighter aircraft with retractable undercarriage. Its structure was a composite of wood, steel and aluminium, covered with fabric. The first prototype flew in late 1933, and serial production of the Type I began in mid-1934. In late October 1936 the first I-16s were delivered to the Spanish Republican forces for deployment in the Civil War, where they were dubbed the 'Mosca' (Fly) by the Republicans and the 'Rata' (Rat) by the Nationalists. The

*The Polikarpov I-16.*

Soviet Union sent a total of 157 machines to Spain, and another 30 were built there under licence. At first, the I-16 was the best fighter aircraft in Spain, but later on proved to be inferior to the more modern Bf 109. It was deployed against the Japanese in the border conflict of 1939 and in the Russo-Finnish Winter War of 1939–40, where it was used both as a fighter and as a fighter bomber. But it was

so hopelessly outclassed by German aircraft that its pilots often resorted to ramming their enemy, and in late 1943 it was permanently withdrawn from front-line service, as better machines were now available. Until then around 7,000 I-16s had been built, including all the different versions.

## MIKOYAN-GUREVICH MIG-1 AND MIG-3

The famous aircraft design team of Mikoyan and Gurevich designed their first combat aircraft, the MiG 140, in 1940, but at first no one would have guessed that they would become so successful. The MiG-1 had its maiden flight on 5 April 1940, and 100 aircraft of this type were produced up to December that year. It was certainly fast, reaching 628 km/h, but it was only lightly armed, with just two 7.62 mm machine guns, and, far more seriously, it was very unstable and had a limited range. An improved version, the MiG-3, was notable for its excellent performance at high altitude, reaching a maximum speed of 640 km/h at 7,800 m, but below 5,000 m its performance was clearly inferior to that of its German counterparts, and its weaponry – one 12.7 mm and two 7.62 mm machine guns – was still inadequate. Production of both fighter models was brought to a halt in the summer of 1942, after 3,322 machines

had been produced, because mass production of the Yak and LaGG fighters had begun in the meantime in the

factories behind the Ural Mountains, and new MiGs did not appear until after the cessation of hostilities.

*A MiG-3 from an unknown unit in winter camouflage.*

| | MiG-3 |
|---|---|
| Type: | Fighter |
| Crew: | 1 |
| Weight when empty/<br>max weight at takeoff: | 2,595 kg/<br>3,350 kg |
| Length/wingspan/height: | 8.27 m/10.2 m/3.5 m |
| Engine(s): | One Mikulin AM 35A V12 engine with 1,350 hp |
| Maximum speed: | 640 km/h at 7,800 m |
| Service ceiling: | 12,000 m |
| Range: | 1,195 kg |
| Weaponry: | 1 x 12.7 mm UBS machine gun, 2 x 7.62 mm ShKAS machine guns fixed in the nose, and an external payload of max. 200 kg, e.g., two 100 kg bombs or eight RS-82 rockets |

# LAVOCHKIN LAGG-1, LAGG-3, LA-5 AND LA-7

The Lavochkin fighter series was one of the most important of such series built by the Soviet Union in the Second World War, second only to the Yak series. All Lavochkin aircraft were made of wood; the company had been developing high-performance fighters made entirely of wood since the 1930s. In conjunction with M.I. Gudkov and W.P. Gorbunov, Lavochkin designed a fighter made entirely of laminated Siberian birch wood, and the prototype had its maiden flight on 30 March 1940. But the aircraft was too hastily developed and had many problems, so only 100 LaGGs were manufactured. The improved LaGG-3 had its maiden flight on 14 June 1940, but its engine was both too heavy and insufficiently powerful, so Lavochkin tested several different engines. Furthermore, when Germany went to war with Russia, the LaGG-3 proved to be inferior to the Bf 109, which led to the development of the La-5. By this time, 6,528 LaGG-3 aircraft had been produced.

Instead of the old V12 engine, the new aircraft (the La-5) had to be completely redesigned to take a Shvetsov ASh 82 radial engine, which meant that it was virtually an entirely new aircraft. The La-5 had its maiden flight in April 1942 and went into production in June that same year. It fared especially well in the southern part of the Eastern Front, where it was dubbed 'the Wooden Saviour of Stalingrad'. Once the improved ASh 82FN engine with direct fuel injection was available in early 1943, the

| | La-7 |
|---|---|
| Type: | Fighter and fighter bomber |
| Crew: | 1 |
| Weight when empty/ max weight at takeoff: | 2,625 kg/ 3,400 kg |
| Length/wingspan/height: | 8.6 m/9.8 m/2.8 m |
| Engine(s): | One 14-cylinder Shvetsov ASh 82FN radial engine with 1,775 hp |
| Maximum speed: | 665 km/h |
| Service ceiling: | 11,800 m |
| Range: | 635 km |
| Weaponry: | 2–3 x ShVAK or B-20 20 mm automatic cannon, and an external payload of max. 200 kg, e.g., two 100 kg bombs or eight RS-82 rockets |

*An La-7 of the 16th Soviet Guard Fighter Wing, Eastern Front, 1945.*

La-5FN was introduced. It had a distinctive forward-facing air intake on the fuselage, as well as a lowered back to allow better rearward visibility. This was the most effective variant of the La-5, helping to turn the tables on the Germans in the summer of 1943. It is claimed that around 10,000 La-5s were built in total. The La-7 was a further development of the La-5, with a completely protected airframe and a new, more aerodynamically efficient oil cooler under the rear of the cockpit. The front-line forces received their first La-7s in mid-1944, and 5,753 of these machines were to be produced.

*The LaGG-3.*

# YAKOVLEV YAK-1, YAK-3, YAK-7 AND YAK-9

| | Yak-3 |
|---|---|
| Type: | Fighter |
| Crew: | 1 |
| Weight when empty/ max weight at takeoff: | 2,105 kg/ 2,660 kg |
| Length/wingspan/height: | 8.49 m/9.2 m/2.42 m |
| Engine(s): | One Klimov VK 105PF 2 V with 1,300 hp |
| Maximum speed: | 655 km/h at 3,100 m |
| Service ceiling: | 10,700 m |
| Range: | 900 km |
| Weaponry: | 1 x 20 mm ShVAK automatic cannon firing through the propeller hub, 2 x 12.7 mm UBS machine guns fixed in the nose, and an external payload of max. 200 kg |

*A Yak-3 in the colours of the Normandy Niemen Squadron – the aircraft pictured is still airworthy today.*

The Soviet fighter series that was produced in the largest numbers in the Second World War was built by the Yakovlev company. The Yak-1 was intended to replace outdated Soviet biplanes. It had its maiden flight on 13 January 1940, and serial production began in December that same year. It was composed of fabric-covered steel rods, with wooden wings and retractable undercarriage. After its first front-line deployment in the summer of 1941, it underwent some improvements: the wing tips were made narrower, and from 1942 the Yak-1B had better all-round visibility, as the back of the fuselage was lowered. Production of the Yak-1

continued until 1943, and 8,721 machines were manufactured. In early 1942 Yakovlev began work on improving the series. Primarily, the aircraft was given a more powerful engine and its weight was reduced: the Yak-3 was the lightest fighter in the Second World War. Its flight tests took place in April 1943, and in August 1944 the first Yak-3 squadrons were ready for service. The Yak proved to be an outstanding fighter and could also be used as a fighter bomber. In fact, it was so effective that in late 1944 the Luftwaffe high command ordered its pilots to avoid engaging Yaks in combat at altitudes of around 5,000 m or less. The Yak was fast and agile, and it could climb rapidly, but

its range left something to be desired. In total, 4,848 Yak-3s were manufactured. The Yak-7 was originally developed as a two-seater training version of the Yak-1, but it was also a front-line fighter, and 6,399 were built. The Yak-9 flew for the first time in 1943, and was manufactured in the largest quantities of all the Yak versions: 16,769 machines were built. It was mainly used as a fighter bomber and long-range escort fighter, and was powered by a slightly more powerful 1,600 hp Klimov VK 107A engine, while the two-seater Yak-9UTI served as a training aircraft. Yaks were flown even after 1945: for instance, by the Communists in the Korean War.

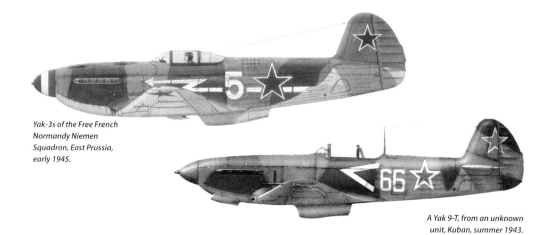

*Yak-3s of the Free French Normandy Niemen Squadron, East Prussia, early 1945.*

*A Yak 9-T, from an unknown unit, Kuban, summer 1943.*

# ILYUSHIN IL-2 AND IL-10 STURMOVIK

The Ilyushin Il-2 was one of the most important combat aircraft in the Second World War, and it is claimed that a total of 36,163 were built, including all the different versions. The first prototype had its maiden flight on 12 October 1940, at which time it was still a single-seater. The first production aircraft were delivered to the Soviet Air Force in May 1941. In the first few months of Germany's invasion of Russia, the Il-2 suffered heavy losses, due to Germany's dominance in the skies. So in 1942 a

*A single-seater Ilyushin Il-2.*

*An Ilyushin Il-2M3 of the 269th Ground Attack Regiment, Kursk, 1943.*

|  | Il-2 |
|---|---|
| Type: | Ground attack aircraft |
| Crew: | 2 |
| Weight when empty/max weight at takeoff: | 4,525 kg/ 6,360 kg |
| Length/wingspan/height: | 8.27 m/10.2 m/3.5 m |
| Engine(s): | One Mikulin AM 38F V12 engine with 1,700 hp |
| Maximum speed: | 410 km/h at 1,500 m |
| Service ceiling: | 4,525 m |
| Range: | 765 km |
| Weaponry: | 2 x 23 mm VYa automatic cannon, 2 x 7.62 mm ShKAS machine guns fixed in the wings, 1 x 12.7 mm UBT machine gun in the rear of the cockpit, and a combined payload of max. 600 kg |

decision was made to introduce the two-seater Il-2M version, in which the observer would be armed with a 12.7 mm machine gun to defend against attacks from the rear. The next important new version was the Il-2M3, which had a more powerful engine and V-shaped (therefore, stronger) wing tips.

The Sturmovik's most important task was to attack armoured vehicles and ground troops, so it had 6–13 mm thick armour all over – to protect its engine,

pilot, fuel tank and, in the two-seater version, observer. The German troops nicknamed it 'Iron Gustav' or 'Black Death', and as well as machine guns and automatic cannon of up to 37 mm calibre, it also carried bombs and RS-82 or RS-132 air-to-surface rockets. The Il-2 originally had a composite structure, but was later made entirely of metal. In addition to the Il-2s flown by the Air Force, the Navy deployed a torpedo bomber version of the aircraft. An improved version, called

the Il-10, was produced from early 1945. The importance of the Il-2 for the Soviet forces is underlined by a telegram from Stalin about delays in delivering the Il-2: 'The Red Army needs Il-2s as it needs air and bread. I demand more machines. That is my final warning!'

## POLIKARPOV PO-2

| | Po-2 |
|---|---|
| Type: | Light night bomber |
| Crew: | 2 |
| Weight when empty/ max weight at takeoff: | 770 kg/ 1,268 kg |
| Length/wingspan/height: | 8.27 m/10.2 m/3.5 m |
| Engine(s): | One 5-cylinder Shvetsov M-11D radial engine with 125 hp |
| Maximum speed: | 130 km/h near ground level |
| Service ceiling: | 1,300 m |
| Range: | 350 km |
| Weaponry: | 1 x 7.62 mm ShKAS machine gun in the rear of the cockpit, and an external payload of max. 300 kg |

*Though nondescript to look at, more Po-2s were manufactured than any other aircraft in the world.*

The Polikarpov Po-2, originally known as the U-2, was designed in 1927 primarily as a flight instruction aircraft, and its prototype had its maiden flight in January 1928. It proved to be easy to fly and to maintain, as well as being very stable, so it was put into serial production in 1930. The frame was made of wood, the front section of the fuselage was covered with laminated wood, and the rear of the fuselage and the wings were covered with fabric. New versions, in addition to the training model, were produced in very little time, including one to spray crops with insecticide, one to transport the sick, a seaplane and a passenger aircraft. When Germany attacked the Soviet Union, around 13,000 Po-2s were in service. Out of necessity many new military versions were produced, including liaison and reconnaissance aircraft. They became famous in their capacity as light bombers for harassing German troops in night raids; because of the noise made by its engine, the Germans nicknamed it the 'Sewing Machine'. It was highly successful, inspiring the Luftwaffe to use dated models which they had seized from the Russians for similar purposes. It is claimed that around 33,000 U-2s and Po-2s were built; this model was manufactured in the largest numbers of any aircraft in history.

## TUPOLEV SB-2

The Tupolev SB-2, also known as the ANT-40, was one of the most modern machines of its kind when it appeared in 1934. With a maximum speed of over 400 km/h, it was faster than most contemporary fighters. Development of the aircraft began in 1933, and the prototype had its maiden flight on 7 October 1934. The second version (hence its SB-2 designation) was introduced in late December 1934. It was put into serial production, and in 1936 the Soviet Union delivered 210 SB-2s to the Republican forces in the Spanish Civil War. The SB-2 also flew missions in the Russo-Japanese border conflict of 1939–40, in the Russo-Finnish Winter War and on the Chinese side against the Japanese. The SB-2s enjoyed only limited success in these conflicts, and they had almost no success whatsoever against the Luftwaffe. Many of the 6,466 machines that had been built were seized by the Germans as they advanced through Russia and were passed on to Bulgaria and Finland, and a few were also used for a short time by the Luftwaffe itself. Yet some remained in front-line service until 1943, after which they served instead as training and liaison aircraft in the rear. A small number of SB-2 aircraft were also built under licence by the Czech firm Avia, which called them B.71s.

*A Chinese SB-2 that flew against the Japanese in 1938.*

| | SB-2bis |
|---|---|
| Type: | Light bomber |
| Crew: | 3 |
| Weight when empty/ max weight at takeoff: | 4,768 kg/ 7,880 kg |
| Length/wingspan/height: | 12.57 m/20.33 m/3.42 m |
| Engine(s): | Two M-103 V12 engines with 950 hp each |
| Maximum speed: | 450 km/h |
| Service ceiling: | 7,800 m |
| Range: | 2,300 km |
| Weaponry: | 3–6 x 7.62 mm ShKAS machine guns and an internal payload of max. 1,000 kg |

# ILYUSHIN DB-3 AND IL-4

*The DB-3.*

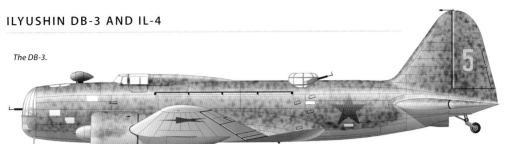

The Ilyushin DB-3 and its improved version, the Il-4, were the most important Soviet long-range aircraft in the Second World War. Development began in 1934, and the first prototype had its maiden flight one year later, powered by two M-85 engines, which were actually French Gnome-Rhône engines built under licence. A second machine underwent flight tests in May 1936 and set five different net load world records between July and September that year. The DB-3 attracted international attention when it flew non-stop from

| | DB-3M | Il-4 |
|---|---|---|
| Type: | Medium-range bomber | Medium-range bomber |
| Crew: | 3–4 | 3 |
| Weight when empty/ max weight at takeoff: | 5,270 kg/ 7,660 kg | 5,800 kg/ 11,300 kg |
| Length/wingspan/ height: | 14.22 m/21.44 m/ 4.19 m | 14.8 m/21.44 m/ 4.1 m |
| Engine(s): | Two M-87B radial engines with 950 hp each | Two M-88B radial engines with 1,100 hp each |
| Maximum speed: | 445 km/h | 430 km/h |
| Service ceiling: | 9,700 m | 9,700 m |
| Range: | 3,800 km | 3,800 km |
| Weaponry: | 3 x 7.62 mm ShKAS machine guns – one in the nose, one in the tail and one in the waist – and an internal or external payload of max. 1,500 kg | 2 x 7.62 mm ShKAS machine guns – one in the nose, one in the tail – 1 x 12.7 mm UBS machine gun in the rear turret, and an internal or external payload of max. 2,500 kg |

*The Il-4.*

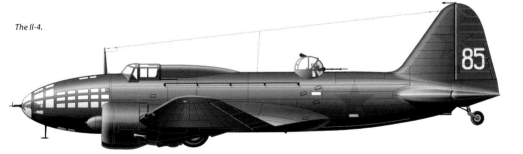

Moscow to the USA, a distance of nearly 8,000 km.

Production of the DB-3b began in 1937. By 1941, 1,528 DB-3s had been manufactured, and there were many different versions including a conventional bomber, a torpedo bomber, and a minelayer for the Navy. The DB-3 was first deployed in the Russo-Finnish Winter War. The Ilyushin Il-4 was an improved version of the DB-3, and the most obvious superficial difference was

its new glazed and pointed nose. It was designed as an all-metal half-shell construction, but later some parts (the outer wings, fuselage and tail) had to be made of wood, as metal was in short supply. This had a negative effect on its flight, but by using more powerful M-88B engines, its flight weight and payload could be increased. The new machine, originally called the DB-3F, flew for the first time in mid-1939, and serial production began early the following

year. Up to 1944, 5,256 machines in the DB-3F/Il-4 series had been built. The Il-4 was deployed in all the major battles on the Eastern Front, where they not only flew long-range bombing missions, but also directly supported the troops on the ground, and it remained in service in the Soviet Air Force until 1949.

## PETLYAKOV PE-2

The Petlyakov Pe-2 was developed from the unsuccessful VI-100 high altitude fighter prototype. It had its maiden flight in late December 1939, and the first production model took off for the first time in November 1940. The Pe-2 was an all-metal low-wing aircraft with a retractable tail wheel, and proved to be an excellent light bomber, but it did not have a pressurized cabin. By the time war broke out, 458 Pe-2s had been delivered, tried and tested. This model became the Soviet Air Force's standard tactical bomber, but it also served as a ground support and reconnaissance aircraft, and as a day and night fighter. Its robust frame meant that it could also be used as a dive-bomber. Before production was halted, 11,427 planes were built. There were various versions of the Pe-2, which mainly differed in their weapon configurations

|  | Pe-2FT |
|---|---|
| Type: | Light bomber |
| Crew: | 3 |
| Weight when empty/ max weight at takeoff: | 6,200 kg/ 8,520 kg |
| Length/wingspan/height: | 12.78 m/17.11 m/3.42 m |
| Engine(s): | Two Klimov VK 105PF V12 engines with 1,260 hp each |
| Maximum speed: | 580 km/h |
| Service ceiling: | 9,000 m |
| Range: | 1,770 km |
| Weaponry: | 2 x 7.62 mm ShKAS machine guns fixed in the wings, 1 x 12.7 mm UBT machine gun in the rear of the cockpit, 2 x 7.62 mm ShKAS waist machine guns, and a combined internal and external payload of 1,000 kg |

and VK-105 engine specifications, and the Pe-3M was a fighter version. From late 1944 the Pe-2 was progressively replaced by the Tu-2.

*The Pe-2.*

## TUPOLEV TU-2

|  | Tu-2 |
|---|---|
| Type: | Medium-range bomber |
| Crew: | 4 |
| Weight when empty/ max weight at takeoff: | 7,474 kg/ 11,360 kg |
| Length/wingspan/height: | 13.8 m/18.86 m/4.55 m |
| Engine(s): | Two 14-cylinder Shvetsov Ash 82FNV radial engines with 1,850 hp each |
| Maximum speed: | 550 km/h |
| Service ceiling: | 9,500 m |
| Range: | 1,400 km |
| Weaponry: | 2 x 20 mm ShVAK automatic cannon fixed in the wings, 3 x 12.7 mm UBT machine guns – and a combined payload of max. 4,000 kg |

The Tupolev Tu-2 was an effective medium-range bomber, but it is notable less for its performance than for the fact that it was designed by Andrei Tupolev in prison – he had been incarcerated at Stalin's behest! Work began on designing a twin-engine bomber to outperform the Junkers Ju 88 in 1937, but it was not until 29 January 1941 that the first Tu-2 had its maiden flight. Engine problems were to blame for this, as was the fact that prison did not provide very good working conditions for the designer. In any event, the first production aircraft were delivered to the Soviet Air Force in November 1942. Its design was simple, with classically elegant lines, and it provided all four crew members with good all-round visibility. Between late 1942 and 1945 1,111 Tu-2s were built, and they were deployed on all fronts, where they acquitted themselves well, thanks to their good flying attributes. In total, 2,527 Tu-2s were built before production was halted in 1948, and aircraft of this type remained in service until the late 1950s. Finally, thanks to his successful design, Tupolev was not only released from prison in 1943, but also awarded the Stalin Prize.

*The Tu-2.*

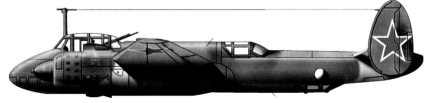

# LOCKHEED P-38 LIGHTNING

The Lockheed P-38 Lightning is one of the best known and most successful American combat aircraft of the Second World War. The standards required in the tender were so high that in 1937–38 they could be met only by installing two engines. Because a turbocharger was to be installed, the aircraft had an unusual double-fuselage design. The first of the prototypes had its maiden flight on 27 January 1939, and after a few pre-production models and a relatively small number of production models had been built, the P38E was delivered in larger

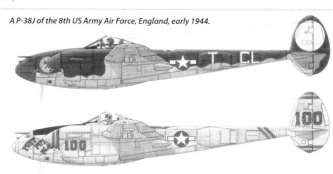

*A P-38J of the 8th US Army Air Force, England, early 1944.*

| | P-38L |
|---|---|
| Type: | Long-range fighter and fighter bomber |
| Crew: | 1 |
| Weight when empty/ max weight at takeoff: | 5,800 kg/ 9,798 kg |
| Length/wingspan/height: | 11.55 m/15.88 m/3.91 m |
| Engine(s): | Two Allison V 1710 111 V12 engines with 1,600 hp each |
| Maximum speed: | 666 km/h at 7,620 m |
| Service ceiling: | 13,410 m |
| Range: | 725 km without extra fuel tanks, 3,620 km with them |
| Weaponry: | 1 x 20 mm Hispano automatic cannon and 4 x 12.7 mm Browning machine guns fixed in the nose, and an external payload of max. 1,816 kg |

*A P-38L of the 5th US Army Air Force, the Philippines, December 1944.*

numbers to the US Army Air Force (USAAF). In the Pacific it proved to be a dangerous adversary for the Japanese A6M Zero. A number of P-38s were delivered to the British, but they were dissatisfied with them as they had no turbochargers. The Luftwaffe first encountered the P-38 in North Africa, and it was deployed as an escort fighter for the 8th USAAF bombers over Germany. In combat with the Bf 109 and Fw 190 the F-38 showed the usual disadvantages expected from a twin-engine fighter, especially limited manoeuvrability, and in this capacity it was replaced by the P-47 and P-51. But because of the heavy weaponry in its nose, rockets and a payload of up to 1,816 kg, it was still a highly effective fighter bomber – after all, the Germans did not give it the nickname 'Fork-Tailed Devil' without reason. The P-38 was also used as a photo reconnaissance aircraft, and of the 9,923 P-38s manufactured in total, around 1,400 (called the F-4 or F-5) were converted for this purpose. Shortly before the end of the war, a night fighter version (the P-38M) was introduced, which had a radar device in its nose, but it flew very few missions.

*This photo clearly shows the P-38's double fuselage design.*

*The American pilots with the most kills, Bong and McGuire, both flew P-38s. On 18 April 1943, a P-38 wing based in the Solomon Islands succeeded in shooting down Japanese Admiral Yamamoto's Mitsubishi G4M.*

# CURTISS MODEL 81/81 P-40 WARHAWK

The P-40 was certainly not one of the best fighter aircraft of the Second World War, yet almost 14,000 were manufactured. The first prototype had its maiden flight on 14 October 1938, and the first serial production machines left the Curtiss factories in May 1940. France had ordered 185 P-40s before its defeat, and these were taken over by the RAF and renamed Tomahawks. Because they could not compete with the Bf 109 due to their weight, they served as training aircraft and fighter bombers in North Africa. The improved P-40 models (Tomahawk II and Kittyhawk I-IV) were also mainly used as fighter bombers in North Africa or the Mediterranean. The P-40s deployed in the Pacific mostly came up against the Japanese A6M Zero, which was a superior fighter and caused them major problems. As part of the Lend-Lease agreement, the P-40 was also delivered to the Soviet Union.

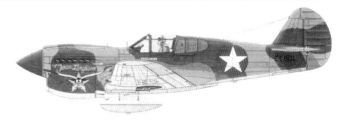

*A P-40E of the 5th US Army Air Force, New Guinea, 1942. Although new P-40 models were introduced with increasingly powerful engines, their performance always lagged behind that of other countries' high-performance fighters.*

|  | P-40N |
|---|---|
| Type: | Fighter bomber |
| Crew: | 1 |
| Weight when empty/ max weight at takeoff: | 2,812 kg/ 4,014 kg |
| Length/wingspan/height: | 10.16 m/11.38 m/3.76 m |
| Engine(s): | One Allison V 1710 81 V12 engine with 1,200 hp |
| Maximum speed: | 552 km/h at 4,570 m |
| Service ceiling: | 9,450 m |
| Range: | 1,738 km |
| Weaponry: | 6 x 12.7 mm Browning machine guns fixed in the wings, and an external payload of max. 681 kg, e.g., three 227 kg bombs |

# BELL P-39 AIRCOBRA

The P-39 was a unique aircraft: it was the first fighter in the world to have landing gear in its nose, and its Allison engine was located not in the nose, but in the middle of the fuselage behind the cockpit, powering the propeller through a long shaft, in which a 37 mm automatic cannon was also installed.

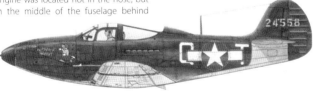

*A P-39L of the 12th US Army Air Force, Tunisia, 1943.*

|  | P-39M |
|---|---|
| Type: | Fighter |
| Crew: | 1 |
| Weight when empty/ max weight at takeoff: | 2,545 kg/ 3,810 kg |
| Length/wingspan/height: | 9.19 m/10.36 m/3.61 m |
| Engine(s): | One Allison V 1710 83 V12 with 1,200 hp |
| Maximum speed: | 621 km/h at 2,900 m |
| Service ceiling: | 10,970 m |
| Range: | 1,050 km |
| Weaponry: | One 37 mm T9 automatic cannon, 2 x 12.7 mm Browning machine guns, 4 x 7.62 mm Browning machine guns, and an external payload of max. 227 kg |

It was designed in this way to accommodate such a heavy weapon, and its mid-engine design promised excellent manoeuvrability. The P-39 prototype made its maiden flight on 6 April 1939, and the first production models were delivered to the front-line units of the USAAF in April 1941. The RAF also ordered P-39s but was disappointed by their performance, so they were mainly deployed in the Mediterranean, where they performed very well. At least half of all 9,504 P-39s were delivered to the Soviets, where they were very successful at low altitudes and in anti-tank operations. The P-36 Kingcobra, which had its maiden flight on 7 December 1942, was a further development of the P-39, with a more powerful engine and improved aerodynamics. Around 3,300 P-63s were built in total, and the French were still using them in Indochina in the early 1950s.

# GRUMMAN F4F WILDCAT

The Grumman F4F Wildcat was the US Navy's first all-metal single-wing fighter with retractable undercarriage. The prototype had its maiden flight on 2 September 1937, but it was not very stable, so the version that went into production in August 1939 had an altered tail. Initially, the Wildcat bore the brunt of the conflict in the Pacific, but, although it was really inferior to the A6M Zero, Wildcat pilots eventually worked out special tactics to cope with its adversary. After the US Navy, the Royal Navy was the second most frequent user of the Wildcat, initially calling it the Martlet, but later changing its name back to the Wildcat in January 1944. From early 1943 the Wildcat was gradually replaced by the Grumman F6F Hellcat as a fighter on the larger aircraft carriers. Even after Grumman had started producing the F6F instead of the Wildcat, General Motors continued to manufacture the latter, calling it the FM-1 and later the FM-2. Because they could take off from

*An F4F-3 of the US Navy VF-3 Squadron based on the USS Lexington, February 1942.*

*As well as being fighters, Wildcats protected convoys, attacked submarines, and supported ground forces.*

| F4F-4 | |
| --- | --- |
| Type: | Carrier-borne fighter and fighter bomber |
| Crew: | 1 |
| Weight when empty/ max weight at takeoff: | 2,612 kg/ 3,607 kg |
| Length/wingspan/height: | 8.76 m/11.58 m/3.62 m |
| Engine(s): | One Pratt & Whitney R 1380 36 Twin Wasp 4-cylinder radial engine with 1,200 hp |
| Maximum speed: | 512 km/h at 5,915 m |
| Service ceiling: | 12,010 m |
| Range: | 1,240 km |
| Weaponry: | 6 x 12.7 mm Browning machine guns fixed in the wings |

short runways, Wildcats were deployed until the end of the war from the smaller aircraft carriers for anti-submarine operations among others. This was in part due to the fact that its external payload was no more than 90.8 kg.

# GRUMMAN F6F HELLCAT

| F6F-5 | |
| --- | --- |
| Type: | Carrier-borne fighter and fighter bomber |
| Crew: | 1 |
| Weight when empty/ max weight at takeoff: | 4,152 kg/ 6,991 kg |
| Length/wingspan/height: | 10.24 m/13.06 m/4.11 m |
| Engine(s): | One Pratt & Whitney R 2800 10W Double Wasp 18-cylinder radial engine with 2,000 hp |
| Maximum speed: | 621 km/h at 7,130 m |
| Service ceiling: | 11,370 m |
| Range: | 2,462 km with 568 litre extra fuel tank |
| Weaponry: | 6 x 12.7 mm Browning machine guns fixed in the wings |

*An F6F-5 of the US Navy VF-84 Squadron based on the USS Bunker Hill, early 1945.*

The F6F Hellcat is unmistakably the F4F Wildcat's successor. The prototype had its maiden flight on 26 June 1942, and the F6F-3 model was put into production in October that year. From January 1943 the Hellcat joined the fighter squadrons based on US aircraft carriers. Although it was larger and heavier than the Wildcat, the F6F had superior flying attributes and heavier weaponry (a total external payload of 908 kg), and it enabled the Americans to gain control of the Pacific skies. Of the US Navy's 6,477 recorded victories in the air, the F6F Hellcat gained 4,947. The Fleet Air Arm (the Royal Navy air force) also put the Hellcat into service. The night fighter version had wing-mounted radar, and the Hellcat also served as an anti-ship and ground attack aircraft, armed with bombs and rockets. The main version of the Hellcat, with 4,402 aircraft produced, was the F6F-3. It was succeeded by the slightly improved F6F-5, of which 6,341 were produced, and the last version in the series was the F6F-5N night fighter. Production continued until November 1945, by which time 12,272 aircraft had been manufactured in total.

# REPUBLIC P-47 THUNDERBOLT

| | P-47D |
|---|---|
| Type: | Long-range fighter and fighter bomber |
| Crew: | 1 |
| Weight when empty/ max weight at takeoff: | 4,513 kg/ 7,938 kg |
| Length/wingspan/height: | 11.02 m/12.43 m/4.47 m |
| Engine(s): | One Pratt & Whitney R 2800 59W Double Wasp 18-cylinder radial engine with 2,535 hp |
| Maximum speed: | 695 km/h at 7,620 m |
| Service ceiling: | 12,495 m |
| Range: | 3,200 km with three additional fuel tanks |
| Weaponry: | 8 x 12.7 mm Browning machine guns fixed in the wings, and an external payload of max. 1,134 kg, e.g., two 454 kg bombs or ten 127 mm rockets, napalm tanks or extra fuel tanks |

*The Republic P-47N Thunderbolt.*

The Republic P-47 Thunderbolt was the largest and heaviest single-engine fighter of its time, and its pilots called it the 'Jug', short for 'Juggernaut', a thoroughly appropriate name. From March 1943 to August 1945, P-47s flew 545,575 missions and destroyed around 7,000 aircraft and 9,000 locomotives, more than 86,000 trucks and around 6,000 armoured vehicles. By contrast, the proportion of P-47s lost in these missions was just 0.7%!

Originally, Alexander Kartveli of the Republic Aviation Company intended to design a light fighter with two machine guns, but reports from Europe about aerial combat experience forced him to rethink, and he based his design around the most powerful engine available at the time, the Pratt & Whitney R-2800. The P-47 had its maiden flight on 6 May 1941, but the aircraft was afflicted by many different problems, so the P-47C was not deployed in Europe until April 1943. The D version of the P-47 was manufactured in the largest quantity (12,602 aircraft built); initially it had a raised tail section (the

*An early P-47 D Razorback.*

Razorback) but later this was lowered and the cockpit had all-round visibility; it was also given a more powerful engine and heavier weaponry. The P47-M, of which 130 were produced, was a high-speed version deployed against German jet fighters, and the P-47N was intended for long-range deployment, hence its larger wings and fuel tanks. In its role as an escort fighter the P-47 was rather less effective than the P-51 Mustang, so it was increasingly used as a fighter bomber. It was outstanding in this role, not only because of its firepower, but also because of its robustness and the fact that its Pratt & Whitney engines could withstand even the most severe hits. In total, 15,677 P-47s were manufactured, including all the different versions, and even after 1945 the Thunderbolt remained in service in numerous air forces worldwide for many more years, especially in South America.

*A P-47D-30 of the 1st Tactical Air Force, France, autumn 1944.*

*A P-47D-5 (Razorback) of the 8th US Army Air Force, England, March 1944.*

*A front view of the colourful 'Tarheel Hal'.*

*In the final phases of the war, Allied aircraft (like this P-47D) were painted with 'invasion stripes' to help troops on their side to recognize them.*

# NORTH AMERICAN P-51 MUSTANG

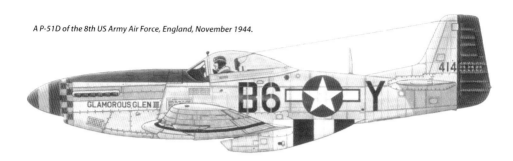

*A P-51D of the 8th US Army Air Force, England, November 1944.*

The P-51 Mustang was arguably the best and most important fighter aircraft in the Second World War, but as with many large machines, this did not appear likely at first. The British Government approached North American Aviation in early 1940, asking them to produce the P-40 under licence for the RAF. But North American Aviation convinced the British that it could produce a much better fighter than the P-40, which was no better than average. After just 117 days of development, the NA-73 took off for the first time on 26 October 1940, powered by an Allison V-1710. The NA-73 was fitted with a special cooler, which not only

encountered less air resistance than the P-40 cooler but also produced more thrust, as well as laminated wings which reduced air resistance further. Consequently, the NA-73, which the RAF called the 'Mustang', was significantly faster than the P-40, but the RAF was far from satisfied, as the Allison engine's performance above 5,000 m was not good enough for the aircraft to be deployed as a fighter. So from May 1942 it was used exclusively as a fighter bomber and a low-altitude reconnaissance aircraft. The USAAF ordered this model nevertheless – the fighter was called the P-51 or P-51A, while the dive-bomber was called the A-36A Apache – and from early

1943 tests began to turn the P-51 into a truly first-class fighter by installing the Rolls-Royce Merlin engine. The result was the P-51B, powered by a Merlin built under licence by Packard in the USA, and the P-51B and C (an identical model built in a different factory) served from late 1943 as long-range escort fighters, protecting the bombers of the 8th USAAF over Germany. Further improvements were made on the basis of combat experience – the Mustang's back was lowered and it was fitted with a teardrop cockpit, which gave the pilot good all-round visibility. This new model, the P-51D, also had a better engine, stronger wings, and two additional 12.7 mm

*The P-51H.*

|  | P-51D |
|---|---|
| Type: | Long-range fighter and fighter bomber |
| Crew: | 1 |
| Weight when empty/ | 3,230 kg/ |
| max weight at takeoff: | 5,262 kg |
| Length/wingspan/height: | 9.84 m/11.29 m/4.1 m |
| Engine(s): | One Packard V 1650 7 V12 engine with 1,600 hp |
| Maximum speed: | 703 km/h at 7,620 m |
| Service ceiling: | 12,500 m |
| Range: | 12,092 km without extra fuel tanks, and 3,302 km with them |
| Weaponry: | 6 x 12.7 mm Browning machine guns fixed in the wings |

*Many P-51s are still flying today and can be seen at air shows.*

calibre machine guns in its wings, giving a maximum external payload of 908 kg. It is impossible to exaggerate the P-51's importance in the US air offensive against Germany. From late 1943 it was a feared opponent at any altitude, and it escorted increasingly large waves of bombers to their targets. Without fighter escorts, the US bombers would have suffered such heavy losses that their missions would not have continued. Although Mustangs were primarily escort fighters, they also attacked ground targets themselves at low altitudes. Mustangs also escorted

Boeing B-29 bombers over Japan, but they were deployed in smaller numbers than over Germany, though their missions there were longer. The Japanese fighters were deployed in typically large numbers, but they were significantly weaker than the technically superior P-51.

In the Second World War the Mustang served almost exclusively as a fighter, fighter bomber and reconnaissance aircraft, and the A-36 was a dive-bomber. In addition to the P-51D, the P-51H, which had a 2,200 hp engine, was used in greater numbers towards the end of the war. After

1945 countless air forces put the P-51 into service, as they could be acquired cheaply from US stocks. The Americans themselves used the P-51 again, this time in the Korean War, where it served as a fighter bomber. The Israelis also used P-51s, as in the 1956 Suez War, and the P-51 remained in service in Latin American countries until the 1980s. In total, 15,586 P-51s were produced, including all the different variants, some of which were built under licence in Australia.

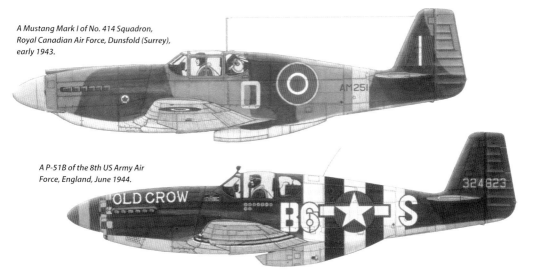

*A Mustang Mark I of No. 414 Squadron, Royal Canadian Air Force, Dunsfold (Surrey), early 1943.*

*A P-51B of the 8th US Army Air Force, England, June 1944.*

## NORTHROP P-61 BLACK WIDOW

The Northrop P-61 Black Widow was the first combat aircraft in the USAAF specifically developed as a night fighter. It was made entirely of metal, and its frame had two long engine gondolas on which the tail was mounted. In 1940, prompted by the German night raids on the United Kingdom, the US Army Air Force ordered a night fighter fitted with radar. By this time, the British had successfully installed an autonomous radar system, the Airborne Intercept (AI) radar, in some of their aircraft. Using data about this device, the Americans developed an improved version which could be installed in the new night fighter.

Northrop introduced a first prototype in May 1942, but various problems prevented serial production until mid-1944. In particular, the machine gun turret on top of the frame caused dangerous vibrations when the guns were fired. But once these problems had been solved, the P-61 proved to be an

*A P-61A during a test flight over California. At first this model was plagued with serious problems.*

|  | P-61B |
|---|---|
| Type: | Night fighter and fighter bomber |
| Crew: | 2–3 |
| Weight when empty/ max weight at takeoff: | 10,637 kg/ 16,420 kg |
| Length/wingspan/height: | 15.11 m/20.11 m/4.47 m |
| Engine(s): | Two Pratt & Whitney R 2800 65 Double Wasp 18-cylinder radial engines with 2,000 hp each |
| Maximum speed: | 589 km/h at 6,100 m |
| Service ceiling: | 11,500 m |
| Range: | 4,820 km with extra fuel tanks |
| Weaponry: | 4 x 20 mm automatic cannon fixed in the chin (under the nose), 4 x 12.7 mm Browning machine guns in a remote-controlled dorsal installation, and an external payload of max. 2,904 kg, e.g., four extra fuel tanks, bombs, or 127 mm rockets |

excellent night fighter, and it was deployed very successfully in Europe and the Pacific. It could also carry an acceptable payload, so it was also deployed as a bomber. Yet, although it had good flying characteristics and shot down a relatively large number of enemy aircraft, only 742 aircraft of this type (including the F-15 Reporter reconnaissance version) were produced, largely because it appeared shortly before the end of the war and was replaced by jet aircraft. The main production model was the P-61B, and there was a P-61C high-speed version, but just 15 of these were delivered to the USAAF. The last P-61s were taken out of service in 1950.

USA

# CHANCE-VOUGHT F4U CORSAIR

*An F4U-1A of the US Navy VF-17 Squadron,
Solomon Islands, in December 1943.*

| | F4U-1 |
|---|---|
| Type: | Carrier-borne fighter and fighter bomber |
| Crew: | 1 |
| Weight when empty/ max weight at takeoff: | 4,074 kg/ 6,350 kg |
| Length/wingspan/height: | 10.16 m/12.5 m/4.9 m |
| Engine(s): | One Pratt & Whitney R 2800 8 Double Wasp 18-cylinder radial engine with 2,000 hp |
| Maximum speed: | 671 km/h at 6,100 m |
| Service ceiling: | 11,247 m |
| Range: | 1,633 m |
| Weaponry: | 6 x 12.7 mm Browning machine guns or 4 x 20 mm automatic cannon fixed in the wings, and an external payload of max. 908 kg, e.g., two 454 kg bombs or six 127 mm rockets |

*An FG-1D Corsair Mark IV of No. 1841 Fleet
Air Arm Squadron based on HMS
Formidable, the Pacific, August 1945.*

The Chance-Vought F4U Corsair is rated by many experts as the best naval combat aircraft in the Second World War. It was deployed by the US Marine Corps and the US Navy, and most Commonwealth countries also flew F4Us. It was designed, above all, for minimal air resistance and maximum speed, using the most powerful engine available at the time. So the Pratt & Whitney R-2800 was installed in the smallest possible airframe. To convert the engine's 2,000 hp into high-speed forward motion, the propeller needed a diameter of more than 4 m. The undercarriage (which had a rear wheel) was also very long, making it very unstable, which was hardly ideal for a carrier-borne aircraft. But its designers came up with a ruse to counteract this problem, giving the aircraft its distinctive gull wings. The prototype had its maiden flight on 29 May 1940, but initially it was not possible to fly the aircraft from carriers, as its engine required a large engine cowling in front of the cockpit, which seriously restricted forward visibility, so the cockpit was raised by 16 cm and the F4U was put into service. Even then, the engine created such a high turning moment during takeoff that it was hard to keep the aircraft on track, which was sometimes too much for inexperienced pilots to handle. This earned the F4U the nicknames 'Ensign Killer' and 'Ensign Eliminator'. Nevertheless, once it was airborne, the F4U was a feared combat aircraft, equally suited to aerial combat and ground attack operations. The F4U-1 Corsair was manufactured under licence by Goodyear (as the FG-1) and Brewster (which called it the F3A-1), and production continued until 1952. The Corsair was deployed by the Americans in the Korean War and by the French Naval Air Force, and even when they were taken out of service, many smaller air forces acquired them.

*A French Navy Corsair,
flown until the 1960s.*

# DOUGLAS TBD DEVASTATOR

| | TBD-1 |
|---|---|
| Type: | Carrier-borne torpedo bomber |
| Crew: | 3 |
| Weight when empty/max weight at takeoff: | 2,804 kg/ 4,624 kg |
| Length/wingspan/height: | 10.67 m/15.24 m/4.6 m |
| Engine(s): | One Pratt & Whitney R 1830 8 Twin Wasp radial engine with 900 hp |
| Maximum speed: | 332 km/h at 2,440 m |
| Service ceiling: | 6,005 m |
| Range: | 700 km with a torpedo/1,150 km with a 454 kg payload |
| Weaponry: | 1 x 7.62 mm or 12.7 mm Browning machine gun fixed in the nose, 1 x 7.62 mm machine gun in the rear of the cockpit, and a 533 mm torpedo or 454 kg bomb carried externally below the fuselage |

The Douglas TBD Devastator was the US Navy's first single wing torpedo bomber and the first all-metal aircraft with hydraulically folding wings in the world. The prototype flew for the first time on 15 April 1935, and in 1937 Douglas delivered the first of 129 machines. Until 1941 the Devastator was the standard American carrier-borne torpedo bomber, but by that time it was clearly no longer the Navy's ideal choice, and its successor, the TBF Avenger, was already being developed. During the Battle of the Coral Sea (7–8 May 1942), the Devastator helped to sink a Japanese aircraft carrier, but it was deployed for

*The Douglas TBD Devastator.*

the last time in the Battle of Midway (4–7 June 1942) when 41 TBDs launched an attack on a Japanese aircraft carrier, only to be shot down one by one by A6M Zero fighters; the remaining Devastators were taken out of service immediately afterwards. Nevertheless, because the Zero fighters were

preoccupied with the TBDs, high-flying Douglas SBD dive-bombers were able to sink or severely damage three Japanese carriers, while suffering only minor losses.

# GRUMMAN TBF AVENGER

| | TBM-3 |
|---|---|
| Type: | Carrier-borne torpedo bomber, bomber and reconnaissance aircraft |
| Crew: | 3 |
| Weight when empty/ max weight at takeoff: | 4,787 kg/ 8,278 kg |
| Length/wingspan/height: | 10.06 m/12.65 m/3.94 m |
| Engine(s): | One Wright Cyclone R 2600 20 14-cylinder radial engine with 1,750 hp |
| Maximum speed: | 430 km/h at 4,570 m |
| Service ceiling: | 7,130 m |
| Range: | 1,820 km |
| Weaponry: | 2 x 12.7 mm Browning machine guns in the wings, 1 x 12.7 mm Browning machine gun in the dorsal turret, 1 x 7.62 mm Browning waist machine gun, and an internal payload of max. 908 kg |

*The TBM-3 Avenger.*

The first TBFs were put into service in January 1942, just one month after Pearl Harbor. Although Grumman had no experience of building them, the company received an order for a torpedo bomber on 8 April 1940. The all-metal prototype flew for the first time on 1 August 1941. Although Grumman were working flat out to produce the TBF, the Navy still needed more machines, so

General Motors took over some of the production (TBFs produced there were known as TBMs). Altogether, 9,836 Avengers were built by Grumman and General Motors. The most important model in the series was initially the TBF-1 (or TBM-1), which was delivered to Navy squadrons from early 1942. The TBF-3 (or TBM-3), which was put into service in mid-1944, was fitted with radar and could

carry 127 mm rockets under its wings. Over 900 TBF/TBM aircraft were delivered to the Royal Navy, which initially renamed them Mark I Tarpoons, only to revert to calling them Mark I Avengers, and 63 were delivered to the New Zealand Air Force. As well as torpedo and bombing raids, Avengers also flew reconnaissance and anti-submarine missions.

# DOUGLAS SBD DAUNTLESS

*The Douglas SBD Dauntless.*

|  | SBD-6 |
| --- | --- |
| Type: | Carrier-borne dive bomber and reconnaissance aircraft |
| Crew: | 2 |
| Weight when empty/ max weight at takeoff: | 2,964 kg/ 4,318 kg |
| Length/wingspan/height: | 10.06 m/12.65 m/3.94 m |
| Engine(s): | One Wright Cyclone R 1820 66 radial engine with 1,350 hp |
| Maximum speed: | 410 km/h at 4,265 m |
| Service ceiling: | 7,680 m |
| Range: | 1,244 km |
| Weaponry: | 2 x fixed 12.7 mm Browning machine guns, 2 x 7.62 mm Browning machine guns, and a payload of max. 762 kg under the fuselage, and max. 295 kg under the wings |

The Douglas SBD Dauntless was the most successful American dive-bomber. The order was given to put it into serial production in April 1939, and the first squadrons were ready to go into service from late 1940. The Dauntless contributed in part to America's victory over the Japanese Navy, and it served the Americans well until late 1944. It distinguished itself in the Battle of the Coral Sea (7–8 May 1942) and in the Battle of Midway (4–7 June 1942), when it managed to sink three Japanese aircraft carriers. Because they could withstand heavy fire, fewer SBDs were lost in the Pacific than any other American aircraft type. The Douglas A-24 Banshee was a land-based version of the Dauntless, and 500 A-24s were delivered to the USAAF from 1940 to 1942, but it proved to be less successful than its carrier-borne counterpart. In total, 5,936 SBDs were manufactured before production was halted in July 1944.

# CURTISS SB2C HELLDIVER

The Curtiss SB2C Helldiver was arguably one of the worst aircraft ever to be manufactured in large numbers. The US Navy and Curtiss had expected very good things from this model, but it was beset with developmental problems and was not put into service until 11 November 1943, though the all-metal prototype with folding wings had first flown in 1940! This prototype was destroyed in a crash,

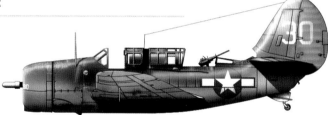

just days before Pearl Harbor, and because the accident was investigated,

*For as long as it was in service, the Helldiver was plagued with problems.*

and the aircraft was redesigned in the light of combat experience, the first production model of the new aircraft did not fly until June 1942. The USAAF took delivery of 900 A-25As (as they were now called) and 26 went to the British, but the latter decided that they were unsuitable and never used them. The Helldiver was ponderous and had a few unpleasant characteristics, especially when taking off and landing; unlike the Dauntless, it was far from popular. In spite of this, around 7,000 Helldivers were produced in total, and it remained in service after 1945.

|  | SB2C-3 |
| --- | --- |
| Type: | Carrier-borne dive bomber and reconnaissance aircraft |
| Crew: | 2 |
| Weight when empty/ max weight at takeoff: | 2,964 kg/ 4,318 kg |
| Length/wingspan/height: | 10.06 m/12.65 m/3.94 m |
| Engine(s): | One Wright Cyclone R 2600 20 14-cylinder radial engine with 1,900 hp |
| Maximum speed: | 472 km/h at 5,180 m |
| Service ceiling: | 8,140 m |
| Range: | 1,930 km |
| Weaponry: | 2 x fixed 20 mm automatic cannons, 2 x 7.62 mm Browning machine guns, and a payload of max. 908 kg internally, and max. 454 kg under the wings |

# DOUGLAS A-20 BOSTON/HAVOC

| | A-20B |
|---|---|
| Type: | Light bomber |
| Crew: | 3 |
| Max weight at takeoff: | 15,867 kg |
| Length/wingspan/height: | 15.24 m/21.34 m/5.64 m |
| Engine(s): | Two Wright Cyclone R 2600 3 14-cylinder radial engines with 1,600 hp each |
| Maximum speed: | 571 km/h at 4,570 m |
| Service ceiling: | 7,700 m |
| Range: | 2,253 km |
| Weaponry: | 4 x 7.62 mm or 2 x 12.7 mm Browning machine guns fixed laterally on the nose, 2 x 7.62 mm Browning machine guns in the rear of the cockpit, and an internal payload of max. 908 kg |

*An A-20B in the USAAF. Note the DB-7 series' slender fuselage.*

The Douglas A-20, known in the factory as the DB-7, was the most important light bomber in the USAAF and was also flown by almost all the Allied air forces. The night fighter developed from the A-20 was called the P-70, and the DB-7 was also used as a reconnaissance aircraft. Its development began in 1937, and the prototype had its maiden flight on 26 October 1938. Although it met all the USAAF's requirements for a new light twin-engine bomber, the Air Force showed no interest in it at first. France was the first customer for the new aircraft, in 1939 placing an order for 100 planes, which was increased to 170 after the war broke out; however, only 70 had been delivered by the time of the German invasion. Some planes were lost, while many escaped to Britain or formed part of the Vichy regime's air force. But most of the aircraft ordered by the French remained in America or were delivered to the RAF, which urgently required bombers and night fighters and called the Douglas machines the Boston and the Havoc. The first version to be produced in large numbers was the A-20B, which was also ordered by the United States Army Air Corps (USAAC), the predecessor of the USAAF. The variant of which most were manufactured was the A-20G (2,850 were built), which had a fixed nose with six 12.7 mm machine guns, a payload of 1,816 kg and a motorized machine gun installation on the fuselage.

Until September 1944, 7,385 machines in the DB-7 series were manufactured, including the P-70 night fighter version. Numerous DB-7s were also delivered to the Soviet Union, as part of the Lend-Lease agreement.

*A Douglas A-20B in the USAAF. The A-20 performed superbly for as long as it was in service. But its first-class aerodynamics were to blame for one of this series' main drawbacks: the fuselage was so narrow that crew members could not change positions in mid-flight. If the pilot was hit, this could be fatal. Hence, the glazed-nose A-20 was fitted with rudimentary controls on the bombardier's side.*

# DOUGLAS A-26 INVADER

| | A-26B |
|---|---|
| Type: | Light bomber |
| Crew: | 3 |
| Weight when empty/ max weight at takeoff: | 10,365 kg/ 15,867 kg |
| Length/wingspan/height: | 15.24 m/21.34 m/5.64 m |
| Engine(s): | Two Pratt & Whitney R 2800 27 Double Wasp 18-cylinder radial engines with 2,000 hp each |
| Maximum speed: | 571 km/h at 4,570 m |
| Service ceiling: | 7,700 m |
| Range: | 2,253 km |
| Weaponry: | 6 x 12.7 mm Browning machine guns fixed in the nose, and 4 x 12.7 mm Browning machine guns in remote-controlled installations and a combined payload of max. 1,816 kg |

The Douglas A-26 Invader was designed as a successor to the A-20. Its prototype flew for the first time on 10 July 1942, and it was put into serial production in April 1944. The 9th US Army Air Force, which deployed Invaders, flew its first missions in Europe in November 1944, and the Invader was also deployed shortly afterwards in the Pacific. By the end of the war, the A-26 had flown around

*The A-26 remained in service in the USAF after 1945.*

11,000 missions in Europe. It was the most manoeuvrable US bomber in the Second World War, and its pilots were delighted, claiming that it handled just like a fighter. Two main versions were produced in the war: the A-26B, which had a fixed nose

and six fixed 12.7 mm machine guns, and the A-26C, which had a glazed nose to house a bombardier (bomb dropper). In total, 1,355 A-26Bs and A-26Cs were built. The Invader was also intensively flown in Korea and Vietnam.

# MARTIN B-26 MARAUDER

The Martin B-26 Marauder was the second American medium-range bomber to be put into service. The prototype had its maiden flight on 25 November 1940, and its unusual nose undercarriage, heavy wings and fast landing speed led to considerable problems. Inexperienced pilots could only control the B-26 with serious difficulty, and it crashed frequently, earning it the nickname 'Widow Maker'. This was not really fair, as fewer than 1% of all B-26s were lost, the lowest figure for any US bomber. The Marauder specialized in precision attacks on air bases, bridges, railroad installations, depots and similar targets, proving to be unusually bulletproof and robust. Most B-26 missions were flown in Europe and the Mediterranean, where these machines flew 129,943 missions and dropped 169,382 tonnes of bombs. In addition, the Marauder's defensive gunners shot down 402 enemy fighters.

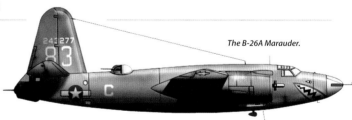

*The B-26A Marauder.*

*As well as the USAAF, the RAF and Free French Air Force flew the B-26. In total, 5,157 B-26s were built, including all the different models (which did not vary significantly).*

| | B-26B |
|---|---|
| Type: | Medium-range bomber |
| Crew: | 5–7 |
| Weight when empty/ max weight at takeoff: | 10,986 kg/ 16,783 kg |
| Length/wingspan/height: | 17.75 m/21.64 m/6.55 m |
| Engine(s): | Two Pratt & Whitney R 2800 43 Double Wasp 18-cylinder radial engines with 1,920 hp each |
| Maximum speed: | 454 km/h at 4,570 m |
| Service ceiling: | 6,400 m |
| Range: | 1,851 km |
| Weaponry: | 5 x fixed and 1 x mobile 12.7 mm Browning machine guns in the nose, 6 x 12.7 mm Browning machine guns and an internal payload of max. 2,359 kg |

# NORTH AMERICAN B-25 MITCHELL

|  | B-25J |
|---|---|
| Type: | Medium-range bomber |
| Crew: | 5 |
| Weight when empty/ max weight at takeoff: | 8,836 kg/ 15,876 kg |
| Length/wingspan/height: | 16.13 m/20.6 m/4.98 m |
| Engine(s): | Two Pratt & Whitney R 2800 43 Double Wasp 18-cylinder radial engines with 1,920 hp each |
| Maximum speed: | 454 km/h at 4,570 m |
| Service ceiling: | 6,400 m |
| Range: | 1,851 km |
| Weaponry: | 5 x 12.7 mm fixed machine guns in the nose, 6 x 12.7 mm machine guns – two in the dorsal turret, two in the tail turret and one on each side – an internal payload of max. 1,361 kg, and eight 127 mm rockets externally |

*The B-25J, which was armed with 12 12.7 mm machine guns, was the final model in this series.*

The North American B-25 Mitchell was the most important American medium-range bomber in the Second World War, and more than 12,000 were deployed in almost all the Allied air forces. The B-25 was developed following an order from the USAAC, and it flew for the first time in January 1939. The first production models were delivered in August 1940, named after General Billy Mitchell, and the B-25's best-known mission was Lieutenant Colonel James Doolittle's raid on Tokyo, known simply as the 'Doolittle Raid', on 18 April 1942. Sixteen B-25Bs took off from the aircraft carrier USS *Hornet*, but they were too large to land on it, so they had to reach China, which they almost all managed to do. Although the raid did not cause any severe damage, it ensured that to protect their country from then on, the Japanese kept interceptor fighters on constant standby, which reduced the number which could be used on the front line. All

*The prototype of the B-25G, which had a 75 mm cannon and two 12.7 mm machine guns in the nose. Because the cannon had to be reloaded manually, this model was unsuccessful. The B-25 was not a convincing anti-ship aircraft until the introduction of the H model, which had an automatic reloading mechanism.*

*A B-25C from the 9th US Army Air Force, Tunisia, April 1943.*

*The B-25B flown by Lieutenant Colonel Doolittle in the Tokyo bombing raid on 18 April 1942.*

the versions from A–D were similar, differing only in their engine specifications or their defensive weapon configurations. The B-25G was notable for the heavy weaponry in its nose (one 75 mm cannon and two 12.7 mm machine guns), and the B-25H was even more heavily armed, with one 75 mm cannon and eight 12.7 mm machine

guns, or just 12 12.7 mm machine guns, in its nose. This version could also carry 127 mm rockets under its outer wing, and it was especially successful in anti-ship operations in the Pacific. The Mitchell was also deployed in the Mediterranean from mid-1942 and in Western Europe from early 1943. The Soviet Union and the United Kingdom also received relatively

large numbers of Mitchells as part of their Lend-Lease agreements with America. The B-25 remained in service beyond the end of the war, and the last USAF Mitchell was not taken out of service until 1960.

## CONSOLIDATED PBY CATALINA

| | PBY-5A |
|---|---|
| Type: | Sea reconnaissance, air-sea rescue and anti-submarine amphibious aircraft |
| Crew: | 9 |
| Weight when empty/ max weight at takeoff: | 9,885 kg/ 16,607 kg |
| Length/wingspan/height: | 19.47 m/31.7 m/6.15 m |
| Engine(s): | Two Pratt & Whitney R 1830 92 Twin Wasp radial engines with 1,200 hp each |
| Maximum speed: | 315 km/h |
| Service ceiling: | 4,000 m |
| Range: | 4,050 km |
| Weaponry: | 5 x Browning machine guns – 3 x 7.62 mm and 2 x 12.7 mm – and an external payload of max. 1,816 kg |

*A Consolidated PBY-5A of the US Coast Guard in San Francisco in 1945.*

The Consolidated PBY Catalina was the Allies' most important sea reconnaissance seaplane, deployed by the US Navy, the Royal Navy, various Commonwealth countries and the Soviet Naval Air Force. The Catalina had its maiden flight in 1935, and the PBY-1 first flew as a US Navy aircraft in October

1936. The PBY-4, which was powered by 1,200 hp twin wasp engines and had a moulded perspex cockpit for the observer or gunner on the rear section of the fuselage, was introduced in 1938. The Catalina was made entirely of metal, with very high wings to protect the engine from spray, and it had retractable auxiliary

floats in its wings, an unusual feature. The PBY-5, which was introduced in 1940, could also take off and land on land or sea. Because of its considerable range, the PBY was perfectly suited for both long-range reconnaissance and naval protection missions. In May 1941 a Catalina discovered the *Bismarck* and led the Royal Navy to it. More than 3,300 Catalinas were produced in total; it was manufactured in the largest numbers of any seaplane.

USA

# BOEING B-17 FLYING FORTRESS

An excellent photograph of a B-17. This one is still airworthy today and features in many air shows. The photograph at the top of the facing page was also taken at an air show.

| | B-17G |
|---|---|
| Type: | Heavy bomber |
| Crew: | 8–10 |
| Weight when empty/ max weight at takeoff: | 14,855 kg/ 29,700 kg |
| Length/wingspan/height: | 22.8 m/31.63 m/5.85 m |
| Engine(s): | Four Wright R 1820 97 Cyclone 9-cylinder engines with 1,200 hp each |
| Maximum speed: | 485 km/h at 4,570 m |
| Service ceiling: | 11,900 m |
| Range: | 6,034 km without bombs, 1,760 km with maximum payload |
| Weaponry: | 12 x 12.7 mm Browning machine guns – two in the chin turret, two in the rear turret, two in the waist turret, and one each in four lateral positions in the nose, in the middle of the fuselage and in the tail – and an internal payload of max. 5,800 kg |

The Boeing B-17 Flying Fortress is one of the best-known American combat aircraft of the Second World War, second only to the P-51 Mustang. Along with the B-24, the B-17 carried out the majority of bomber attacks on occupied Europe with the 8th US Army Air Force. The prototype of the B-17 had its maiden flight on 18 July 1935.

This model was originally designed to patrol the American coast, so early models did not really merit the name 'Flying Fortress'. At first the designers believed that the model would certainly reach high speeds and altitudes, because it was the first turbocharged bomber in the world. But the RAF's experience in Europe prompted a different approach: the E version (which had its maiden flight on 5 September 1941) was redesigned with stronger armour and heavier firepower, and its side fins were moved further forward. The 8th US Army Air Force's first operation in occupied Europe

was a daylight raid in France on 17 August 1942. The B-17E, of which 512 were built, seated 10 men, and two versions based upon it were built from May 1942 to July 1945 by Boeing, Douglas and Lockheed. The F-series, of which 3,405 were produced, had even stronger armour and heavier weaponry than its predecessor, and it was first deployed on 27 January 1943. From the autumn of 1943, the G version was the most important model in the series, and

The B-17F proved to be too vulnerable in the face of frontal attacks by the Luftwaffe, which is why the B-17G was fitted with a 2 x 12.7 mm MG chin turret.

USA

8,680 were manufactured. To protect it from frontal attacks from fighters, it had a third, remote-controlled turret under its nose, and with a total of 13 12.7 mm Browning machine guns, it was the most heavily armed version of the B-17. Flying Fortresses flew into battle in a tight formation (a 'battle box') and welcomed oncoming German fighters with a hail of heavy machine gun fire. But they suffered great losses when deployed without a fighter escort. For example, when they raided a ball-bearing factory in Schweinfurt and the Messerschmitt factory in Regensburg, 60 out of 376 bombers were shot down, and another 176 were damaged to some extent. Consequently, the USAAF suspended all unaccompanied bombing raids in the autumn of 1943, and they were not resumed until early 1944, when they were escorted by the new Mustang fighters. The Flying Fortress could survive very heavy fire, was easy to manoeuvre, and was very popular with its crews because it was so reliable.

There were also special variants of the B-17: a photo reconnaissance aircraft, an air-sea rescue aircraft and a VIP transporter. It also served as a patrol and weather reconnaissance plane for British Coastal Command, which just called it the 'Fortress'. The Luftwaffe also flew a few which it had seized for demonstration purposes, to instruct its fighter pilots. It was also called the Do 200 and used in the 200th German Bomber Wing to carry agents. Altogether, 12,731 B-17s were manufactured; when production was at its peak, 16 were being built daily.

*A B-17G with open bomb bay.*

*This B-17G had no chin or ventral turret – instead, it was fitted with radar under the fuselage.*

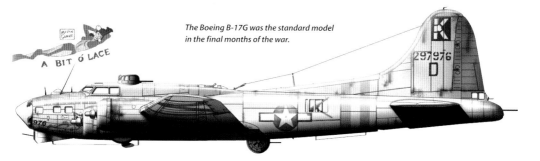

*The Boeing B-17G was the standard model in the final months of the war.*

# CONSOLIDATED B-24 LIBERATOR

The Consolidated B-24 Liberator has always been rather overshadowed by the legendary B-17 Flying Fortress, although significantly more B-24s – 19,203 in total – were actually produced. The B-24 was developed because an order came from the USAAF for a bomber that could surpass the B-17's load capacity and range. The prototype had its maiden flight on 29 December 1939, and the model was noted for its voluminous fuselage with two tail fins, and its high, very slender wings with a Davis design to ensure maximum lift, which gave the B-24 its considerable range (around 7,400 km). But the wing load was also considerable, which made the aircraft very difficult to fly, and taking off in a fully laden B-24 was a real challenge for a pilot. Even once airborne, the B-24 was not very stable, so it was not easy for the pilot of a damaged B-24 to save himself.

The first production models were delivered to the RAF in 1941, which received 1,694 B-24s in total. Because of their long range, the RAF deployed Liberators in Atlantic patrols, where they attacked submarines and protected convoys. For this they were fitted with ASV radar and four 20 mm machine guns in a gondola under the fuselage. The B-24

*A Consolidated B-24J over Friedrichshafen, 1944–45.*

also fulfilled the same role in the US Navy, where it was called the PB4Y, but a large proportion of B-24s were deployed as heavy bombers in the Pacific, in the Mediterranean and over continental Europe, particularly Germany. Along with the B-17 they formed the backbone of the US daytime bombing units, but because the B-24 could not reach the same altitudes as the Boeing model, they mostly flew separately.

The B-17 also had a better reputation than the B-24 for sustaining damage in battle. Nevertheless, an analysis of the numbers of 8th US Army Air Force bombers lost in Europe shows that fewer B-24s were lost than B-17s. The first major production model was the B-24D, which had a glazed nose with a manually

operated machine gun and a retractable machine gun turret on the underside of the fuselage. On the basis of combat experience, models from the B-24H onwards had a nose turret with two 12.7 mm machine guns. The standard model from 1944 onwards, and the one that was manufactured in the greatest numbers, was the B-24J, which had a maximum payload of 5,450 kg. The same model also served as a passenger and freight aircraft, which was called the Consolidated C-87. An improved version of the B-24 with a simple side fin, called the Consolidated Privateer, was built for the US Navy, where it served as a sea reconnaissance aircraft and bomber.

| | B-24J |
|---|---|
| Type: | Heavy bomber |
| Crew: | 10 |
| Weight when empty/ max weight at takeoff: | 17,250 kg/ 27,216 kg |
| Length/wingspan/height: | 21.16 m/33.55 m/5.49 m |
| Engine(s): | Four Pratt & Whitney R 1830 65 Twin Wasp radial engines with 1,200 hp each |
| Maximum speed: | 480 km/h at 8,500 m |
| Service ceiling: | 9,150 m |
| Range: | 3,380 km with 2,270 kg payload |
| Weaponry: | 10 x 12.7 mm Browning machine guns – two in the nose turret, two in the dorsal turret, two in the ventral turret, two in the tail turret and one each in two lateral positions in the middle of the fuselage |

This photograph of an unarmed B-24 in a flight instruction unit clearly shows this aircraft's long, thin wings.

A B-24J Liberator of the 15th US Army Air Force over Mühldorf, southern Germany, 19 March 1945.

The B-24D.

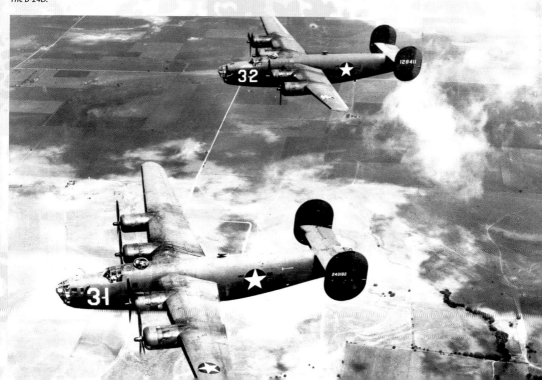

# BOEING B-29 SUPERFORTRESS

| | B-29 |
|---|---|
| Type: | Heavy bomber |
| Crew: | 10 |
| Weight when empty/ max weight at takeoff: | 31,815 kg/ 56,245 kg |
| Length/wingspan/height: | 30.18 m/43.05 m/9.02 m |
| Engine(s): | Four Wright R 3350 23 23A 41 97 Cyclone turbocharged radial engines with 2,200 hp each |
| Maximum speed: | 576 km/h at 7,620 m |
| Service ceiling: | 10,200 m |
| Range: | 5,200 km |
| Weaponry: | 8 x 12.7 mm Browning machine guns – two in each of four remote-controlled installations on the top and bottom of the fuselage – 3 x 12.7 mm Browning machine guns or two machine guns and one 20 mm automatic cannon in a manned tail position |

*The B-29 had an extensive array of defensive weaponry, but its weapons were often removed in 1945, as there was no longer any threat from enemy fighters.*

The Boeing B-29 Superfortress was the largest and best-performing bomber to be deployed in the Second World War, and its maximum takeoff weight – including an internal payload of 9,072 kg – was more than twice that of the B-17. The origins of the B-29 date back to 1940, when the USA expected the United Kingdom to fall to the Germans, prompting the Americans to develop a long-range bomber that could strike at targets in Europe. Boeing's design for the aircraft broke new ground technologically: it was the first plane in the world to have a pressurized cabin as standard. It also had four aerodynamically efficient weapons installations, which were remote controlled by gunners in the fuselage. B-29s built by Bell even had radar fitted in the rear section. In short, constructing the B-29 was the most complex and comprehensive production programme that there had ever been. Thousands of subcontractors contributed components and parts to a complex aircraft, which – as could only have been expected – had to overcome some initial problems. The B-29 prototype had its maiden flight on 21 September 1942. Its wings had a high aspect ratio and

were fitted with enormous Fowler flaps to minimize its landing speed. But initially there were severe problems with the cooler for the Wright radial engines. The first models were delivered in 1943,

but they were not deployed in combat until June 1944.

Because of its considerable range, the B-29 was exclusively deployed in the Pacific. At first, it carried out high-altitude precision raids on Japanese industrial targets by day, but these were mostly unsuccessful on account of unfavourable weather and wind conditions. After General Curtis LeMay took command of the USAAF, however, he changed tactics and deployed B-29s for night raids instead. Because precision raids were even harder by night than by day, they flew at low altitudes and carpet-bombed Japanese cities, which were made largely of wood, killing hundreds of thousands of people. The most devastating of these raids was the bombing of Tokyo, in which more people probably died in one night than in the atomic bomb attack on Hiroshima, which was also carried out by a B-29 (as was the attack on Nagasaki). By the end of the war, 2,132 Superfortresses had been delivered to the USAAF. Production continued after 1945, and in total, 3,790 B-29s were built.

*The B-29's clean lines can be seen clearly in this photograph.*

# CURTISS C-46 COMMANDO

| | C-46 |
|---|---|
| Type: | Transporter |
| Crew: | 4 |
| Weight when empty/ max weight at takeoff: | 13,302 kg/ 23,154 kg |
| Length/wingspan/height: | 23.96 m/32.91 m/6.62 m |
| Engine(s): | Two Pratt & Whitney R 2800 34 Double Wasp radial engines with 2,000 hp each |
| Maximum speed: | 394 km/h at 4,000 m |
| Service ceiling: | 8,412 m |
| Range: | 2,900 km |
| Capacity: | Up to 40 people or an equivalent freight load |

*A Curtiss C-46 flying over the Chinese mountains.*

The Curtiss C-46 Commando was the military version of the Curtiss CW-20 civil aircraft. It was unusual in that its fuselage was made up of two circular segments, which meant that there was enough room for passengers and freight. From the front the frame looked like a figure of eight. After Pearl Harbor the USAAF established that it urgently needed transporter aircraft, so it duly ordered the Curtis 200 CW-20B (its military designation was the C-46A Commando). It had a side door for loading freight and a stronger cabin floor, as well as folding seats, and models from the C-46B onwards were powered by Pratt & Whitney R-2800 engines. Because of its range and robustness, the Commando was deployed primarily in Asia and the Pacific, and the US Marines called it the RSC-1. The C-46 also served after 1945 – for instance, in the Berlin Airlift and the Korean War – and the last C-46s were not taken out of service until 1955. Even nowadays, ex-military C-46 aircraft are flown as civil aircraft in the developing world.

# DOUGLAS C-47 SKYTRAIN/DAKOTA

The Douglas C-47 Skytrain was a military version of the Douglas DC-3. The DC-3 had its maiden flight in December 1935 and was a very innovative aircraft for its time; it is still in service (to some extent) today. The C-47 had a stronger cabin floor, more powerful engine and larger freight doors than the DC-3, and it was the Allies' most important transporter aircraft in the Second World War. It was used as a transporter, a tug, an air ambulance and a passenger aircraft, and was also used to drop paratroopers. It could carry a freight load up to 2,722 kg or 28–35 people. The RAF called their C-47s the 'Dakota', and there were also many different designations for this type in the USA – for example, the US Navy called it the R4D. There was also a special freight version with a wider double cargo door to facilitate loading and unloading, and countless other variants. The DC-3 was built under licence by the Soviets, who used it intensively during the war, as the Lisunov Li-2, and Nakajima also built a few variants of the DC-3 for military use. Even after 1945, the C-47 remained in service for a long time throughout the world; for instance, the Americans flew them in the Berlin Airlift.

*A C47-A of the 9th US Army Air Force, England, June 1944.*

| | C-47A |
|---|---|
| Type: | Transporter |
| Crew: | 4 |
| Weight when empty/ max weight at takeoff: | 7,650 kg/ 11,800 kg |
| Length/wingspan/height: | 19.65 m/28.96 m/5.17 m |
| Engine(s): | Two Pratt & Whitney R 1830 92 Twin Wasp radial engines with 1,200 hp each |
| Maximum speed: | 370 km/h at 2,950 m |
| Service ceiling: | 7,070 m |
| Range: | 3,420 km |

**SHIPS**

# U-486

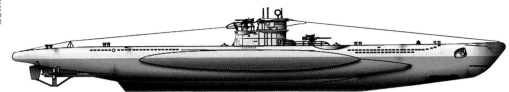

*U-486 was sunk off Bergen on 12 April 1945.*

The 700-plus Type VII U-boats built in a number of different versions between 1935 and 1945 formed the backbone of the German Navy's U-boat fleet. The different models were designated A to F; of these, VIIC was produced in the largest numbers (663) and bore the brunt of the war in the Atlantic and Mediterranean. At first these submarines achieved great success but as Allied countermeasures such as radar and ASDIC/sonar improved, and the seas were more systematically patrolled from the air, losses increased. From 1942–43 onwards, the number of anti-aircraft guns carried by the U-boats was significantly increased and the 88 mm gun often removed. Numbers of 20 mm and 37 mm anti-aircraft guns were mounted on the aft of the vessel in single, twin or sometimes even quadruple configurations. A strengthening of the pressure hull enabled the diving depth to be increased to 200 m and retractable snorkels started to be fitted in 1943. This allowed the batteries to be recharged while the U-boat was submerged and enabled large distances to be covered safely using the diesel engine. In addition, passive radar warning receivers were designed to ensure that threats were identified in good time. Nonetheless, of a total of 40,600 U-boat crew, 30,246 failed to return and 5,338 were taken prisoner. Although 2,882 merchant vessels – totalling over 14 million GRT (gross registered tons) – and 175 warships were sunk by German U-boats, 784 out of 863 submarines were lost.

*U-486* went on only two patrols in the North Sea and English Channel, sinking four ships totalling around 20,000 GRT before being sunk by British submarine HMS *Tapir* on 12 April 1945.

| | Type VIIC U-boat |
|---|---|
| Commissioned: | 22.04.1944 |
| Fate: | sunk by torpedoes from British submarine HMS *Tapir* off Bergen on 12.04.1945 |
| Displacement: | 790 tons/871 tons submerged |
| Length/beam/draught: | 67.1 m/6.2 m/4.8 m |
| Armour sides/deck: | none |
| Engines (surfaced/submerged): | two MAN diesel engines delivering 3,200 hp/two electric motors delivering 750 hp |
| Maximum speed: | 17.6 knots (7.6 knots submerged) |
| Range: | 8,500 nm at 10 knots surfaced/80 nm at 4 knots submerged |
| Crew: | 44 (later up to 57 due to increasing number of anti-aircraft guns) |
| Armament: | 4 x forward and 1 x stern 533 mm torpedo tubes (14 torpedoes or mines), 1 x 8.8 cm gun and 1 x 2 cm anti-aircraft gun |
| Diving depth: | 100 m |

**U-35 *was a Type VIIA submarine sunk in the North Sea by British destroyers on 29 November 1939.***

## U-107

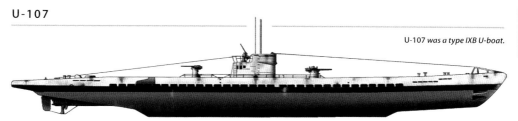

*U-107 was a type IXB U-boat.*

With over 200 vessels in seven different variants, Type IX was the second-largest class of U-boat in the German Navy. Because of its good seafaring capability and extensive range (initially 10,500 nm and in the later variants 31,500 nm at 10 knots), Type IX was deployed predominantly off the US coast, in the South Atlantic and in the Indian Ocean. As with Type VII, the different variants represented successive improvements to the original version, even if the differences were slight. Type IX was also equipped with a snorkel and its anti-aircraft capability was steadily increased during the course of the war. *U-107* was built in 1940 and sank 39 ships totalling 216,795 GRT during its 14 patrols. She was sunk with the loss of her entire crew on 18 August 1944 west of La Rochelle by a British Sunderland.

|  | Type IXB U-boat |
|---|---|
| Commissioned: | 08.10.1940 |
| Fate: | sunk in the Atlantic on 18.08.1944 |
| Displacement: | 1,051 tons/1,178 tons submerged |
| Length/beam/draught: | 76.5 m/6.76 m/4.7 m |
| Armour sides/deck: | none |
| Engines (surfaced/ submerged): | two MAN diesel engines delivering 4,400 hp /two electric motors delivering 1,000 hp |
| Maximum speed: | 18.2 knots (7.7 knots submerged) |
| Range: | 12,000 nm at 10 knots surfaced/80 nm at 4 knots submerged |
| Crew: | 48 (later up to 60 due to increasing number of anti-aircraft guns) |
| Armament: | 4 x forward and 1 x stern 533 mm torpedo tubes (22 torpedoes or 6 torpedoes and 32 mines), 1 x 10.5 cm, 1 x 3.7 cm and 1 x 2 cm anti-aircraft guns |
| Diving depth: | 150 m |

## U-2511

|  | Type XXI U-boat |
|---|---|
| Commissioned: | 29.09.1944 |
| Fate: | surrendered to the United Kingdom at the end of the war |
| Displacement: | 1,610 tons/1,833 tons submerged |
| Length/beam/draught: | 76.6 m/8 m/6.86 m |
| Armour sides/deck: | none |
| Engines (surfaced/ submerged): | two MAN diesel engines delivering 4,000 hp/two electric motors delivering 5,000 hp and two electric motors for stealth maneuvers delivering 226 hp |
| Maximum speed: | 15.5 knots (17.5 knots submerged) |
| Range: | 14,000 nm at 10 knots surfaced/420 nm at 4 knots submerged |
| Crew: | 57 |
| Armament: | 6 x forward 533 mm torpedo tubes (23 torpedoes or 17 torpedoes and 12 mines), 4 x 3 cm or 2 cm anti-aircraft guns |
| Diving depth: | 200 m |

The Type XXI, also known as the 'Elektroboot', was intended to restore the U-boats' command of the seas. In order to achieve a greater underwater speed, the hulls and conning towers of these boats were streamlined and the performance of the electric motors and batteries dramatically increased. Type XXI boats also boasted a fast torpedo reload device and comprehensive sonar and electronics systems. To speed up production, the boats were designed to be pre-manufactured inland and assembled at the coast. Because of their numerous technical innovations, however, there were serious delays in the production programme. Although an order for 200 units (later increased to 1,300) was issued in June 1943, by the end of the war only 113 had been commissioned. The Type XXI pointed the way forward for U-boat construction and many of the features developed for this class of submarine were adopted in post-1945 vessels. *U-2511* completed just one patrol before surrendering to the British in Norway.

U-2511.

GERMANY

# CLASS S-12 AND S-100 SCHNELLBOOTE (E-BOATS)

The German Navy's torpedo boats ('Schnellboote' or 'S-Boote') were known by the Allies as E-boats (an abbreviation of 'enemy boat') and are widely regarded as excellent examples of their type. Because the Versailles Treaty had imposed severe restrictions on the German Navy, considerable energy was devoted to the development of these fast patrol boats as they were not covered by it. Different classes of E-boat, which nevertheless resembled each other closely, were built from 1933 onwards. All had a wooden hull and aluminium frame, two forward torpedo tubes and three diesel (generally Mercedes-Benz) engines. Their anti-aircraft defences were continually upgraded as aircraft gradually took over as the main threat. The most important type from 1943 onwards was the S-100 class, of which 74 had been built by the end of the war. Vessels of the S-100 class had an armoured bridge to help them withstand air attack. Around 200 E-boats of all types were built. They were used mainly to attack coastal shipping around the British Isles at night but were also deployed in the Mediterranean and Black Sea. From around 1943 the main burden of the surface war at sea fell to the E-boat fleet as the German Navy's larger ships either had already been destroyed or could no longer operate with any realistic prospect of success. Losses of E-boat crew were correspondingly high although the boats themselves proved extremely robust.

|  | S12 (S-7 class) | S-100 class |
|---|---|---|
| Commissioned: | 31.08.1935 | – |
| Fate: | surrendered to USA at the end of the war | – |
| Displacement: | 92 tons | 122 tons |
| Length/beam/draught: | 31.91 m/4.9 m/1.2 m | 34.94 m/5.28 m/1.67 m |
| Armour sides/deck: | none | bridge, 12 mm |
| Engines: | three MB502 diesel engines delivering 3,960 hp | three MB501A/511 diesel engines delivering 7,500 hp |
| Maximum speed: | 37 knots | 42 knots |
| Range: | 600 nm | 700 nm |
| Crew: | 22 | 30–32 |
| Armament: | 2 x 533 mm torpedo tubes (2 torpedoes), 1 x 2 cm anti-aircraft gun, 1 x 7.92 mm MG | 2 x 533 mm torpedo tubes (4 torpedoes), 1 x 2 cm anti-aircraft gun on the forecastle, 1 x 2 cm double anti-aircraft gun amidships and 1 x 3.7 cm or 4 cm anti-aircraft gun aft |

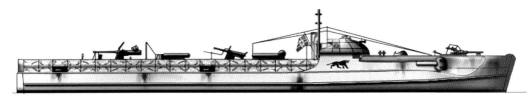

*An E-boat of the S-100 class. The panther was the emblem of the 4th Schnellboot Flotilla.*

*S-12 in the Baltic before the war. This vessel survived the war unscathed and went to the Americans as war booty.*

# Z 4 RICHARD BEITZEN

Z 4 Richard Beitzen.

Because such vessels were initially prohibited under the Versailles Treaty, the 16 Type 34 and 34A destroyers were the first ships of their kind to be built in Germany since the First World War. A new feature was their high-pressure superheated steam technology. Whereas the ship engines of other countries were subject to a maximum boiler pressure of 20 atm, boilers were developed in Germany that could withstand pressures of up to 110 atm in order to generate more power in a smaller space. This system proved very unreliable, however. The high pressure meant that cracked pipes were common, and the ships were also considered not very seaworthy. At the start of the war the *Richard Beitzen* was deployed in the Bay of Danzig but was switched in 1940 to minelaying operations off the British coast. In 1942 she took part in Operation Cerberus, the breakout of German warships *Scharnhorst*, *Gneisenau* and *Prinz Eugen* from the Channel. She spent the rest of the war in Norway, where she was severely damaged in an air attack in March 1945. *Z 4* was surrendered to the United Kingdom at the end of the war and scrapped in 1949.

| Type 34A destroyer | |
|---|---|
| Launched/commissioned: | 30.11.1935/13.05.1937 |
| Fate: | surrendered to the United Kingdom at the end of the war |
| Displacement: | 2,232 tons |
| Length/beam/draught: | 119 m/11.3 m/3.82 m |
| Armour sides/deck: | none |
| Engines: | two steam turbines delivering 70,000 shp |
| Maximum speed: | 38 knots |
| Range: | 1,900 nm at 19 knots |
| Crew: | 325 |
| Armament: | 5 x 12.7 cm guns, 4 x 3.7 cm anti-aircraft guns, 6 x 2 cm anti-aircraft guns, 8 x 533 mm torpedo tubes, 4 depth charge launchers, up to 60 mines |

# Z 25

The Type 36 destroyer was a development of the Type 34. Reduction of top weight, a flatter superstructure and a widening of the hull resulted in a more seaworthy vessel. The engine was also improved. Type 36A was equipped with 150 mm main guns instead of the 127 mm armament. *Z 25* served initially in northern Norway but was transferred to France to take part in Operation Cerberus at the beginning of 1942. Afterwards she returned to northern Norway, making up destroyer group Arktis with *Z 24* and *Z 26*. In April 1942, *Z 25* and *Z 24* damaged British cruiser HMS *Edinburgh* so badly that she had to be abandoned. From March 1943, *Z 25* provided U-boats with protection in the Bay of Biscay and in summer 1944 was moved to the Baltic, where she remained until the end of the war.

| Type 36A destroyer | |
|---|---|
| Launched/commissioned: | 16.03.1940/30.11.1940 |
| Fate: | surrendered to France |
| Displacement: | 2,232 tons |
| Length/beam/draught: | 127 m/12 m/3.92 m |
| Armour sides/deck: | none |
| Engines: | two steam turbines delivering 70,000 shp |
| Maximum speed: | 38 knots |
| Range: | 2,500–2,900 nm at 19 knots |
| Crew: | 332 |
| Armament: | 5 x 15 cm guns, 4 x 3.7 cm anti-aircraft guns, 6 x 2 cm anti-aircraft guns, 8 x 533 mm torpedo tubes, 4 depth charge launchers, up to 60 mines |

*Z 25 was surrendered to France at the end of the war and remained in service as the* Hoche *until 1958.*

# ADMIRAL GRAF SPEE

|  | Panzerschiff (pocket battleship) of the *Deutschland* class |
|---|---|
| Launched/commissioned: | 30.06.1934/06.01.1936 |
| Fate: | scuttled in the River Plate, Uruguay, on 17.12.39 |
| Displacement: | 12,100 tons |
| Length/beam/draught: | 188 m/21.7 m/7 m |
| Armour sides/deck: | max. 80 mm/45 mm |
| Engines: | eight MAN 9-cylinder diesel engines delivering 55,400 hp |
| Maximum speed: | 28 knots |
| Range: | 9,100 nm at 19 knots |
| Crew: | 1,150 |
| Armament: | 6 x 28 cm guns in two 3-gun turrets, 8 x 15 cm guns, 6 x 10.5 cm anti-aircraft guns, 8 x 3.7 cm anti-aircraft guns, 8 x 2 cm anti-aircraft guns, 8 x 533 mm torpedo tubes, 2 Arado AR196 aircraft |

*The guiding principle behind the* **Admiral Graf Spee** *was that she should be 'faster than stronger ships and stronger than faster ships'.*

*In 2004 an initiative was begun to raise parts of the wreck of the* **Admiral Graf Spee**, *which lies in shallow water.*

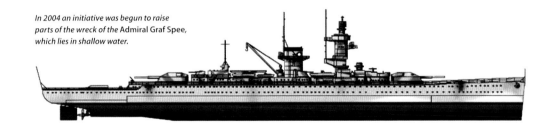

The Versailles Treaty prohibited Germany from possessing warships with a displacement of more than 10,000 tons. As this ruled out the construction of battleships, an alternative was sought. This gave rise to a new type of vessel that was faster than a battleship and more powerful than a cruiser. In the English-speaking world, this concept became known as the 'pocket battleship'. The idea worked because the major maritime powers were focused on the classes of ship defined in the Washington Naval Treaty. With a maximum speed of 28 knots, the *Graf Spee* and her sister ships the *Admiral Scheer* and the *Deutschland* (renamed the *Lützow* in November 1939) were indeed faster than most battleships

and with six 280 mm guns were more heavily armed than heavy cruisers. An innovative feature was their diesel propulsion, which extended their range and reduced the amount of smoke that they generated.

When war broke out the *Graf Spee* was stationed in the South Atlantic fully equipped and immediately began commerce raiding. By December 1939 she had sunk nine merchant ships totalling 50,089 GRT. On 13 December 1939 she was located by the British heavy cruiser HMS *Exeter* and light cruisers HMS *Ajax* and HMS *Achilles* off the Argentinian coast. During the ensuing battle the *Exeter* was badly damaged and all the other ships were hit too. The *Graf*

*Spee* was immediately withdrawn to Montevideo (Uruguay). As the German ship could only remain in harbour for 72 hours and the battle damage could not be repaired within this space of time, Captain Hans Langsdorff (who had been tricked into thinking the enemy forces lying in wait outside the harbour were stronger than they actually were) took the decision to scuttle the *Graf Spee* just beyond the mouth of the River Plate on 17 December 1939. The crew were imprisoned in Argentina and Captain Langsdorff took his own life on 20 December.

# ADMIRAL HIPPER

The *Admiral Hipper* gave her name to a whole class of heavy German cruisers that included the *Blücher*, the *Prinz Eugen*, the *Seydlitz* and the *Lützow*. The *Blücher* was lost during the invasion of Norway in 1940, barely three years after launch. The *Prinz Eugen* made a name for herself fighting alongside the *Bismarck* in 1941 and ended her days as a target ship for atomic bomb tests. The *Seydlitz* was due to be converted into an aircraft carrier but the work was never finished. The *Lützow* was sold to the Soviet Union in 1940, towed there in a semi-finished state and never completed. These ships were

inadequately armed and armoured for their size (nearly 14,000 tons) and did not have sufficient range. Although she had been commissioned at the end of April 1939, the *Hipper* was still not fully operational by the following September. She eventually received her baptism of fire during the invasion of Norway (Operation Weserübung) in April 1940. On 8 April she encountered HMS *Glowworm* and sank the British destroyer during the ensuing battle. In June 1940 the *Hipper* took part alongside the *Scharnhorst* and the *Gneisenau* in Operation Juno, during which three smaller enemy ships were

sunk. After this she patrolled the seas between North Cape and Spitzbergen as a commerce raider, sinking one freighter. On 30 November 1940 she broke out to the Atlantic, where she inflicted damage on heavy cruiser HMS *Berwick* and sank 15 freighters during the course of two cruises. She was then moved to Norway (via Germany) and deployed unsuccessfully against convoy PQ17 in July 1941. On 30 November 1942 she set out to attack convoy JW51B in the company of pocket battleship *Lützow* (not to be confused with the *Hipper*-class heavy cruiser of the same name mentioned above) and six destroyers. On New Year's Eve the German flotilla engaged the British escorts, which defended the convoy successfully, sinking a German destroyer and damaging the *Hipper*. Hitler is said to have raged at the outcome of the battle. The *Hipper* was consequently decommissioned on 1 April 1943, only to be recommissioned as a training ship a year later. On 30 January 1945, she sailed with 1,530 refugees on board from Gotenhafen (present-day Gdynia in Poland) to Kiel, where she was hit by a bomb on 3 April. On 3 May she was scuttled in dock.

| Heavy cruiser of the *Hipper* class | |
|---|---|
| Launched/commissioned: | 06.02.1937/29.04.1939 |
| Fate: | scuttled in Kiel on 03.05.1945 |
| Displacement: | 13,900 tons |
| Length/beam/draught: | 195 m/21.3 m/7.7 m |
| Armour sides/deck: | max. 80 mm/max. 30 mm |
| Engines: | three steam turbines delivering 132,000 hp |
| Maximum speed: | 32.5 knots |
| Range: | 6,800 nm at 19 knots |
| Crew: | 1,600 |
| Armament: | 8 x 20.3 cm guns in four double turrets, 12 x 10.5 cm anti-aircraft guns, 12 x 3.7 cm anti-aircraft guns, 8 x 2 cm anti-aircraft guns, 12 x 533 mm torpedo tubes, 3 Arado AR196 aircraft |

*The **Admiral Hipper** was plagued by engine problems throughout her entire operational life.*

# BISMARCK

The *Bismarck* and her sister ship the *Tirpitz* were the German Navy's largest vessels and its only fully fledged battleships as the artillery of the *Scharnhorst* and the *Gneisenau* was far inferior to that of any likely opponents. The Anglo-German Naval Agreement of 1935 allowed Germany to build battleships with a displacement of up to 35,000 tons and the *Bismarck* was duly laid down on 1 July 1936. As a result of numerous changes implemented during her construction, however, she ended up displacing 45,950 tons. In their day, the *Bismarck* and the *Tirpitz* were the world's most advanced battleships; the Royal Navy possessed nothing like them as its battleships (with a few exceptions) all dated from before 1918.

After being commissioned on 24 August 1940, the *Bismarck* did not become fully operational until spring 1941. On 18 May 1941 she set out with the *Prinz Eugen* on a merchant shipping raid in the Atlantic. After stopping in Norway, however, the ships were spotted by British reconnaissance aircraft and cruisers and placed under constant surveillance. The battlecruiser HMS *Hood* and the new battleship HMS *Prince of Wales* were sent to the southern exit of the Denmark Strait in order to intercept the German flotilla. The ensuing battle on 24 May 1941 resulted in the sinking of the *Hood* and the disabling of the

The **Bismarck** *in the Atlantic, photographed from the* **Prinz Eugen.**

*Prince of Wales*, which was forced to disengage. While the *Prinz Eugen* was unscathed, three hits from the *Prince of Wales* destroyed one of the *Bismarck's* forward tanks causing fuel to leak out. The *Bismarck's* failure to refuel in Norway now came back to haunt her as it ruled out longer operations. Admiral Karl Lütjens decided to separate the two German ships, leaving the *Prinz Eugen* to hunt merchant ships while the *Bismarck* made directly for St Nazaire in France. A feint succeeded in allowing the two vessels to escape observation by

the British cruisers but an RAF Catalina flying boat later spotted the now unaccompanied *Bismarck*. On 26 May Swordfish torpedo bombers from HMS *Ark Royal* scored a hit on the *Bismarck's* rudders, rendering her unmanoeuvrable.

On the morning of 27 May a British battle group comprising battleships HMS *King George V* and HMS *Rodney* and a number of cruisers and destroyers cornered the *Bismarck*. By the end of a 90-minute battle the German battleship was a floating wreck that ought to have been sunk by torpedoes. Her engines

*The* **Bismarck** *fires a broadside at HMS* **Hood***, 24 May 1941.*

| Battleship of the *Bismarck* class | |
| --- | --- |
| Launched/commissioned: | 14.02.1939/24.08.1940 |
| Fate: | scuttled in the Atlantic on 27.05.1941 after being badly damaged by British units |
| Displacement: | 45,590 tons |
| Length/beam/draught: | 250.5 m/30 m/10.5 m |
| Armour sides/deck: | max. 320 mm/max. 170 mm |
| Engines: | three steam turbines delivering 150,170 hp |
| Maximum speed: | 30.1 knots |
| Range: | 8,100 nm at 19 knots |
| Crew: | approx. 2,200 |
| Armament: | 8 x 38 cm guns in four double turrets, 12 x 15 cm guns, 16 x 10.5 cm anti-aircraft guns, 16 x 3.7 cm anti-aircraft guns, 20 x 2 cm anti-aircraft guns, 6 x 533 mm torpedo tubes, 4–6 Arado AR196 aircraft |

*The* Bismarck *had large aerial identification markings on her bow and stern.*

*Although it is impossible to hide a ship of this size, the* Bismarck's *camouflage was designed to mislead enemies about her size and speed.*

were still working but four hits from close range had penetrated her side armour. It is thought that Admiral Lütjens then ordered the ship to be scuttled with explosives and by opening the sea valves. The *Bismarck* sank at 10.36 with the loss of all but 118 of her crew.

The *Tirpitz*, the *Bismarck's* sister ship, spent most of her operational life at anchor in Norwegian fjords or unsuccessfully hunting convoys in the North Sea. In September 1943 she was severely damaged by British midget submarines and thereafter became the target of repeated attacks by RAF bombers. On 12 November 1944, Avro Lancaster bombers dropped 6-ton Tallboy bombs on the battleship, two of which scored direct hits while a number of near misses gashed her hull.

The ship capsized with the loss of 1,204 of the 2,094 crew.

*The* Bismarck *in a Norwegian fjord.*

GERMANY

# SCHARNHORST

| | Battleship of the *Scharnhorst* class |
|---|---|
| Launched/commissioned: | 03.10.1936/07.01.1939 |
| Fate: | sunk by British units in the North Sea on 26.12.1943 |
| Displacement: | 31,500 tons |
| Length/beam/draught: | 234.9 m/30 m/10.5 m |
| Armour sides/deck: | max. 350 mm/max. 100 mm |
| Engines: | three steam turbines delivering 160,000 hp |
| Maximum speed: | 31.5 knots |
| Range: | 10,000 nm at 15 knots |
| Crew: | 1,800 |
| Armament: | 9 x 28 cm guns in three triple turrets, 12 x 15 cm guns, 14 x 10.5 cm anti-aircraft guns, 16 x 3.7 cm anti-aircraft guns, 38 x 2 cm anti-aircraft guns, 6 x 533 mm torpedo tubes, 4 Arado AR196 aircraft |

The *Scharnhorst* and her sister ship the *Gneisenau* were originally intended to be large 'Panzerschiffe' (pocket battleships) but were developed into full battleships in order to match the French *Dunkerque* class. They were the first new ships to significantly exceed the Versailles Treaty limit of 10,000 tons. Political considerations (a desire not to upset the United Kingdom) meant the calibre of the ships' main guns was limited to 280 mm. The *Scharnhorst* and the *Gneisenau* were therefore underarmed although it was planned to upgun them to 380 mm main guns at a later stage.

Until 1942, these two ships spent nearly all their time together. In 1939 they sank the British auxiliary cruiser HMS *Rawalpindi* off Iceland. During the invasion of Norway they engaged British battlecruiser HMS *Renown* and both the *Gneisenau* and the *Renown* were damaged. From 4 to 10 June 1940 the *Scharnhorst* and the *Gneisenau* took part alongside the *Admiral Hipper* and four destroyers in Operation Juno, during which the British aircraft carrier HMS *Glorious*, the two destroyer escorts HMS *Ardent* and HMS *Acast*, a tanker, a troop carrier and the minesweeper

HMS *Juniper* were all sunk. The *Scharnhorst* was hit by a torpedo which knocked out its middle and starboard engines and aft triple gun turret. In December 1940 the two battleships switched their attention to merchant shipping in the Atlantic, sinking 22 vessels totalling 115,600 GRT. Both ships subsequently remained in Brest until February 1942, where they became the targets of repeated bombing by the RAF. On 11 February they therefore attempted to break out of the Channel for Germany accompanied by the *Prinz Eugen*. The breakout was successful although both the *Scharnhorst* and the *Gneisenau* suffered mine damage. The *Scharnhorst* continued to Norway while the *Gneisenau* was bombed in Kiel and decommissioned. On 25 December 1943, the *Scharnhorst* set out to attack a convoy in the company of five destroyers. Heavy British units, including the new battleship HMS *Duke of York*, located the *Scharnhorst* with their superior radar equipment and sank her on 26 December. All but 36 of her crew perished.

*Although classed as such, the Scharnhorst was not a fully fledged battleship.*

# EUGENIO DI SAVOIA

*The* Eugenio di Savoia *in 1939.*

A long with the other ships in the *Duca d'Aosta* class of light cruiser, the *Eugenio di Savoia* was considered well balanced and very seaworthy. Particularly impressive was her speed, which was that of a destroyer. Her armament and armour were on a par with those of other light cruisers. Only her range was limiting but this was not so important as her field of operations was the Mediterranean rather than the Atlantic. The *Eugenio di Savoia* took part in all the major battles fought by the Italian Navy between 1940 and 1943, survived the war unscathed and was awarded to Greece as war reparations. She remained in service as the *Helli* until she was scrapped in 1964.

| Light cruiser of the *Duca d'Aosta* class | |
|---|---|
| Launched/commissioned: | 16.03.1935/16.01.1936 |
| Fate: | surrendered to Greece after the war |
| Displacement: | 8,747 tons |
| Length/beam/draught: | 186.9 m/17.5 m/6.5 m |
| Armour sides/deck: | max. 70 mm/max. 35 mm |
| Engines: | two steam turbines delivering 110,000 hp |
| Maximum speed: | 36.5 knots |
| Range: | 3,900 nm at 14 knots |
| Crew: | 578 |
| Armament: | 8 x 15.2 cm guns in four double turrets, 6 x 10 cm anti-aircraft guns, 8 x 3.7 cm anti-aircraft guns, 12 x 13.2 mm anti-aircraft MGs, 6 x 533 mm torpedo tubes, up to 185 mines, 2 Arado AR196 aircraft |

# ANDREA DORIA

*SS* Andrea Doria.

T he *Andrea Doria* was a battleship in the *Caio Duilio* class. She had originally been commissioned in 1916 but was comprehensively modernized between 1937 and 1940, receiving new engines and top works. Her hull was also extended by some 10 m and her armament updated (the old 305 mm guns were rebored to 320 mm and new secondary and anti-aircraft guns were fitted). Her war was typical of that of most surface vessels of the Italian Navy: other than a number of unsuccessful interventions against British convoys, she saw very little active service. Her operational life ended in March 1942.

| Battleship of the *Caio Duilio* class | |
|---|---|
| Launched/commissioned: | 30.03.1913/13.06.1916 |
| Fate: | used as a training ship after the war; scrapped in 1957 |
| Displacement: | 29,000 tons |
| Length/beam/draught: | 186.9 m/28 m/10.4 m |
| Armour sides/deck: | max. 70 mm/max. 35 mm |
| Engines: | two steam turbines delivering 85,000 hp |
| Maximum speed: | 27 knots |
| Range: | 3,400 nm at 20 knots |
| Crew: | 1,495 |
| Armament: | 10 x 32 cm guns in two double and two triple turrets, 12 x 13.5 cm guns, 10 x 9 cm anti-aircraft guns, 19 x 3.7 cm anti-aircraft guns, 12 x 2 cm anti-aircraft guns |

Following the Italian surrender in September 1943, she was taken to Malta before returning to Italy in June 1944, where she served as a training ship. She was finally scrapped in 1957.

## I-400

The *I-400* was a submarine in the *Sen Toku* class. The three vessels hold the record as the largest conventionally powered submarines ever to be built and were designed to attack the Panama Canal. Each of their three Aichi M6A1 aircraft could carry a torpedo or up to 800 kg of bombs and was housed in a watertight, pressure-resistant hangar. The planes were launched from a catapult located in front of the tower and all three could be assembled, fuelled, armed and launched within 45 minutes of surfacing. Following the German example, the *I-400* was equipped with a snorkel and was coated with a 1 cm thick, rubber-like substance designed to absorb radar and sonar

*In 2005 a submarine of the Sen Toku class similar to the I-400 was discovered off Hawaii.*

signals. The war ended before the *I-400* could be used in combat. She was

| Submarine cruiser of the *Sen Toku* class | |
| --- | --- |
| Launched/commissioned: | 18.01.1944/15.12.1944 |
| Fate: | surrendered to the USA after the war; used as a target ship and sunk in 1946 |
| Displacement: | 5,223 tons, 6,560 tons submerged |
| Length/beam/draught: | 122 m/12 m/7 m |
| Armour sides/deck: | none |
| Engines: | four diesel engines delivering 7,700 hp, two electric motors delivering 2,400 hp |
| Maximum speed: | 18.75 knots (6.5 knots submerged) |
| Range: | 35,000 nm at 14 knots |
| Crew: | 144 |
| Armament: | 8 x 533 mm torpedo tubes, 1 x 14 cm cannon, 10 x 2.5 cm anti-aircraft guns, 3 Aichi M6A1 Seiran airplanes |
| Diving depth: | 100 m |

surrendered to the USA and was sunk in 1946 during target practice.

## ISOKAZE

*The Isokaze shared the same fate as all but one of the Kagero-class destroyers.*

The *Isokaze* was a Japanese destroyer of the *Kagero* class. Thanks to their combination of seaworthiness, good range, firepower and speed, the 19 destroyers in this class were regarded as the Japanese Navy's most successful

| Destroyer of the *Kagero* class | |
| --- | --- |
| Launched/commissioned: | 19.06.1939/30.11.1940 |
| Fate: | severely damaged by US carrier planes on 07.04.1945 and scuttled near Okinawa |
| Displacement: | 2,490 tons |
| Length/beam/draught: | 118.5 m/10.8 m/3.8 m |
| Armour sides/deck: | none |
| Engines: | two steam turbines delivering 52,000 hp |
| Maximum speed: | 35 knots |
| Range: | 5,000 nm at 18 knots |
| Crew: | 240 |
| Armament: | 6 x 12.7 cm dual purpose guns, up to 28 x 2.5 cm anti-aircraft guns, 4 x 13.2 mm anti-aircraft MGs, 8 x 609 mm torpedo tubes, 36 depth charges |

ships of their type although their lack of radar and sonar equipment reduced their effectiveness as the war progressed. Of the 19, 18 were eventually lost, including the *Isokaze*, which sank on 7 April 1945 after taking part in almost all the Japanese Navy's operations in the Pacific. The *Isokaze* was one of the *Yamato's* escort destroyers. While making for Okinawa, the flotilla was attacked by US carrier planes and the *Isokaze* was so badly damaged that she had to be scuttled by the destroyer *Yukikaze*.

# KONGO

The *Kongo*, which gave her name to a class of four capital ships, was built in 1912–13 in the United Kingdom. She was the last major Japanese warship to have been

(October) and in 1944 engaged US units during the Battle of Leyte Gulf. She was sunk by US submarine *Sealion* (SS-315) near Taiwan on 21 November 1944. Heavy seas prevented all but 237 members of the crew from being saved.

built abroad. Between 1929 and 1931 and 1936 and 1937 the *Kongo*-class ships were comprehensively rebuilt, receiving new engines, reinforced deck armour, torpedo bulges and additional anti-aircraft guns. Previously classed as battlecruisers, the vessels were reclassified after their refits as fast battleships. The *Kongo* was initially involved in operations against Borneo, Celebes and Sumatra before heading for Ceylon. In 1942 she took part in the battles of Midway (June) and Guadalcanal

*Note the **Kongo's** torpedo bulges, which were added later but could not protect her against the USS **Sealion**.*

| Battleship of the *Kongo* class | |
|---|---|
| Launched/commissioned: | 18.05.1912/16.08.1913 |
| Fate: | torpedoed and sunk by USS *Sealion* (SS-315) near Taiwan on 21.11.1944 |
| Displacement: | 36,600 tons |
| Length/beam/draught: | 222 m/31 m/9.7 m |
| Armour sides/deck: | max. 203 mm/max. 51–127 mm |
| Engines: | four steam turbines delivering 136,000 hp |
| Maximum speed: | 30 knots |
| Range: | 9,800 nm at 18 knots |
| Crew: | 1,437 |
| Armament (1944): | 8 x 35.6 cm guns, 4 x 15.2 cm guns, 4 x 12.7 cm anti-aircraft guns, up to 118 x 2.5 cm anti-aircraft guns, 3 carrier planes |

# ISE

| Battleship of the *Hyuga* class | |
|---|---|
| Launched/commissioned: | 12.11.1916/15.12.1917 |
| Fate: | badly damaged in Kure by US carrier planes and scuttled |
| Displacement: | 35,350 tons |
| Length/beam/draught: | 219.6 m/33.8 m/9.3 m |
| Armour sides/deck: | max. 305 mm/max. 51–120 mm |
| Engines: | four steam turbines delivering 80,825 hp |
| Maximum speed: | 25.3 knots |
| Range: | 9,450 nm at 16 knots |
| Crew: | 1,463 |
| Armament: | 8 x 35.6 cm guns in four double turrets, 16 x 12.7 cm anti-aircraft guns, up to 104 x 2.5 cm anti-aircraft guns, 22 aircraft |

*The **Ise** after her refit, which lasted from September 1942 until September 1943.*

The *Ise* was a battleship of the *Hyuga* class and a veteran of the First World War modernized between 1935 and 1937. After the Battle of Midway in June 1942, the *Ise* and *Hyuga* were converted into carrier battleships in an attempt to compensate for Japan's loss of aircraft carriers. Two of the ships' original six main gun turrets were removed and replaced by a hangar, flight deck and catapults

from where up to 22 planes could be launched which would land on 'proper' aircraft carriers after carrying out their missions. This plan could not be fully realized as the necessary aircraft could not be delivered and so small numbers of flying boats were used instead. The *Ise* and *Hyuga* were both hit by bombs in Leyte Gulf on 26 October 1944. They were sent to Kure (Japan) where on 28 July 1945 they were attacked and severely damaged by aircraft from US carriers *Lexington* and *Ticonderoga*. They were then scuttled in shallow water and scrapped on the spot in 1946.

# YAMATO

The Yamato in 1942.

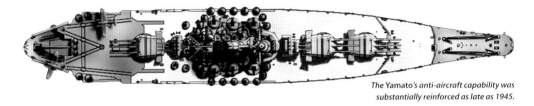

The Yamato's anti-aircraft capability was substantially reinforced as late as 1945.

The *Yamato* and her sister ship the *Musashi* (of her other sister ships the *Shinano* was converted into an aircraft carrier and the *Kii* was never completed) were the largest and most heavily armed and armoured battleships the world had ever seen and yet both were sunk by carrier planes. After quitting the League of Nations in 1934 and withdrawing from the Washington Naval Treaty at the end of 1936, Japan started planning a class of super battleship capable of outdoing any imaginable opponent. The plan was designed in particular to force the USA to retaliate by building battleships so large they would not be able to pass through the Panama Canal. As all the US shipyards capable of building and repairing such large vessels were located on the East Coast, this would have given the Japanese an enormous strategic advantage. The designs for the *Yamato* class contained many new features. These included the so-called Kanpon hull line designed to avoid transverse stresses and the extremely unusual shape of the hull itself with its low drag beneath the water line. Its armour was designed to withstand 406 mm shells and 1,000 kg bombs dropped from a height of 3,500 m. Furthermore these ships were regarded as particularly well protected under water as their side armour was continued all the way down to the bottom of the ship, gradually decreasing in thickness from 410 to 75 mm. For the main armament the designers chose a 46 cm L/45 gun, the largest, most powerful weapon ever to arm a ship. The armour-piercing shells fired by these guns weighed 1,460 kg and could penetrate 60 cm of steel from a distance of 24 nautical miles (44 km). The *Yamato* was the Japanese flagship at the Battle of Midway but she had no contact with the enemy. On 25 December 1943 she was hit by a torpedo from US submarine *Skate* (SS-305) and put in for repairs at Kure where her 15.5 mm side turrets were replaced by extra 120 mm anti-aircraft guns and a new radar system was fitted.

On 24 October 1944 the *Yamato* and *Musashi* took part in the Battle of Leyte Gulf. Together with the *Kongo* they sank US escort carrier *Gambier Bay* and three destroyers. The *Musashi* was sunk by carrier planes later that day while the *Yamato* was hit by three bombs that caused only minor damage. The repairs were again carried out at the Kure shipyard and her light anti-aircraft defences were further strengthened. In April 1945 the *Yamato* received orders to attack the US invasion fleet off Okinawa.

As it was thought unlikely in the Japanese Navy that she would survive

| Battleship of the *Yamato* class | |
| --- | --- |
| Launched/commissioned: | 08.09.1940/16.12.1941 |
| Fate: | sunk by US carrier planes on 07.04.1945 |
| Displacement: | 69,646 tons |
| Length/beam/draught: | 263.5 m/38.9 m/10.8 m |
| Armour sides/deck: | max. 410 mm/max. 200–250 mm |
| Engines: | four steam turbines delivering 165,000 hp |
| Maximum speed: | 28 knots |
| Range: | 7,500 nm at 16 knots |
| Crew: | 3,332 |
| Armament (1945): | 9 x 46 cm guns in three triple turrets, 6 x 15.5 cm guns, 24 x 12.7 cm anti-aircraft guns, up to 150 x 2.5 cm anti-aircraft guns, 12 rocket launchers each with 28 x 12 cm unguided anti-aircraft rockets, 7 aircraft |

*The* Yamato *under construction.*

*The* Yamato *during trials, October 1941.*

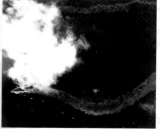

*The* Yamato *caught in a hail of bombs from the attacking US carrier planes. US Navy photographs.*

the attack, only enough fuel was taken on board for the outward journey, not for the journey back. On 7 April 1945 she was attacked by 386 US carrier planes on her way to Okinawa and suffered 13 torpedo and eight bomb hits. Her hull was further damaged by numerous near misses. At 14.23 the *Yamato* capsized and an explosion in her forward ammunition store split her in two. Only 269 crew members were saved.

# KAGA

**W**ork started on the *Kaga* in 1921. She was originally intended to be a battle cruiser but because of the limitations imposed by the Washington Naval Treaty, she could not be commissioned as such and was converted into an aircraft carrier (completed in 1928). In December 1941 she was part of the Japanese fleet that attacked Pearl Harbor. Along with the *Akagi* she provided support for the invasion of Rabaul in January 1942 and shortly afterwards hit a reef and had to be repaired. The following month, aircraft from the *Kaga* and *Akagi* attacked Darwin in northern Australia and sank

nine ships including USS *Peary*. At the Battle of Midway the *Kaga* was bombarded by SBD Dauntless dive-

bombers from the USS *Enterprise*, which caused her to burst into flames and sink shortly afterwards.

| Aircraft carrier | |
|---|---|
| Launched/commissioned: | 17.11.1921/31.03.1928 |
| Fate: | sunk by US carrier planes at the Battle of Midway on 04.06.1942 |
| Displacement: | 38,813 tons |
| Length/beam/draught: | 260.7 m/31.3 m/9.44 m |
| Armour sides/deck: | max. 280 mm/max. 102–152 mm |
| Engines: | four steam turbines delivering 127,000 hp |
| Maximum speed: | 31.25 knots |
| Range: | 10,000 nm at 16 knots |
| Crew: | approx. 2,000 |
| Armament: | 10 x 20.3 cm guns in casemate mounts, 16 x 12.7 cm anti-aircraft guns, 22 x 2.5 cm anti-aircraft guns, 72 aircraft (plus 25 dismantled planes in reserve) |

*The* Kaga.

# AKAGI

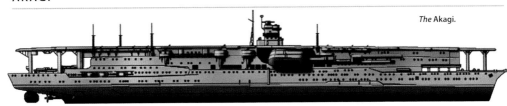

*The* Akagi.

**L**ike the *Kaga*, the *Akagi* was begun as a battlecruiser and because of the

Washington Naval Treaty ended up as an aircraft carrier. After taking part in the

attack on Pearl Harbor, she was involved in the invasion of Rabaul and the Bismarck Islands. She also participated in the attack on Darwin in Australia and engaged with Allied naval forces off Sumatra and in the Indian Ocean. During the Battle of Midway she was attacked by dive-bombers from the USS *Enterprise* and *Yorktown* and caught fire. This caused ammunition and aviation fuel to explode and the burnt-out wreck was sunk by torpedoes from Japanese destroyers the following day.

| Aircraft carrier | |
|---|---|
| Launched/commissioned: | 22.04.1925/27.03.1927 |
| Fate: | badly damaged by US carrier planes during the Battle of Midway on 04.06.1942 sunk by escort destroyers on 05.06.1942 |
| Displacement: | 37,080 tons |
| Length/beam/draught: | 260.68 m/31.8 m/9.1 m |
| Armour sides/deck: | max. 254 mm/max. 102–152 mm |
| Engines: | four steam turbines delivering 133,000 hp |
| Maximum speed: | 31.2 knots |
| Range: | 8,200 nm at 16 knots |
| Crew: | approx. 2,020 |
| Armament: | 6 x 20.3 cm guns in casemate mounts, 12 x 12.7 cm anti-aircraft guns, 28 x 2.5 cm anti-aircraft guns, 66 aircraft (plus 25 dismantled planes in reserve) |

# SURCOUF

*The* Surcouf *was a true submarine cruiser and was the largest and heaviest submarine in the world in her day.*

Before the Second World War, the *Surcouf* was the largest submarine in the world. Not only was she armed with torpedoes; she also had two 203 mm cannon mounted in a turret forward of her conning tower and an aircraft housed in a watertight, pressure-resistant hangar behind the conning tower. Having avoided falling into German hands by escaping to the United Kingdom, the *Surcouf* fought on the side of the Free French forces during the Second World War. On 18 February 1942 she sank with all hands lost following a collision with a US merchantman in the vicinity of the Panama Canal.

|  | Submarine cruiser |
|---|---|
| Launched/commissioned: | 18.11.1929/15.12.1932 |
| Fate: | sank as the result of a collision on 18.02.1942 |
| Displacement: | 2,880 tons/4,304 tons submerged |
| Length/beam/draught: | 110 m/9 m/7.2 m |
| Armour sides/deck: | none |
| Engines: | two diesel engines delivering 7,600 hp and two electric motors delivering 3,400 hp |
| Maximum speed: | 18.5 knots (10 knots submerged) |
| Range: | 12,000 nm at 10 knots |
| Crew: | 150 |
| Armament: | 8 x 551 mm torpedo tubes (10 torpedoes), 4 x 400 mm torpedo tubes (4 torpedoes), 2 x 20.3 cm guns, 2 x 3.7 cm anti-aircraft guns, 4 x 13.2 mm anti-aircraft MG, 1 aircraft |
| Diving depth: | 100 m |

# RICHELIEU

|  | Battleship of the *Richelieu* class |
|---|---|
| Launched/commissioned: | 17.01.1939/15.06.1940 |
| Fate: | used as a training ship from 1955; scrapped in 1968 |
| Displacement: | 37,832 tons |
| Length/beam/draught: | 247.85 m/33.08 m/9.9 m |
| Armour sides/deck: | max. 330 mm/max. 190 mm |
| Engines: | four steam turbines delivering 179,000 hp |
| Maximum speed: | 32.6 knots |
| Range: | 9,836 nm at 16 knots |
| Crew: | 1,550 |
| Armament (after 1943): | 8 x 38 cm guns in two quadruple turrets, 9 x 15.2 cm guns, 12 x 10 cm anti-aircraft guns, 56 x 4 cm anti-aircraft guns, up to 50 x 2 cm anti-aircraft guns, 3 aircraft |

The *Richelieu* was one of the most advanced ships of her day. An unusual feature was the way her main guns were concentrated into two quadruple turrets on her forecastle and her secondary guns into three triple turrets aft. The reason for this was that it kept the dimensions of the ship – and thus of the areas that needed armour-plating – within limits. Shortly after being commissioned, the *Richelieu* was transferred to Dakar to escape capture by the Germans. As there was no indication at first that she would fight on the side of the Free French forces, she was attacked in Dakar by aircraft from British carrier HMS *Hermes* and later by the battleship HMS *Barham*. In November 1940 she then joined the Free French forces whereupon she was directed to New York for repairs and refitting, which lasted until October 1943. Initially she served in the Mediterranean, later with the British Home Fleet, and ultimately in the Far East. After a brief return to France she remained in Asian waters until the end of the war.

*Note the* Richelieu's *unusual concentration of heavy artillery on her forecastle.*

## HMS UPHOLDER

The first U-class submarines were built as unarmed practice targets for anti-submarine vessels. They were later fitted with six and then four bow torpedo tubes as it was soon realized that their size made them ideal for operations in the North Sea and Mediterranean. Forty-six U-class vessels and 20 of the very similar V-class submarines were built. Under the command of Lieutenant Commander Malcolm Wanklyn, HMS *Upholder* sank over 90,000 tons of German and Italian shipping in the Mediterranean. The *Upholder* went missing on 14 April 1942, presumed sunk by an Italian anti-submarine vessel.

*HMS Upholder was one of the Royal Navy's most successful submarines.*

| U-class submarine | |
|---|---|
| Launched/commissioned: | 08.07.1940/31.10.1940 |
| Fate: | lost in action on 14.04.1942 |
| Displacement: | 648 tons/730 tons submerged |
| Length/beam/draught: | 59.69 m/4.8 m/4.8 m |
| Armour sides/deck: | none |
| Engines: | two Paxman diesel engines delivering 615 hp and two electric motors delivering 825 hp |
| Maximum speed: | 11.75 knots (9 knots submerged) |
| Range: | 4,050 nm at 10 knots (23 nm at 8 knots submerged) |
| Crew: | 33 |
| Armament: | 4 x 533 mm torpedo tubes (8 torpedoes), 1 x 7.62 mm anti-aircraft gun |
| Diving depth: | 60 m |

## HMCS LA MALBAIE

*Corvettes of the Flower class performed an invaluable role guarding the convoys that were Britain's lifeline.*

When the Royal Navy realized at the outbreak of war that it had a shortage of escort and anti-submarine vessels, it turned to the design for a commercial whaling boat, the main advantages of which were its compact size and simple construction. British shipyards built 145 *Flower*-class corvettes, and 120 were built in Canada. Although conditions on these ships were extremely severe and seasickness was rife, they proved their mettle on arduous and monotonous patrol duties in the North Atlantic. During the first half of the war *Flower*-class corvettes formed the backbone of Britain's and Canada's convoy escort fleets. HMCS *La Malbaie*, pictured here, was one of them. She performed her duties steadfastly between mid-1942 and the end of the war, doing her bit to keep a close watch over the North Atlantic.

| Corvette of the *Flower* class | |
|---|---|
| Launched/commissioned: | 25.10.1941/28.04.1942 |
| Fate: | decommissioned on 28.06.1945 |
| Displacement: | 980 tons |
| Length/beam/draught: | 63.5 m/10 m/3.4 m |
| Armour sides/deck: | none |
| Engines: | triple-expansion steam engine delivering 2,750 hp |
| Maximum speed: | 16 knots |
| Range: | 3,500 nm at 12 knots |
| Crew: | 85 |
| Armament: | 1 x 10.2 cm dual purpose gun, 1 x 4 cm anti-aircraft gun, 2 x 2 cm anti-aircraft gun, 2 x Hedgehog spigot mortar dischargers, 2–4 depth charge projectors |

# HMS COSSACK

*HMS Cossack had the distinction of fishing the Bismarck's ship's cat (named Oscar) out of the Atlantic.*

HMS *Cossack* was a *Tribal*-class destroyer. This class comprised 27 ships of which 16 were built for the United Kingdom, eight for Canada and three for Australia. As Britain's 16 were among the Royal Navy's most advanced and powerful destroyers, they were used intensively and 12 were lost. HMS *Cossack* was involved in the Royal Navy's attempt to prevent Germany's invasion of Norway and was subsequently deployed to protect convoys in the Atlantic. In May 1941 she was part of the battle group charged with sinking the *Bismarck*. On 24 October 1941 she was badly damaged by a torpedo from German submarine *U-563* while escorting a convoy. A tug attempted to tow the *Cossack* to Gibraltar but it ended in disaster when she sank west of Gibraltar three days later with the loss of 159 crew.

| Destroyer of the *Tribal* class | |
|---|---|
| Launched/commissioned: | 08.06.1937/07.06.1938 |
| Fate: | torpedoed and sunk by *U-563* west of Gibraltar on 24.10.1941 |
| Displacement: | 1,850 tons |
| Length/beam/draught: | 114.9 m/11.13 m/3 m |
| Armour sides/deck: | none |
| Engines: | two steam turbines delivering 44,000 hp |
| Maximum speed: | 36 knots |
| Range: | 5,700 nm at 17 knots |
| Crew: | 190 |
| Armament: | 8 x 12 cm dual purpose guns, 1 x 4 cm quadruple anti-aircraft gun, 2 x 12.7 mm quadruple anti-aircraft MGs, 4 x 533 mm torpedo tubes, 1 depth charge rack, 2 depth charge launchers |

# HMS TRUMPETER

HMS *Trumpeter* was built in the USA as a *Bogue*-class escort carrier but was supplied to Britain under the Lend-Lease Agreement, where this type of carrier was known as the *Ameer* class. The *Bogue*-class ships were converted freighters and were used mainly for escorting convoys and hunting submarines. A total of 46 were built in two phases. These and many other escort carriers performed an invaluable service for the Allies as they liberated larger aircraft carriers for more important tasks and provided effective aid in the hunt for German U-boats.

*Escort carriers like HMS Trumpeter helped the Allies avert the U-boat threat.*

| Escort aircraft carrier of the *Ameer* class | |
|---|---|
| Launched/commissioned: | 15.12.1942/04.08.1943 |
| Fate: | decommissioned on 19.06.1946 |
| Displacement: | 7,800 tons |
| Length/beam/draught: | 151 m/21.2 m/7.9 m |
| Armour sides/deck: | none |
| Engines: | one steam turbine delivering 8,500 hp |
| Maximum speed: | 18 knots |
| Range: | not known |
| Crew: | 890 |
| Armament: | 2 x 12.7 cm dual purpose guns, 10 x 4 cm anti aircraft guns, 20 x 2 cm anti-aircraft guns, up to 24 aircraft |

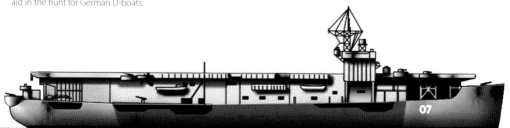

## HMS MANCHESTER

HMS *Manchester* was a powerful, modern ship commissioned on 4 August 1938. She experienced a baptism of fire during the Royal Navy's unsuccessful attempt to prevent the German invasion of Norway and served thereafter mainly as a convoy escort. In 1942 Malta came under siege and needed urgent supplies. A convoy of 14 merchant vessels and several warships including HMS *Manchester* attempted to break through to the island in August 1942 but Italian patrol boats and aircraft spotted the flotilla and attacked. On 13 August two torpedoes fired by the Italian ships disabled the cruiser with the loss of 15 crew. With its engines out of action, HMS *Manchester* drifted

|  | Light cruiser of the *Gloucester* class |
| --- | --- |
| Launched/commissioned: | 12.04.1937/04.08.1938 |
| Fate: | scuttled off the Tunisian coast on 13.08.1942 after being torpedoed by an Italian patrol boat |
| Displacement: | 9,650 tons |
| Length/beam/draught: | 180 m/19.7 m/6.3 m |
| Armour sides/deck: | max. 124 mm/max. 51 mm |
| Engines: | four steam turbines delivering 82,500 hp |
| Maximum speed: | 32 knots |
| Range: | 8,400 nm at 15 knots |
| Crew: | 750 |
| Armament: | 12 x 15.2 cm guns in four triple turrets, 8 x 10.2 cm anti-aircraft guns, 8 x 4 cm anti-aircraft guns, 8 x 12.7 mm anti-aircraft MGs, 6 x 533 mm torpedo tubes, 2 aircraft |

towards the Tunisian coast and the order was given to scuttle her. Captain Drew was court-martialled for his decision and was never given another command.

*Mounting 12 x 152 mm cannon, HMS* Manchester *was heavily armed for a light cruiser.*

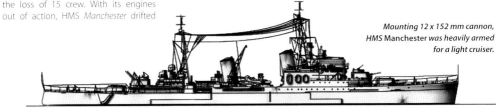

## HMS EXETER

|  | Heavy cruiser of the *York* class |
| --- | --- |
| Launched/commissioned: | 18.07.1929/21.07.1931 |
| Fate: | sunk by Japanese cruisers in the Java sea on 01.03.1942 |
| Displacement: | 8,520 tons |
| Length/beam/draught: | 175.6 m/17.7 m/6.2 m |
| Armour sides/deck: | max. 76 mm/max. 51 mm |
| Engines: | four steam turbines delivering 80,000 hp |
| Maximum speed: | 32 knots |
| Range: | 8,500 nm at 14 knots |
| Crew: | 630 |
| Armament (from 1941): | 6 x 20.3 cm guns in three double turrets, 8 x 10.2 cm anti-aircraft guns, 16 x 4 cm anti-aircraft guns, 6 x 533 mm torpedo tubes, 2–3 aircraft |

HMS *Exeter*, the fourth Royal Navy ship of that name, was a heavy cruiser in the *York* class. She made a name for herself during the Battle of the River Plate on 13 December 1939. Fighting alongside light cruisers HMS *Ajax* and HMS *Achilles*, HMS *Exeter* succeeded in damaging the far more strongly armed *Admiral Graf Spee* to such an extent that the pocket battleship was forced to take refuge in Montevideo. The *Exeter* sustained such bad damage herself that she only just made it to the Falklands for emergency repairs, which were completed in January 1940. After returning to Devonport for full repairs, which were not finished until March 1941, she was transferred to the Far East, where she was sunk on 1 March 1942 by Japanese cruisers and destroyers while defending the Dutch East Indies (Indonesia).

*HMS* Exeter *made a name for herself during the battle with the* Graf Spee.

# HMS WARSPITE

HMS *Warspite*, a battleship of the *Queen Elizabeth* class, was built during the First World War and took part in the Battle of Jutland in 1916. Between 1934 and 1937 she underwent extensive modernization, which involved replacing her engines, increasing her armour and replacing much of her secondary armament with extra anti-aircraft guns. Her superstructure was also modified in order to allow her to accommodate aircraft. At the outbreak of war in 1939 the *Warspite* was on patrol in the Mediterranean and she was immediately ordered to rejoin the Home Fleet. In 1940 she took part in the British attack on Narvik, the Norwegian iron ore port, sinking a number of vessels including a German destroyer. She was then sent back to the Mediterranean, where she was involved with sister ships HMS *Barham* and HMS *Valiant* in the sinking of Italian cruisers *Zara*, *Pola* and *Fiume* on 24 March 1941. On 22 May that year, she was badly damaged by German dive-bombers off Crete and sailed to the USA for repairs.

After a short tour of duty in the Pacific, the *Warspite* rejoined the Mediterranean fleet in April 1943, taking part in the Allied landings on Sicily in July and at Salerno in September, where she was seriously damaged by German Fritz X guided missiles. One of the missiles penetrated

*HMS Warspite, a veteran of the First World War, was nearly sunk by German Fritz X guided missiles.*

|  | Battleship of the *Queen Elizabeth* class |
|---|---|
| Launched/commissioned: | 26.11.1913/19.03.1915 |
| Fate: | decommissioned in March 1946 |
| Displacement: | 31,500 tons |
| Length/beam/draught: | 196.8 m/31.7 m/9.7 m |
| Armour sides/deck: | max. 330 mm/max. 102 mm |
| Engines: | four steam turbines delivering 80,000 hp |
| Maximum speed: | 23 knots |
| Range: | 4,200 nm at 14 knots |
| Crew: | approx. 1,180 |
| Armament: | 8 x 38.1 cm guns in four double turrets, 8 x 15.2 cm, 8 x 10.2 cm anti-aircraft guns, 32 x 4 cm anti-aircraft guns, 15 x 2 cm anti-aircraft guns, 16 x 12.7 cm anti-aircraft MGs, 2–3 aircraft |

her deck armour amidships and passed through a further six decks before finally exploding and ripping an enormous hole in her hull through which 5,000 tonnes of water flooded. The outcome was complete engine failure and the loss of power for all systems. The *Warspite* was towed to Malta but the subsequent repairs put her out of action for nine long months.

In June 1944 the battleship supported the Normandy landings. On 13 June, while returning to the United Kingdom to have her worn-out gun barrels replaced,

she struck a mine and was again badly damaged. Following provisional repairs she took part once more in the shelling of coastal positions in France during the Normandy landings. The *Warspite* was decommissioned in March 1946 and eventually scrapped.

# HMS HOOD

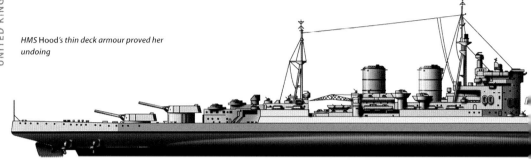

*HMS* Hood's *thin deck armour proved her undoing*

For many years, HMS *Hood* was considered the largest and most powerful battleship in the world. Initially planned as an out-and-out battlecruiser, her armour was strengthened on the basis of lessons learned at the Battle of Jutland in 1916. Her deck armour nevertheless remained relatively weak

and ultimately proved her undoing. HMS *Hood* was modernized between 1929 and 1931. She was the pride of the Royal Navy and spent a significant amount of time on official tours to other countries. At the outbreak of war she was with the Home Fleet and took part in the hunt for the *Scharnhorst* and *Gneisenau* in the Atlantic

in November 1939. In May 1941 the *Hood* and HMS *Prince of Wales* were given the task of preventing the *Bismarck* and the *Prinz Eugen* from breaking out into the Atlantic. They encountered their opponents in the Denmark Strait south of Greenland on the morning of 24 May: two British battleships against a German

# HMS PRINCE OF WALES

| | Battleship of the *King George V* class |
|---|---|
| Launched/commissioned: | 03.05.1939/31.03.1941 |
| Fate: | sunk by Japanese aircraft east of Malaya on 10.12.1941 |
| Displacement: | 38,000 tons |
| Length/beam/draught: | 227.1 m/31.4 m/10.9 m |
| Armour sides/deck: | max. 381 mm/max. 177 mm |
| Engines: | four steam turbines delivering 110,000 hp |
| Maximum speed: | 28 knots |
| Range: | 14,500 nm at 10 knots |
| Crew: | 1,521 |
| Armament (1941): | 10 x 35.6 cm guns in two quadruple and one double turret, 12 x 13.3 cm dual purpose guns, 49 x 4 cm anti-aircraft guns, 8 x 2 cm anti-aircraft guns, 2 aircraft |

*HMS* Prince of Wales *had barely been in service for nine months when she was sunk on 10 December 1941.*

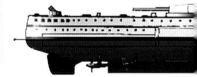

Along with her sister ships the *Duke of York*, the *Howe* and the *Anson*, the *King George V*-class battleship HMS *Prince of Wales* had the most advanced design of all the Royal Navy's battleships in the Second World War. Opting instead for stronger armour, and not wishing to inflame the naval arms race even further, a decision had been taken during the design phase in the 1930s to arm

the battleship with guns no greater than 356 mm. Twelve of these were originally planned but it came to be considered more important to strengthen the ship's horizontal protection and so the number of main guns was limited to ten, organized in a brand new configuration of two quadruple turrets and one double. Another innovation was the decision to

dispense with secondary armament in favor of a new dual purpose 133 mm gun designed for use against both air and sea targets.

The *Prince of Wales* had only just been commissioned when she was sent with HMS *Hood* to prevent the *Bismarck* and the *Prinz Eugen* from breaking out into the Atlantic and was badly damaged in the ensuing battle. A hit from the *Bismarck*

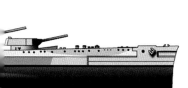

| | Battlecruiser |
|---|---|
| Launched/commissioned: | 22.08.1918/05.03.1920 |
| Fate: | sunk by the *Bismarck* south of Greenland on 24.05.1941 |
| Displacement: | 41,200 tons |
| Length/beam/draught: | 262.2 m/31.7 m/8.9 m |
| Armour sides/deck: | max. 305 mm/max. 51 mm, 102 mm in places |
| Engines: | four steam turbines delivering 150,000 hp |
| Maximum speed: | 32 knots |
| Range: | 5,200 nm at 18 knots |
| Crew: | 1,419 |
| Armament (1941): | 8 x 38.1 cm guns in four double turrets, 6 x 14 cm guns, 14 x 10.2 cm anti-aircraft guns, 24 x 4 cm anti-aircraft guns, 20 x 12.7 cm anti-aircraft MGs, 5 launchers for unguided anti-aircraft rockets |

battleship and cruiser. Six minutes into the battle, the *Bismarck* hit the *Hood*'s aft ammunition magazine with the fifth salvo from her 381 mm guns, causing an enormous explosion that swept the *Hood*'s main aft turrets and top deck into the sea. The ship sank swiftly with the loss of all but three of her crew.

The reason she succumbed so quickly can be attributed to her original battlecruiser configuration whereby high speeds were achieved at the expense of adequate deck armour. This meant the *Bismarck*'s shells were able to penetrate her ammunition magazines with hardly any resistance.

The badly damaged *Prince of Wales* disengaged and the subsequent fate of the *Bismarck* and *Prinz Eugen* is described elsewhere in the book.

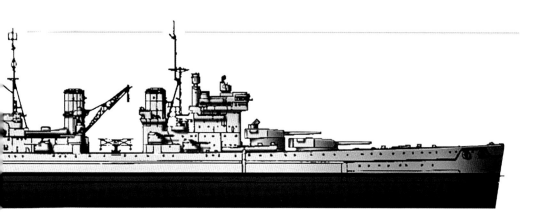

killed the entire bridge crew with the exception of the captain and a signalman. Other hits took out the forward artillery control station and penetrated the side armour, letting in some 500 tonnes of water. The ship then disengaged. Once repaired, the *Prince of Wales* carried the British Prime Minister Winston Churchill to Canada in August 1941 for a meeting with President Roosevelt.

In autumn 1941 the battleship was transferred to South-East Asia. On 10 December 1941 the *Prince of Wales* and the battlecruiser HMS *Repulse*, sailing out of Singapore, were sunk off the east coast of the Malay Peninsula by bombs and torpedoes from Japanese aircraft. The fate of these two ships made it only too apparent that there was little even modern, well-armoured battleships

with good anti-aircraft weaponry could do to defend themselves against a concentrated air attack.

# HMS ARK ROYAL

HMS *Ark Royal* was the Royal Navy's first modern aircraft carrier. Her flight deck was no longer simply constructed over the hull but was an integral part of the overall structure. The ship had two hangars positioned one above the other which could accommodate a total of 60–72 aircraft (depending on type) and two catapults. Another feature was her side and horizontal armour, without which there would have been more room for aircraft. After the start of the war in September 1939 the *Ark Royal* was sent with other British vessels to try to prevent German warships from breaking out into the Atlantic. During the course of this mission she was torpedoed by German submarine *U-39* and narrowly escaped being sunk. This was because the three torpedoes fired at her detonated prematurely. After taking part in the unsuccessful attempt to thwart the German invasion of Norway, during which aircraft from the carrier sank the German light cruiser *Königsberg*, the *Ark Royal* was transferred to the Mediterranean and then the Atlantic. In

| | Aircraft carrier |
|---|---|
| Launched/commissioned: | 13.04.1937/16.12.1938 |
| Fate: | torpedoed by *U-81* east of Gibraltar on 13.11.1941, sinking the following day |
| Displacement: | 22,000 tons |
| Length/beam/draught: | 248.3 m/28.88 m/8.5 m |
| Armour sides/deck: | max. 114 mm/max. 64 mm |
| Engines: | three steam turbines delivering 102,000 hp |
| Maximum speed: | 31 knots |
| Range: | 7,600 nm at 20 knots |
| Crew: | 1,580 |
| Armament (1941): | 16 x 11.4 cm anti-aircraft guns, 48 x 4 cm anti-aircraft guns, 32 x 12.7 mm anti-aircraft MGs, 60–72 aircraft |

May 1941 she joined the Royal Naval flotilla hunting the *Bismarck*. On 26 May Swordfish torpedo bombers from the carrier scored a hit on the *Bismarck*'s rudder machinery, rendering the battleship unmanoeuvrable. On 13 November 1941 the *Ark Royal* was attacked by German submarine *U-81* and was hit amidships. An attempt was made to tow the carrier to Gibraltar but on 20 November the vessel capsized and sank 20 miles from her destination.

One interesting piece of trivia is that the *Ark Royal* was home to Oscar, the *Bismarck*'s cat, which had been rescued by the destroyer HMS *Cossack*, which itself had been torpedoed a few months later. The animal had thus brought little luck to the three ships that were its home, but survived the sinking of each one and was eventually given a new home by the harbourmaster of Gibraltar.

*HMS Ark Royal after being torpedoed by German submarine U-81.*

# HMS ILLUSTRIOUS

*HMS* Illustrious.

HMS *Illustrious* gave her name to a class of four aircraft carriers (*Illustrious*, *Victorious*, *Formidable* and *Indomitable*) that stood out above all for their comprehensive armour. Their hull and hangar sides were 102 mm thick, their flight deck 76 mm and their hangar floor 51 mm. The *Illustrious*-class carriers were therefore shorter than the *Ark Royal* and in order to keep the weight to within reasonable limits and improve stability, had no second hangar deck. This meant that at first only 36 aircraft could be carried (though this number could rise to 54 if aircraft were parked on the flight deck).

HMS *Illustrious* had a turbulent history. Her most famous action was without doubt the attack carried out by her Swordfish torpedo bombers during the night of 11–12 November 1940 on the Italian fleet as it lay at anchor in Taranto, resulting in the sinking of one battleship and the crippling of two others. On 10 January the *Illustrious* was hit eight times by dive-bombers and suffered heavy damage. She then sailed to Malta for repairs, where she was damaged again in another air attack. Once emergency repairs had been carried out, she was moved to Alexandria and then Norfolk, Virginia, where she lay in dock until the beginning of 1942. She then had a tour of duty in the Indian Ocean, where she took part in the invasion of Madagascar, before returning to the Mediterranean and taking part in the Salerno landings in 1943. After yet another spell in the shipyard, the

| Aircraft carrier of the *Illustrious* class | |
|---|---|
| Launched/commissioned: | 05.04.1939/23.05.1940 |
| Fate: | decommissioned at the end of 1954 |
| Displacement: | 23,100 tons |
| Length/beam/draught: | 224 m/29.2 m (waterline)/8.5 m |
| Armour sides/deck: | max. 102 mm/max. 76 mm (flight deck), 51 mm (hangar floor) |
| Engines: | three steam turbines delivering 110,000 hp |
| Maximum speed: | 30.5 knots |
| Range: | 11,000 nm at 14 knots |
| Crew: | 1,200 |
| Armament (1941): | 16 x 11.4 cm anti-aircraft guns, 48 x 4 cm anti-aircraft guns, 50 x 2 cm anti-aircraft guns, 36–54 aircraft |

*The heavy armour of the* Illustrious *class proved extremely effective.*

*Illustrious* was stationed in the Far East where she was hit twice in kamikaze attacks but protected from serious damage by the strength of her armour. After the war the *Illustrious* remained in service with the Royal Navy. She was finally decommissioned at the end of 1954 and scrapped in 1956.

# USS WAHOO (SS-238)

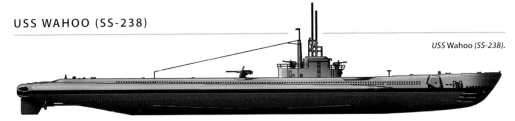

*USS* Wahoo *(SS-238).*

The *Gato* class was the backbone of the US submarine fleet and its underwater war against Japan. Over 200 vessels of this highly effective design had been ordered by 1945, achieving a level of success on a par with that of the German U-boat fleet. USS *Wahoo* (SS-238) was one of the most successful of all the US Navy's submarines, sinking 22 Japanese ships with a total GRT of 69,000 during the course of her seven patrols. Nineteen of these sinkings (with a GRT of 55,000) occurred under her second commander, Dudley 'Mush' Morton. Morton, however, is a controversial figure as he ordered his men to shoot at the survivors of the troop carrier *Buyo Maru* as they drifted on the sea after the loss of their ship on

26 January 1943. The *Wahoo* was sunk by a Japanese anti-submarine aircraft

north of Hokkaido in the Sea of Japan on 13 October 1943 during its seventh patrol.

| *Gato*-class submarine | |
|---|---|
| Launched/commissioned: | 14.02.1942/15.05.1942 |
| Fate: | sunk by Japanese aircraft on 11.10.1943 |
| Displacement: | 1,525 tons, 2,424 tons submerged |
| Length/beam/draught: | 95 m/8.3 m/4.6 m |
| Armour sides/deck: | none |
| Engines: | four diesel engines delivering 5,400 hp, four electric motors delivering 2,740 hp |
| Maximum speed: | 20.3 knots (8.75 knots submerged) |
| Range: | 11,000 nm at 10 knots (96 nm at 2 knots submerged) |
| Crew: | 60 |
| Armament: | 10 x 533 mm torpedo tubes (six forward, four aft, 24 torpedoes), 1 x 10.2 cm dual purpose gun, 2 x 2 cm anti-aircraft gun |
| Diving depth: | 90 m |

# PT-309

During the Second World War the US Navy used two types of fast patrol boat which were produced in large numbers. One was built by the Higgins yard in New Orleans, the other by Elco in New Jersey. Seven hundred boats were built in total and were used mainly in the Pacific, the English Channel and the Mediterranean. PT-309 was one of the boats built by Higgins and was commissioned at the end of January 1944. While the boat was in New York awaiting transfer to Europe, her commander, Lieutenant Barker, met Frank Sinatra, who agreed to the vessel being named *Oh Frankie*. While in the Mediterranean, the patrol boat achieved astonishing success without losing a single man. During the course of 75 operations she sank five enemy boats and captured an Italian patrol boat. Today PT-309 is on display in the Admiral Nimitz Museum in Friedricksburg, Texas.

*PT-309:* **Oh Frankie.**

| *Higgins*-type motor torpedo boat | |
|---|---|
| Commissioned: | January 1944 |
| Fate: | decommissioned after the war, now a museum boat |
| Displacement: | 43 tons |
| Length/beam/draught: | 23.77 m/6.07 m/1.6 m |
| Armour sides/deck: | none |
| Engines: | three Packard gasoline engines delivering 4,050 hp |
| Maximum speed: | 41 knots |
| Range: | 520 nm at 35 knots |
| Crew: | 11 |
| Armament: | 4 x torpedoes, 1 x 4 cm anti-aircraft gun, 2 x 2 cm anti-aircraft guns, 4 x 12.7 mm anti-aircraft MGs |

# USS DOWNES (DD-375)

*USS* Downes *(DD-375) before the attack on Pearl Harbor.*

The USS *Downes* was one of 22 *Mahan*-class destroyers built for the US Navy between 1935 and 1937. During the Japanese attack on Pearl Harbor she was so badly damaged that under normal circumstances she would have been scrapped. As destroyers were urgently needed, however, an almost completely new ship was built using every possible reusable part and recommissioned under the same name on 15 November 1943. She then served in the Pacific until the end of the war, when she was decommissioned and broken up.

| Destroyer of the *Mahan* class | |
|---|---|
| Launched/commissioned: | 22.04.1936/15.01.1937 |
| Fate: | decommissioned on 17.12.1945 |
| Displacement: | 1,500 tons |
| Length/beam/draught: | 104 m/10.7 m/2.8 m |
| Armour sides/deck: | none |
| Engines: | two steam turbines delivering 49,000 hp |
| Maximum speed: | 37 knots |
| Range: | 6,500 nm at 12 knots |
| Crew: | 158 |
| Armament (1941): | 5 x 12.7 cm dual purpose guns, 4 x 12.7 mm anti-aircraft MGs, 12 x 533 mm torpedo tubes, 2 depth charge racks |

# USS FLETCHER (DD-445)

The USS *Fletcher* (DD-445) gave her name to a class of 175 destroyers built for the US Navy between 1942 and 1944. The *Fletcher* class is held to be the best Second

*USS* Fletcher *(DD-445).*

World War destroyer of her type, and after the war many ships of the same extremely successful design were sold to navies all over the world. A number of *Fletcher*-class ships even remained in service into the 1990s. USS *Fletcher* spent the war in the Pacific, taking part in almost every major US operation there. On 11 February 1943 she sank Japanese submarine *RO-102* with depth charges and on 14 February 1945 was slightly damaged by Japanese coastal batteries in Manila Bay. After the war she remained in service with the US Navy until she was decommissioned in 1969.

| Destroyer of the *Fletcher* class | |
|---|---|
| Launched/commissioned: | 03.05.1942/30.06.1942 |
| Fate: | decommissioned in 1969 |
| Displacement: | 2,083 tons |
| Length/beam/draught: | 112 m/12 m/4.2 m |
| Armour sides/deck: | none |
| Engines: | two steam turbines delivering 60,000 hp |
| Maximum speed: | 38 knots |
| Range: | 6,500 nm at 15 knots |
| Crew: | 273 |
| Armament (1941): | 5 x 12.7 cm dual purpose guns, 4 x 2.8 cm anti-aircraft guns, 4 x 2 cm anti-aircraft guns, 10 x 533 mm torpedo tubes, depth charge racks |

# USS BIRMINGHAM (CL-62)

*USS* Birmingham.

The USS *Birmingham* was a light cruiser of the *Cleveland* class of which 27 units were built, the largest production run of any class of cruiser ever. Another nine ships in the *Cleveland* class were completed not as cruisers but as *Independence*-class carriers. The *Cleveland* class stood out for the strength of its anti-aircraft armament and was widely regarded as a highly successful, well-balanced design.

USS *Birmingham* was deployed mainly in the Pacific, sustaining damage there on a number of occasions. After being commissioned at the end of January 1943, she was initially sent to the Mediterranean where she supported the Sicily landings in July 1943. The cruiser was then assigned to the Pacific Fleet. On 8 November Japanese aircraft scored hits against her with two bombs and a torpedo off the island of Bougainville, forcing her to retire for repairs, which took until February 1944. After rejoining the Pacific Fleet she took part in numerous operations and survived them all unharmed. During the Battle of Leyte Gulf she was attempting to support the light aircraft carrier USS *Princeton*, which had been badly damaged in a bomb attack, when the carrier was ripped apart by an enormous explosion. The USS *Birmingham* was also badly damaged, suffering 426 fatalities, 237 wounded and sections of her upper works destroyed. After another spell in the shipyard, lasting until January 1945, she took part in the invasion of Iwo Jima and Okinawa. On 4 May 1945 she was

the target of several kamikaze attacks. After she had shot down three aircraft, a fourth hit her bow causing serious damage that left 51 dead and 81 wounded. The necessary repairs took until August 1945. After the war the USS *Birmingham* returned to San Francisco where she was mothballed on 2 January 1947.

| Light cruiser of the *Cleveland* class | |
|---|---|
| Launched/commissioned: | 20.03.1942/29.01.1943 |
| Fate: | mothballed on 02.01.1947 |
| Displacement: | 10,800 tons |
| Length/beam/draught: | 186 m/20.2 m/7.6 m |
| Armour sides/deck: | max. 127 mm/max. 51 mm |
| Engines: | four steam turbines delivering 100,000 hp |
| Maximum speed: | 33 knots |
| Range: | 8,000 nm at 15 knots |
| Crew: | 1,200 |
| Armament: | 12 x 15.2 cm guns in four triple turrets, 12 x 12.7 cm anti-aircraft guns, 28 x 4 cm anti-aircraft guns, 10 x 2 cm anti-aircraft guns, 4 aircraft |

*The USS* Birmingham *after her first spell in the shipyard in February 1944.*

# USS INDIANAPOLIS (CA-35)

The captain of the USS Indianapolis was court-martialled and dismissed from the Navy after the sinking of his ship. He was accused of not taking any measures to protect it from U-boat attack.

The USS *Indianapolis* was a cruiser in the *Portland* class (which comprised just two vessels) and spent the entire war in the Pacific. She took part in numerous operations and was flagship of the 5th Fleet of Admiral Raymond A. Spruance. In 1945 the *Indianapolis* took part in the landings on Iwo Jima and Okinawa. On 31 March, while pouring pre-invasion fire on to Okinawa, she was hit by a kamikaze pilot and damaged but was able to make it under her own steam to the Mare Island naval shipyards on the west coast of the USA. When the repairs were finished the cruiser was tasked with carrying atom bomb components to Tinian.

After carrying out this mission the *Indianapolis* sailed to Leyte via Guam. On

the way there she was hit amidships by two torpedoes from Japanese U-boat *I-58* at 00.15 hours on 30 July 1945. The ship capsized within 12 minutes although nearly 900 seamen initially managed to survive the sinking. It had not been possible to put out a distress call and for some obscure reason the ship was not immediately missed by her port of destination. The survivors floated in the sea, mostly without lifeboats or lifejackets,

for three days (during which time they were exposed to shark attacks) before being spotted by chance by a patrol aircraft. The last of the 317 shipwrecked seamen were fished out of the Pacific on the fifth day after the sinking.

*The USS Indianapolis photographed on 20 April 1942 off the Mare Island Marine Arsenal.*

| | Heavy cruiser of the *Portland* class |
|---|---|
| Launched/commissioned: | 07.11.1931/15.11.1932 |
| Fate: | sunk by Japanese submarine *I-58* on 30.07.1945 |
| Displacement: | 10,110 tons |
| Length/beam/draught: | 186.3 m/20.2 m/7.4 m |
| Armour sides/deck: | max. 127 mm/max. 63.5 mm |
| Engines: | four steam turbines delivering 107,000 hp |
| Maximum speed: | 32.75 knots |
| Range: | 10,000 nm at 15 knots |
| Crew: | 1,199 |
| Armament: | 9 x 20.3 cm guns in three triple turrets, 8 x 12.7 cm anti-aircraft guns, 26 x 4 cm anti-aircraft guns, 20 x 2 cm anti-aircraft guns, 4 aircraft |

USA

# USS MISSOURI (BB-63)

*The USS Missouri.*

The USS *Missouri* was a battleship in the *Iowa* class. The original intention was to build six ships in the class but in the end only four were completed (the *Iowa*, *New Jersey*, *Missouri* and *Wisconsin*). These were the largest and most powerful battleships ever built in the USA. They were intended mainly as escorts for the US aircraft carrier groups, providing protection against enemy surface units and air attack, and had a fittingly high top speed of 33 knots – making them the fastest ships of their type in the world. During the design process, greater emphasis was placed

*The USS* **Missouri** *firing a broadside from her mighty 406 mm guns.*

USA

on the strength and steadfastness of the vessels than on upgrading their weaponry. Thus the deck armour was 355 mm thick while the lower, 152 mm strength deck in the vicinity of the boiler rooms was dispensed with. This was the first time the thickness of a battleship's horizontal armour had ever exceeded that of its side armour. The *Iowa*-class ships were also equipped with quadruple torpedo bulkheads and a triple hull bottom to protect them against mines. The ships' guns could fire 1,200 kg shells a distance of 21 nautical miles (39 km). The rapid construction time of these ships (32–41 months) highlights the strength of the US shipbuilding industry during the war.

The USS *Missouri* was commissioned on 11 June 1944 and after crew training she was made flagship of the Pacific Fleet. One of her first missions was to provide covering fire for the invasions of Iwo Jima and Okinawa. On 11 April 1945 a Japanese A6M Zero managed to penetrate the *Missouri*'s anti-aircraft defences and slammed into the ship. Fortunately this caused only superficial damage as the point of impact was the vessel's side rather than her upper deck. During the attack on Okinawa, the *Missouri* shot down five enemy aircraft and damaged a further six. In July 1945 the ship attacked a section of the Tokyo battle group and shelled industrial targets in Japan. As flagship of the Pacific Fleet, the *Missouri* played a role of historic importance on 2 September 1945 when a Japanese delegation came aboard as the battleship lay at anchor in Tokyo Bay to sign the instrument of surrender. The Second World War in Asia was finally over.

In the years after 1945 the *Missouri*, like the other ships in the *Iowa* class, alternated between reserve status and active service whenever the USA was at war. She and her sister ships took part in the Korean and Vietnam wars, for example, in which their main role was to shell coastal targets. All the ships of this class underwent a thorough refit in the 1980s. Their light anti-aircraft weaponry was stripped out and radar-guided Phalanx anti-aircraft systems, Tomahawk

| Battleship of the *Iowa* class | |
|---|---|
| Launched/commissioned: | 29.01.1944/11.06.1944 |
| Fate: | now a museum ship in Pearl Harbor |
| Displacement: | 48,500 tons |
| Length/beam/draught: | 270.43 m/32.98 m/11.6 m |
| Armour sides/deck: | max. 310 mm/max. 355 mm |
| Engines: | four steam turbines delivering 212,000 hp |
| Maximum speed: | 33 knots |
| Range: | 16,600 nm at 15 knots |
| Crew: | 2,800 |
| Armament (1945): | 9 x 40.6 cm guns in three triple turrets, 20 x 12.7 cm anti-aircraft guns, 80 x 4 cm anti-aircraft guns, 49 x 2 cm anti-aircraft guns, 4 aircraft |

*Admiral Chester Nimitz, Commander in Chief of the Pacific Fleet, signing the Japanese surrender on board USS Missouri on 2 September 1945*

cruise missiles and Harpoon anti-ship missiles fitted. Their electronics were also fully upgraded. In this form the *Missouri* took part in the first Gulf War in 1991, during which she launched cruise missiles against Iraq. In 1992 the ship was definitively decommissioned and is now a museum ship in Pearl Harbor. The *New Jersey* and *Wisconsin* have also been transformed into museums although the

second of these has been maintained in a reactivable state. The *Iowa* is part of the US reserve fleet and is currently at anchor in the vicinity of San Francisco.

# USS ALABAMA (BB-60)

*Today the USS Alabama is a floating museum.*

The USS *Alabama* was a battleship of the *South Dakota* class, which comprised four ships (*South Dakota*, *Indiana*, *Massachusetts* and *Alabama*). These ships had been planned even before the Second World War against a background of US rearmament. Their construction, however, was influenced by the Washington Naval Treaty, which was still in force at the time and limited battleships to a maximum 35,000 tons. As a consequence the desired strength and firepower could only be achieved at the expense of speed. In order to save weight, the hull was kept short (207.5 m). This resulted in poor manoeuvrability but was accepted in exchange for extra armour. The superstructure was also squeezed but this in turn offered the advantage that the ship's silhouette was kept as low as possible.

The USS *Alabama* joined the British Home Fleet in spring 1943, undertaking operations in the North Sea. After returning to Norfolk, Virginia, in August 1943, she set sail for the Pacific, taking part with aircraft carrier groups in the battle for the Gilbert Islands in the Philippine Sea, the Battle of Leyte Gulf, and the battle for the Marshall Islands. In 1945 the *Alabama* was involved in carrier attacks on Formosa (now Taiwan) and Japan itself as well as in the invasion of Okinawa. As the ship and her crew survived all of these combat operations without sustaining any damage, the *Alabama* was nicknamed the 'Lucky A'. She was decommissioned on 9 January 1947 and remained in reserve in Bremerton until finally being struck from the register of naval vessels on 1 June 1962. On 16 June 1964 she was transferred, fittingly, to the State of Alabama and has lain at anchor near Mobile as a floating museum since September that year.

| Battleship of the *South Dakota* class | |
|---|---|
| Launched/commissioned: | 16.02.1942/16.08.1942 |
| Fate: | now a museum ship near Mobile, Alabama |
| Displacement: | 38,000 tons |
| Length/beam/draught: | 207.5 m/32.9 m/11 m |
| Armour sides/deck: | max. 310 mm/max. 184 mm |
| Engines: | four steam turbines delivering 130,000 hp |
| Maximum speed: | 27.5 knots |
| Range: | 15,000 nm at 15 knots |
| Crew: | approx. 2,200 |
| Armament (1945): | 9 x 40.6 cm guns in three triple turrets, 20 x 12.7 cm anti-aircraft guns, 48 x 4 cm anti-aircraft guns, 42 x 2 cm anti-aircraft guns, 3 aircraft |

# USS COPAHEE (CVE-12)

| Escort carrier of the *Bogue* class | |
|---|---|
| Launched/commissioned: | 21.10.1941/15.06.1942 |
| Fate: | mothballed on 05.07.1946 and struck from the navy register in 1961 |
| Displacement: | 7,800 tons |
| Length/beam/draught: | 151 m/21.2 m (waterline)/7.9 m |
| Armour sides/deck: | none |
| Engines: | one steam turbine delivering 8,500 hp |
| Maximum speed: | 17 knots |
| Range: | no data |
| Crew: | 890 |
| Armament (1943): | 2 x 12.7 cm dual purpose guns, 16 x 4 cm anti-aircraft guns, 27 x 2 cm anti-aircraft guns, up to 24 aircraft |

The USS *Copahee* was an escort carrier built as part of the first sequence of 46 *Bogue*-class ships. These carriers were based on the hulls of converted freighters and were used mainly for escorting convoys, hunting submarines and the transportation of aircraft. A number were also lent to the Royal Navy (where they were designated *Attacker* or *Ameer*-class vessels). Their typical complement of aircraft was 12 Grumman Wildcat fighters and nine Grumman Avenger torpedo bombers. The *Copahee* spent the war in the Pacific and survived all her operations unharmed. She was mothballed in 1946.

*The USS* Copahee *transporting captured Japanese aircraft to the USA, July 1944.*

## USS SAIDOR (CVE-117)

The USS *Saidor* was an escort carrier in the *Commencement Bay* class, which was intended to comprise 33 ships. As they only started being built shortly before the end of the war, however, only 19 of the vessels were ultimately commissioned. These vessels represented the perfect escort carrier solution and eliminated many of the problems of the other classes. This was largely due to the fact that, although they were based on a large tanker design, thought was given at an early stage to later uses and the carriers of this class were the only ones to remain in service after 1945. The *Saidor* arrived too late to be used in the Second World War but served as a platform for photographic reconnaissance aircraft during the Bikini Atoll atomic tests. She was mothballed in 1947.

*The USS* Saidor *was finished too late to be used in the Second World War.*

| Escort carrier of the *Commencement Bay* class | |
|---|---|
| Launched/commissioned: | 17.03.1945/04.09.1945 |
| Fate: | mothballed on 12.09.1947 and struck from the navy register in 1970 |
| Displacement: | 11,370 tons |
| Length/beam/draught: | 176.04 m/22.86 m (waterline)/9.35 m |
| Armour sides/deck: | none |
| Engines: | two steam turbines delivering 16,000 hp |
| Maximum speed: | 19 knots |
| Range: | no data |
| Crew: | 1,066 |
| Armament (1943): | 2 x 12.7 cm dual purpose guns, 36 x 4 cm anti-aircraft guns, 20 x 2 cm anti-aircraft guns, up to 33 aircraft |

# USS LEXINGTON (CV-2) AND USS SARATOGA (CV-3)

*The aircraft carrier USS Lexington off Hawaii in 1933.*

The USS *Saratoga* and her sister ship USS *Lexington* were the US Navy's first aircraft carriers. Originally they were both intended to be battlecruisers but could not be completed as such because of the limitations imposed by the Washington Naval Treaty. A decision was therefore taken to convert the ships, on which work had already begun, into aircraft carriers. Both ships escaped the attack on Pearl Harbor as they were on manoeuvres in the Pacific at the time.

The *Saratoga* was torpedoed by a Japanese submarine on 11 January 1942 and had to spend several months in the shipyard. Her four double 203 mm gun turrets forward and aft were replaced by 127 mm guns arranged in pairs and her light anti-aircraft weaponry was strengthened. This work prevented the *Saratoga* from taking part in the Battle of Midway. In August 1942 the carrier was involved in the Guadalcanal landings and shortly afterwards in operations in the Solomon Islands, where she was hit by another submarine torpedo on 31 August. Following repairs, the *Saratoga* was operational again in December 1942 and took part in attacks on Japanese bases on Rabaul and the Gilbert Islands. After the occupation of the Marshall Islands at the beginning of 1944, the carrier was assigned to the British Eastern Fleet, taking part in a number of operations. After this came another spell in the shipyard before the carrier rejoined the US Pacific Fleet. On 21 February 1945 the Saratoga was badly damaged during the assault on Iwo Jima by three bomb and as many kamikaze hits and once

| Type: aircraft carrier | USS *Lexington* (1942) | USS *Saratoga* (from 1944) |
|---|---|---|
| Launched/commissioned: | 03.10.1925/14.12.1927 | 07.04.1925/16.11.1927 |
| Fate: | damaged by Japanese carrier planes in the Coral Sea and then sunk by US destroyers | sunk on 25.07.1946 while being used as a target ship for atomic bomb tests |
| Displacement: | 33,000 tons | 35,000 tons |
| Length/beam/draught: | 270.7 m/32.2 m/ 9.7 m | 274.7 m/39.6 m/ 9.7 m |
| Armour sides/deck: | 152 mm/flight deck 25 mm strength deck 51 mm | 152 mm/flight deck 25 mm strength deck 51 mm |
| Engines: | four steam turbines delivering 210,000 hp | four steam turbines delivering 212,000 hp |
| Maximum speed: | 33.9 knots | 34.5 knots |
| Range: | 10,000 nm at 10 knots | 10,000 nm at 10 knots |
| Crew: | 2,122 | 3,300 |
| Armament (1943): | 12 x 12.7 cm dual purpose guns, 20 x 2.8 cm anti-aircraft guns, 20 x 2 cm anti-aircraft guns, up to 90 aircraft | 16 x 12.7 cm dual purpose guns, 96 x 4 cm anti-aircraft guns, 32 x 2 cm anti-aircraft guns, up to 80 aircraft |

USS Lexington,
1938.

USS Lexington *around 1934.*

more had to spend a substantial period of time in dock.

After these repairs she did not return to active service, however, but was initially mothballed and then used as a target ship during the atomic tests in the vicinity of Bikini Atoll and sunk on 25 July 1946.

Shortly after Pearl Harbor the *Lexington* took part in the defence of Wake Island

and then spent time in the shipyard, where she also swapped her 203 mm guns for dual purpose 127 mm guns. In May 1942 the carrier was tasked with preventing the Japanese landings at Port Moresby and a battle with Japanese carriers ensued in the Coral Sea. Although the *Lexington*'s aircraft had played an important part in the sinking of the

Japanese aircraft carrier *Shoho*, she was so badly hit by carrier planes on 8 May 1942 that she caught fire and had to be abandoned by her crew. The survivors were rescued by the destroyer USS *Phelps*, which then sank the *Lexington* with four torpedoes. The USS *Lexington* was thus the first aircraft carrier to be lost by the USA.

*The USS* Saratoga *before her major refit in 1942. Her 203 mm guns can still be seen forward and aft of her island.*

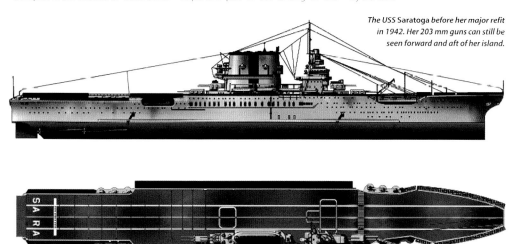

*The call sign 'SARA' is clearly discernible in the view from above.*

USA

# USS HORNET (CV-8)

| | Aircraft carrier of the *Yorktown* class |
|---|---|
| Launched/commissioned: | 14.12.1940/21.10.1941 |
| Fate: | badly damaged by Japanese carrier planes off the Santa Cruz Islands on 26.10.1942 and sunk by Japanese destroyers the next day |
| Displacement: | 20,200 tons |
| Length/beam/draught: | 252.5 m/34.7 m/8.8 m |
| Armour sides/deck: | 102 mm/51 mm |
| Engines: | four steam turbines delivering 120,000 hp |
| Maximum speed: | 32.5 knots |
| Range: | 10,500 at 15 knots |
| Crew: | 2,919 |
| Armament (from 1943): | 8 x 12.7 cm dual purpose guns, 16 x 2.8 cm anti-aircraft guns, 24 x 12.7 mm anti-aircraft MGs, up to 96 aircraft |

*USS **Hornet** on 27 October 1941, shortly after her completion.*

The USS *Hornet* (CV-8) was one of the *Yorktown* class of four aircraft carriers, the others being the *Yorktown*, the *Enterprise* and the smaller *Wasp*. The reason the *Wasp* was smaller was that anything over 14,000 tons would have exceeded the upper limit for the US carrier fleet under the Washington Naval Treaty. Overall, these vessels are regarded as having been highly successful, versatile carriers. During the early part of the war they bore the brunt of the bitter fighting in the Pacific with the result that by the end of 1942 all of them other than the *Enterprise* had been lost.

The *Hornet* was commissioned on 20 October 1941 and sailed out of port just a few months later with two large B-25 Mitchell bombers on board. To the astonishment of the crew, the bombers took off out at sea from the ship, the first time any aircraft of this size and weight had ever achieved such a feat. By the beginning of April 1942, training was complete and the *Hornet* set sail with a complement of 16 B-25 bombers for Japan. Its mission was the famous raid on the Japanese mainland of 18 April 1942 led by Lieutenant Colonel James Doolittle. The *Hornet* also took part in the Battle of the Coral Sea and the Battle of Midway. Although her aircraft did not hit any Japanese carriers, they sank a destroyer and inflicted serious damage on two cruisers as well as inflicting lighter damage on a number of other ships. Following this the *Hornet* took part in the fighting in the Solomon Islands, where her aircraft severely damaged the Japanese ships *Shokaku*, an aircraft carrier, and *Chikuma*, a cruiser. The *Hornet* came under such severe attack herself from Japanese dive-bombers and torpedo bombers that she had to be abandoned, with the loss of 111 lives. Japanese destroyers sank the drifting wreck with torpedoes on 27 October 1942.

# USS FRANKLIN (CV-13)

The USS *Franklin* was one of the 23 vessels of the *Essex* class. This was the largest class of aircraft carrier ever built, although not all its number were used during the war. These ships formed the core of the US fast carrier battle groups of the second half of the war and played an important role in the victory over Japan. The *Essex* class was a direct development of the *Yorktown*-class carriers, though freed from the constraints of the Washington Naval Treaty, which meant they could be bigger and heavier. An innovation that has survived to this day was the deck-edge aircraft lift, which interferes far less with flight operations. These aircraft carriers were considered

*The burning USS **Franklin** photographed from the USS Santa Fe.*

the best of their day. Most of them were modernized after the war and remained in service for decades. The USS *Lexington* (CV-16) served as a training ship until 1991.

The USS *Franklin* was commissioned on 31 January 1944 and after testing and training joined the Pacific Fleet in June that year. There she took part in numerous landing operations and assaults on Japanese bases. On 13 September the carrier narrowly escaped serious damage when she was missed by two torpedoes, while a kamikaze pilot hit her at such a flat angle that his burning aircraft glanced off the flight deck and skidded into the sea. While supporting the assault on the Philippines a bomb hit the deck lift, causing light damage to the ship, and during the Battle of Leyte the carrier was hit again by kamikaze bombers – this time so badly that she had to return to the USA for repairs.

| Aircraft carrier of the *Essex* class | |
|---|---|
| Launched/commissioned: | 14.10.1943/31.01.1944 |
| Fate: | decommissioned in 1964 |
| Displacement: | 27,100 tons |
| Length/beam/draught: | 264.9 m/44.96 m/10.4 m |
| Armour sides/deck: | 102 mm/flight deck 38 mm, strength deck 63.5 m |
| Engines: | four steam turbines delivering 150,000 hp |
| Maximum speed: | 33 knots |
| Range: | 15,000 at 15 knots |
| Crew: | 3,448 |
| Armament (from 1943): | 12 x 12.7 cm dual purpose guns, 32 x 4 cm anti-aircraft guns, 46 x 2 cm anti-aircraft guns, 80–100 aircraft |

In March 1945 the *Franklin* was just 50 nautical miles (approximately 90 km) from Japan. On the morning of 19 March a single Japanese aircraft broke through the cloud cover and hit the carrier with two 250 kg bombs, which passed through the flight deck and set fire to fuel and ammunition in the hangar below. The ship went up in flames and all her power failed; 724 of the company were killed and 264 wounded. Despite listing chronically, the *Franklin* was prevented from sinking – in part thanks to the USS *Santa Fe* (CL-60), which had sped on to the scene to help.

Although the aircraft carrier was repaired, she never again saw active service, remaining instead in reserve until 1964, when she was struck from the ships register.

# INDEX

# PICTURE CREDITS

Belgium, 101b Deutsches Wehrkundearchiv, Herford, Germany, 102t Vincent Bourguignon, Rochefort, Belgium, 102ml Deutsches Wehrkundearchiv, Herford, Germany; artist: Grzegorz Jackowski, 102mr Vincent Bourguignon, Rochefort, Belgium, 103m Vincent Bourguignon, Rochefort, Belgium, 103b Vincent Bourguignon, Rochefort, Belgium, 104t Shutterstock, Inc., 104m Vincent Bourguignon, Rochefort, Belgium, 104b Vincent Bourguignon, Rochefort, Belgium, 105t Vincent Bourguignon, Rochefort, Belgium, 105mr Deutsches Wehrkundearchiv, Herford, Germany, 105b Deutsches Wehrkundearchiv, Herford, Germany, 106t Vincent Bourguignon, Rochefort, Belgium, 106ml Vincent Bourguignon, Rochefort, Belgien, 106mr Vincent Bourguignon, Rochefort, Belgium, 107mr Vincent Bourguignon, Rochefort, Belgium, 107bl Vincent Bourguignon, Rochefort, Belgium, 108t Vincent Bourguignon, Rochefort, Belgium, 108m Vincent Bourguignon, Rochefort, Belgium, 108b Corbis Corporation, 109t Vincent Bourguignon, Rochefort, Belgium, 109m Vincent Bourguignon, Rochefort, Belgium, 109b Corbis Corporation, 110t Vincent Bourguignon, Rochefort, Belgium, 110b Vincent Bourguignon, Rochefort, Belgium, 111t Deutsches Wehrkundearchiv, Herford, Germany; artist: Grzegorz Jackowski, 111b Public Domain, 112t Vincent Bourguignon, Rochefort, Belgium, 112b Vincent Bourguignon, Rochefort, Belgium, 113tl Deutsches Wehrkundearchiv, Herford, Germany, 113tm Deutsches Wehrkundearchiv, Herford, Germany, 113b Vincent Bourguignon, Rochefort, Belgium, 114t Shutterstock, Inc., 114ml Deutsches Wehrkundearchiv, Herford, Germany, 115t Deutsches Wehrkundearchiv, Herford, Germany; artist: Grzegorz Jackowski, 115m Deutsches Wehrkundearchiv, Herford, Germany; artist: Grzegorz Jackowski, 115b stock.xchng, 116t Vincent Bourguignon, Rochefort, Belgium, 116bl Deutsches Wehrkundearchiv, Herford, Germany, 116br Deutsches Wehrkundearchiv, Herford, Germany, 117t Vincent Bourguignon, Rochefort, Belgium, 117b Deutsches Wehrkundearchiv, Herford, Germany, 118b Deutsches Wehrkundearchiv, Herford, Germany, 119t Deutsches Wehrkundearchiv, Herford, Germany; artist: Grzegorz Jackowski, 119m Vincent Bourguignon, Rochefort, Belgium, 119b Vincent Bourguignon, Rochefort, Belgium, 120t Vincent Bourguignon, Rochefort, Belgium, 120b Vincent Bourguignon, Rochefort, Belgium, 121t Vincent Bourguignon, Rochefort, Belgium, 121b Vincent Bourguignon, Rochefort, Belgium, 122t Deutsches Wehrkundearchiv, Herford, Germany, 122m Oliver Missing, Vallendar, 122b Oliver Missing, Vallendar, 123t Vincent Bourguignon, Rochefort, Belgium, 123m Vincent Bourguignon, Rochefort, Belgium, 124t Jaap Meijer, Assen, the Netherlands, National Archives and Record Administration, USA, 124b Vincent Bourguignon, Rochefort, Belgium, National Archives and Record Administration, 125t Shutterstock, Inc., 125bl Vincent Bourguignon, Rochefort, Belgien, 125br Vincent Bourguignon, Rochefort, Belgium, 126b National Archives and Record Administration, USA, 127t Oliver Missing, Vallendar, 127m Public Domain, 127b Oliver Missing, Vallendar, 128t Vincent Bourguignon, Rochefort, Belgium, 129tr Vincent Bourguignon, Rochefort, Belgium, 129b Public Domain, 130t Deutsches Wehrkundearchiv, Herford, Germany; artist: Grzegorz Jackowski, 130b National Archives and Record Administration, USA, 131tl Vincent Bourguignon, Rochefort, Belgium, 131tr National Archives and Record Administration, USA, 131h Vincent Bourguignon, Rochefort, Belgium, 132mr Vincent Bourguignon, Rochefort, Belgium, 132br Vincent Bourguignon, Rochefort, Belgium, 133t Oliver Missing, Vallendar, 133m National Archives and Record Administration, USA, 133b National Archives and Record Administration, USA, 134m Vincent Bourguignon, Rochefort, Belgium, 135t Vincent Bourguignon, Rochefort, Belgien , 135b Vincent Bourguignon, Rochefort, Belgium, 136m Vincent Bourguignon, Rochefort, Belgium, 137t Vincent Bourguignon, Rochefort, Belgium, 137m Vincent Bourguignon, Rochefort, Belgium, 137b National Archives and Record Administration, USA, 138m Vincent Bourguignon, Rochefort, Belgium, 138b Vincent Bourguignon, Rochefort, Belgien , 139t Vincent Bourguignon, Rochefort, Belgium, 139b Corbis Corporation, 140–141 Corbis Corporation, 142t Deutsches Wehrkundearchiv, Herford, Germany, 142b Deutsches Wehrkundearchiv, Herford, Germany, 143t Deutsches Wehrkundearchiv, Herford, Germany, 143m Deutsches Wehrkundearchiv, Herford, Germany, 143b Deutsches Wehrkundearchiv, Herford, Germany, 144t Vincent Bourguignon, Rochefort, Belgium, 144b Deutsches Wehrkundearchiv, Herford, Germany, 145t Vincent Bourguignon, Rochefort, Belgium,

145b Deutsches Wehrkundearchiv, Herford, Germany, 146t Deutsches Wehrkundearchiv, Herford, Germany, 146b Deutsches Wehrkundearchiv, Herford, Germany, 147t Deutsches Wehrkundearchiv, Herford, Germany, 147b Deutsches Wehrkundearchiv, Herford, Germany, 148t Deutsches Wehrkundearchiv, Herford, Germany, 148b Deutsches Wehrkundearchiv, Herford, Germany, 149t Deutsches Wehrkundearchiv, Herford, Germany, 149b Deutsches Wehrkundearchiv, Herford, Germany, 150ml Deutsches Wehrkundearchiv, Herford, Germany, 150mr Deutsches Wehrkundearchiv, Herford, Germany, 150b Deutsches Wehrkundearchiv, Herford, Germany, 151tr Deutsches Wehrkundearchiv, Herford, Germany, 151ml Deutsches Wehrkundearchiv, Herford, Germany, 151bl Deutsches Wehrkundearchiv, Herford, Germany, 151bm Deutsches Wehrkundearchiv, Herford, Germany, 151br Deutsches Wehrkundearchiv, Herford, Germany, 152tr Deutsches Wehrkundearchiv, Herford, Germany, 152b Deutsches Wehrkundearchiv, Herford, Germany, 153t Vincent Bourguignon, Rochefort, Belgium, 153b Philippe Carmoy, Frankreich, 154b Vincent Bourguignon, Rochefort, Belgium, 155t Corbis Corporation, 155b Vincent Bourguignon, Rochefort, Belgium, 156t Vincent Bourguignon, Rochefort, Belgium, 156b Vincent Bourguignon, Rochefort, Belgium, 157t Shutterstock, Inc., 157b Vincent Bourguignon, Rochefort, Belgium, 158t Vincent Bourguignon, Rochefort, Belgium, 158b Deutsches Wehrkundearchiv, Herford, Germany, 159t Deutsches Wehrkundearchiv, Herford, Germany, 159b Deutsches Wehrkundearchiv, Herford, Germany, 160t Corbis Corporation, 160b Vincent Bourguignon, Rochefort, Belgium, 161t Vincent Bourguignon, Rochefort, Belgium, 161b Corbis Corporation, 162t Vincent Bourguignon, Rochefort, Belgium, 162b Deutsches Wehrkundearchiv, Herford, Germany, 163t Oliver Missing, Vallendar, 163b stock.xchng, 164m Oliver Missing, Vallendar, 164b Oliver Missing, Vallendar, 165t Oliver Missing, Vallendar, 165b Corbis Corporation, 166t Shutterstock, Inc., 166b Deutsches Wehrkundearchiv, Herford, Germany, 167t Shutterstock, Inc., 167b Deutsches Wehrkundearchiv, Herford, Germany, 168t Deutsches Wehrkundearchiv, Herford, Germany, 168b Deutsches Wehrkundearchiv, Herford, Germany, 169t Vincent Bourguignon, Rochefort, Belgium, 169b Vincent Bourguignon, Rochefort, Belgium, 170t Corbis Corporation, 170b Shutterstock, Inc., 171t Vincent Bourguignon, Rochefort, Belgium, 171bl National Archives and Record Administration, USA, 171br National Archives and Record Administration, USA, 172t National Archives and Record Administration, USA, 172b Vincent Bourguignon, Rochefort, Belgium, 173t National Archives and Record Administration, USA, 173b National Archives and Record Administration, USA, 174t Shutterstock, Inc., 174b Shutterstock, Inc., 175mr Deutsches Wehrkundearchiv, Herford, Germany, 175bl Deutsches Wehrkundearchiv, Herford, Germany, 175br Deutsches Wehrkundearchiv, Herford, Germany, 176–177 Corbis Corporation, 178t Deutsches Wehrkundearchiv, Herford, Germany, 178b Vincent Bourguignon, Rochefort, Belgien , 179t Deutsches Wehrkundearchiv, Herford, Germany, 179b Vincent Bourguignon, Rochefort, Belgium, 180mr Deutsches Wehrkundearchiv, Herford, Germany, 180ml Deutsches Wehrkundearchiv, Herford, Germany; artist: Grzegorz Jackowski, 180bm Deutsches Wehrkundearchiv, Herford, Germany, 180br Deutsches Wehrkundearchiv, Herford, Germany, 181t Public Domain, 181b Vincent Bourguignon, Rochefort, Belgium, 182mr Peter Woodcock/Norman Yates, England, 182b Shutterstock, Inc., 183bl Corbis Corporation, 183br Public Domain, 184t Corbis Corporation, 184b Public Domain, 185tl Oliver Missing, Vallendar, 185tr Oliver Missing, Vallendar, 185b Public Domain, 186tr iStock International Inc., 186b Corbis Corporation, 187t Corbis Corporation, 187b US Air Force, 188–189 Corbis Corporation, 190b Public Domain, 191t Corel Stock Photo, 191m Corel Stock Photo, 191b Corel Stock Photo, 192m Corel Stock Photo, 192b Corel Stock Photo, 193t Corel Stock Photo, 193b Deutsches Wehrkundearchiv, Herford, Germany; artist: Grzegorz Jackowski, 194m Deutsches Wehrkundearchiv, Herford, Germany; artist: Grzegorz Jackowski, 194b US Air Force, 195t Corel Stock Photo, 195b Corel Stock Photo, 196t Corel Stock Photo, 196b Vincent Bourguignon, Rochefort, Belgium, 197b US Air Force, 198t Vincent Bourguignon, Rochefort, Belgium, 198b Deutsches Wehrkundearchiv, Herford, Germany; artist: Grzegorz Jackowski, 199t Deutsches Wehrkundearchiv, Herford, Germany, 199b Deutsches Wehrkundearchiv, Herford, Germany, 200t Deutsches Wehrkundearchiv, Herford, Germany; artist: Grzegorz Jackowski, 200b Vincent Bourguignon, Rochefort, Belgium,